THE WORTHINGTONS OF FAILSWORTH

AND THEIR DESCENDANTS

THE WORTHINGTONS OF FAILSWORTH

AND THEIR DESCENDANTS

PHILIP MICHAEL WORTHINGTON
BSc(Eng), CEng, FICE

PHILLIMORE

2005

Published by
PHILLIMORE & CO. LTD
Shopwyke Manor Barn, Chichester, West Sussex, England

ISBN 1 86077 289 7

Printed and bound in Great Britain by
ANTONY ROWE LTD
Chippenham, Wiltshire

CONTENTS

5. FAMILY OF ARTHUR GEORGE WORTHINGTON OF THE TRANSVAAL

6. LINE OF JONATHAN ERNEST WORTHINGTON OF BEAUMONT

7. LINE OF ANDREW JUKES WORTHINGTON OF LEEK

11. LINE OF JOSEPH WORTHINGTON OF WOODHOUSES

12. LINE OF DANIEL WORTHINGTON OF AUDENSHAW

LIST OF PEDIGREES

PREFACE

Research on the subject matter of this book was started sometime before 1902 by my first cousin once removed – Percy W.L. Adams, JP. By 1917 he had traced the ancestors of his mother back to Thomas Worthington of Failsworth, Lancashire, who died in 1648. I inherited his papers and publications and thus started my work with much of the genealogy complete. I have carried on the research since 1948 during which time some additional cadet lines have been discovered and much biographical material has come to light.

I am indebted to many archivists, family members and others who have responded to my questions and pleas for information. Of the professional researchers I wish to mention in particular Mrs Pamela M. Barnes of Lakeland Genealogy, PO Box 304, Howick, Natal, for work in South Africa and J. Derek Skepper, BA, MEd, MPhil, of 87 Kiln Lane, St Helens, Lancashire, for his work in Lancashire and Cheshire. Mrs Betty Y. Crosskill (born Worthington) co-ordinated communications with all members of the family in Natal, South Africa, and provided much biographical material on three generations of the Natal Worthingtons. My wife, Mrs Judith S.M. Worthington, researched records in Gloucestershire and Australia; my sister Mrs M.E. Valentine Gibson, proofread and commented on my first manuscript draft; my brother Brigadier Andrew R. Worthington checked and commented on my second manuscript draft, and my half-brother Stuart G. Worthington and half-sister Mrs Rosalie F. Courage proofread the first typeset draft. I thank all of them for their valuable contributions. I also thank Stuart for his considerable research and genealogical checks.

The College of Arms were involved in the earlier work on the book, particularly during the 1960s and 1970s. The college entered a three-generation pedigree of Philip Jukes Worthington in their records; they established proof of the line back to the Worthingtons of Old Trafford near Manchester and subsequently granted arms in 1975.

The scope of the book is the history of Thomas Worthington of Failsworth and as many of his direct Worthington descendants as have come to light for a total of 12 generations. The history is not exhaustive; indeed information is still being uncovered as the book goes to press. The great improvements currently being made by archivists in indexing their records will almost certainly make further research rewarding in the future. The pedigrees in the book show the Worthington descendants up to date, beyond the 12th generation (as far as is known) but the biographical articles do not extend beyond the twelfth. The descent of associated families such as those of Worthington daughters are not given, but brief notes on the direct ancestors of the spouses of Worthington sons and daughters are given where known.

Prior to the British adoption of the Gregorian calendar in 1752, it was the custom to date the year from Lady Day (then called Our Lady's Day). Thus, 31 December 1655 was followed by 1 January 1655 and so on until 24 March 1655 which was followed by 25 March 1656. Much confusion has been caused by the change as some historians convert old years to the new system and some do not. I have used the convention of quoting both ancient and modern usage for dates occurring between 1 January and 24 March prior to 1752. For example 12 February 1722-3 refers to the year 1722 by the old system.

The value of money has changed so much over the centuries that money has little meaning unless it can be related to some real value of the period. Footnotes have therefore been given to convert money to the equivalent number of days of agricultural labour, labour having been considered the most meaningful basis of value. Conversion factors are given in Appendix A.

Philip M. Worthington
1 January 2005

The Knoll House
Knossington
Oakham
Rutland
LE15 8LT

INTRODUCTION

Origin of the family

Failsworth lies 23 miles east-south-east of the township of Worthington in Lancashire, and 60 miles north-west of the township of Worthington in Leicestershire. These two townships named Worthington were the original independent sources of families bearing the same name. For generations past it has been presumed that the Worthingtons of Failsworth emanated from the Lancashire township; that is certainly more likely partly because of the shorter distance and partly because Manchester, only six miles from Failsworth, was an attraction for migration generally. It is much less likely that a branch of the Worthington of Worthingtons in Leicestershire would have migrated north-westwards.

By 1400 there were Worthington lines settled at Worthington in Lancashire, and at Shevington, Blainscough and Crawshaw, all within

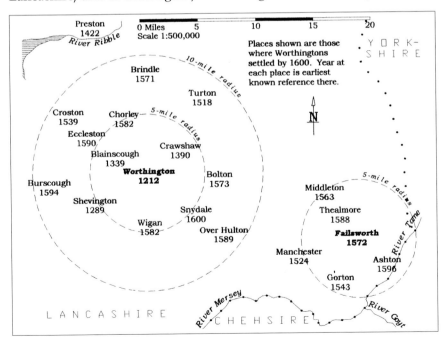

1 *Expansion and migration in Lancashire to 1600.*

three miles of Worthington. By 1600 this expanding cluster increased to 15 or more Worthington lines, within 10 miles of the township of Worthington. However, by that time a smaller cluster of six or more Worthington lines had developed within five miles of Failsworth – an area lying on the east side of Manchester. These two separate clusters accounted for a high proportion of all Worthingtons in Lancashire at that time. Thus it is suggested that just one Worthington – perhaps with wife and children – migrated to the Failsworth area in or before the 16th century, and that he gave rise to the local branches.

Worthingtons in and around Failsworth

The earliest known reference to a Worthington in Failsworth is that of 1572 in which Thomas Worthington appears as a husbandman (Article 1.1). How long the family had already been there is not known, nor is the size or exact location of Thomas' land. However, there is evidence that the farm passed down, father to son, for five generations or more. The family expanded so that by 1719 there were cadet lines settled at Woodhouses, Audenshaw and Werneth, all within four miles of Failsworth, and another at Old Trafford only seven miles away (chapters 11, 12, 9 and 3 respectively). In due course the family became common carriers as well as husbandmen. This was a natural progression as carrying involved horses, wagons, horse handlers and labourers, all of which were available on the farm. The earliest reference to carrying in the family is dated 1668; but 40 to 50 years later, the Worthingtons of Audenshaw, Old Trafford, Werneth and Rochdale all had carrying businesses.

Migration in England

Some years after one line of the Worthingtons had moved to Old Trafford, the canal revolution began. England's second commercial canal, the Bridgewater, was opened to navigation in 1761. During the next 20 to 30 years an extensive network of canals was developed over much of England. A Worthington son at Old Trafford wisely switched to carrying by horse-drawn canal barges, and he moved southwards along one of his carrying routes to Stourport in Worcestershire. Stourport was a leading centre for transhipment between the canals and the River Severn, thus attracting import and export business. There, that branch of the family for two generations developed a transport business extending over the West Country, the Midlands and the North of England.

The network of railways built during the 19th century seriously eroded the profitability of the canals, and the Worthingtons wisely sold their interest in the canal carrying business sometime before 1850. The decision was momentous, bringing to a close the family's occupation in transport for some seven generations over the previous two centuries. One son used his proceeds of the sale to buy a coalmine at Llancaiach, South Wales, from which he supplied fuel for the

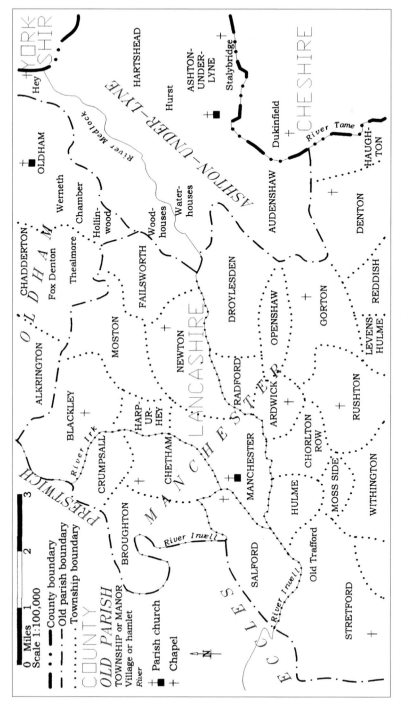

2 *Townships near Failsworth.*

railways. A younger son had already deserted the carrying business to enter the textile industry which was then in the early years of mechanisation, based on steam power. By 1838 he had moved to Leek in Staffordshire where he acquired and expanded a textile mill. He and his descendants owned or held major interests in the mill for four generations.

The family in Natal

Meanwhile, a son of the branch in Llancaiach, migrated with his wife and family to the colony of Natal (now called KwaZulu-Natal) in southern Africa, where he gave rise to a large branch of the family which still flourishes. British settlement in Natal had started in a small way in 1824 at Port Natal (now called Durban). The capital city of Pietermaritzburg was founded in 1838. Natal was declared British territory in 1843 and received full status as a separate colony in 1856. Thus, when the first Worthington arrived in Pietermaritzburg in about 1874 the colony was still young and in the process of being stocked with a flow of English settlers and immigrants. However, he was a second-generation settler so did not have the advantage of acquiring a large tract of land, as had been enjoyed by the earlier settlers.

As might be expected, the Worthingtons of Natal were more adventurous and restless than the Worthingtons of England. For example, two sons joined the rush for gold in the Transvaal. Other Worthingtons set up businesses or professional offices in Beaumont, Dundee and Durban.

Lines and cadet lines

This history is arranged by lines of succession – father to eldest son and so forth until the line fails to produce an heir male. Such a line of Worthingtons and siblings are treated in a chapter of their own and shown in a corresponding pedigree. A younger son who produces a son becomes the founder of a cadet line; he and his line of eldest sons are treated in a separate chapter with their siblings and in a corresponding pedigree.

It is noteworthy that long lines of succession were often sustained in the earlier centuries but much less so in the 20th century. This is because families have become smaller so the chances of producing a son are substantially less. Correspondingly, large unit families led to heiresses and co-heiresses being rare, but now with smaller unit families heiresses are abundant, and they have the tendency to transfer assets from one extended family to another.

It is also noteworthy that the tendency of a whole line to reside in one place and follow the same career has also decreased. Land, businesses and so forth can now be more easily sold, so that each generation is freer to move away and pursue favourite or opportunistic careers. The era of individualisation has arrived.

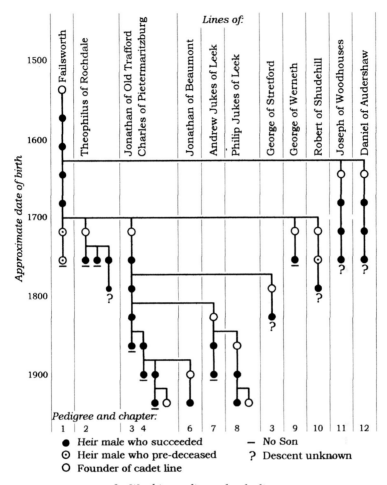

3 *Worthington line and cadet lines*

Heraldry

The earlier Worthington lines of Worthington, Blainscough and Crawshaw in Lancashire, of Braunston in Lincolnshire and of Springfield in Essex all had armorial bearings registered at the College of Arms between 1536 and 1664-5 (1). Descendants of the Worthingtons of Failsworth had the tradition that they were descended from one of these ancient Lancashire families; so they used similar bearings. It is known that Jonathan Worthington of Stourport, Worcestershire, born in 1756 and his half-brother Andrew Jukes Worthington of Leek, Staffordshire, used a goat as a crest on notepaper, silver and so forth, as did various of their descendants. Their assumed bearings were:

4 *Arms of Lancelot Jukes Worthington, granted 1975.*

Arms – Argent 3 Dung Forks erect Sable.
Crest – On a Wreath of the Colours a Goat passant Argent holding in the mouth a sprig of Oak proper fructed Or.
Motto – Virtute Dignus Avorum.

Their arms were the same as those of the Worthingtons of Worthington, but their crest had slight differences from any of the five ancient lines. The goat of the Worthingtons of Worthingtons was statant and browsing at nettles erect vert. Whereas the goat of the Worthingtons of Essex had in the mouth a sprig of oak, the goat was statant and its horns were or.

On 30 May 1975 Garter Principal King of Arms and Clarenceux King of Arms granted bearings to Lancelot Jukes Worthington of Leek (Article 8.2) and his descendants with due and proper differences according to the Laws of Arms:

Arms – Argent on a Pale between two Dung Forks erect Sable a Dung Fork erect Argent.
Crest – On a Wreath of the Colours a Goat passant Argent holding in the mouth a Leek and with a Leek erect proper behind the raised sinister foreleg.
Motto – Virtute Dignus Avorum.

It is thought that the Worthingtons of Worthington originally chose dung forks as a pun on the family name. In medieval times the word 'worthing' was Lancashire dialect for dung. Choice of the browsing goat may have been to add to the image of the family's attachment to husbandry. The motto was, no doubt, based on a double pun, as 'virtus' (having the ablative singular case of 'virtute') means courage or, figuratively moral worth. 'Dignus' (which takes the ablative whilst retaining for its relating noun the meaning of the accusative case) translates as worthy of. 'Avorum' (the genitive plural of avus) means of ancestors. The motto can thus be translated as 'Be worthy of the worth of my ancestors'.

CHAPTER 1

WORTHINGTONS OF FAILSWORTH

1.1 Thomas

The earliest known reference to a Worthington in Failsworth, Lancashire, appears in the court rolls for the manor of Newton, Lancashire, on 21 October 1572. The entry was: 'That Wm. Smythe, Richard Clughe, Francys Kempe and Thos Worthington had trespassed in putting their beasts onto the common, being of Faylisworth, without license.'[1] Newton is adjacent to the west side of Failsworth, both townships lying within the ancient ecclesiastical parish of Manchester.[2] About a year later another entry was made in the rolls:

> We have great wrong by certain neighbours of Faylisworth, and Drylesdon, William Smythe, Richard Cloughe, Francis Kempe, Ralph Thorpe, Thos Worthington with others which do not only eat up our common but also geate their cattle upon the same, contrary to all right and custom.

A similar entry appears about 1580 when each culprit was fined 12 pence.[*] In a further entry of 19 April 1583 the common was more fully described as 'the common of Newton Heath' when their fines were set at four pence for each offence. However, on 8 November 1583 and 20 October 1586 the fines were eight pence each. These entries had appeared over a 14-year period, so it seems that the lord of Newton was more interested in income from the fines than removing the cattle.

When Thomas wrote his Will in 1588, his wife was Elizabeth; it was presumably by her that he produced three sons and one daughter namely:[3]

Forename	Key dates	Article
Ralph	Second marriage 1613	1.2
Richard		1.3
Nicholas	Died 1636-7	1.4
Margaret	Married 1574, died 1578-9	1.5

Unfortunately there are no registers of the Collegiate Church of Manchester (now Manchester Cathedral) earlier than 1573, so the dates of Thomas's marriage to Elizabeth and the baptisms of their children remain unknown. However, the marriage of their daughter, Margaret, in 1574 suggests that Thomas and Elizabeth may have married in the early 1540s and that Thomas may have been born in the 1520s.

---

[*] Equivalent to three man-days of agricultural labour.

PEDIGREE 1 – THE WORTHINGTONS OF FAILSWORTH, LANCASHIRE

Thomas Worthington; b. circa 1525, d. 1588. (Art. 1.1) = Elizabeth ...; d. 1591-2

Margaret, dau. =(1) Ralph Worthington; (Art 1.2) =(2) Anne Taylor; d. 1613-4
of Jeffrey Hall; m(2) 1613. (Art 1.2)
d.1610

=(3) ...

Richard Worthington. (Art. 1.3)

Nicholas Worthington; d. 1636-7 (Art 1.4) = Isabel, dau. of ... Somester

Margaret; m. 1574 Ellis Buerdsell & had issue, d. 1578-9. (Art. 1.5)

Ralph Worthington; m. 1615-6 d. 1668. (Art. 1.6) = Jane, dau. of Nicholas Wolsencroft; bap. 1588-9, d. 1668

Thomas Worthington; d. 1592. (Art. 1.7)

Alice; bap. 1594. (Art. 1.8)

Thomas Worthington; bap. 1596. (Art.1.9)

Mary; bap. 1602. (Art. 1.10)

Anne; bap. 1604-5. (Art. 1.11)

James Worthington; bap. 1610. (Art. 1.12)

Richard Worthington; bap. 1615. (Art. 1.13)

Robert Worthington; bap. 1617

Elizabeth; bap. 1620

Nicholas Worthington; b. circa 1620, m. 1655, d. 1697. (Art.1.14) = Hannah, dau. of George Bardsley; d 1710-1

Joseph Worthington; (Arts 1.15 & 11.1) = ...

Pedigree 11

Daniel Worthington; m. 1669, d. 1708-9. (Arts 1.16 & 12.1) = Alice, dau. of Richard Jones; bap. 1644-5, d. 1709

Pedigree 12

John Worthington. (Art 1.17)

Thomas Worthington. (Art. 1.18)

Ralph Worthington; living 1668. (Art 1.19)

John Worthington; b. 1656, d. young. (Art. 1.20)

A son; bap. 1658, d. young

Rebecca, dau. of Robert Thorpe; bap. 1657-8, m(1) 1680 Roger Kenyon =(1) Daniel Worthington; bap. 1665-6, =(2) Mary, dau. of John Occleston; b. 1657, m(1) 1677-8 John Billingham & had issue, d. 1747
m(1) 1684, m(2) 1719 without issue, d. 1732-3. (Art. 1.21)

A son; bap. 1672

2

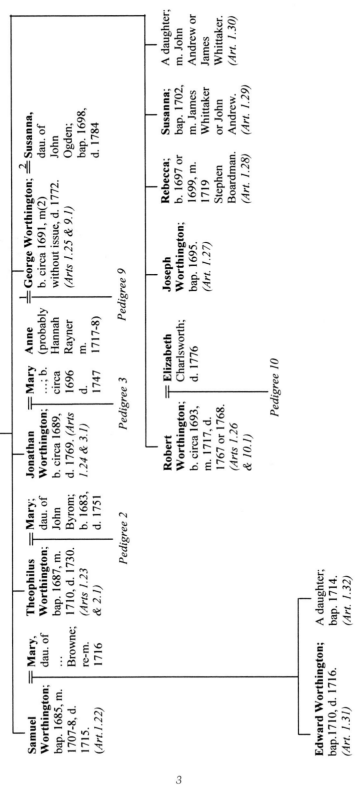

Samuel Worthington; bap. 1685, d. 1707-8, d. 1715. (*Art.1.22*)

= **Mary,** dau. of ... Browne; re-m. 1716

Theophilus Worthington; bap. 1687, m. 1710, d. 1730. (*Arts 1.23 & 2.1*)

= **Mary;** dau. of John Byrom; b. 1683, d. 1751

Pedigree 2

Jonathan Worthington; b. circa 1689. (*Arts 1.24 & 3.1*)

= **Mary** ...; b. circa 1696 d. 1747

Anne (probably Hannah Rayner) m. 1717-8

Pedigree 3

George Worthington; b. circa 1691, m(2) without issue, d. 1772. (*Arts 1.25 & 9.1*)

= **2 Susanna,** dau. of John Ogden; bap. 1698, d. 1784

Pedigree 9

Robert Worthington; b. circa 1693, m. 1717, d. 1767 or 1768. (*Arts 1.26 & 10.1*)

= **Elizabeth** Charlsworth; d. 1776

Pedigree 10

Joseph Worthington; bap. 1695. (*Art. 1.27*)

Rebecca; b. 1697 or 1699, m. 1719 Stephen Boardman. (*Art. 1.28*)

Susanna; bap. 1702, m. James Whittaker or John Andrew. (*Art. 1.29*)

A daughter; m. John Andrew or James Whittaker. (*Art. 1.30*)

Edward Worthington; bap.1710, d. 1716. (*Art. 1.31*)

A daughter; bap. 1714. (*Art. 1.32*)

The Will of 'Thomas Worthington of Failsworth, husbandman' was dated 21 May 1588 and proved at Chester on 19 June the same year. The Will is in frail condition and parts are missing, but the following are abstracts.[4]

> ... To be buried in the pishe Church Yard of Manchester. I bequeath unto my wife the third pte of my goodes and also after my fourth brynginge I give unto my three sonnes my pte quallie to be dealt amongst them. Also I give unto Katheryn Smythe 2 shillings.[*] Also I geve unto John Buerdsell 12 pence. Also I geve unto my three sonnes the other third pte of my goodes... Also I give unto my two sonnes Richard Worthington and Nicholas Worthington the ground I have taken of Mr William Radcliffe of Foxdenton, Esquire, which lyeth on Thealmore to be dealt with equally betwixt them... I give to Elizabeth Mellor 12d ...

Thomas's daughter Margaret is not mentioned in the Will because she had died in 1578-9. She had married Ellis Buerdsell in 1574, so that may explain the bequest to John Buerdsell. But who was Katherine Smythe? Could she have been another daughter who possibly married a relative of William Smythe, the co-grazier of Newton Heath? The executors of the Will were 'my Wiffe, Elizabeth, and Ralph Worthington my eldest sonne'.

Thomas paid £48[†] for the land on Thealmore, of which £4 was still due. A yearly rent of 13s. 4d. was still payable. Thealmore (sometimes called Theale Moss) lies in the southern part of the manor of Chadderton with Foxdenton, about 2 miles north-west of Failsworth. It was part of the estate of William Radcliffe of Foxdenton Hall who held the Foxdenton third of the manor.[5] The Radcliffes had held the whole manor from about 1367 until 1454 when Elizabeth, one of the three daughters and co-heiresses of Sir James de Radcliffe inherited her third part. The third was retained in the family when she married her cousin Robert Radcliffe. The passage of Thomas's interest in Thealmore to his younger sons is only explained by the general rule that his real estate in Failsworth would have passed to his eldest son. So universal was the rule whereby land passed to the eldest son that it was not customarily mentioned in Wills.

Thomas was buried at the Collegiate Church of Manchester on 16 May 1588, the entry in the register being 'Thos Worthington of Failsworth husbandman'.

An inventory of his goods was taken on 7 June 1588 and kept with his Will, but the inventory has remained in good condition. His livestock consisted of 50 cows, two swine, two geldings, three mares, and two hives of bees. There was corn and barley, carts, harness and saddles, ploughs and furrows and other outdoor equipment. The household goods included much brass valued at £4 and some pewter,

---

[*] Equivalent to five man-days of agricultural labour.
[†] Equivalent to 2,500 man-days of agricultural labour.

silver and ironware. The total value of his goods and chattels was put at £134 10s. 2d.[*]

Elizabeth continued to live as a widow for a further three years. She was buried on 22 February 1591-2 at the Collegiate Church, the entry in the register being 'Elizabeth widowe of Thomas Worthington'.

SECOND GENERATION – FAMILY OF THOMAS AND ELIZABETH

1.2 Ralph

Ralph Worthington, the eldest son of Thomas Worthington and his wife Elizabeth (Article 1.1), was probably born during 1560s. His first wife was Margaret, daughter of Jeffrey Hall, yeoman, of Newton, Lancashire and his wife Alice.[5] Evidence of Ralph's marriage appears in Jeffrey's Will dated 1 February 1598.[4]

> ... and I give and bequeath to my sonne in lawe Ralphe Worthington and Margaret his wiffe.... pounds and I give and bequeath.... Hollande my sonne in law and his wife ... pounds ...

The missing words in this abstract result from damage to the edges of the Will. Jeffrey had inherited his land from his father, George Hall in 1570, as recorded by the court leet of Manchester held on 4 October 1570:[1]

> The Jurie doothe presente George Hall to be departed syns the last court and that Jeffere Hall his sonne is his heire and of Laufull agge and is redie to doe all soche servys as for hym is due.

The registers of the Collegiate Church of Manchester show that Ralph and Margaret had six children, namely:[6]

Forename	Date of baptism	Date of burial	Article
Thomas		11 November 1592	1.7
Alice	1 November 1594		1.8
Thomas	21 November 1596		1.9
Mary	20 June 1602		1.10
Anne	3 March 1604-5		1.11
James	11 November 1610		1.12

The entry for the last of these reads 'James sone to Ralphe Worthington of Failsworth'. According to P.W.L. Adams there was a further son Ralph – the eldest and heir.[3] However, his baptism remains unknown and some uncertainty remains; the subject is discussed more fully later. (Article 1.6)

Alas, Margaret died in childbirth when delivering James. She was buried at the Collegiate Church on 10 November 1610, the day before James's baptism. The entry in the register is 'Margaret wife of Ralph Worthington of Faylesworth'.

---

[*] Equivalent to 6,700 man-days of agricultural labour.

Ralph re-married on 26 October 1613 at Middleton church, Lancashire, the entry in the register being 'Raffe Worthington and Anne Taylor', but she died within four months. She was buried at Middleton on 17 February 1613-4, the entry in the register being 'Uxor Raff Worthington'. It is possible that Anne had previously been the wife of Edmund Taylor; an entry in the register of marriages in 1601 at the Collegiate Church reads 'Edmund Taylier and Anne Massey by licence'. A generation later there was an Edmund Taylier, fuller, of Middleton whose son was also named Edmund. This is shown by the Will of Edmund Taylier dated 2 June 1637.[4]

Ralph married once more; he had a further child baptised at the Collegiate Church, namely:

Forename	Date of baptism	Article
Richard	2 April 1615	1.13

The entry in the register is 'Richard son to Ralphe Worthington of Faylesworth'. Two further children were baptised at the same church – Robert on 25 May 1617 and Elizabeth on 27 November 1620, but they were described as children of 'Ralph Worthington of Manchester'. The dates fit well as siblings of Richard. The place name can be explained either by a move to Manchester in the meantime, or simply because 'Manchester' in the register is referring to the name of the parish in which Failsworth lies. The pedigree published by P.W.L. Adams shows Ralph as having yet another son, George (article 13.2) who lived at Newton and had eight children. However, George's baptism has not yet been discovered. The evidence of his place in the family is firstly that he is quoted as nephew to Nicholas Worthington, innkeeper of Manchester, in the letters of administration following Nicholas's death (Article 1.4) and secondly that Newton is only a mile or so from Failsworth. However, it is not proved beyond doubt that Nicholas, innkeeper, is the same Nicholas as the third son of Thomas.

Ralph was one of the two constables of Failsworth – the officers of the lord's court responsible especially for law and order. In 1616, however, they were failing in their duties as shown in the records of the *Manchester Quarter Sessions* of 11 April 1616 'A precept to the Constables of Faylesworth to appear at the next Quarter Sessions to answer their default in execution of their offices'.[1] On 6 September 1616 a further entry was made: 'A precept to apprehend Ralphe Worthington the constable of Faylesworth to appear at the next Sessions'. Again, the following day, 7 September 1616 appears:

Ralphe Worthington bound over with Thomas Lomas of Failsworth as surely to appear at the next Sessions or in the meantime pay the sum of money taxed upon his Township towards the building of a House of Correction.

Perhaps the default was part of an attempt by the residents of Failsworth to avoid the tax.

1.3 Richard

Richard Worthington, the second son of Thomas Worthington and Elizabeth his wife (Article 1.1), is first referred to in his father's Will made on 21 May 1588. Thomas had bequeathed his leased land at Thealmore to Richard and his brother Nicholas between them equally. Richard occupied and farmed the land, presumably making some financial arrangement with Nicholas (Article 1.4), whose career took a different course.

Richard was involved in a three-cornered dispute concerning the tithes due from his land, which had been enclosed and 'Lately Improved out of Theyle Moore'.[7] James Ashton, who held a third of the manor of Chadderton cum Foxdenton, claimed that the tithes were due to him as he had a lease of the right to the tithes from the Collegiate Church of Manchester. The college claimed that James did not have such a lease and that the tithes were due to them. Richard had not paid the tithes to either party. An early meeting on the subject was held on 18 May 1596 at the church when:

> ... personallie appeared James Ashton of Chaderton, Esq., Edmund Chaderton and James Chetame gent, with Ric. Worthington, all parties to a cause concerning ye right of tithes coming and remening upon a parcel of land nowe in ye tenure and occupation of ye said Worthington and they everie on of theime did submite theime selves to thorder, Judgement, dome and award of Nicholas Banaster of Althame and William Ashton of Clegg Esqrs. and did consent that this cause would stand in state as ye same doth nowe without prejudice to any party...

The parties thus signed an agreement to have the matter settled by the arbitrators, after which the decision would be published in the ecclesiastical court of Chester. However, the matter was not settled so simply; it laboured on for more than two years – with the aid of solicitors. In due course, the bishop of Chester approached the court of the Duchy of Lancaster at Westminster Palace which in turn appointed commissioners to investigate the matter. The College claimed strongly against the right of James Ashton to take the tithes; for example they wrote:

> Concerning our Sutte at Chester for Tythes come of Theilemore ... betwixt Mr Asheton and us, neither in the spiritual courte, nor within any other court within her majesty's dominion. For whatever sinister means hath bene used by the said Mr Asheton to procure a sentens at haste against Worthington ... had not colour nor tytle in the matter ...

It seems that by 1599 a settlement out of court had been reached in which James Ashton was to enter into an indenture with the College to lease the right of tithes in return for a small annual rent. Richard Worthington would then pay the tithes to James and also pay compensation for loss of earlier tithes. Accordingly, Richard wrote to his solicitors:

Mr Powell, Touching the Suite oy tithes Dependinge in your courte betwixte Mr Asheton and me, I have yelded to him for same because I have neither can clayme (as you know) any right there unto. And he is at the mediation of my goode friends contended to referre what charges be due unto him for delaying the tithes to the arbitrements of Christopher Tonge and James Traves yeoman. I doe therefore hartilye requyre you to staye any further proceedings therein. In full truste whereof with many thanks for your paynes taken in this my suite, I committe you to god. Theylemore this viijth of October 1599. Your lovinge Clyennte, Richard Worthington, his mark.

It appears that the Worthingtons had left Thealmore by 1614, by which time Richard may have died. The record of the assessment of that year to raise funds to enable King Charles I to disband and pay off the English and Scottish armies included an entry for Chadderton thus:[8] 'John Ogden, Thealmore, £10 2s. 0d.[*] The assessment was at the rate of 1s. 0d. for each £5 of annual income (that is one percent).[8]

1.4 Nicholas

As has been mentioned, P.W.L. Adams considered that Nicholas Worthington, son of Thomas Worthington and Elizabeth his wife (Article 1.1) was the same person as Nicholas Worthington of Manchester, innkeeper. An abstract from this Nicholas's Will dated 10 June 1626 and proved at Chester on 9 February 1636-7 in which he is described as 'Nicholas Worthington of Manchester, yeoman, alehouse keeper' reads:[4]

… my goode shalbee devided into twoe equal pte whereof one pte I doe reserve to my selfe and the other pte I doe give unto my now lovinge wyffe Issabell Worthington. Also whereas I had a basebegotten sonne of the bodye of one Anne Bewdsell late of Openshawe deceased called by the name of Ralph Bewdsell alias Ralph Worthington, it is my will that the saide Ralph shall not medle with any pte of my goode but onlie that I give him one suit of apparel of myne and 2s in money in regard I have heretofore been at charge of him and given him certen somes of money.

He then made various bequests out of his own part, including 12d.[†] to each of his godchildren, 5s. to his 'lovinge frinde Mr Adam Byron of Salford gent' and his sword and dagger to John Leigh. Isabel was the sole executrix and received all the residue. When probate was granted 'Jacobi Worthington' and 'Georgij Worthington', nephews of Nicholas, signed on behalf of 'our Arnte his wiffe'. Isabel was a sister of Nicholas Somester of Gorton, Lancashire, who was appointed overseer of the Will.

The basebegotten son mentioned in Nicholas's Will may have been the boy baptised at St Michael's Church, Ashton-under-Lyne on

---

[*] Equivalent to 250 man-days of agricultural labour.
[†] Equivalent to one man-day of agricultural labour.

26 December 1597. The entry in the register was 'A childe nunc of Nicholas Worthington, base'. Although it appears that Nicholas and Isabel had no children to survive them, they may have had a son. An entry of 16 May 1602 in the register of baptisms at the Collegiate Church reads 'Rauffe son to Nicholas Worthington', but there is also a burial there six years later – 'An infant of Nycholas Worthington of Mancr'. That was on 23 June 1608.

The inventory of Nicholas's goods taken on 31 January 1636-7 adds some colour to his inn. The rooms mentioned were 'the bodie of the house … the parlour … the chamber over the house … the chamber over the parlour … the brewhouse … the butterie … the sellor'. There were barrels, woodenware, long tables, settles, benches, 'throwne chairs', other chairs, buffet stools and one 'fooles chaire'. There was also a 'musket, bandaleers and a headpiece'. The total value was £362 14s. 2d.,[†] but of this £242 5s. 3d. consisted of debts owing by 54 of his customers 'as appeareth by bonds and bills'.

There is not yet any corroborative evidence that Nicholas the innkeeper was the son of Thomas and Elizabeth Worthington of Failsworth. P.W.L. Adams assumed that there was such evidence because of the reference to Jacobi and Georgij Worthington who signed their Uncle Nicholas's letters of administration. Adams linked Jacobi with James Worthington, the youngest son of Ralph Worthington by his first wife Margaret. Although Nicholas the innkeeper is likely to be the son of Thomas and Elizabeth, there is another possibility – Nicholas Worthington, husbandman, of Chadderton. Chadderton lies about three miles north-west of Failsworth. An inventory of his goods was taken on 10 April 1644 and administration of his affairs was granted to Thomas Worthington of Chadderton, linen webster.[4]

1.5 Margaret

Margaret Worthington, daughter of Thomas Worthington and Elizabeth his wife (Article 1.1) of Failsworth married Ellis Buerdsell. The wedding was on 13 July 1574 at the Collegiate Church, Manchester, the entry in the register being 'Elize Buerdsell and M'grett Worthington istius'. Ellis had had a previous wife, 'Jone', who had been buried at the same church on 18 March 1573-4. Alas, Margaret had less than four years of married life; she was buried at the Collegiate Church on 8 March 1578-9, the entry being 'Margaret wife to Elize Buerdsell of Gorton'. Ellis lived a further 10 years before being buried at the same church on 26 April 1588, the entry being 'Elize Buerdsell of Gorton hou'.

Both Margaret and Ellis had died before Margaret's father wrote his Will, which explains why neither is mentioned. But John Buerdsell, presumably their son, did receive a bequest.

---

[*] Equivalent to 8,300 man-days of agricultural labour.

THIRD GENERATION – FAMILY OF RALPH (SENIOR)

1.6 Ralph (junior)

Ralph Worthington of Failsworth, hereafter called 'Ralph senior' (Article 1.2) son and heir of Thomas Worthington, husbandman of Failsworth (Article 1.1) was succeeded in due course by Nicholas Worthington, husbandman of Failsworth (Article 1.14). It is reasonable to presume, therefore, that Nicholas was a direct descendant of Ralph senior. Ralph senior's first marriage was probably about 1590, as his infant son Thomas was buried in 1592 and the baptisms on record of his other children range from 1594 to 1615 or later. Nicholas Worthington's marriage was in 1655, some 65 years after that of Ralph senior. Nicholas could, therefore, have been either the grandson or great-grandson of Ralph senior. P.W.L. Adams assumed that Nicholas was the grandson and that the generation between them was filled by Ralph Worthington, shoemaker of Middlewood in the parish of Ashton-under-Lyne, Lancashire, hereafter called 'Ralph junior'.[3] Ralph junior was married in 1615-6 which would be well spaced from that of his father at about 24 years, but with a long interval of about 41 years to the marriage of his son Nicholas.

The baptism of Ralph junior is not known, but if he were the eldest son and heir of Ralph senior he would have been born before 1596 when his younger surviving brother Thomas was baptised. On 10 February 1615-6 Ralph junior married Jane daughter of Nicholas Wolsencroft of Failsworth and his wife Isabel (born Holmes). Ralph and Jane's wedding was at the Collegiate Church of Manchester, the entry in the register being 'Ralph Worthington and Jane Wolsencroft huius'. Jane had been baptised at the same church on 2 February 1588-9, so she married at the age of 27 years. According to Ralph junior's Will made on 7 May 1668, he and Jane produced six sons; in order of mention they are:

Forename	Bequest	Article
Joseph	£40[*]	1.15
Daniel	£10	1.16
John	Cow and third of residue	1.17
Ralph	Four horses for carrying	1.19
Nicholas	Third of residue	1.14
Thomas	Third of residue	1.18

The order of mention does not appear to indicate the order of seniority. However, Nicholas was the first named executor and inherited the farm at Failsworth, so it is presumed he was the eldest.

The Will, which is beautifully written on vellum and remains in excellent condition, is as follows:[4]

> In the name of God Amen, The seventh day of May in the 20th year of the reign of our most gracious Sovereign Lord Charles the Second by the grace of god king of England Scotland France and Ireland, defender of

---

[*] Equivalent to 800 man-days of agricultural labour.

the faith Anno Domi 1668, I Ralph Worthington of Middlewood within the parrish of Ashton-under-Lyne in the countie of Lancaster, Shoemaker being amongst many other causes moved with the consideration of frailtie and uncertantye of the lyves of all people in general and especially of myne owne lyfe in particulary fynding myselfe to growe in years whereby I am admonished to make my selfe readie as well in the preparation of my soule to God as by his disposition of my earthly substance in this world, doe in my perfect and sound memorie and understanding, thanks bee given to Almightie god for the same make ordayne publish and declare this my last will and testament in manner and form following. That is to say first and principally I render and bequeath my soule to my lord god and creator firmely trusting that by the death and passion of his deerly beloved sonne Christ Jesus and by his onely <u>mersie</u> and mediation for me I shall live and partake with his belessed saints in his heavenly kingdom of those celestial joyes which of his eternall goodness he hath prepared for his elect, of which number through his infinit grace and mercie I doe confidently and stedfastly hope and believe that I am one. And my bodie commend and leave to Christian burial in such decent sorte as my executors hereafter herein named shall thinke befitting. And as concerning the disposition of my temporal estate which Almighty god of his bounteous liberalitie hath bestowed on mee, my will and mynde is the same shall be bestowed and distributed as followeth. First it is my will and mynde that all such debts as of right or in conscience shalbe due and oweing by mee at the time of my decease to anie person or persons whatsoever, my herriot, probate of this is my present testament, exhibiting of an inventorye, and all necessaries costs charges and expenses concerning the same shalbe paid and discharged out of my whole goods. Item I give and bequeath to Jane my loveing wiefe my best bedstead with the ffetherbed, boulsters, pillows, bedclothes and all other the furniture both woolen and lynnen thereunto belonging, and it is my will and mynde that she shall have noe more of my goods, because I have given here a full competencie in my cottage or tenements for the terme of her natural life in pure widowhood to her owne desire and contentment in the terme mentioned or conteyned in the same indentures of lease shall so long they continue. Item I give and bequeath to my sonne Joseph Worthington the sume of ffortie pounds of lawfull money of England. Item I give and bequeath unto my sonne Daniel Worthington the sume of Ten pounds of lyke lawfull money of England. Item I give and bequeath to my sonne John Worthington that Cowe that I formerly hyred forth to one Edward Kennerly. Item I bequeath to every childe that I am Grandfather to the sume of fyve shillings* of lyke lawfull money of England. Item I give and bequeath to my sonne Ralph Worthington all my horses, geldings and mares that have been usually employed for carrying. Item all the rest residue and remainder of my goods cattells and chattels and debtes of what name, nature or condition so ever or in whose hands or custodie soever the same shalbee or remayne at the tyme of my decease (bee the same more or less) I give and freely bequeath to my three sonns Nicholas Worthington, John Worthington and Thomas Worthington equally to be devyded amonst them. Item I constitute and ordayne and

---

* Equivalent to five man-days of agricultural labour.

make my sonnes Nicholas Worthington and Daniel Worthington my
true and lawfull executors of this my present testament and lastly, I
doe frustrate and make voyed all former and other wills, gifts, legarcys
and bequests and doe publish this to be my last will and testament
touching the disposing of my temporal goods.

In a codicil, Ralph junior bequeathed 10 shillings to John Cropper, five
shillings to Margaret wife of John Berrie and his 'best stockings, doublet,
breeches and jumpe' to his sonne John. Ralph junior was buried at St
Michael's Church, Ashton-under-Lyne on 25 May 1668, the entry in the
register being 'Ralph Worthington, Waterhouses'. An inventory of his
goods was taken on 4 June 1668 and the Will was proved at Chester on
17 June 1668. The inventory included a little mare, four carrying horses
given to his son Ralph, corn sold to Ralph, saddles and harness, one
swine, 18 kyne, poultry, a harrow and dung pile. It appears, therefore,
that Ralph junior had three strands to his career – shoemaking, carrying
and farming. Apart from one piece of leather, nothing connected with
shoemaking was listed, but perhaps he had retired, sold the business,
or passed it to one of his sons. The herriot mentioned in the Will also
shows that he held land by feudal tenure, but it is not known whether
this was for the land at Failsworth or Middlewood.

Jane, who had been married for 52 years, lived as a widow for six
months. She was buried aged 79 years on 15 November 1668 at St
Michael's Church, Ashton-under-Lyne, the entry being 'Jane Worthington,
Waterhouses, widow'.

The evidence concerning the connection of Ralph junior with the
Worthingtons of Failsworth can now be reviewed. The presumed succession
can be summarised in four generations, thus:

a) Thomas Worthington, husbandman, of Failsworth;
b) His son Ralph Worthington senior of Failsworth;
c) His son Ralph Worthington junior, shoemaker of Middlewood;
d) His son Nicholas Worthington, husbandman of Failsworth.

Any doubt about this lineage arises firstly because Ralph junior is a
shoemaker not living in Failsworth, secondly because the baptism of
Ralph junior is unknown while those of five of his siblings are on
record, and thirdly, because there is a gap of about 41 years between
the marriages of Ralph junior and his presumed son Nicholas. However,
the evidence in favour of the lineage is:

a) Known dates concerning Ralph senior and Ralph junior match well;
b) The second wife of Ralph senior of Failsworth was a widow at
   Middlewood who died in 1613-4 about four months after the marriage
   of Ralph junior. Ralph junior could have been introduced to Middlewood
   by his stepmother, or gone to look after her interests;
c) The wife of Ralph junior of Middlewood came from Failsworth;
d) Ralph junior bequeathed his carrying horses to his son Ralph (the
   third Ralph) while Nicholas's son Daniel was to become a carrier.

Middlewood is not shown on modern maps, but it lay in the northern district of the old parish of Ashton-under-Lyne, within two miles of both Failsworth and Waterhouses. In addition to being a shoemaker Ralph junior had husbandry interests and could well have held land in Failsworth, managed or used by another member of the family. It is just possible there was an additional generation between Ralph junior and Nicholas, but appropriate records of baptisms, marriages, and burials have not come to light.

1.7 Thomas
If Ralph Worthington junior (Article 1.6) were the eldest son of Ralph senior and Margaret his first wife (Article 1.2), it is likely that Thomas Worthington was the second son. An entry of 8 December 1592 in the register of burials at the Collegiate Church, Manchester reads 'Thomas son to Rauffe Worthington'. He was not baptised there and probably died at or soon after birth.

1.8 Alice
Alice Worthington, the eldest daughter of Ralph Worthington senior and Margaret his first wife (Article 1.2), was baptised on 1 November 1594 at the Collegiate Church, Manchester. The entry in the register was 'Alice daughter to Rauffe Worthington'.

1.9 Thomas
Thomas Worthington, third son of Ralph Worthington senior and Margaret his first wife (Article 1.2), was baptised on 21 November 1596 at the Collegiate Church, Manchester. The entry in the register was 'Thomas son of Rauffe Worthington'. He was given the same name as his elder brother who died nearly four years earlier. (Article 1.7)

This Thomas may be the Thomas Worthington who became a linenweaver of Failsworth. He wrote his Will on 14 April 1671.[4] In the Will he referred to Margaret, his wife, whom he appointed sole executrix. A Thomas Worthington had married 'Margaret Bardisley' on 4 October 1631 at the Collegiate Church. He also referred to 'James Whitehead my son in law' and 'Robert Gilliam my sonne in law of Manchester'. Robert in turn, had two daughters – Mary and Martha. The inventory of Thomas's goods shows that his residence included a barn, house, loom house, parlour, buttery and chamber. In the loom house there were:

> Great pair of loomes with treddles & pullices.
> Lesser pair of loomes with treddles and pullices.
> Shuttles, temples, and brushes.
> Rath and steads.
> Two wheels, two standards and two pairs of blaids.
> Sonnel and wisbetts. Bill, a homer and a pair of pincers.
> Shore shaft warping walls with rings.

1.10 Mary
Mary Worthington, the second daughter of Ralph Worthington senior and Margaret his first wife (Article 1.2), was baptised on 20 June 1602 at the Collegiate Church of Manchester. The entry in the register was 'Mary daughter to Rauffe Worthington'.

1.11 Anne
Anne Worthington, the third daughter of Ralph Worthington senior and Margaret his first wife (Article 1.2), was baptised on 3 March 1604-5 at the Collegiate Church of Manchester. The entry in the register was 'Anne daughter to Rauffe Worthington'.

1.12 James
James Worthington, the fourth son of Ralph Worthington senior and Margaret his first wife (Article 1.2), was baptised on 11 November 1610 at the Collegiate Church, Manchester. The entry in the register was 'James son to Rauffe Worthington of Faylsworth'. His mother Margaret died in childbirth and was buried the previous day at the same church.

'Joseph son of James Worthington' baptised on 26 May 1650 at the Collegiate Church may be a son of the James treated in this article. If so, James would have been 39 years of age at the time. This connection remains in doubt. (Article 1.15)

1.13 Richard
Richard Worthington, the fifth son of Ralph Worthington senior (Article 1.2) but the first by his presumed third wife, was baptised on 2 April 1615 at the Collegiate Church, Manchester. The entry in the register was 'Richard son to Rauffe Wothington of Faylesworth'.

FOURTH GENERATION – FAMILY OF RALPH AND JANE

1.14 Nicholas
Nicholas Worthington of Failsworth, husbandman, presumed to be the eldest son of Ralph Worthington and Jane his wife (Article 1.6), was certainly heir to Thomas Worthington and Ralph senior his son. (Articles 1.1 and 1.2) This may have been the Nicholas Worthington who signed the protestation oath of 1641. A Thomas Worthington also signed for the same geographical section, and 10 other Worthingtons signed for other sections.[1] On 30 September 1655 Nicholas married Hannah at St Michael's Church, Ashton-under-Lyne, the entry in the register being 'Nicholas son of Ralph Worthington, Waterhouses, and Anna daughter of George Bardsley, Hurst'. Hurst was a hamlet lying half a mile north of Ashton-under-Lyne, within the parish. The marriage was confirmed at the groom's church – the Collegiate Church of Manchester – on 15 October 1655. They produced at least four children, their baptisms being spread over 14 years:

Forename	Date of birth	Date of baptism	Article
John	28 August 1656	14 September 1656	1.20
A son		1658	
Daniel		February 1665-6	1.21
A son		1672 (between June and November)	

John was baptised at the bride's church – St Michael's – the entry in the register being 'John son of Nicholas Worthington of Failsworth born 28 August'. The three younger sons were baptised at All Saints' Church, Newton.[9]

Nicholas had interests in Waterhouses as well as Failsworth. He was assessed as a resident of Waterhouses for the poor rate of 1691 for the parish of Ashton-under-Lyne.[10]

Nicholas was buried on 16 October 1697 at All Saints' Church after 42 years of married life. He had not written a Will, but a letter of administration was granted to Daniel Worthington and Samuel Bardsley – presumably Daniel's uncle or cousin.[4] In the letter Nicholas was described as Nicholas Worthington 'late of Failsworth in ye sd county of Lancaster, husbandman'. Hannah had given her approval to the administrators, thus:[4]

> This may certifie to whom it may concern that I Hannah Worthington of Failsworth in the parish of Manchester and County of Lancaster, widow and relict of Nicholas Worthington late of Failsworth aforesaid deceased doo give my full consent and desire my sonne Daniel Worthington of Newton in ye said county, carrier, and Samuel Bardsley of Manchester aforesaid, yeoman, may have ye administration of my late husband Nicholas Worthington estate. As witness my hand and seale this nyneteenth day of October Anno Dm 1697.

Hannah lived as a widow for 13 years. She was buried at All Saints' Church, Newton on 21 March 1710-1: 'Ann Widow to Nicholas Worthington late of Failsworth'.

1.15 Joseph

Joseph Worthington, one of the younger sons of Ralph Worthington junior of Middlewood and Jane his wife (Article 1.6), was mentioned in his father's Will made on 7 May 1668. Ralph and Jane had married in 1615-6 and Joseph was a younger son, so he would have been born sometime between 1618 and the late 1620s.

P.W.L. Adams assumed that this Joseph was the Joseph Worthington who married Elizabeth Barlow on 13 January 1669-70 at the Collegiate Church, Manchester, and gave rise to a new cadet line of husbandmen and yeomen at Woodhouses in the parish of Ashton-under-Lyne. (Chapter 11 and Pedigree 11.) But Adams may not have then known that there was another Joseph in the district who could have married Elizabeth Barlow and founded the Woodhouses line; he was baptised as 'Joseph son of James Worthington' on 30 May 1650 at the Collegiate Church.

This second Joseph was probably the son of James Worthington (Article 1.12), the fourth son of Ralph Worthington senior and Margaret his wife. Thus, the two possible Josephs may also have been first cousins. The evidence in favour of each of the two contenders for the role of Joseph Worthington of Woodhouses can best be assessed by listing all relevant references in chronological order. The following chronology includes all known references between 1620 and 1690 to (a) any Joseph Worthington within, say, seven miles of Failsworth and Middlewood and (b) all Worthingtons in Woodhouses:

> 1650, 30 May – 'Joseph son of James Worthington' was baptised at the Collegiate Church, Manchester.
> 1668, 7 May – Ralph Worthington wrote in his Will '... to my son Joseph Worthington the sume of fforte pounds'.
> 1669-70, 13 January – 'Joseph Worthington and Elizabeth Barlow huius' were married at the Collegiate Church, Manchester.
> 1676, November – 'Ralph son of Joseph Worthington' was baptised at All Saints' Chapel, Newton.
> 1684, October – '... daughter of Joseph Worthington' was baptised at All Saints' Chapel, Newton.
> 1684-5, 11 March – 'Anne child of Joseph Worthington de Woodhouses' was buried at Ashton-under-Lyne church.
> 1686 – 'Elizabeth dau. of Joseph Worthington of Failsworth' was baptised at Newton church.
> 1686, 8 October – 'Elizabeth daughter of Joseph Worthington of Failsworth' was buried at Ashton-under-Lyne church.

The Collegiate Church of Manchester lies four miles west-south-west of Woodhouses, Middlewood lies two miles north-west of Woodhouses, the border of Failsworth lies a quarter of a mile west of Woodhouses, Newton chapel lies a mile and a half west of Woodhouses, and Ashton-under-Lyne church lies two miles south-east of Woodhouses. While geographical considerations tend to favour P.W.L. Adams' assumption, they do not provide firm evidence. More convincing evidence of the same conclusion is obtained by considering the churches at which Joseph Worthington of Woodhouses had his children baptised and buried. His children were baptised at Newton in 1676, 1679, 1684 and 1686, while he had children buried at Ashton-under-Lyne in 1684-5 and 1686. This was a clear custom. Newton was probably used for normal church-going because it was nearer to Woodhouses than Ashton, while Ashton could have been used for burials because Ralph Worthington junior of Middlewood was buried there. It would have been natural for the family to wish to be buried together. This strongly suggests that Joseph of Woodhouses was the son of Ralph Worthington junior of Middlewood. No good reason has been devised to explain why the other Joseph – baptised and married at Manchester – should have had this curious custom.

It has not been possible to trace the parentage of Elizabeth Barlow because there were several women of that name at the time. For example, there were Elizabeth Barlow baptisms at the Collegiate Church, Manchester, in 1641, 1642, 1643 and 1650, the girls being respectively the daughters of Robert, James, George and Robert Barlow. The family of Joseph Worthington and Elizabeth his wife can be summarised as follows:

Forename	Date of baptism	Date of burial	Article
Joseph	30 May 1676 probably		11.2
Ralph	November 1680		11.3
Anne	October 1684	11 March 1684-5	11.4
Elizabeth	1686	3 October 1686 probably	11.5

All the baptisms were at All Saints' Church, Newton. The register is in a dilapidated condition, particularly at the left-hand side, so that some dates and forenames are missing. Both burials were at St Michael's Church, Ashton-under-Lyne. For that of Anne, Joseph Worthington is described as 'de Woodhouses' but for that of 'Eliz' he was described as 'de Failesworth'!

Joseph senior died in 1721 and was buried on 24 July that year at St Michael's Church, Ashton-uner-Lyne. He must have been at least 93 years of age. His widow, Elizabeth Worthington of Woodhouses, lived for a further five months, being buried on 15 January 1721-2 at the same church. Joseph's cadet line – the Worthingtons of Woodhouses – is discussed later (Chapter 11).

1.16 Daniel

Daniel Worthington, one of the younger sons of Ralph Worthington junior and Jane his wife (Article 1.6), was appointed executor of his father's Will made on 7 May 1668. Ralph and Jane were married in 1615-6, so Daniel is likely to have been born between 1618 and the late 1620s. On 20 May 1669 he married Alice, daughter of Richard Jones of Flixton, Lancashire, which lies seven miles south-west of Manchester. Alice was then 24 years of age, having been baptised on 21 January 1644-5 at the Collegiate Church. The wedding also took place at the Collegiate Church. They produced a son:

Forename	Date of baptism	Article
Ralph	22 May 1670	12.2

His baptism was at St Michael's Church, Ashton-under-Lyne. The entry in the register was 'Ralph son of Daniel Worthington de Waterhouses', so Daniel was still living in the village where his father held property. In due course, however, Daniel and his family moved to Audenshaw, five miles south of Failsworth where he became a farmer. They were presumably there by 2 July 1680 when 'William Haigh late servant of Daniel Worthington' was buried at St Michael's Church, Ashton-under-Lyne.[6] Described as a yeoman of Audenshaw, Daniel wrote his Will on 9 February 1702-3.[4] He made bequests to his four grandchildren, 'Daniel, Alice, Ralph and John Worthington', to be paid to them following Alice's death or to each of them on reaching the age of 21 years if later. The grandson Daniel was singled out for a bequest of a 'cupboard, table, coach chair and barke stool which stand together on one side of the house', but these goods were to remain in Alice's use for the remainder of her life. After payment of the 'Lord's herriott', Alice was to enjoy the yearly income of the estate for life. There was an unusual provision that she could bequeath up to £30* of the estate to 'such person or persons as she shall think meet'. The remainder was to pass to his son Ralph.

Study of the inventory of Daniel's goods prepared on 21 April 1709 suggests that Ralph and his family were living in the same farmhouse as Daniel and Alice, but probably separated by well defined rooms. Daniel's rooms included the parlour, the chamber over the parlour, and the 'chamber over the house'. But Daniel also had furniture and effects 'in Ralph's chamber' including a musket and sword. It appears that most of the farming interests had already passed to Ralph, but Daniel retained a few animals and still owned some of the equipment. Daniel may have been a carrier at one stage of his life as he still had a coal cart, a corn cart, a 'turf cart', and some spare wheels. The turf cart was presumably for carrying peat fuel. These three carts were valued at only 16s. 8d.,† so were presumably old and disused.

Daniel was buried at St Michael's Church, Ashton-under-Lyne on 15 or 18 March 1708-9. His widow lived for a further 12 weeks as shown in an entry of 10 June 1709 in the register of the Old Presbyterian Chapel at Dukinfield, Cheshire: 'Alice Worthington widow of Daniel Worthington of Audenshaw who died this spring'.[11] Dukinfield lies about two miles to the east of Audenshaw just over the county boundary.

Daniel's cadet line – the Worthingtons of Audenshaw – is discussed later (Chapter 12).

1.17 John

John Worthington, one of the youngest sons of Ralph Worthington junior and Jane his wife (Article 1.6), was to inherit a cow and one third of the residue of his father's personal estate according to the Will made on 7 May 1668. It may have been this John Worthington who had two daughters baptised at All Saints' Church, Newton – Ales, baptised in 1670 and another daughter baptised on 31 August 1673. The remainder of the date of the first baptism and the forename of the second are missing because of damage to the register. Another possibility is that this is the John Worthington who settled at Brinnington, in the parish of Stockport, Cheshire. Brinnington lies five miles south of Failsworth and about three miles south-east of Audenshaw, just over the county boundary between Lancashire and Cheshire. John's wife was Hannah, and they had five children, all baptised at Dukinfield Chapel, Cheshire:[11]

---

* Equivalent to 570 man-days of agricultural labour.
† Equivalent to 16 man-days of agricultural labour.

Forename	Date of baptism
Jonathan	10 February 1679
Samuel	5 June 1682
Joshua	4 February 1684
Daniel	2 October 1687
Hannah	19 April 1691

Identity of this John Worthington of Dukinfield with John the brother of Daniel (Article 1.16) could explain the otherwise odd burial of Daniel's widow Alice at Dukinfield when her husband had been buried three months previously at Ashton-under-Lyne.

John Worthington of Brinnington died on 11 October 1706 and was buried three days later at the Old Presbyterian Chapel. His Will dated 8 March 1705 and proved at Chester on 17 October 1706 shows that he called himself 'John senior' and that he had a son also called John. The only other children mentioned in the Will are son Samuel Worthington and son Hugh Worthington of Macclesfield who was appointed the sole executor. John junior may have been the eldest son, as his father had already given him a moiety of his 'messuage with the housing and buildings'. The other moiety was bequeathed to his widow Hannah for life. That property was leased from Sir Robert Dukinfield by an indenture dated 29 September 1674. John senior also held a clage or field called Ashebotham in Reddish, Lancashire, which he leased from Sir Edward Coke by an indenture of 28 October 1674. That clage he bequeathed to Hannah for life and then to his son Samuel.

1.18 Thomas
Thomas Worthington, one of the younger sons of Ralph Worthington and Jane his wife (Article 1.6), was mentioned in his father's Will made on 7 May 1668. He inherited a third of the residue of Ralph's personal estate.

1.19 Ralph
Ralph Worthington, one of the younger sons of Ralph Worthington junior and Jane his wife (Article 1.6), was mentioned in his father's Will made on 7 May 1668. Ralph the son may have been a carrier, as he was bequeathed four horses 'usually used for carrying'.

FIFTH GENERATION – FAMILY OF NICHOLAS AND HANNAH

1.20 John
John Worthington, the elder son of Nicholas Worthington and Anna or Hannah (Article 1.14) was born on 28 August 1656 and baptised on 14 September 1656 at St Michael's Church, Ashton-under-Lyne. Presumably John died young; he was certainly dead by the time administration of his father's estate was granted in 1697, as Daniel was then heir and, apparently, the only surviving child.

1.21 Daniel

Daniel Worthington, the third son (but later heir) of Nicholas Worthington and Hannah his wife (Article 1.14) was baptised in February 1665-6 at All Saints' Chapel, Newton. On 3 July 1684, at the age of 18 years, Daniel married Rebecca the daughter of Robert Thorpe of Hathershaw, in the parish of Oldham, Lancashire. Rebecca was eight years older than Daniel, having been baptised on 14 March 1657-8 at St Mary's Church, Oldham, Lancashire. Rebecca's father wrote his Will when Rebecca was only three years of age.[4] She was to receive continuing schooling and a third of his personal estate; her brother Isake Thorpe was to receive another third and succeed to land held (presumably copyhold) of the lord of the manor. Rebecca married firstly Roger Kenyon of Lymm, Cheshire, about 17 miles south-west of Failsworth. The wedding took place on 17 December 1680 at St Mary's Church, Prestwich, Lancashire. Alas, the marriage lasted 16 months only; Roger wrote his Will on 21 April 1682 which was proved at Chester on 26 May 1682.[12] Roger was a linen webster, but they also had a small holding with livestock. He bequeathed the whole of his estate to Rebecca although there was a provision that, if Rebecca was with child or children at the time of his death, Rebecca would have received one third and the child or children two-thirds.

Rebecca had been unlucky with her father and her first husband, but with Daniel she found security. Their wedding was at St Leonard's Church, Middleton, and they produced nine or ten children:

Forename	Date of birth	Date of baptism	Article
Samuel		December 1685	1.22
Theophilus		18 September 1687	1.23
Jonathan			1.24
George			1.25
Robert			1.26
Joseph		8 September 1695	1.27
Rebecca	7 April 1697	23 April 1699	1.28
Susanna		24 April 1702	1.29
A daughter			1.30

Samuel and Theophilus were baptised at All Saints' Church, Newton, Daniel being described as 'of Failsworth'. However, Joseph, Rebecca and Susanna were baptised at Dob Lane Chapel, Failsworth, while Daniel was a carrier of Newton! Perhaps Daniel and Rebecca changed their allegiance to the chapel because it was Presbyterian and became United Brethren following the cooperation between the Presbyterians and the Independents about 1693. An outstanding minister – Nathaniel Scholes – was incumbent there from 1691 to 1702. The entries in the register for the birth of a Rebecca and the baptism of a Rebecca could relate to the same daughter, but it would have been unusual in this period to delay a baptism for two years. It is more likely that the first

Rebecca died before she could be baptised and that the next daughter, who arrived about two years later, was given the same name.

Daniel and his family moved from Failsworth to Waterhouses, a mile or two eastwards into the parish of Ashton-under-Lyne, sometime after 1687 while retaining his carrying business at Newton. Perhaps he moved there following the death of his father, Nicholas, who was a resident of Waterhouses in 1691. (Article 1.14) Waterhouses was a charming village lying on the north-west bank of the River Medlock; in Victorian times it became a favourite picnic site for Manchester families.[14] A picture of it was used to illustrate a fictitious place called 'Daisy Nook' in the book *A Day Out* by B. Brierly, so Waterhouses acquired the new name Daisy Nook. Daniel held his 'messuage and tenement with appurtenances' in Waterhouses, together with a 'little house and croft' on the other side of the river. The tenure was in the form of a lease for three lives, held of Henry Booth, 1st earl of Warrington, PC, chancellor of the exchequer.

Rebecca must have died sometime between 1702 and 1719 because Daniel re-married on 28 May 1719. His new wife was Mary, the daughter of John Occleston, senior, and sister of John Occleston junior of Mere, Cheshire. Daniel was then about 53 years of age while Mary was about 61, having been baptised on 10 December 1657 at St Mary's Church, Rosthorne (later called Rostherne), which is less than two miles north-east of Mere.[13] The Occleston family had been settled there for several generations, as shown by the monumental inscriptions in Rostherne churchyard. A licence had been issued at Chester on 23 May 1719.[14] In the list of bondsmen Daniel himself was described as a 'yeoman of Newton', while the second bondsman was 'John Gardiner, carrier of Newton'. Presumably John Gardiner was Daniel's manager or business partner. The wedding took place at St Mary's Church, Rostherne. Mary had previously married at that church on 10 January 1677-8 John Billingham, yeoman farmer of Garwood, Rostherne, and had produced by him four children – John, William, Mary and Elizabeth. However, John had died, his Will being made on 22 January 1701-2 and proved on 5 August 1702 at Chester.[12]

Daniel died aged 66 years and was buried on 13 January 1732-3 at St Michael's Church, Ashton-under-Lyne. By his Will dated 11 December 1731 and proved at Chester on 9 June 1733 his widow, Mary, was to have the little house and croft for life.[4] Subject to this arrangement, the whole of his real estate passed into trust for 21 years for the benefit of his grandson Samuel Worthington (the second son of Daniel's second son, Theophilus) who was then aged 17 years (Article 2.4). Daniel's first two sons had pre-deceased him; so had his eldest son's only son and his second son's eldest son; so Samuel had become Daniel's heir male. After 21 years the trust was to end and the estate to pass unfettered to Samuel – at the age of about 33 years. After bequests of personal estate to Daniel's daughters or their widowers, the residue of the personal estate was divided equally among Daniel's three surviving sons – Jonathan, George, and Robert. (Articles 1.24, 1.25 and 1.26 respectively). An inventory and valuation of Daniel's 'goods, chattels and cattle' was taken on 11 November 1731, Robert Worthington being one of the signatories. The items are arranged under 16 headings as follows:

> In the house
> In the Great Battery
> In the Parlour
> In the Dining Room
> In the Little Buttery
> In the Kitchen
> In the Chamber over the Parlour
> In the Chamber over the House
> In the New Chamber
> In the Chamber over the Kitchen
> In the Closett over the Porch
> Out of Doors
> In the Barn
> In the Carthouse
> In the Porch
> In the Garden

The contents were valued at £132 11s. 3d.[*]

Mary lived for a further 14 years. Her attachment to Mere, or her family there, appears to have been great, for she was buried in Rostherne churchyard on 4 December 1747. The monumental inscription is: 'Here lies the body of Mary Worthington (widow) sister to John Occleston of Meire December 4th 1747 aged near 91 years'.

SIXTH GENERATION – FAMILY OF DANIEL AND REBECCA

1.22 Samuel

Samuel Worthington, the eldest son of Daniel Worthington and Rebecca his first wife (Article 1.21), was baptised in December 1685 at All Saints' Church, Newton. The entry in the register was 'Samuel son [of] Daniel Worthington of Failsworth'. On 17 February 1707-8, at the age of 22 years, Samuel married Mary, a sister of Francis Browne, yeoman, of Prestwich, Lancashire, a township lying about seven miles west-north-west of Failsworth. The wedding took place at the Collegiate Church, Manchester. They produced two children.

Forename	Date of baptism	Date of burial	Article
Edward	14 April 1710	21 September 1716	1.31
A daughter	December 1714		1.32

Edward was baptised and buried at the Collegiate Church, Manchester, but the daughter, (unnamed in the register) was baptised at St Matthew's Chapel, Stretford, Lancashire.

---

[*] Equivalent to 2,600 man-days of agricultural labour.

In due course, Samuel became tenant of the 'Old Trafford Demesne', the freehold of which was held by the de Trafford family, lords of the manor of Stretford. There he ran his carrying business and farmed 207 acres of land. The earliest known reference to his occupancy of the farm is in the *Stretford Court Book*, the entry for 4 March 1712 being:[15]

> We order Samuel Worthington occupant of the Old Trafford Demesne to ditch betwixt the Great Meir Hey and Moor Hey Yate before 24th day of June next in pain of 2s. 6d.*

Samuel died at the age of 29 years; he was buried at the Collegiate Church, Manchester on 1 April 1715. He had written his Will four days previously – on 28 March 1715.[4] The wording of the preamble, although in part standard legal form for the times, gives an interesting glimpse of his religion and state of mind:

> In the name of God Amen, I Samuel Worthington of Stretford in the County of Lancashire, Carrier, being of sound and perfect mind and memory, thanks be therefore given to Almighty God, doe make and ordain this my Last Will and Testament in manner and forme following and first and principally I commend my soule into the hands of Almighty God hoping through the merits, death and passion of my Blessed Saviour and Redeemer Jesus Christ to have full and free pardon and forgiveness of all my sins and to inherit Everlasting Life. And my body I commit to the Earth to be decently buried at the discretion of my Executors hereafter named as touching disposition of all such temporall estate as it has pleased Almighty God to bestowe upon me ...

He bequeathed £120[†] to his son, Edward, the income to be accumulated or used for his education and the capital to pass when he reached the age of 21 years or marriage, whichever came first. All the remainder of his estate passed to Mary his wife. Mary, Daniel (Samuel's father), and Francis Browne (Mary's brother), were three of the four executors. The Will was proved at Chester on 21 May 1715. An inventory of his goods and chattels was valued professionally at £297 1s. 1d. as follows:

	£	s.	d.
Goods in the house	8	6	8
Goods in the Best Chamber	5	4	4
Goods in the Red Chamber	1	10	0
Goods in the Parlour	7	0	2
Goods in the Kitchen	2	11	9
Goods in the Buttery	0	18	0
In Linnens	3	7	0
In the Stable	7	8	2
In the Barne in corn and hay	11	5	0
In Cattle	71	13	4
Two Colts	19	0	0
Carts and Wheels	7	0	0

* Equivalent to three man-days of agricultural labour.
† Equivalent to 5,700 man-days of agricultural labour.

In corn and cheese in the house	12	18	4
In corn on ye ground	13	8	4
Debts supposed to be good	120	0	0
In wearing apparel	5	0	0
In hustlem'ts	0	10	0
Sume	297	1	1

Mary was potentially in a predicament, holding the carrying business and a substantial farm, but Samuel's younger brother, Jonathan (the third son of Daniel), came to the rescue. He took on the carrying business and farm, presumably giving Mary an undertaking to pay for the assets involved over a period of time.

Mary re-married within a year of Samuel's death and Edward, her son, died soon afterwards. Mary's second husband was John Harrison, yeoman, of Stretford. A licence was issued at Chester on 7 April 1716 and they were married later the same day at the Collegiate Church, Manchester. Mary had three children by John, namely Mary who was baptised on 17 March 1716-7, Ann baptised on 7 August 1720, and Samuel baptised on 20 May 1722. All three baptisms were at St Matthew's Chapel, Stretford. It is noteworthy that their son should have been given the same name as Mary's former husband.

1.23 Theophilus

Theophilus Worthington, the second son of Daniel Worthington and Rebecca his first wife (Artcicle 1.21), was baptised on 18 September 1687 at All Saints' Church, Newton, the entry in the register being 'Theophilus son of Daniel Worthington of Failsworth'. Like his elder brother Samuel, Theophilus became a carrier, but ran his business from Rochdale, a town lying eight miles north of Failsworth. Indeed, four of the five sons of Daniel were carriers. (Articles 1.22, 1.24 and 1.25)

On 6 June 1710, at the age of 22 years, Theophilus married Mary, the only daughter of 'Mr John Byrom, linen draper, of Manchester'. Mary was four years older than Theophilus, having been baptised on 19 June 1683 at the Collegiate Church of Manchester. Her mother, also named Mary, did not long survive the delivery, and was buried on 21 June 1683 at the Collegiate Church. Alas, Mary junior also lost her father when she was five years of age. In his Will dated 3 January 1689 and proved in February 1689 he was described as 'gentleman'. He bequeathed all his 'messages, bergages, tenements, lands, rents, reversions, services and hereditaments' in Manchester to his 'sonne William Byrom and the heires of his bodye'.[4] In default of such heirs the estate was to pass to his daughter Mary Byrom and her heirs. Failing both his children and their heirs, the estate was to pass to John's cousin Edward Byrom, gentleman, of Manchester, 'and his heirs for ever'. John had other properties described as 'messuages, cottages, clanshares and hereditaments with their ... appurtenances'. These were to be sold to provide an increased personal estate of which £400* was to pass to Mary, £300 to William and £20 to Edward (who was appointed executor). The remainder was to be divided equally between William and Mary. Theophilus and Mary produced seven children, at least six of whom were baptised at St Chad's Church, Rochdale:

Forename	Date of baptism	Article
Mary	20 May 1711	2.2
Daniel	9 August 1713	2.3
Samuel	15 June 1715	2.4
Thomas	15 June 1715	2.5
John	3 June 1716	2.6
Rebecca	14 February 1718-9	2.7
Jonathan	Unknown	2.8

The parson, it appears, had difficulty with the father's name, spelling it variously, 'Theoffelus' and 'Offelus'. For the first two baptisms the family was described as 'of Blackwater' and for the remainder as 'of Rochdale'. However, Blackwater was part of Rochdale and it appears that the family always resided at Blackwater, where Mary was living as a widow at her death in 1751.

Theophilus died aged 43 years and was buried at St Chad's Church on 16 September 1730. His Will was dated 4 September 1730 when he was already 'sick and weak of body, but of sound and perfect mind and memory...'.[4] He bequeathed the whole of his estate to his wife:

> ...wherewith to bring up my children and to give them as they arrive
> at age of Twenty one years or be marryed, whichever first shall happen,
> such proportion as she thinks convenient ...

However, she was to reserve one third part of his estate for herself. The executors were his widow Mary and his younger brother Jonathan Worthington. An inventory of his goods and chattels was taken on 26 March 1731 which was valued at £154 8s. 6d.† consisting of:

	£	s.	d.
14 horses and gears	63	0	0
2 cows, 1 plough and 4 harrows	7	18	0
Stone trough	5	12	6
6 carts and 4 pairs of wheels	12	0	0
Hay	26	10	6
In the house			
Fire iron, tongues, fender and crow	0	10	0
Iron things and brass ladles	0	4	0
4 Brass panes, a brass pot and Iron pot	1	1	0
Frying pan and chalfindishes	0	3	0
Copper cann, saucepanne and 2 brass pots	0	8	0

---

* Equivalent to 8,000 man-days of agricultural labour.
† Equivalent to 3,000 man-days of agricultural labour.

1 dipper and 6 candlesticks	0	2	6
Salt, pye and candle box and coach chair and cushion	0	11	0
4 chairs, 3 tables, clock and case	3	17	0
Warming pan and 8 spitts	0	4	0
In the Parlour			
2 Bedsteads and bedding, fire iron and tongues	3	17	6
7 chairs, chest, 2 little tables, chest of drawers	1	14	0
Nest of drawers, 1......, linen	2	7	6
In the Buttery			
Table and seats, 1 doz of trenchers, shelves and pots	0	14	0
Pewter, wooden things and bottles	1	18	0
Chamber over the milk house			
1 bedstead and bedding, chest and 2 buffills	0	17	0
Chamber over the house			
2 bedsteads and bedding, chest and chair, hack saddle, 4 saddles	4	2	0
Chamber of the Parlour			
Fire iron, bedstead and bedding, presse and 5 chairs	6	2	0
1 table and cheese board, 1 sleeping glass, pictures	0	11	0
Two bussills	0	2	0
In the shop			
Counter and shelves	0	5	0
1 chest, 3 measures, weights and scales	2	17	0
Hustlements			
Purse and apparale	7	0	0
sume	154	8	6

Mary lived as a widow for 20 years. She died aged 53 years and was buried on 4 June 1751 at St Chad's Church. She had signed her Will on 16 April 1737 – 14 years before her death.[4] Although the state of her family had moved on in the meantime, the Will shows her strong sense of responsibility to the younger children who had not yet flown the nest. She wrote:

> ... whereas my sons Thomas Worthington and Jonathan Worthington are bound apprentices and I am to find them cloaths during that time, it is my will and mind that the Rents of the Dwelling House and Barn Bay, Cart house and Stable at the Lane Side on the top of Blackwater Street within Spotland go towards finding Thomas Worthington and Jonathan Worthington with Cloaths during their apprenticeships and for and towards the maintenance of my son Samuel Worthington till such times as the Estate called Waterhouses that his Grandfather Daniel Worthington left him comes clear; And then I do discharge him Samuel Worthington from having any more of my Estate. And when Jonathan Worthington is loose from his apprenticeship and my son Samuel's estate comes to him it is my will and mind that the aforesaid Housing be valued and that the value thereof be equally divided amongst Thomas Worthington, John Worthington, Jonathan Worthington, Mary Worthington and Rebecca Worthington my children, and it is my mind that some of them buy the same if they all be willing that it be sold ...

Daniel, the son not mentioned, had presumably died before the Will was written (Article 2.3). Mary specifically referred to her 'pitch pillion and side saddle' which she bequeathed to her two daughters. By a codicil dated 29 May 1751, within days of her death, she appointed her son Jonathan and daughter Rebecca executors in place of her son John who had died. She also appointed her brother-in-law Jonathan Worthington as overseer.

Theophilus's cadet line is discussed later (Chapter 2).

1.24 Jonathan

Jonathan Worthington, the third son of Daniel Worthington and Rebecca his first wife (Article 1.21), was born about 1689. Unfortunately the date and place of his baptism are unknown. His two elder brothers had been baptised at All Saints' Chapel, Newton, but parts of the register for the period are badly damaged and unreadable. The Newton register of marriages is also in poor condition between 1712 and 1718 which may be why the marriage of Jonathan to Mary has not been traced. Mary had been born about 1696 so was some six years younger than Jonathan. They produced six daughters and one son:

Forename	Date of baptism	Date of burial	Article
Mary	15 February 1718-9		3.2
Rebecca	19 March 1720-1	30 April 1727	3.3
Hannah	17 May 1724	12 July 1730	3.4
Jonathan	17 July 1726		3.5
Rebecca	20 July 1729		3.6
Hannah	23 April 1732		3.7
Susanna	18 August 1734		3.8

Jonathan and Mary were described as 'of Stretford' in the 1724 entry, as 'carrier' in 1732 and as 'of Trafford' in 1734. All the children were baptised at St Matthew's Chapel, Stretford.

When Jonathan's eldest brother, Samuel (Article 1.22), died in 1715, Jonathan took on the carrying business and the tenancy of Old Trafford demesne. This must have been by some family arrangement because Samuel had an heir – Edward Worthington (Article 1.31) then nearly five years of age. Edward died the following year leaving his uncle Theophilus (Article 1.23) as the next heir male, but Theophilus already had a carrying business at Rochdale. Perhaps Jonathan had already been working with Samuel at Old Trafford – perhaps in partnership.

On 3 March 1717-8, Jonathan was directed by the court baron of Stretford, thus:[15]

> We order Jonathan Worthington leccupant of Trafford Demesne to ditch the end of the Great Coppy adjoining the Oxe Hayeys and overcrosse the lane leading from Trafford to Moor Hey betwixt the first day of May next in pain of 10s.*

---
* Equivalent to 10 man-days of agricultural labour.

Again, on 21 October 1719, George Fletcher and Jonathan Worthington were ordered to 'ditch betwixt Houghe Moss and Mr Broom's house in pain of 13s. 4d each'. On 8 July 1723 Jonathan and two other occupants of Mr Broom's Moss Roome were ordered to 'ditch and slaine their Cross Trenches and side Trenches and pull up their Plattings upon the Parke Moss'.

Jonathan's wife, Mary, died at the age of 51 years. She was buried on 30 March 1747 in the family grave at St Matthew's Chapel, Stretford, where two of her daughters already lay. The grave was railed in, north of the front gate of the Old Chapel Yard.

A glimpse of Jonathan's business is given in the pocket book of John Collier, junior, the painter and author who wrote under the name 'Tim Bobbin'. An entry for 29 May, probably in the year 1764, shows that Jonathan had commissioned John to paint a sign and name for his business: The entry reads:[16]

	£	s.	d.
May 29. To a sign	1	10	0
To a board over the post with 88 gold letters		8	0
	1	18	0*

On the following page appear amounts owing by Jonathan to John Collier, thus:

Jona Worthington p con	£	s.	d.
Ap 13, 1756 by carriage of 12 cheeses from Northwich to Rochdale		4	2
Ap 30, by Jacky's box to Chester		3	2
May 14, by carriage of 12 cheeses from Northwich to Rochdale		3	3
Sep 9, Pints of.... of...		1	0
Apr 22, 1756 A small parcel			10
		12	5
Apr 13 1757, Punch &c.		1	8
22 ...			6
22 May. Ale Punch Dinner		1	8
8 July		2	0
24 Aug		1	9
1758 Sep		4	0
July .... Ale		1	2
March 5		0	9
17 April Ale		1	6
17 ... punch Ale, corn hey &c.		1	6
Total reced of Jon Worthinton	1	8	11
His sign & Board come to	1	18	0
June 18 1764. Remains due to me	0	9	1

It is interesting that these debts appear to have remained unsettled over the period 1756 to 1764! On another page, which is over-scored,

---

* Equivalent to 35 man-days of agricultural labour.

Jonathan is described as 'Jon Worthington of Manchester and Halifax Carrier'. This has led to the suggestion that the 88 gold letters consisted of JONATHAN WORTHINGTON, CARRIER, MANCHESTER & HALIFAX on both sides of the board. John Collier, who lived from 1708 to 1786, was the son of the Reverend John Collier, chaplain of St Matthew's Chapel, Stretford, 'a poor country curate whose stipend never amounted to £30 per annum'.

Jonathan died on 31 July 1769 aged 79 years, and was buried in the family grave at St Matthew's Chapel, Stretford, where his wife and three daughters were already buried. The stonework there was inscribed:

> Here resteth the Body of Jonathan Worthington who departed this life
> July ye 31 1769 aged
> 79 years.
> Mary his wife buried March the 30th Ao Domi 1747 aged 51 years
> Rebecca the daughter of Jonathan Worthington of Stretford who
> departed this life April ye
> 29th 1727.
> Hannah his daughter who departed this life July ye 10th 1730.
> Also Susanna his daughter who departed this life June ye 26th 1756.

It appears that Jonathan had already retired by handing the business and farm to his son. He may also have moved to a residence in Manchester. He described himself in his Will dated 22 January 1767-8 as 'yeoman of Manchester'.[4] He bequeathed to his son the property on the west side of Dawson Square, Manchester, consisting of 'a burgage or dwelling house, warehouses and other buildings'. Land which Jonathan held at Sale, Cheshire, was placed in trust, the income being for the benefit of his daughter Mary Hesketh. After her death the income was to be used to bring up her two children by Thomas Hesketh until the age of 21 years when they would inherit the land. Jonathan also held land in Irlam within Barton upon Irwell, Lancashire, which was placed in trust for the benefit of his daughter Hannah Wright and her two children. There was ample provision for the education of Jonathan's grandchildren until they reached the age of 21 years. Jonathan also bequeathed to his son the pew 'with all its rights and privileges' which he had purchased from the warden and fellows of the College of Christ, Manchester. Jonathan referred in his Will to a silver tankard which was to pass to his daughter Rebecca, the wife of George Worthington (Article 9.5); the remaining silver was to pass to Jonathan's daughter Mary. A chest of drawers was bequeathed to Jonathan's servant Mary Bancroft, if she was still in his service at the time of death.

Jonathan's cadet line is discussed later (Chapter 3).

1.25 George
George Worthington, the fourth son of Daniel Worthington and Rebecca his first wife (Article 1.21), was born about 1691. His baptism is unknown,

probably because the church register of the period is badly damaged and unreadable (Article 1.24).

Like his three elder brothers, George was a carrier. In the oldest surviving Manchester directory, published in 1772, there appears a section giving a list of 'stop coaches, wagons and their owners'. It includes: 'York – George Worthington, Sun Shudehill, Satuday.' Shudehill lies about a quarter of a mile east of the Collegiate Church. At this time George senior would have been about 81 and George junior about 48 years of age. George junior would clearly have been more active in the management of the business but his father may still have been a partner; he was described as 'carrier' at the time of his death. The regular weekly run to York was advertised as a public service, but contract work would have proceeded throughout the week.

George's first wife was Anne. A search for a record of the marriage in the church registers of Lancashire did not produce a result, but a further search along his carrying route to York yielded the following entry at the parish church of Birstall, West Yorkshire: 'George Worthington and Hannah Rayner', the date being 1 January 1717-8. Birstall lies six miles south-west of Leeds, on the old route. George and Anne produced four children:

Forename	Date of baptism	Article
Mary		9.2
Hannah	13 September 1719	9.3
Phoebe	11 October 1721	9.4
George	8 March 1723-4	9.5

The baptisms of Hannah, Phoebe, and George took place at St Mary's Church, Oldham, Lancashire. For each, George senior was described as 'of Werneth'. The record for George junior gives the most information – 'George son of George and Anne Worthington of Wernith'. Werneth lies two miles north-east of Failsworth, within the parish of Oldham, Oldham being on the old road from Manchester to York. It is thought that the family lived at Werneth Hall; certainly George junior lived at the hall in his time (Article 9.5).

George senior married secondly Susanna, daughter of John Ogden and Susannah his wife of Foxdenton. Susanna was about seven years younger than George, having been baptised on 22 May 1698 at St Mary's Church, Oldham. John Ogden's Will, in which he is styled yeoman, was made on 11 November 1723 and proved in 1727; it shows that he held his farm by lease from Alexander Radcliffe, Esq.[4] Another John Ogden of the same family had by 1641 become the occupant of the Thealmore farm in Foxdenton, taking over from Richard Worthington (Article 1.3). George and Susanna had no children.

George senior died aged about 82 years and was buried on 19 March 1772 at St Mary's Church, Oldham. He was then described as 'of Maygate Lane'. He had not made a Will, but power of administration was granted to George junior on 24 March 1772 by the Consistory Court of Chester.[4] Susanna had renounced her right in favour of her stepson 'George Worthington, carrier, of Werneth' in a document of 21 March 1772.

'Mrs Susanna Worthington, widow of Highfields' in Oldham died aged 86 years and was buried on 23 February 1784 at St Mary's Church. Her Will was dated 1783 with a codicil dated 8 February 1784.[4] She held the freehold of two messuages and tenements with 'closes, fields, and parcels of land' called 'Frankenhurst' and 'Fearnbed' in Chadderton, Lancashire. These she bequeathed to her sister Martha Ogden who was occupant of one of the properties. Susanna also held a messuage and tenement with closes, fields and lands called 'Top of the Edge' in Royton, Lancashire which were in the occupation of her niece and nephew, Elizabeth and John Clegg, yeoman. The freehold of this property Susanna devised to her other sister Hannah Taylor. Susanna had inherited Top of the Edge from her father, John Ogden, who had entered into a lease whereby coalmining could proceed beneath the land in return for a rent and a royalty of a quarter of the value of the coal and cannel mined. Susanna bequeathed the rent and quarterage from this source to her niece Mary Scholes who was living with Susanna, and no doubt looking after her, at the end of her life.

George's short-lived cadet line – the Worthingtons of Werneth – is discussed later (Chapter 9).

1.26 Robert

Robert Worthington, the fifth son of Daniel Worthington and Rebecca his wife (Article 1.21), was born about 1693. In 1717 he married Elizabeth Charlsworth of Ashton-under-Lyne, the wedding being at St Peter's Church, Blackley, near Manchester. They produced three sons and one daughter, namely:

Forename	Date of baptism	Article
George	29 April 1722	10.2
Jonathan		10.3
Robert		10.4
Elizabeth		10.5

George was baptised at All Saints' Church, Newton, the entry in the register being 'George, son of Robert Worthington of Failsworth, slaughterer, and Elizabeth his wife'. How Robert's career developed from being the Failsworth slaughterer in his mid-20s is not known, but in his 60s he was described as 'yeoman of Manchester'. That was his style in his Will made on 15 July 1764.[4] 'Robert Worthington of Manchester' was buried on 7 January 1768 at St Michael's Church, Ashton-under-Lyne. Ashton as the burial place may have been chosen because his son Jonathan lived there (Article 10.3). Robert's Will was proved on 25 January 1768 at Chester. It shows that Robert held and lived at a 'messuage or dwelling house with lands' at Shudehill, Manchester. His elder brother George Worthington ran his carrier service to York from the *Sun* at Shudehill, and it is possible that Robert had some connection with it. Robert left all his property and personal estate to his wife who was still living there when she wrote her Will on 12 May 1770.[4] She died about 1776 and her Will was proved at Chester on 12 August of that year. By her Will all the Shudehill property and all her personal estate was to be placed in trust with instructions that they be sold. The proceeds were to be distributed to her only surviving son, George, her three grandchildren (issue of her second son, Jonathan) and her widowed daughter-in-law Elizabeth. Her nephew George Worthington of Werneth (Article 9.5) and her son-in-law Joseph Lion (Article 10.5) were appointed trustees.

Robert's cadet line is treated later (Chapter 10).

1.27 Joseph

Joseph Worthington, the sixth son of Daniel Worthington (Article 1.21) by Rebecca his first wife, was baptised on 8 September 1695 at Dob Lane Chapel, Failsworth.[18] The entry in the register reads: 'Joseph Worthington son of Daniel Worthington of Nuton.' No other references to Joseph have come to light, and he is not mentioned in his father's Will dated 11 December 1731. It seems likely, therefore, that Joseph died young without issue.

1.28 Rebecca

Rebecca Worthington, daughter of Daniel Worthington and Rebecca his first wife (Article 1.21), was born on 7 April 1697 and baptised on 23 April 1699 at Dob Lane Chapel, Failsworth. It was unusual at this period for a child not to be baptised for two years, but it was also unusual to note the date of birth in the registers. The entries are separate, that for the birth being 'Rebeckah Worthington was borne 7 day of April: daughter of Daniel Worthington', and that for the baptism being 'Rebeckah Worthington daughter of Daniel Worthington of Newton'. They may have been separate daughters, the first having died young.

Rebecca married at the age of 20 or 22 years on 1 October 1719 to Stephen Boardman of Eccles, Lancashire, the wedding taking place at the Collegiate Church, Manchester. It appears that they produced children: a Will of 1783 refers to a David Boardman and his wife Mary 'niece of Susanna Worthington', and in 1767-8 a Thomas Boardman, chapman, was occupying Jonathan Worthington's property in Dawson Square, Manchester (Article 1.24).

Rebecca was mentioned in her father's Will made on 11 December 1731:[4]

> ... I give to Rebeccah wife of the said Stephen Boardman if she survives her said husband whitch same sume I will shall be paid to her within three months after her husband's death if she be then living ...

1.29 Susanna

Susanna Worthington, the second daughter of Daniel Worthington and Rebecca his first wife (Article 1.21), was baptised on 24 April 1702 at Dob Lane Chapel, Failsworth, the entry in the register being 'Suanne Worington the douter of Daniel Worthington of Nuton'. The event was also recorded at All Saints' Chapel, Newton.

In his Will dated 11 December 1731, Susanna's father Daniel made bequests to his three sons-in-law, James Whittaker, John Andrew and Stephen Boardman.[4] Stephen Boardman was the husband of Rebecca (Article 1.28) so Susanna's husband would have been either James Whittaker or John Andrew.

1.30 A daughter

There was another daughter of Daniel Worthington and Rebecca his first wife (Article 1.21). Her husband was either John, Andrew or James Whittaker, both being mentioned as sons-in-law of Daniel (Article 1.29).

SEVENTH GENERATION – FAMILY OF SAMUEL AND MARY

1.31 Edward

Edward Worthington, the only son of Samuel Worthington and Mary his wife (Article 1.22), was baptised on 14 April 1710 at the Collegiate Church of Manchester. He died at the age of six years and was buried on 21 September 1716 at the same church.

Edward's father had died young about 18 months earlier on 1 April 1715 – leaving Edward as heir to his grandfather, Daniel Worthington (Article 1.21). It seems likely that Edward's only sister also died young. Also his mother re-married five months before young Edward's death. The grandparents must have considered the demise of this line a disaster. Edward's place as male heir and potential future representative of all six generations from Thomas Worthington of Failsworth (Article 1.1) was taken by his uncle Theophilus Worthington (Article 1.23).

1.32 A daughter

A daughter to Samuel Worthington and Mary his wife was baptised at St Matthew's Chapel, Stretford, Lancashire, in December 1714, the entry in the register curiously being 'daughter to Samuel Worthington of Stretford, baptised December'. P.W.L. Adams stated that her name was Mary but his reason is not known.[3] The daughter's mother, Mary, had a daughter by her second marriage named Mary, so either Samuel's daughter died young or was not named Mary.

When Samuel, her father, wrote his Will on 17 March 1715 he mentioned only one child – Edward his son. Thus, it seems likely that the daughter was already dead.

CHAPTER 2

LINE OF THEOPHILUS WORTHINGTON
OF ROCHDALE

2.1 Theophilus

Theophilus Worthington, the second son of Daniel Worthington and Rebecca his first wife (Article 1.21), was baptised in September 1687 at All Saints' Church, Newton. Theophilus's life has already been discussed (Article 1.23). He and Mary his wife produced six children.

SECOND GENERATION – FAMILY OF THEOPHILUS AND MARY

2.2 Mary

Mary Worthington, the eldest daughter of Theophilus Worthington and Mary his wife (Article 1.23), was baptised on 20 May 1711 at St Chad's Church, Rochdale, Lancashire.[1]

On 10 April 1746, at the age of about 34 years, Mary married John Fieldes (or Fildes), tobacconist of Toad Lane, Rochdale. John was nine years younger than Mary, having been baptised on 26 December 1720 at St Chad's Church. The entry in the register was 'John Filds of Toad Lane'. They had obtained a licence from the diocese of Chester the previous day when Thomas Lord, grocer of Rochdale, was John's co-bondsman.[2] The entry in the register of licences reads: '... john Fildes licensed to marry Mary Worthington spinster of Rochdale' at St Mary's Chapel, Rochdale. St Mary's was a satellite of St Chad's Church where the registers were kept. John was a younger son of 'John Fildes the Elder of Rochdale ... Yeoman' who wrote his Will on 16 September 1757.[3] He then held an estate consisting of his house and farm, several cottages and a croft at 'Yate near Cronkashaw' and several more cottages at Chapel Hill. At the farm there was a dyehouse, a frizzing mill and several other buildings – probably for the production of leather. The real estate descended to the eldest son, Jonathan, but a life annuity of £8[*] was to be paid to John out of the estate's rentals and a further annuity of £12 was to be paid to a third son James.

John and Mary produced two children, both being baptised at St Mary's Chapel:

Forename	Date of baptism
Mary	1 October 1747
John	27 September 1750

---

[*] Equivalent to 150 man-days of agricultural labour.

PEDIGREE 2 – LINE OF THEOPHILUS WORTHINGTON OF ROCHDALE, LANCASHIRE

Theophilus Worthington; bap. 1687, m. 1710, d. 1730. *(Pedigree 1 & Arts 1.23 & 2.1)* ═ **Mary**, dau. of John Byrom; b. 1683, d. 1751

| **Mary**; bap. 1711, m. 1746 John Fieldes & had issue, d. 1760. *(Art. 2.2)* | **Daniel Worthington**; bap. 1713, d. 1729. *(Art. 2.3)* | **Samuel Worthington**; bap. 1715, d. 1757 un-m. *(Art. 2.4)* | **Thomas Worthington**; bap. 1715, d. 1765. *(Art. 2.5)* | **John Worthington**; bap. 1716, d. 1744. *(Art. 2.6)* | **Rebecca**; bap 1718-9, m. 1752 Richard Tunnadine & had issue, d. 1756. *(Art. 2.7)* | **Jonathan Worthington**; m. 1743-4. *(Art. 2.8)* ═ **Jane Holt** |

Rebecca; bap. 1750   **Theophilus Worthington**; bap. 1753

Alas, 'Mary wife of John Fildes of Toad Lane' died when her children were only 12 and nine years of age. She was buried on 13 March 1760 at St Chad's Church, Rochdale.

2.3 Daniel
Daniel Worthington, the eldest son of Theophilus Worthington and Mary his wife (Article 1.23), was baptised on 9 August 1713 at St Chad's Church, Rochdale. The entry in the register was: 'Daniel, son of Theoffelus Worthenton of Blackwater'. Daniel died at the age of 15 years and was buried on 16 April 1729.

2.4 Samuel
Samuel Worthington, the second son of Theophilus Worthington and Mary, his wife (Article 1.23), was baptised on 15 June 1715 at St Chad's Church, Rochdale. His first cousin, Edward Worthington (Article 1.31) died without issue in 1716, and Samuel's father Theophilus Worthington died in 1730: so Samuel was the heir when his grandfather Daniel Worthington (Article 1.21) died in 1732-3. He also became representative of the line of all six generations from Thomas Worthington of Failsworth (Article 1.1). Thus it was that Samuel inherited the Waterhouses estate, described as 'Messuages and Tenement Closes, Fields and parcels of Land thereunto belonging in the hamlets of Waterhouses and Woodhouses' in the parish of Ashton-under-Lyne, Lancashire. The estate was held for three lives under lease from the earl of Warrington.

Samuel died unmarried at the age of 42 years and was buried on 3 January 1757 at St Chad's Church. In the register he was described as 'of Baitings'. Baitings referred to *Baitings Inn* on the Rochdale to Halifax road – one of the routes over which his father would have operated his carrying business.[4] He had prepared his Will 16 months earlier when he was described as '… late of Rochdale but now of Manchester in the County of Lancaster, Yeoman'.[3] He left the Waterhouses estate in trust, the trustee being his brother-in-law Richard Tunnadine of Manchester, gentleman (Article 2.7). Samuel instructed the trustee to have the lease from the earl extended. The income was to pass to his youngest brother, Thomas, for his life and then onto his youngest brother Jonathan for his life. Afterwards, the estate was to be sold and the proceeds paid equally to all the children of Samuel's two sisters – Mary Fieldes and Rebecca Tunnadine. The children would only receive their shares on reaching the age of 21 years, but in the meantime the income was to be applied to their education and maintenance.

2.5 Thomas
Thomas Worthington, the third son of Theophilus Worthington and Mary his wife (Article 1.23), was baptised on 15 June 1715 at St Chad's Church, Rochdale. The fact that he was baptised on the same day as his

brother Samuel (Article 2.4) suggests that they were twins. However, it is just possible that Samuel was about a year older but was not baptised until Thomas had arrived. Identical twins are suggested by the fact that Samuel, in his Will, devised his wearing apparel to Thomas.

When Thomas's mother Mary (Article 1.23) made her Will as a widow on 16 April 1737 he was a 'bound apprentice'. During his apprenticeship he received half of the rents of the dwelling house, barn bay, cart house, and stables in Blackwater Street, Rochdale – the place from which his father had operated his carrying business until his death in 1730.

Thomas succeeded as head of the family on the death of his brother Samuel in 1757. At the same time he would have succeeded to the income for life from the Waterhouses estate – if the lease from the earl had been extended as instructed. He died at the age of 49 years and was buried on 19 May 1765 at St Chad's Church.

2.6 John
John Worthington, the fourth son of Theophilus Worthington and Mary his wife (Article 1.23), was baptised on 3 June 1716 at St Chad's Church, Rochdale. He died at the age of 28 and was buried on 4 May 1744 at St Chad's. It is presumed that he died unmarried, as neither a widow nor children are mentioned in the Will or codicil of his mother made in 1739 and 1751 respectively. Furthermore, the Will of his elder unmarried brother Samuel (Article 2.4) specifically mentions all his surviving siblings but does not mention any widow or child of John.

2.7 Rebecca
Rebecca Worthington, the younger daughter of Theophilus Worthington and Mary his wife (Article 1.23), was baptised on 14 February 1718-9 at St Chad's Church, Rochdale, the entry in the register being 'Rebeckah daughter of Offelus Worthenton of Rochdale'.[1] She married at the age of 33 years Richard Tunnadine of Manchester. The wedding was on 21 June 1752 at St Chad's Church. The marriage licence, which had been issued at Chester, reads 'Richard Tunnadine licensed to marry Rebeccah Worthington, spinster of Rochdale, at the parish church of Rochdale'.[2] Richard's co-bondsman was John Merriot, innholder of Rochdale. Richard and Rebecca produced one son:

Forename	Date of baptism	Place of baptism
Richard	17 August 1756	St Anne's Church, Manchester

Alas, Rebecca only lived for four more months; she was buried at the Collegiate Church, Manchester on 20 November 1756. Her son died aged six years and was buried on 8 September 1958 at the same church.

After being a widower for seven years, Richard Tunnadine took as his second wife Frances Crowther, described in the banns register as 'of this parish and town of Stockport, spinster'.[5] They were married on 2 June 1763 at the Collegiate Church of Manchester and produced a son also named Richard who was baptised in 1764 at St Anne's Church, Manchester. Richard senior died in 1794 or 1795; he made his Will on 18 November 1794 and it was proved on 4 March 1795 at Chester.[2] In the Will he was described as a gentleman of Manchester. He was a shareholder of the Liverpool and Leeds Navigation Company and held pews 49 and 54 at St Peter's Church, Manchester. He bequeathed all to his wife Margaret with a provision that if she remarried his estate would descend to their daughter Margaret Frances. Presumably Margaret was Richard's third wife, both Frances and Richard Tunnadine junior having died.

2.8 Jonathan

Jonathan Worthington, the fifth son and youngest child of Theophilus Worthington and Mary his wife (Article 1.23), was probably born about 1719. No record of his baptism has been found. He was a bound apprentice aged 18 years when his mother prepared her Will on 16 April 1737. On 1 February 1743-4 he married Jane Holt by licence at St Chad's Church, Rochdale. The licence had been issued earlier the same day; in it Jonathan was described as 'Jonathan Worthington, joiner of Spotland in Rochdale parish'. Jane may have been the daughter of Edward and Ann Holt; if so she would have been 16 years of age at the time of the marriage, having been baptised on 15 December 1727 at St Chad's Church. Alternatively, Jane may have been Jane, daughter of James and Ann Holt – baptised only five weeks later on 21 January 1727-8. Holt was a prolific name in the district. Jonathan's co-bondsman was John Holt, tradesman of Spotland.

A 'Jonathan Worthington, joyner' had two children who were baptised at the Collegiate Church, Manchester:

Forename	Date of baptism
Rebecca	14 October 1750
Theophilus	11 March 1753

It is likely that this Jonathan is the Jonathan son of Theophilus Worthington for two reasons: firstly, the choice of the names Rebecca and Theophilus, and secondly, the fact that he was a joiner. Perhaps the family had left Rochdale for Manchester, where there would have been a bigger market for joinery.

CHAPTER 3

LINE OF JONATHAN WORTHINGTON
OF OLD TRAFFORD

3.1 Jonathan

Jonathan Worthington, the third son of Daniel Worthington and Rebecca his first wife (Article 1.21), was born about 1689. His life has already been discussed (Article 1.24). He and Mary his wife produced six daughters and one son.

SECOND GENERATION – FAMILY OF JONATHAN AND MARY

3.2 Mary

Mary Worthington, the eldest daughter of Jonathan Worthington and Mary his wife (Articles 1.24 and 3.1), was baptised on 15 February 1718-9 at St Matthew's Chapel, Stretford, Lancashire.[1] Her Will shows that she had married firstly Thomas Shaw and produced by him one son and one daughter, bearing their parents' forenames:[2]

Forename	Surname	Date of birth
Thomas	Shaw	Before 1758
Mary	Shaw	Before 1758

Neither the record of the marriage nor the baptisms of the two children have come to light, possibly because some of the registers of Stretford Chapel are missing – such as those of 1739 and 1742 to 1746.

Mary married secondly on 9 June 1758 Thomas Hesketh at the Collegiate Church of Manchester (now Manchester Cathedral) where the entry in the register was 'Thomas Hesketh dealer in cattle of Chorlton-cum-Hardy and Mary Shaw widow of Manchester by licence'. The bond had been issued at Chester the previous day, thus:[3]

> Bondsmen Thomas Hesketh dealer in cattle of Manchester, Abraham Taylor blacksmith of Manchester. The above bound Thomas Hesketh a widower aged 21 and upwards licensed to marry at the Collegiate Church.

Thomas had a daughter Martha by his previous marriage. Mary and Thomas produced two children of their own:

Forename	Surname	Date of birth
Thomas	Hesketh	Unknown
Edmund	Hesketh	Unknown

PEDIGREE 3 – LINE OF JONATHAN WORTHINGTON OF OLD TRAFFORD, LANCASHIRE

Jonathan Worthington; b. circa 1689, d. 1769. (*Pedigree 1 & Arts 1.24 & 3.1*) ═══ **Mary** ...; b. circa 1696, d. 1747

Mary; bap. 1718-9, m(1) Thomas Shaw & had issue, m(2) 1758 Thomas Hesketh & had issue, d. 1778. (*Art. 3.2*)

Rebecca; bap. 1720-1, d. 1727. (*Art 3.3*)

Hannah; bap. 1724, d. 1730. (*Art. 3.4*)

Jonathan Worthington; b. 1726, m. 1750, d. 1793. (*Art. 3.5*) ═══ **Susanna**, dau. of John Lloyd; b. 1725, m(1) 1746 John Steward without issue, d. 1783.

Rebecca; bap. 1729, m. 1749 George Worthington, d. 1791 without issue. (*Arts 3.6 & 9.5*)

Hannah; bap. 1732, m. 1754 Thomas Wright & had issue. (*Art. 3.7*)

Susanna; bap. 1734, d. 1756, un-m. (*Art. 3.8*)

John Lloyd Worthington; b. 1753, d. 1758. (*Art. 3.10*)

George Worthington; b. 1758, m. 1779. (*Art. 3.12*) ═══ **Hannah Worral**.

Daniel Worthington; b. 1759, m. 1783, d. 1806. (*Art. 3.13*) ═ **Jane**, dau. of Samuel Hesketh; bap. 1763, d. 1821

John Lloyd Worthington; b. 1760, d. 1795 un-m. (*Art. 3.14*)

Jonathan Worthington; b. 1756, m(1) 1789, m(2) 1802, d. 1821. (*Art. 3.11*) — (1) **Sarah**, dau. of Aaron York, b. 1769, d. 1796. — (2) **Elizabeth**, dau. of Richard Jukes; b. 1770, d. 1861.

Article 3.12

Samuel Worthington; b. 1761, d. 1762. (*Art. 3.15*)

Thomas Worthington; bap. 1762, d. 1804. (*Art. 3.16*)

Mary; b. 1764. (*Art. 3.17*)

Susanna; b. 1766, d. 1766. (*Art. 3.18*)

Samuel Worthington; b. 1768. (*Art. 3.19*) ═══ ...

Jonathan Worthington; b. 1751, d. 1751. (*Art. 3.9*)

George Worthington; b. 1790, d. 1802. *(Art. 3.20)*

Jonathan Worthington, JP; b. 1792, m. 1826, d. 1860. *(Art. 3.21)* = Anne Maria, dau. of Samuel Bartnett; bap. 1796, d. 1876.

Sarah Yorke; b. 1793, m. 1818 John Gardner, FRCS, & had issue, d. 1869. *(Art. 3.22)*

Harriet Rebecca; b. 1795, d. 1799. *(Art. 3.23)*

Mary Anne; b. 1796, d. 1802. *(Art. 3.24)*

George Worthington; b. 1802, d. 1803. *(Art. 3.25)*

Emma Susanna; b. 1804, m. 1824 Thomas Halcomb & had issue, d. 1874 *(Art. 3. 26)*

Eliza; b. 1805, d. 1827 un-m. *(Art. 3.27)*

Jane Jukes; b. 1807, d. 1883 un-m. *(Art. 3.28)*

Marianne; b. 1809, m. 1846 Richard Cooper, MRCS, & had issue, d 1885. *(Art. 3. 29)*

Andrew Jukes Worthington; b. 1810, m. 1839, d. 1873. *(Arts. 3.30 & 7.1)* = Sarah Booth, dau. of Thomas Pemberton, JP; b. 1814, d. 1877

Pedigree 7

Jonathan Yorke Worthington, Captain; b 1827, m. 1860, d. 1902 without issue. *(Art. 3. 31)* = Henrietta Charlotte, dau. of Valentine Bryan; b. 1828, m(1) 1852 Francis Charles Annesley, Captain, without issue, m(2) 1854 Robert Bridgeman Wigstrom without issue, m(3) 1856 Rowland Edward Cooper & had issue, d. 1896

George Samuel Worthington; bap. 1829, d. 1881 un-m. *(Art. 3. 32)*

Mary Jane; bap. 1830, d. 1859 un-m. *(Art. 3.33)*

Richard Jukes Worthington; b. 1832, d. 1862 un-m. (Art. 3. 34)

Lucy Anne; b. 1833, m. 1866 Edward Rushworth Keele & had issue, d. 1907. *(Art 3.35)*

Charles Worthington, JP (New Zealand); b. 1835, m. 1858, d. 1904. *(Arts 3.36 & 4.1)* = Penelope Jane, dau. of John Scott; b. 1834, d. 1901

Sarah Caroline; b. 1837, m. 1864 Augustus Halifax Ferryman, General, CB, Chevalier de la Légion d'Honeur (France) & had issue, d. 1921. *(Art. 3. 37)*

Pedigree 4

The name Thomas had become a habit in the family. Mary's deceased husband was Thomas, her current husband was Thomas, and two of her living sons were concurrently Thomas. The arrangement must have led to confusion and much hilarity. Mary's second husband died in 1766, then being described as 'grazier of Chorlton'. He had not made a Will, but administration of his estate was granted at Chester to Mary his widow, Richard Tunnadine of Manchester, gentleman, and George Worthington of Werneth, carrier. Richard was the husband of Mary's first cousin Rebecca (Article 2.7) and George was Mary's first cousin and husband of her sister Rebecca (Articles 9.5 and 3.6).

When her father Jonathan died in 1769, Mary inherited income for life from Jonathan's 'Messuage or tenement lands' at Sale, Cheshire, and George Worthington was the trustee. After Mary's life, the income was to be used for the maintenance and education of her two children Thomas and Edmund Hesketh. When both children reached the age of 21 years they would inherit the freehold of the property.

After being a widow for 12 years, Mary died on 31 December 1778. She was buried at St Mary's Church, Manchester on 3 January 1779, the entry in the register being 'Mary Hesketh widow late of Chorlton'. A gravestone was erected to her memory; the inscription, part of which is illegible, reads:[4]

> Here lieth the body of Mary Hesketh widow who departed this life on 31st December 1778 in the 60th year of her age. Edmund ... April 25th 1803

Presumably her son Edmund Hesketh was buried with her; the church register shows that he was buried on 27 April 1803.

By her Will dated 15 February 1772 and proved at Chester on 7 September 1779, she made a large bequest to her 'daughter-in-law Martha Hesketh' calculated according to the proportion of her late father's estate which would rightly have been due to her.[2] Daughter-in-law was the old description of the modern step-daughter: terminology to distinguish between a child's spouse and a spouse's child were not in general use at the time. Mary also made bequests to her son Thomas Shaw and Mary. The residue was placed in trust for the 'maintenance, education and bringing up of her two sons Thomas Hesketh and Edmund Hesketh'. Thomas and Edmund would inherit the capital absolutely when the younger had reached 21 years of age. The executor and trustee was George Worthington of Werneth, carrier (Article 9.5).

3.3 Rebecca

Rebecca Worthington, the second daughter of Jonathan Worthington and Mary his wife (Articles 1.24 and 3.1), was baptised on 19 March 1720-1 at St Matthew's Chapel, Stretford. She lived for six years and was buried at the same chapel on 30 April 1727. The entry in the register of burials reads 'Rebekah daughter of Jonathan Worthington and Mary his wife'.

3.4 Hannah

Hannah Worthington, the third daughter of Jonathan Worthington and Mary his wife (Articles 1.24 and 3.1), was baptised on 17 May 1724 at St Matthew's Chapel, Stretford. In the register she was described as 'Anna ye daughter of Jonathan Worthington and Mare his wife'. Like her elder sister, Rebecca, she lived for six years only. She was buried on 12 July 1730 at St Matthew's Chapel, the entry in the register being 'Hannah daughter of Jonathan Worthington, carrier of Old Trafford'.

3.5 Jonathan

Jonathan Worthington, the only son of Jonathan Worthington and Mary his wife (Articles 1.24 and 3.1), was born on 4 July 1726 and baptised on 17 July 1726 at St Matthew's Chapel, Stretford. Old Trafford was his home for the whole of his childhood where, no doubt, he helped in his father's business of carrying by horse-drawn coaches and wagons. One of the carrying routes was the Bristol run which was about 140 miles as the crow flies. However, many goods were transhipped at Bewdley in Worcestershire, where transport could more economically be in trows – shallow-draught, single-masted sailing boats. Bewdley lies on the west bank of the River Severn about 90 miles south of Stretford; it was the most northerly substantial port on the river, although some boats could reach Shrewsbury during the wetter seasons.

Perhaps it was on business visits to the port that Jonathan met Susanna, only daughter and heiress of John Lloyd of Wribbenhall, Worcestershire, and Susanna his wife. This Susanna senior may have been born Watkins: there is an entry in the marriage register of St Martin's Church, Hereford, for 15 April 1727 'John Lloyd and Susanna Watkins'. Wribbenhall lies on the east bank of the River Severn opposite Bewdley. John was styled 'trowman' and had his carrying business on the river, with a warehouse and seven houses and tenements in Bewdley.[5] Susanna was nearly the same age as Jonathan, having been born on 3 August 1725 and baptised on 8 September 1725 at All Saints' Chapel, Wribbenhall.[6] They were married by licence on 18 July 1750 at St Andrew's Church, Ombersley, Worcestershire, near the Severn about nine miles down stream of Wribbenhall.[7] Susanna had married previously on 14 October 1746 John Steward of Wribbenhall, their wedding having been at Hartlebury church, Worcestershire. John died two years later without issue. He had been the only child of John and Mary Steward of Wribbenhall who continued to regard Susanna as their daughter-in-law for the rest of their lives. Indeed, John senior bequeathed in his Will made on 10 April 1766 '£200* and a silver pint to his daughter-in-law Susanna Worthington of Manchester'.[8] John also bequeathed £50 each to Susanna's children Jonathan and Mary Worthington (the eldest surviving son and daughter).

---

* Equivalent to 3,400 man-days of agricultural labour.

Jonathan and Susanna produced nine sons and two daughters, the first eight children being sons:

Forename	Date of birth	Date of baptism	Article
Jonathan	2 September 1751	6 September 1751	3.9
John Lloyd	11 July 1753	27 July 1753	3.10
Jonathan	14 April 1756		3.11
George	28 February 1758	4 March 1758	3.12
Daniel	8 June 1759	12 June 1759	3.13
John Lloyd	4 March 1760	11 May 1760	3.14
Samuel	19 August 1761	28 August 1761	3.15
Thomas		27 August 1762	3.16
Mary	20 September 1764	17 October 1764	3.17
Susanna	29 January 1766	30 January 1766	3.18
Samuel	2 April 1768	28 April 1768	3.19

The first two children were baptised at Wribbenhall, but both died young. The baptism of the third has not yet come to light. Samuel was baptised at St Anne's Church, Manchester. All the other children were baptised at St Matthew's Chapel, Stretford.

John Lloyd's property in Bewdley was held copyhold of the lord of the manor of Bewdley, so when John died the property was inherited by Susanna as his heiress (Article 3.11). Jonathan's father died in 1769 from which time Jonathan was the sole proprietor of the carrying business and the occupant of the farm at Old Trafford. The earliest Manchester directory, published in 1772, lists 'Jonathan Worthington, Windmill, Deansgate, Wednesday' under 'stop coaches and wagons operating from the town'.[9]

An assignment of a mortgage dated 4 December 1777 shows that Jonathan Worthington 'wagoner of Old Trafford' held a 99-year lease of land and buildings in Stanley Barn Close in Manchester.[10] The land measured 620 square yards, being approximately 30 yards by 20 yards. On the west side the property was bounded by the king's highway linking Manchester to Stockport. This property remained with Jonathan until he died in 1793. On 8 June 1778 Jonathan and his son Jonathan Worthington junior, both of Old Trafford, carriers, and Thomas Preston of Manchester, whalebone cutter, entered into an indenture to acquire 'messuages and dwelling houses, shop, hereditaments and premises with appurtenances in Deansgate, Manchester'.[10]

Jonathan's house and farm had been leased by the Worthingtons from the de Trafford family since 1712 or earlier, when Jonathan's uncle, Samuel Worthington, was the tenant (Article 1.22). The lease was due to expire on 1 February 1784, so Jonathan Worthington and John Trafford negotiated a seven-year renewal which they engrossed in an indenture dated 11 May 1782.[11] The estate was described as '... All Housing, Outbuildings, Folds, Crofts, Orchards and Gardens on the south side of the Duke of Bridgewater's new cut or canal, Closes, Fields and parcels of land ...'. The rights to fell trees and extract minerals were excluded from the lease, but up to 19 acres of the land could be filled in any one year. A curious clause was added just before signing which required Jonathan 'to keep a cock and dog as often as required by the said John Trafford'. The rent was agreed at £200.* There is some doubt about the extent of the estate. The indenture quotes a total of 128 acres 31 square perches, but a survey of the Trafford estate made in 1782 quotes 207 acres, 2 roods and 22 square perches statutory measure for the same fields, as follows:[12]

	a.	r.	p.
Mr Jon Worthingtons house, outbuildings, folds, garden lane and orchards	9	0	16
Horse steads	11	3	18
Great Clay Field	12	3	5
Higgin Heath	13	0	39
Little Clay Field	8	1	20
Hopyard	3	3	35
Coppy Meadow	14	1	36
Nearer Ley	12	3	19
Further Ley	8	0	34
Shear Meadow	7	0	4
Broad Field	13	2	30
New Hey	11	3	2
Little Coppy	10	0	13
Middle Coppy	11	3	23
Further Coppy	12	2	39
Little Barn Croft	1	0	34
Little Cows Croft	2	0	18
Horse Pasture	9	2	34
Great Cows Field	16	1	19
Mill Field	16	0	24
Survey	207	2	22

Plans of the 1782 estate show that the land lay on both sides of Trafford Lane which led from Old Trafford to Chorlton. The house and farm buildings adjoined the Duke of Bridgewater's canal. Less than two years before the re-negotiation it was announced in the *Manchester Mercury* that 260 trees were for sale at Mr Worthington's farm at Old Trafford.[13]

Susanna died on 25 February 1783. The *Manchester Mercury* reported: '... On Sunday sen'night Mrs Worthington wife of Jonathan Worthington of Old Trafford died'.[13] Jonathan was still in business in 1788 when he was listed as a carrier in *Lewis's 1788 Directory of Salford and Manchester*, thus: 'Worthington, Jonathan – Birmingham, Bewdley & Bristol, every Thursday, at his warehouse, Mulberry Street. – Book-keeper Mr Worthington, jun.'[9] Which of Jonathan's six surviving sons was the book-keeper is not known, but it would not have been

---

* Equivalent to 2,800 man-days of agricultural labour.

the eldest, Jonathan junior, as he was already in the canal carrying business (Article 3.11). Thomas Worthington is one possibility, as there is some evidence that he later provided a similar service for Jonathan junior at Stourport, Worcestershire (Article 3.16).[13] Sometime afterwards Jonathan retired from his business and the farm, and moved to Manchester. Certainly his ecclesiastical allegiance moved from St Matthew's, Stretford, to St John's in Manchester. Also Jonathan's style changed from 'carrier' to 'gentleman'. He died 10 years after Susanna, on 10 June 1793. A monument was erected in St John's churchyard with the inscription:

> Here lies Jonathan Worthington who died the 10th June 1793 in the 67th year of his life. Also Susanna wife of Jonathan Worthington who died 25th January 1783 in the 58th year of her life. Also John Lloyd Worthington their son who died 15th October 1795 in the 36th year. Also their son Daniel Worthington who died 9th April 1806 in the ... Also ...

The remainder of the inscription is illegible.

Jonathan's Will with two codicils was made on 5 November 1792 and proved at Chester on 29 July 1793.[2] The executors and trustees were Richard Tunnadine of Manchester, gentleman, Joseph Williamson of Stretford, yeoman and Edmund Hesketh of Failsworth, timber merchant. Richard was Jonathan's first cousin-in-law (Article 2.7) and Edmund was Jonathan's nephew (Article 3.2). It is interesting that Jonathan's eldest son, Jonathan, is not mentioned – perhaps because he had moved away to Worcestershire and achieved substantial success as a carrier in his own right (Article 3.11). The Will makes provisions for Jonathan senior's other sons and daughters, and provisions for his sons' children. He bequeathed to his daughter Mary his dwelling house, warehouse etc in St James's Square, Manchester, occupied by a tenant. The dwelling house and other premises in Deansgate passed, subject to certain conditions, to his son George who was already in occupation. Another dwelling house and premises in Deansgate called York Minster, then occupied by Messrs. Gilbert and Worthington (Article 3.11), were placed in trust for the benefit of Samuel Worthington and his family. Jonathan's pew in St Mary's Church, Manchester, was passed to his sons John Lloyd Worthington and Samuel Worthington and his daughter Mary Worthington. Jonathan's other pew at St John's Church, Manchester, was passed to his sons George Worthington and Samuel Worthington.

3.6 Rebecca

Rebecca Worthington, the fourth daughter of Jonathan Worthington and Mary his wife (Articles 1.24 and 3.1), was baptised on 20 July 1729. On 14 May 1749, at the age of 19 years, she married by licence her first cousin George Worthington (Article 9.5) at the Collegiate Church of Manchester.[3] George was the only son of Rebecca's uncle,

George Worthington of Werneth. Both George senior and George junior were carriers. It is likely that both Georges in turn lived at Werneth Hall, but certainly George junior and Rebecca were living there in 1788.

On 29 March 1788, after 38 years of married life, 'Mr Worthington of Werneth hall ... was dragged from his horse one night on a lonely part of [Newton] Heath and robbed and murdered' (Article 9.5). Rebecca was then 58 years of age, and they had not produced any children. She lived as a widow for three years during which time she moved to the village of Hollinwood in the parish of Oldham – about one and a half miles south-west of Werneth Hall. She was buried on 8 December 1791 at St Mary's Church, Oldham, the entry in the register being 'Mrs Rebecca Worthington of Hollinwood widow of the late Mr George Worthington of Werneth'.

Rebecca's Will was made on 12 April 1791 and proved on 13 February at Chester.[2] She made bequests and established annuities for many family members and others. The three sisters of George Worthington and their children and her own brothers and sisters and their children were included. To her '... old and faithful servant Mary Bancroft' she gave a life annuity together with:

> ... the bedstocks bedcloathes bedding and belongings whereon she now usually sleeps, and also two pairs of good sheets. A chest of drawers made of oakwood and the New Cupboard which now stand thereon Six Mahogany Chairs, an Oval Mahogany dining table and looking glass And also such other necessary things as my executor hereafter named may think proper for the purpose of furnishing a room for her to dwell in.

All the residue of her estate, including a house called Moor Lee, near Oldham, and a messuage and tenement in Shudehill were bequeathed to her nephew Jonathan Worthington, who was appointed sole executor.

3.7 Hannah

Hannah Worthington, the fifth daughter of Jonathan Worthington and Mary his wife (Articles 1.24 and 3.1), was baptised at St Matthew's Chapel, Stretford, on 23 April 1732.[1] On 22 December 1754 she married Thomas Wright of Stretford at the Collegiate Church of Manchester, an additional wedding ceremony being held the following day at St Matthew's Chapel. The register of marriages described Thomas as husbandman, but the marriage licence obtained at Chester three days earlier described him as 'yeoman of Stretford', his co-bondsman being George Lathom, yeoman of Stretford.[3] Thomas had six children by 'Hannah', their births ranging from 20 August 1749 to 26 August 1760. For example, the entry in the register for the second child was 'Rebecca daughter of Thomas Wright of ye great stone and Hannah his wife privately baptised'. The question was once asked why Thomas and Hannah were married after the birth of the first three children. The answer now appears to be that Thomas had married a Hannah Shawcross at the Collegiate Church of Manchester on 16 August 1746 and that she provided the first three children. She presumably died after she delivered the third child. Thomas and Hannah (born Worthington) produced:

Forename	*Date of baptism*	*Date of burial*
Jonathan	23 August 1756	
Mary		October 1759
Mary		26 August 1760

Hannah's step-children were Thomas Wright baptised on 20 August 1749, Rebecca Wright baptised on 1 April 1751 and John Wright baptised on 24 September 1752. All six baptisms and the two burials were at St Matthew's Chapel, Stretford.[1] It may have been the same Thomas Wright who was warden of Stretford Chapel in 1747.

Hannah and Thomas were still living on 22 January 1767 when her father, Jonathan Worthington (Article 1.24) made his Will.[2] He provided that his Irlam property should be held in trust for the benefit of Hannah and her children; but he did not trust Thomas Wright with money. In providing a further income, being interest on £400,* he wrote:

> ... into the hands of my said daughter Hannah Wright for and during the term of her natural life Exclusive of her Husband who is to have no power to give five or dispose of or intermeddle with the same or any part thereof nor liable to be husbands debts or incumbrances the better to supporting herself and maintaining and educating and bringing up all and every her child and children ...

That this problem with Thomas may already have existed for many years is indicated by an indenture lease dated 8 May 1758 and a release of the following day in which Jonathan had previously placed the Irlam property in trust. Hannah's elder brother and sister – Jonathan and Mary – were the trustees who held the property for the benefit of Hannah after the death of Jonathan senior 'in consideration of the Natural Love and Affection' which he bore her. Jonathan retained the right to determine how and when the freehold of the property should pass. This he did in his Will – to Hannah's children equally.

3.8 Susanna
Susanna Worthington, sixth daughter and youngest child of Jonathan Worthington and Mary his wife (Articles 1.24 and 3.1), was born on 22 July 1734 and baptised on 18 August 1734 at St Matthew's Chapel, Stretford.[1] She died aged 21 years and was buried on 3 July 1756 at the same chapel. The entry in the register reads 'Susanna daughter of Jonathan Worthington, carrier'.

---

* Equivalent to 6,800 man-days of agricultural labour.

THIRD GENERATION – FAMILY OF JONATHAN AND SUSANNA

3.9 Jonathan

Jonathan Worthington, eldest son of Jonathan Worthington and Susanna his wife (Article 3.5), was born on 2 September 1751 and baptised on 6 September 1751 at Wribbenhall, Worcestershire.[8] He died aged six weeks on 18 October 1751 and was buried the same day.

3.10 John Lloyd

John Lloyd Worthington, the second son of Jonathan Worthington and Susanna his wife (Article 3.5), was born on 11 July 1753 and baptised on 27 July 1753 at Wribbenhall.[6] He was named after his maternal grandfather, John Lloyd of Wribbenhall. Alas, John junior died aged four years 11 months on 1 July 1758.

3.11 Jonathan

Jonathan Worthington, the third son of Jonathan Worthington and Susanna his wife (Article 3.5), was born on 14 April 1756.[14] His two elder brothers (Articles 3.9 and 3.10) had died by July 1758, so Jonathan became the eldest surviving son at the age of two years. Much of his childhood was spent at Old Trafford. No doubt he became familiar with his father's carrying business – the road networks, the warehouses, horses, wagons and office work. It would have been a formulative period which contributed later to his own success as a carrier.

In 1759 Francis Egerton, the 3rd Duke of Bridgewater, built a canal from his coalmines at Worsley seven miles eastwards to Manchester. So low was the cost of canal transport compared with road that the price of coal in Manchester halved. This was an early stage in the transport revolution in which a network of canals was developed throughout the country linking navigable rivers and many industrial towns. This led in turn to rapid growth of trade and to loss of business on many of the road routes. The canal age had begun. In 1782 Jonathan, then described as 'road carrier', entered into partnership with John Gilbert to form a canal-carrying company called 'Worthington and Gilbert'.[15] There has been much debate as to whether Gilbert was John Gilbert senior, who was the Duke of Bridgewater's agent, a member of parliament and a member of the Canal Committee, or his son John Gilbert junior. According to P. Leach's work on the Gilberts published by the University of Keele in 1989, Jonathan's partner was John senior, while John junior was running a separate carrying business on the Trent and Mersey canal.[16] He pointed out that Jonathan continued the business on his own account after John senior's death. Worthington and Gilbert, based at Manchester, initially concentrated on the Manchester to Stockport run which had been opened about 1772 by completion of the Staffordshire and Worcestershire canal. This canal joined the River Severn where the

5   *The canal basin at Stourport in 1776. Detail from 'Perspective View of Stourport, 1776'*
by J. Sherriff. By courtesy of Bewdley Museum Service.

River Stour joins the Severn. Canal basins, wharves and warehouses
were built there for trans-shipment of goods between the narrow horse-
drawn canal barges to the larger sailing trows navigating the River
Severn. Indeed, Stourport was a new Georgian town within the parish
of Lower Mitton, which developed for the new trade. It was first called
'Stour Port', soon afterwards 'Stourport' and from 1936 'Stourport-on-
Severn'. Until 1782 Hugh Henshall and Co had been the sole private
canal carriers on that route, paying dues to the canal proprietors, but
now they faced competition.[17] Sometime after Worthington and Gilbert
were established, Hugh Henshall and Co commented:

> His Grace's people are all very partial to Worthington; his boats can
> discharge in two hours, while ours must lie a day or more under their
> cargo for want of proper assistance to discharge them.

An indenture of 1 December 1785 shows that from 25 December that
year 'Jonathan Worthington and John Gilbert' leased a warehouse in
Stourport for three years from the Staffordshire and Worcestershire
Canal Navigation Company.[18] The warehouse had the number nine
painted on the door. They had the use of the 'wharf with crane'
between the warehouse and canal basin. The rent was £30[*] a year. By

---
[*] Equivalent to 400 man-days of agricultural labour.

the same indenture, Jonathan and John entered into an agreement as to their maximum charges for 'housing, porterage, craneage, weighing and turning in and out of goods' for each of 46 classes of goods. The first of these classes was merchandise measured by the ton (such as coal, bricks, metals, hemp and grindstones). Other classes included butts of liquor, hogsheads of grocery or cider, timber, mahogany and other hardwoods, sacks of corn and hundredweights of cheese. Another lease between the canal navigation company and 'Jonathan Worthington Boatowner' dated 5 December 1799 shows that, in addition to Warehouse 9, Jonathan held warehouses one and two, being two-thirds of the Old Iron Warehouse lying on the south side of the Old Basin Wharf.[18] He also shared with the canal navigation company the 'counting houses' which were adjacent to the south side of the Old Iron Warehouse.

Sometime before 1791 Worthington and Gilbert had established a warehouse at the termination of the duke's canal at Castlefield, Manchester.[9] The relative size of the carriers working from the Castlefield Quay at about this time is indicated by the assessments on the warehouses for local taxation as follows:[19]

Occupant	Assessment(£)	Rate (£ s. d.)
Duke of Bridgewater	120	18 0 0
Matthew Pickford	10	1 10 0
Gilbert and Worthington	50*	7 10 0
H Henshall and Company	50	7 10 0

The warehouse shared by Matthew Pickford, Gilbert & Worthington and H. Henshall & Co. consisted of five storeys. Barges could be floated into the building through arches so that goods could be handled by crane to or from any of the floors. The warehouse was demolished in 1960. (The name Worthington and Gilbert was sometimes reversed to 'Gilbert and Worthington' in Manchester, but the name Worthington always appeared first in Worcestershire.) Around 1791 the duke's clerks at Preston Quay, Manchester were book-keeping for Worthington and Gilbert, who paid the duke £40[†] for a year's work.[20]

When Jonathan's father, Jonathan Worthington of Manchester (Article 3.5), made his Will on 5 November 1792, 'Richard Shenton and Messrs. Gilbert and Worthington were using a dwelling house and premises in Deansgate, Manchester'. The property was leased from Jonathan senior in return for rent. By 1795 Worthington and Gilbert were operating a fleet of 23 boats.[20]

On 31 December 1789 Jonathan married Sarah, the younger daughter of Aaron York and Mary his wife of Stourport, the wedding being at St Michael's Chapel, Lower Mitton. The chapelry of Lower Mitton in which Stourport developed was part of the ancient parish of Kidderminster.

---

* Equivalent to 600 man-days of agricultural labour.
† Equivalent to 500 man-days of agricultural labour.

6 *Jonathan Worthington, Senior, of Stourport*

7 *Sarah, daughter of Aaron Yorke and first wife of Jonathan Worthington*

Jonathan was then aged 43 years and Sarah 20 having been born on 26 September 1769. The entry in the register of marriages reads:[21]

> Jonathan Worthington, bachelor, and Sarah York, spinster, both of this parish by licence with the consent of parents. In the presence of Aaron York sen., Aaron York, jun., Richard Dickens.

Aaron York senior was a partner in the firm of Glover and York of Stourport, wharfingers and merchants, whose main business was carrying on the river in trows as far as Gloucester or Bristol and then onwards in larger sailing vessels. On one occasion a vessel called 'The Hero' belonging to Glover and York foundered on the Sheperdine Sounds near Bristol, the cargo being valued at £25,000.* Aaron also had some canal carrying interest on his own account. On 24 December 1789 – only a week before the wedding – he published a five-page paper entitled *An Answer to the Comparative Statement, lately circulated by the Schemers of the Intended Worcester Canal.*[22] In the paper he made a strong argument, with market assessments and comparative costings, against a new canal from Birmingham to Worcester on the grounds that the existing Staffordshire and Worcestershire Canal was already economical and fulfilling the market need at a cost which could not be bettered. In the introduction he wrote:

---

* Equivalent to 250,000 man-days of agricultural labour.

... it becomes the duty of everyone acquainted with the subject to endeavour to expose those misrepresentations, and to lay before the Public a true state of the different conveyances, that the Public may decide impartially thereon. And as almost the whole of my days have been spent in the Carrying Trade, both on the River and Canal Navigations, I may be allowed credit for some knowledge of both; and therefore without further apology, I shall proceed to correct the misrepresentations ...

Aaron's lobbying may have contributed to delaying the construction of the Birmingham and Worcester Canal. Work did not start until 1795 and the Worcester end was not completed until 1815 because of financial difficulties. When completed it took a substantial amount of business from Stourport because it provided a more direct route from Birmingham and it joined the River Severn some 12 miles further south where the water was deeper. Indeed the dividends paid by the Staffordshire and Worcestershire Canal fell from 31 percent a year between 1811 and 1815 to 24 percent a year in 1816 and 1817.[15] Aaron had in 1787 built York House in a commanding position close to and overlooking the Stourport canal basin. It was said to be the first house to be built in the new town of Stourport. Later, the street in which the house stands was named York Street. The house still stands and is now used by one of Stourport's medical practices. In 1788 Aaron's name headed the petition to the bishop of Worcester for a licence to establish a Wesleyan chapel in Stourport; the licence was granted on 8 October 1788. The last letter John Wesley wrote was addressed to Aaron; Wesley died on 2 March 1799 before posting it. It reads:[23]

Dear Sir, On Wednesday, March 17th, I propose, if God permits, to come from Gloucester to Worcester and on Thursday the 18th to Stourport. If our friends at Worcester are displeased, we cannot help it. Wishing you and yours all happiness. I am dear sir, your affectionate servant, John Wesley.

Jonathan and Sarah's nuptial home was probably adjacent to York House. 'A plan of Stourport...' surveyed in May 1802 shows that Mr Worthington held a house, garden and outbuildings adjacent to the garden of York House where Mrs York still lived.[24] Jonathan and Sarah produced two sons and three daughters, namely:[21]

Forename	Date of birth	Date of baptism	Aticle
George	20 September 1790	22 November 1790	3.20
Jonathan	2 August 1792	16 January 1793	3.21
Sarah Yorke	30 June 1793	13 July 1793	3.22
Harriet Rebecca	12 March 1795	9 April 1795	3.23
Mary Anne	14 September 1796	31 October 1796	3.24

All the baptisms took place at St Michael's Church, Lower Mitton. (The old chapel was rebuilt in 1792 and designated a church.) Alas, after giving birth to these five children in her seven years of marriage, Sarah died on 22 December 1796 – 12 weeks after the birth of the fifth.

8 *Elizabeth, born Jukes, and her family in 1821. Left to right: Andrew Jukes Worthington, Elizabeth, Marianne, Emma, Jane and Eliza.*

Sarah was then aged 27 years. She was buried on 28 December, being the second person to be buried in the York family tomb at St Michael's Church, her only brother Aaron York junior being the first. They were joined by Aaron York senior three months later – on 23 March 1797.[25] Thus it was that Sarah, prior to her death, and her elder sister, Ann the wife of John Izon, brassfounder, of Bower Brook Hall, Kings Norton, Warwickshire, became co-heiresses of Aaron.[26]

Jonathan remained a widower for five years before marrying, on 18 February 1802, Elizabeth the third daughter of Richard Jukes and Jane his wife of Cound, Shropshire. Jonathan was then aged 56 years whilst Elizabeth was 32, having been born on 19 September 1770 and baptised on 24 September 1770 at St Peter's Church, Cound. The Jukes family had been settled for at least 250 years at Cound and Berrington, both within six miles south-east of Shrewsbury. Richard was directly descended from William Jukes of Berrington who died in 1525 owning houses in Cound.[27] Elizabeth's mother was Jane, the second daughter of Andrew Dodson of Cressage, Shropshire. One of Elizabeth's brothers was Richard Jukes of High Street, Stourport, medical practitioner and surgeon. Charles Hastings (later Sir Charles Hastings, Kt, MD, DCL, founder of

9   *Moorhill, Worcestershire (Stourport), the home of Jonathan Worthington.*

the British Medical Association) served his apprenticeship with Richard Jukes and his partner Kenrick Watson for two years commencing in September 1810.[28] Indeed, in 1967 the Association held its centenary celebration at St Michael's Church, Lower Mitton, when a wreath was laid on Richards's cenotaph. Jonathan and Elizabeth's wedding took place at St Michael's Church by licence.[21] Richard Jukes and Hannah Worthington, Jonathan's aunt (Article 3.9), were the witnesses.

Thus Elizabeth became step-mother to Jonathan's three surviving children by Sarah. Elizabeth then bore Jonathan a further six children, namely:[21]

Forename	Date of birth	Date of baptism	Article
George	1802	13 December 1802	3.25
Emma Susanna	1804	30 May 1804	3.26
Eliza	1805	3 November 1805	3.27
Jane Jukes	17 April 1807	23 June 1807	3.28
Marianne	17 April 1809	19 April 1809	3.29
Andrew Jukes	22 December 1810	23 December 1810	3.30

All the births were at Moorhill and all the baptisms were at St Michael's Church. Jonathan had built Moorhill on an eminence overlooking the river, with 50 acres of ground sloping down to the water. The house stood a mile from the wharf – on Long Lane running from Lickhill Manor to Hartlebury. More land was acquired later. The *Cambrian Traveller's Guide* of 1813 described 'Mr Worthington's residence', as a new mansion.[29] Another gazette published two years later described Moorhill as one of nine 'gentlemen's seats' in Stourport.[30] By 1811 the population of Stourport had grown to 2,352 people living in 464 houses. It appears that Moorhill was a well run and happy house, the whole family remaining closely knit throughout their lives. Andrew John Jukes, son of Elizabeth's brother, Dr Andrew Jukes, wrote as an old man in a letter of 8 June 1891 to Philip Jukes Worthington (Article 7.8) the following words about Elizabeth: '…I can never forget or repay all her love and care during my early Moorhill days. I have seen few like her …' Andrew at the age of five and his younger brother Mark Richard Jukes had come to live at Moorhill while his parents were in India. Again, on 28 December 1895, Andrew wrote to Philip:

> … you don't know what pleasure it gives me to hear from one who bears your name. It brings back to me all those early days and years I spent at Moorhill when your dear father was a boy and your aunts were there as girls. Memories of later days have faded away. Everything connected with Moorhill of those days, and with the dear ones who lived there, is as fresh to my memory as if it had happened yesterday …

Andrew's younger brother Mark had no doubt had similar happy recollections. He gave his fourth son 'Worthington' as his sole forename, despite the lack of a Worthington ancestor. This son later became the Reverend Worthington Jukes, MA, rector of Shobrooke, Devonshire.[27]

The various York and Worthington business interests were noted in a list of 1793 of 61 'inhabitants and trades of and to Stourport …' who entered into an Association 'for the mutual protection and defence of each other's property and for the effectual prosecution of all felonies …'[31] The list included Cowel and York, Aaron York, York and Co, York and Worthington, and John Worthington. The John was presumably a misprint for Jonathan. Richard Jukes was also on the list, and Jonathan's grandfather's family interests still appeared to be represented by Wilden and Lloyd, and G. Lloyd. These were the days of the vigilantes in somewhat lawless times; another 36 years were to pass before Sir Robert Peel started the movement towards the modern police forces. This Stourport Association was the forerunner of the 'Stourport Severn Association' concerned mainly with the protection of fishing and other rights in the river. At a meeting of the committee held on 30 September 1811 at the Coffee Room, Stourport, it was resolved unanimously that the Reverend Reginald Pynder and Jonathan Worthington, Esq.,[32]

> be appointed delegates from this Association to the General Meeting, and that those Gentlemen be requested to attend at such place as shall be fixed on for assembling the central Committee.

Not all in the affairs of Jonathan's business ran smoothly. A letter of 9 October 1796 from 'Messrs Gilbert and Worthington' survives concerning late delivery to Manchester of a boiler manufactured by Boulton and Watt for Mr Taylor:[33]

> Mr Forman, Sr, I am sorry we have been so unfortunate respecting the boiler from Dudley port, but from various stoppages upon that part of the canal we have not been able to send a boat that way. I did send one to take it the next morning after I received Mr Lodges letters and he had not got half way to D Port but was informed that a culvert had blown which stopped the passage. More than a week and it would have gone the beginning of last week but another stoppage has taken place which will not be open again till this evening. I have offered some of the men that come with coal boats five shillings exclusive of fr't to bring it to Birm'm and we could then have sent it the other road, but they would not undertake it. Shall send a boat tomorrow certain to take it and will be at Manchester this day week – am s'r y'r obd't serv't, B'n Jeavons.

Jonathan's partnership with John Gilbert continued until John's death in 1812 after which Jonathan owned the whole business. For at least 12 years after Aaron's death in 1797, his business continued to run separately; that is shown by a collection for the purchase of a town clock which was built by Samuel Thorp in 1813. 'Messrs. York & Co' and 'J. Worthington, Esq.' contributed £7 7s. 0d.* each.[34] The clock, now known as the 'Basin clock' still remains above one of the basin buildings. Subsequently, however, the York business was merged with Worthington's; 'York and Worthington' was listed under canal carriers to Stourport in the Worcester directory of 1820. In the same year the general entry in the directory for Worthington was:

> Worthington & Co. Fly boats from James Bromley's warehouse, Lowesmoor, to Birmingham, Wolverhampton, Stafford, The Potteries, Congleton, Warrington, Liverpool, Manchester, and the intermediate places from whence goods are forwarded by respectable carriers, to all parts of Cheshire, North Wales, Westmoreland, Cumberland and parts of Scotland adjacent. Agent G. Wood.

A blue-printed earthenware plate manufactured between 1800 and 1820 depicts a canal scene surrounded by the names of 16 English carriers.[35] Below the scene appears the following verse:

> Pickford, Beach and Snell's are jolly lads and true ones
> Kenworthy, and Worthingtons, you'll likewise find true blue ones
> Wakeman, Green and Ames, amiss you never find Sirs
> Holt's, Crocket and Salkeld's will sail as fast as the wind Sirs
> True heated and jolly ones you'll find with Heath and Crawley
> Sturtland's, Henshall's, Alkin's too, can likewise use theirs mauley
> So likewise can the boatmen all, and drink their can of flip Sirs,
> They'll drink their grog, and toast their lass and then they'll crack their
>   whip Sirs.

---

* Equivalent to 80 man-days of agricultural labour.

When Jonathan's mother, Susanna, died in 1783, he inherited from her three dwelling houses and a warehouse at Severn Side in Bewdley, Worcestershire. These properties, which were held of the lord of the manor of Bewdley under the ancient system of copyhold, had formerly been in the possession of Jonathan's grandfather, John Lloyd, and had been inherited by Susanna as his only child (Article 3.5). On 7 November 1807 Jonathan appeared in person at the court baron of the manor to have his inheritance confirmed:[36]

> … To whom the Lord by his Steward aforesaid have seizing thereof by the rod according to the custom of the said manor. To have and to hold the same with the appurtenances unto the said Jonathan Worthington the son, his heirs and assigns for ever according to the Custom of the said manor. Paying therefore yearly to the Lord sixpence at the usual times Heriot when it shall happen Suit of Court and all other customs and services therefore due and of right accustomed, and the said Jonathan Worthington, the son being present in court is thereof accordingly admitted Tenant and did his fealty.

Two days later on 9 November 1807 Jonathan leased the dwellings but not the warehouse to Joseph Tythe of Wribbenhall, victualler, for 500 years for a premium of £135* paid immediately and a rent thereafter of one penny a year.[36]

Lewis's 1820 directory lists 'Worthington Jonathan Gent' for Stourport, but also lists 'Worthington Mrs, coffee rooms, New Street'.[37] The coffee rooms of Stourport were then a notable institution where public and private meetings were held. Jonathan's wife Elizabeth may have managed them.

In 1821 heavy defalcations were discovered at the Manchester branch of the business. Jonathan went there to investigate but died at his hotel on 21 June 1821 after two days' illness.[38] He was then aged 65 years. He was buried on 29 June 1821 in the family tomb at St Michael's Church, Lower Mitton, the York tomb having now become the York and Worthington tomb. No Will had been prepared but letters of administration were granted on 27 January 1822 by the Consistory Court of Chester. A further grant was made at Canterbury on 21 February 1822. The grants of administration were to Jonathan Worthington his eldest son, Elizabeth his widow having renounced.[2] The family continued to live at Moorhill until 1825, shortly before Jonathan junior's marriage (Article 3.21). Elizabeth with her son Andrew and her three unmarried daughters then moved to Malvern, Worcestershire.[39] It appears that Elizabeth lived there for about 20 years until her youngest daughter Marianne married in 1846 (Article 3.29). Elizabeth and Jane, her one remaining unmarried daughter, then went to live with Elizabeth's eldest daughter Emma Susanna and her husband Thomas Halcombe at High Trees Farm in the Savernake Forest (Article 3.26). The move also brought her nearer to her married step-daughter Sarah Yorke Gardner who was living in Marlborough (Article 3.22).

---

* Equivalent to 1,500 man-days of agricultural labour.

In 1851 Elizabeth and Jane moved to The Wood House in Lockwood Lane, about a mile north-east of Cheadle, Staffordshire, where they lived for the remainder of Elizabeth's life. She presumably moved there to be near her daughter Emma Halcomb and her family (Article 3.26), who had moved to the district from Marlborough, and to be near her son Andrew (Article 3.30) and his family who lived at Leek, Staffordshire, about eight miles to the north. The Wood House, a three-storey, seven-bedroom house built of stone, remained a private residence until 1939 when it was requisitioned by the Royal Air Force for the duration of the Second World War for use as an administrative headquarters. In 1985 it became a Christian centre and retreat for the Cheadle Methodist Church.[40]

Elizabeth died aged 90 years at The Wood House on 1 June 1861. She had the choice of being buried in the York-Worthington family tomb at Lower Mitton where her husband and three of her children were already buried, or at Leek where her son Andrew and his family were settled. She chose to look forwards and accordingly a vaulted tomb was constructed in the churchyard of St Luke's Church in which she was the first to be interred. A stained glass window depicting the crucifixion was installed to her memory in the church, together with a memorial inscription.[41] Beneath it is a brass plaque to the memory of her son Andrew Jukes Worthington and his wife Sarah, and beneath that there is another brass plaque to the memory of Elizabeth's grandsons, Ernest Andrew Worthington, Walter Moore Worthington, and Philip Jukes Worthington (Articles 7.3, 7.6 and 7.8). In her Will dated 15 September 1858 she left her household goods, furniture, and wine to her unmarried daughter Jane. Her silver was to be divided equally, by weight, between her four surviving children. After certain bequests and special arrangements, the residue of her estate was placed in trust for the benefit of her four children, except that her daughter Marianne's share was to be £1,000* less than each of the others because she had received a marriage settlement of that amount. Much of the Will is preoccupied with providing for the possibility of Jane becoming married and having a family, although she was then 51 years of age. Perhaps Elizabeth had long had a strong desire to see Jane comfortably married, like her brothers and sisters. Elizabeth left bequests to her three god-children – Sarah Yorke Worthington Reid, George Samuel Worthington, and Charles Henry Halcomb. The first two of these were step-grandchildren and the third a grandson (Articles 3.22, 3.32 and 3.26).

3.12 George
George Worthington, the fourth son of Jonathan Worthington and Susanna his wife (Article 3.5), was born on 28 February 1758 and baptised at St Michael's Chapel, Stretford, on 4 March 1758.[1] On 16 September 1779,

---

* Equivalent to 8,000 man-days of agricultural labour.

at the age of 21 years he married Hannah Worrall of Manchester. The wedding took place at the Collegiate Church of Manchester. Marriage bonds had been filed at Chester the previous day when George was described as 'farmer of Stretford'.[3] Probably this description related to work he was doing for his father on the farm at Old Trafford which lay within the parish of Stretford. George's co-bondsman was 'Charles Barnes, taylor of Mancherster'. Hannah was described as 'Hannah Worrall a spinster of Manchester aged 21 and upwards'.

George and Hannah produced seven children, namely:

Forename	Date of baptism	Church in Manchester
Mary	23 February 1781	St Anne's
Hannah	18 October 1782	St Anne's
John	12 August 1787	Collegiate
George	14 August 1791	Collegiate
Ann	25 March 1792	Collegiate
William	30 March 1794	Collegiate
Eliza	23 March 1795	St Anne's

All were described in the registers as children of 'George Worthington and Hannah' except for Ann who was described as 'Ann daughter of Hannah Worthington'.

In 1792 George was occupying a 'dwelling house and other premises' in Deansgate, Manchester, owned by his father, Jonathan (Article 3.5). Jonathan had offered to convey the property to George in return for a mortgage of £400,* but George was apparently reluctant. When making his Will on 5 November 1792, Jonathan crystallised the situation by stating that, if the deal was not completed before his death, the property would be bequeathed to John Lloyd Worthington (Article 3.14) – one of George's younger brothers.

3.13 Daniel

Daniel, the fifth son of Jonathan Worthington and Susanna his wife (Article 3.5), was born on 8 June 1759 and baptised on 12 June 1759 at St Michael's Chapel, Stretford.[1] On 13 November 1783, then aged 24 years, Daniel married Jane daughter of Samuel Hesketh at the Collegiate Church of Manchester. Jane was then aged 20 years having been baptised on 26 February 1763 at St Clement's Church, Chorlton-cum-Hardy. The entry in the marriage register is 'Daniel Worthington, husbandman, township of Stretford, and Jane Hesketh, spinster and minor, township of Withington by licence'. The witnesses were Ann Holt and Richard Sheraton. The marriage licence, given by the bishop of Chester on 11 November 1783, shows that Samuel Hesketh, farmer, gave his consent and approbation.[3] Withington, then a rural village, lies about five miles south-south-west of Stretford. Daniel's co-bondsman for the licence was Richard Thornton of Manchester, publican.

---

* Equivalent to 5,000 man-days of agricultural labour.

Daniel was presumably working on his father's farm at the Old Trafford demesne. He died after 22 years of married life and was buried on 13 April 1806 at St John's Church, Manchester, the entry in the register being 'Daniel Worthington, labourer, 47, fever'.[1] He was buried in the family grave there, with his parents and his younger brother John Lloyd Worthington. An inscription was added to the stone monument (Article 3.5). It is not yet known whether he had children.

Jane lived for a further 15 years as a widow. Her father, described as 'yeoman of Withington', wrote his Will on 26 November 1811; he held 'cottages and dwelling houses with land and appurtenances in Ashton-upon-Mersey, Cheshire'.[2] When he died on 20 October 1812, these properties were divided equally among Samuel's four sons and his only daughter 'Jane Worthington widow'. Jane died aged 59 years and was buried on 9 December 1821 at St John's Church, Manchester.[1]

3.14 John Lloyd

John Lloyd Worthington, the sixth son of Jonathan Worthington and Susanna his wife (Article 3.5), was born on 4 March 1760 and baptised at St Matthew's Chapel, Stretford, on 11 May 1760.[1] He was brought up on his father's farm at Old Trafford and later became a farmer at Moss Side, about a mile to the east of Trafford. That is shown by the assignment of mortgage of 8 March 1794 in which John Lloyd Worthington and Samuel Worthington, 'both farmers of Moss Side, children of Jonathan Worthington deceased were executors of Jonathan Worthington wagoner of Old Trafford, deceased'.[42]

John died unmarried at the age of 36 years and was buried on 18 October 1795 at St John's Church, Manchester. The parish register notes 'decline' as the cause of death. He was buried in the family grave there with his parents, an inscription being added to the stone monument (Article 3.5). No Will had been made but administration of his estate was granted by the Chester Consistory Court to his only surviving sister, Mary Worthington spinster (Article 3.17) on 22 October 1795.[2] John was then described as 'yeoman deceased'. Mary's bondsmen in applying for the letter of administration were James Whitaker, gentleman, and Richard Fryer, warehouseman, both of Manchester.

3.15 Samuel

Samuel Worthington, the seventh son of Jonathan Worthington and Susanna his wife (Article 3.5), was born on 19 August 1761 and baptised on 28 August 1761 at St Matthew's Chapel, Stretford.[1] He died at the age of six months on 19 February 1762 and was buried on 21 February 1762 at St Matthew's Chapel.

3.16 Thomas

Thomas Worthington, the eighth son of Jonathan Worthington and Susanna his wife (Article 3.5), was baptised at St Matthew's Chapel, Stretford, on 27 August 1762.[1]

It is thought that this Thomas Worthington lived in Stourport and worked with his elder brother Jonathan (Article 3.11) in the canal carrying business. A Thomas Worthington married Ann Wantling on 8 October 1799 at St Jame's Church, Hartlebury, which lies about two miles south-east of Stourport. Both Thomas and Ann were described as being of the parish of Hartlebury, which included Upper Mitton. No children of Thomas and Ann have been traced. Thomas Worthington was buried on 9 April 1804 at St Michael's Chapel, Lower Mitton.[22] If he were the younger brother of Jonathan, he would have been 41 years of age.

Ann Worthington married a James Harper at Ribbesford on 6 August 1804, less than four months after Thomas's death. Ribbesford lies adjacent to the north-west side of Stourport. As no other Worthingtons have come to light in the region, apart from Jonathan and his family and Thomas and Ann, it is almost certain that this Thomas was Jonathan's brother.

3.17 Mary

Mary Worthington, the elder daughter of Jonathan Worthington and Susanna his wife (Article 3.5), was born on 20 September 1764 and baptised on 17 October 1764 at St Matthew's Chapel, Stretford.[1] Her younger sister Susanna (Article 3.18) died aged three days leaving Mary as the only girl amongst six surviving brothers. She was still a spinster at the age of 31 years when, on 22 October 1795, she was appointed administratrix of the goods, chattels and credits of her elder brother John Lloyd Worthington (Article 3.14). Mary was then living in Manchester. When her father had died in 1793 he had bequeathed to her his '... messuage or dwelling house, warehouse and premises with their appurtenances ...' in St James's Square, Manchester. This property was let at the time to Mr Singard who became her tenant.

3.18 Susanna

Susanna Worthington, the younger daughter of Jonathan Worthington and Susanna his wife (Article 3.5), was born on 29 January 1766 and baptised on 30 January 1766 at St Matthew's Chapel, Stretford.[1] She died aged three days on 1 February 1766 and was buried on 4 February at St Matthew's Chapel.

3.19 Samuel

Samuel Worthington, the ninth son and youngest child of Jonathan Worthington and Susanna his wife (Article 3.5), was born on 2 April 1768. He was baptised on 28 April 1768 at St Ann's Church, Manchester, the entry in the register being 'Samuel son of Jonathan and Shusanah

Worthington'. Samuel was 24 years of age when his father made his Will.[2] The Will made certain financial provisions for Samuel, 'his present wife' and any of their children. However the wife and children were not named and it is not certain that any children had already been born. Samuel also inherited all of Jonathan's wearing apparel.

The deed of assignment of a mortgage dated 8 March 1794, associated with Jonathan's Will, refers to John Lloyd Worthington and Samuel Worthington, both farmers of Moss Side.[42] Perhaps they were in partnership. They jointly inherited with their sister Mary their father's pew at St Mary's Church, Manchester.

FOURTH GENERATION – FAMILY OF JONATHAN OF STOURPORT

3.20 George

George Worthington, the eldest son of Jonathan Worthington and Sarah his first wife (Article 3.11), was born on 20 September 1790 and baptised on 22 November 1790 at St Michael's Chapel, Lower Mitton.[22] He died aged 11 years on 24 March 1802, and was buried in the Yorke-Worthington tomb at St Michael's Chapel. During his lifetime the old chapel had been rebuilt.

3.21 Jonathan

Jonathan Worthington, the second son of Jonathan Worthington and Sarah his first wife (Article 3.11), was born on 2 August 1792 and baptised on 16 January 1793 at St Michael's Church, Lower Mitton.[22] His elder brother George (Article 3.20) died when Jonathan junior was nine years of age after which Jonathan was the eldest surviving son.

'Rejoicings at Stourport' for the 'Glorious Peace' were reported in the local press in June 1814, following the Treaty of Paris and the imprisonment of Napoleon Bonaparte on the island of Elba.[32] Dinners for all with roast ox and plum pudding were the order of the day. A local charity ensured that all the workers of the town had a free dinner including up to four pints of ale for each man and two for each woman. At 3.00 p.m. on 17 June 1814 a public dinner was also held at the *Stourport Inn* for which tickets were 12 shillings[*] each. The eight stewards for the event included Jonathan Worthington junior then aged 21 years, his future father-in-law Samuel Barnett, his future uncle-in-law Richard Jukes, and Richard's partner Kenrick Watson (Article 3.11). Little did they know that the following March Napoleon would land in France, raise an army and engage in the battle of Waterloo.

Jonathan junior inherited the canal carrying business when his father died seven years later, and the business continued to prosper under the name 'Worthington and Company'. In 1740, the company operated a

---

[*] Equivalent to seven man-days of agricultural labour.

10   *Anne Maria, born Barnett, in 1864, at the age of 68 years.*

canal carrying service from Stourport to Derby, Nottingham, Leicester, Gainsborough and Hull on Tuesdays, Thursdays and Saturdays, and to Liverpool, Manchester and Chester on Thursdays and Saturdays.[43] The company's Birmingham branch was listed at Great George Street. Jonathan was also a merchant, perhaps through the same company. He is described as merchant in the baptism records at St Michael's Church in 1826 and 1829 and 'carrier and merchant' in 1830 and 1832.

On 2 August 1826 – his 34th birthday – Jonathan married Anne Maria, daughter of Samuel Barnett and Mary his wife (born Jukes). Mary was an elder sister of Jonathan's step-mother Elizabeth (Article 3.11), so Anne was first cousin to all Jonathan's half-siblings.[27] Samuel Barnett described himself as merchant in his Will made on 25 May 1831.[44] The Worcester Directories of 1820 and 1822 describe him as maltster, and he was also a carrier on the River Severn. Perhaps all three activities constituted parts of the business which he ran in partnership with his eldest son, John Barnett. A likely scenario is that imported grain was transported up the River Severn from Bristol, Cardiff and Newport, and that some of the barley was purchased and converted into malt for onward sale through the canal system. The Barnett family home was at New Street, Lower Mitton, and consisted of the dwelling house, malthouse, gardens, outbuildings, and parcels of land before and behind the house. Pigot and Co's *London and Provincial New Commercial Directory* for 1822-3 shows, amongst others, the following firms operating in Stourport:[45]

> *Wharfingers, general agents and conveyancers:*
> Barnett, Meaby and Co
> Barnett, Meaby and Worthington
> Worthington and Co
> *Wharfingers and general agents:*
> York and Worthington
> *Malsters:*
> Barnett, Samuel

By 1835 Barnett, Meaby and Co had become 'Barnett and Co.'; also Barnett, Meaby and Worthington had become 'Barnett and Worthington'. York and Worthington were then situated at the Hop Market.

Jonathan and Anne's wedding took place at St Michael's Church, Lower Mitton.[21] Moorhill was their nuptial home, Jonathan's step-mother having conveniently moved to Great Malvern the previous year taking her unmarried daughters with her (Articles 3.11 and 3.27 to 3.29). At Moorhill, Jonathan and Anne produced a family of four sons and three daughters:

Forename	Date of birth	Date of baptism	Article
Jonathan Yorke	25 June 1827	27 June 1827	3.31
George Samuel		5 March 1829	3.32
Mary Jane		26 July 1830	3.33
Richard Jukes	10 January 1832	21 January 1832	3.34
Lucy Anne	11 December 1833	16 December 1833	3.35
Charles	16 July 1835	21 September 1835	3.36
Sarah Caroline	30 October 1837	27 December 1837	3.37

All the baptisms took place at St Michael's Church.[21]

There is reference to Jonathan as church warden in 1827. At the general quarter-sessions of Worcestershire held at the Guildhall, Worcester, on 30 June 1834 'Jonathan Worthington Esquire' was one of 35 men appointed 'justices of our said Lord the King ...' (King William lV): '... to keep the Peace in the said County and also to hear and determine divers, felonies, trespasses and other misdemeanours and offences in the said County committed'.[46] Stourport's celebrations of Queen Victoria's coronation day in July 1838 started early in the morning with a salute by cannon and continued throughout the day with a procession, church service, sport, feasting and smoking. A local newspaper continued:[32]

> At the Swan Inn 86 gentlemen sat down to an excellent dinner at which Jonathan Worthington Esq. presided and J Danks, Esq. officiated as vice president. The evening was passed in a most pleasing and satisfactory manner and the company did not separate till a late hour.

According to *Bentley's Directory* of 1840 'York and Worthington, wharfingers' were listed at the wharf. There was a 'Jos. Worthington, water carrier' at Moorhill as well as 'Jonathan Worthington, Esq. magistrate'.[43] The identity of Jos. remains a mystery but the entry may have been an erroneous duplicate entry for Jonathan. At the national census taken in 1841, those residing at Moorhill were Jonathan Worthington, carrier, Anne his wife, their four youngest children aged nine, seven, six and four years, a civil engineer (not born in the country), three male servants and four female servants.[47]

By 1840 construction of the railway network throughout England and Wales was well advanced, and during the following years it became increasingly clear that the canals could not compete. Profits dropped sharply, and – wisely – Jonathan decided to sell the business. There is no mention of Worthington and Company in *Billings Directory* of 1855; also *Littlebury's Directory* of 1879 records that Worthington and Company was entirely in the hands of the Severn and Canal Carrying Shipping and Steam Towing Co. Ltd.[48] Moorhill was also put up for sale in a single lot by auction at the *Lion Hotel*, Kidderminster, Worcestershire at 3pm on 27 June 1844. The auctioneer's notice of sale described the property as:[38]

> ... a mansion of importance, seated on an eminence in Park-like Grounds, the property and residence of Jonathan Worthington, Esq. who is about to leave the same, with requisite domestic offices, coach house, stabling, very superior agricultural buildings, cottages, gardens, hot and green houses, plantations, pleasure grounds and upward of 105 acres of excellent meadow, orchard and arable land ...

The principal rooms on the ground floor included an oval drawing room 27 feet by 20 feet, a dining room 26 feet by 18 feet, a breakfast room 20 feet by 17 feet and a study 17 feet by 15 feet, all with solid mahogany doors. There was also 'a spacious hall, with Corinthian columns' with a geometrical stone staircase leading to 'a very spacious and well lighted landing place around which are the principal bed chambers (six in number) besides a dressing room'. Also upstairs were a school room, night nursery, housemaid's closet, a commodite, three servants' bedrooms, and a second staircase. There was a walled garden containing fruit trees, a summer house and a vinery 42 feet by 18 feet. The estate was bought for £10,000* by James Arthur Taylor, a deputy lieutenant for Worcestershire. A separate five-day sale took place on the site for the contents, including 'choice wines, a cabinet collection of minerals and fossils, books and live and dead farming stock'. By 1871 Moorhill was the home of John Brinton, the well-known carpet manufacturer; he re-named the house 'Moor Hall' and made substantial extensions – adding a conservatory at one end and a tower at the other.[49] During the First World War the house was used as a convalescent home for officers, but afterwards it lost its way and attempts to sell it in 1917

---

* Equivalent to 110,000 man-days of agricultural labour.

and 1924 failed. It was finally sold for demolition in 1938. In 1994 the cellars of the old house re-appeared when a three-foot hole opened in Moorhill Drive.

After leaving Moorhill, the family moved to Llancaiach House, Llancaiach, in the parish of Gelligaer, near Nelson, Glamorgan. They were certainly there by 1848. Jonathan had entered into partnership with Andrew Duncan and John Garston. The business, which ran the Llancaiach Colliery and had an office in Cardiff, was known for some years as Duncan and Co. Hunts' *Mineral Statistics* for the years 1854 and 1855 shows that the colliery was owned by Gamster and Worthington, but later Jonathan became the sole proprietor. He also owned three farms there. His move was astute; the demand for coal was rising fast, partly to fire the steam-powered railway trains which were displacing the horse-drawn canal barges. How the opportunity came is not known, but the estate is only 15 miles up valley from Cardiff on the River Severn, and coal from Llancaiach may have been shipped up the Severn to Stourport for onward transport via the canal network.

Old maps of Llancaiach show the colliery shaft, engine house, cooling pond, smithy, coke ovens and cottages. They also show tram roads leading to the slag tip and Llancaiach railway station. There is some confusion as to which of two houses was Llancaiach House. According to one authority writing in 1901 Llancaiach House was the castellated stone mansion which stands a few hundred yards north (uphill) of the shaft: it had been built in the Tudor period by Edward Pritchard who was high sheriff of Glamorgan in 1599.[50] On the oldest maps the house is called 'Llancaiach Ucha' and in recent times 'Llancaiach Fawr'. The name 'Llancaiach House' now applies to another large house – probably the colliery manager's, lying about 200 yards south of the shaft (downhill).

In 1849 the family also had a house in Cheltenham, Gloucestershire – then a rapidly expanding Regency town. A list of the resident gentry of the town for 1849 records 'Worthington, J.' as occupier of 7 Oriel Terrace.[51] He had not been there in 1848 when Lady Pepys occupied the house, nor was he there in 1851 when the national census showed that it had 10 residents. Perhaps the Worthingtons rented the house for a season or a year.

In 1859, Jonathan placed the running of his concerns at Llancaiach into the hands of his second son George Samuel Worthington (Article 3.32) while he, Anne and their daughters Lucy and Sarah returned to Cheltenham. They lived for the first year or so at 1 Promenade Terrace before settling at Arundel Villa. The villa built about 1852 was the second of eight large semi-detached houses known as Bays Hill Villas, lying on the west side of Bays Hill Road. Number 1 and Arundel Villa constituted the first pair of a four-storey building on the corner of St George's Road and Bays Hill Road, with their fronts facing Fauconberg

which later became part of Cheltenham Ladies' College. By 1885 the villa had been renamed 'Arundel House'; by 1915 the pair of houses had been merged into one, known as Arundel House, today the main office of Kraft Foods Limited. Jonathan regarded this as his second home; his Will, dated 10 April 1860, begins:

> This is the last will and testament of me Jonathan Worthington of Llancaiach in the County of Glamorgan, but now residing at Arundel Villa, Cheltenham, in the County of Gloucestershire, Esquire ...

Alas, Jonathan did not enjoy Arundel Villa for long; he died at Cheltenham on 12 April 1860 and was buried at St Peter's Church, Leckhampton, near Cheltenham on 17 April 1860. His second daughter Lucy wrote from Leek, Staffordshire, on 31 May 1860 to her friend Mary Jane Burne who was then staying with 'A Dudley, esq. The Manor House, Neston, Cheshire':

> ... It has indeed been a sad sad grief to us. Papa's health gradually failed from February when he had an epileptic fit. The second one on the night of 11 April proved fatal – he had only been in bed eight days. He was quite aware of his own danger and had no fear of death but rather welcomed it as a messenger of God to release him from pain and suffering. What we all endured that night no tongue can even tell – to see a loved one suffering is so dreadful. Poor Mama bore up wonderfully and my three brothers were great comforts to her and us. I cannot even now realise the fact that dearest Papa is gone. I could not help thinking all that night how rejoiced dearest Kits would be to welcome him and perhaps unseen by our mortal eyes she stood waiting to receive him ...

Kits was Jonathan's eldest daughter, Mary Jane, who had pre-deceased him (Article 3.33).

In his Will of 10 April 1860, witnessed by his butler, George Chepellas, Jonathan appointed his three eldest sons, Yorke, George and Richard as his trustees and executors (Articles 3.31, 3.32 and 3.34). The assets were to be held in trust to provide an income for Anne for the maintenance of herself and their two surviving unmarried daughters. On the death of Anne £3,000[*] was to be held in trust for each of the daughters (Articles 3.35 and 3.37) and for the education and benefit of any children they may have. The residue of the estate was for the three sons – Yorke, George and Richard. Jonathan was very reserved about leaving anything for the benefit of his fourth son, Charles, who had already shamed the family and shown serious weaknesses (Article 3.36). Charles was then married but had not yet produced a grandchild. In his Will Jonathan directed that £1,000 capital could be made available to Charles '... at the option of my said Executors'. Jonathan's estate was not wound up for a further 16 years when George and Yorke published a notice pursuant to Chapter 35 of the Property Act of 1859. Any person with

---

[*] Equivalent to 30,000 man-days of agricultural labour.

a claim against the estate was required to send details to the executors' solicitor, Benjamin Matthews of Cardiff.[52]

Anne continued to live at Arundel Villa for seven more years; she was still there in 1867. The residents on the day of the national census return for 1861 were Anne, described as 'proprietor of colliery', Caroline her daughter, Mary Barnett her unmarried sister, Hannah Berber visiting from East India, George Chisnell (probably a new name for George Chepella the butler) and two female servants.[51] From 1868 to 1872 she was living at 6 Royal Well Terrace, Bays Hill, Cheltenham.[51] The national census of 1871 shows her there aged 74 years with her lady's maid Rose Mustoe aged 19 years.[51] Presumably Anne had a flat or rooms. The head of the household was Thomas Ryder, boot and shoe maker aged 49 years; he had with him his wife, daughter, two sons and two domestic servants. From 1873 to 1876, Anne lived at 1 Promenade Terrace – the house in which she, Jonathan, and their two surviving daughters had lived for a year when in 1859 they moved from Wales.[51] She died at 3 Promenade Terrace on 23 March 1876 at the age of 79 years.[52] She was buried at St Peter's Church, Leckhampton, on 30 March 1876. By her Will dated 17 March 1864 she left her estate to three of her children – Yorke, Charles and Lucy. The other two surviving children, George and Caroline, were not included although George was appointed an executor.

3.22 Sarah Yorke

Sarah Yorke Worthington, the eldest daughter of Jonathan Worthington (Article 3.11) by his first wife Sarah, was born on 30 June 1793 and baptised on 13 July 1793 at St Michael's Church, Lower Mitton. She was the first member of the family to have Yorke as a second forename – a practice which was to continue in the family for six further generations. It is not known why the name was spelt 'Yorke' when her grandfather Aaron's surname was spelt 'York'. If it were to give a feminine touch, the idea must have been quickly lost because 'Yorke' was used equally for male and female Worthington descendants. Indeed, it came to be thought that Yorke was the surname of the ancestral family; for example Jonathan Yorke Worthington wrote in a letter of 1895 that the name '…comes through my grandmother from the Yorkes of Beverley…' (Article 7.14). Sarah's mother died when she was only three years of age, and she had a step-mother, Elizabeth, from the age of nine years.

On 16 November 1818, at the age of 25 years, Sarah married John Gardner of Marlborough, Wiltshire, a younger son of Charles Gardner of Ombersley, Worcestershire. John was then aged 28 years, having been born on 15 May 1790 at Ombersley. He had been a member of the Royal College of Surgeons since 15 May 1812. On 25 December 1812 he was appointed assistant surgeon to the 1st Foot Guards and was present with his regiment at the battle of Waterloo in 1815.[53] On 10 October 1816 he transferred to the 52nd Regiment of Foot with whom he served until 12 November 1830 when he commuted to half-pay. The wedding was at St Michael's Church, Lower Mitton, the register being signed by the bride's father Jonathan, her elder brother 'Jonathan Worthington Junr', her half-sister Eliza Worthington, her uncle Richard Jukes and her cousin Eliza Izon. Sarah and John produced two daughters:

Forename	Date of baptism
Sarah Yorke Worthington	13 December 1819
Caroline Anne	5 February 1821

Sarah was born at Marlborough and baptised at St Mary's Church, Marlborough; Caroline was baptised at St Peter and St Paul's Church, Marlborough. Pigot and Co's *London and Provincial New Commercial Directory for 1822-3* shows John Gardner as a surgeon of Kingsbury Street, Marlborough.[45]

In 1829 John was elected a licentiate of the Society of Apothecaries. In 1830, the year of his partial release from military service, John was elected mayor of Marlborough, and he was mayor again in 1834. John Halcomb, the father-in-law of Sarah's half-sister Emma Susanna (Article 3.26) had been mayor in three earlier years. In 1840 John was appointed surgeon to the Wiltshire Yeomanry and on 26 August 1844 he was promoted fellow of the Royal College of Surgeons.[53] From 1843 to 1848 he was medical attendant to Marlborough College and from 1849 to 1859 he was the school's consulting surgeon.[54]

The 1851 national census return shows that Sarah and John were then living at 222 Kingsbury Street, Marlborough St Peter, John being noted as alderman and FRCS.[55] Also residing there at the time were their daughter Sarah Reid aged 31 years and her son John Reid aged five years. There were three living-in servants, namely Michael Cook aged 45 years, Ann Banett aged 28 and Elizabeth Shile aged 22.

John made his Will on 24 August 1852 at Marlborough, 20 years before he died.[56] His horses and carriages were to pass to his wife. Sometime between signing the Will and signing its first codicil on 27 May 1859, John had inherited the Chapel Estate at Ombersley from his elder brother Thomas Gardner who had in turn inherited it from their father Charles Gardner. By the codicil the estate was to pass to the heirs male of John and Sarah's daughter – Sarah Yorke Worthington Reid, and failing such heirs was to return to the Gardner family 'according to their respective seniority in tail male'. By that time Sarah junior had married Edward Maitland Reid and was sole heiress, her younger sister having died unmarried.[42] John Gardner's executors were Sarah and her nephew George Samuel Worthington of Cardiff (Article 3.32). His solicitor was John Halcomb, presumably a relation of Thomas Halcomb – Sarah's half-brother-in-law who also lived at Marlborough (Article 3.26).

John retired by 1856 when they moved to 13 Priory Street, Cheltenham – a three-storey semi-detached house near Cheltenham College. The national census return for 1861 lists the household thus:[51]

John Gardner, head	Age 70	Landed proprietor
Sarah Y Gardner, wife	67	Fundholder
Sarah Y Reid, daughter	41	Fundholder
John M Reid, grandson	15	Scholar
Michael Cook, servant	55	Butler to family
Mary Lony, servant	35	Housemaid
Ellen Gore, servant	24	Cook

The butler had been born at Marlborough, so it appears he had moved with the family to Cheltenham.

Sarah died on 28 July 1869 at the age of 76 years. She was buried on 3 August 1869 at St Andrew's Church, Ombersley. John continued to live at 13 Priory Street; at the 1871 census John aged 80 was there as a widower accompanied by his daughter Sarah and three servants, including Michael Cook his butler.[51] John died on 15 October 1872 and his body was taken to Ombersley where it was buried with that of his wife, Sarah. Although he had not lived at Ombersley since he married Sarah, he returned in death to the place of his ancestors. Their grave is the nearest to the south-west corner of the church building and the inscription reads:

> Blessed are the dead which die in the Lord. Sacred to the memory of Sarah Yorke Gardner, wife of John Gardner Esquire of this parish; born at Stourport June the 30th 1793, died at Cheltenham July the 28th 1869. Sacred also to the memory of John Gardner Esq're, eldest son of the late Charles Gardner of Parsonage in this Parish, who died at Cheltenham Oct 15th 1872, aged 82. Also their daughter Sarah, widow of E. M. Reid, died August 29th 1890 aged 84.

There are many other Gardner graves and a tomb in the churchyard relating to the 18th, 19th and 20th centuries. The family had held land in Northampton within the manor of Ombersley at least since 1761.[57]

3.23 Harriet Rebecca
Harriet Rebecca Worthington, the second daughter of Jonathan Worthington (Article 3.11) by Sarah his first wife, was born on 12 March 1795 and baptised on 9 April 1795 at St Michael's Church, Lower Mitton.[21] She died on 22 February 1799 aged three years and was buried in the York-Worthington family tomb at St Michael's Church.

3.24 Mary Anne
Mary Anne Worthington, the third daughter and youngest child of Jonathan Worthington (Article 3.11) by Sarah his first wife, was born on 14 September 1796 and baptised on 31 October 1796 at St Michael's Church, Lower Mitton.[21] She died on 12 January 1802 aged five years

and was buried on 15 January 1802 in the York-Worthington family tomb at St Michael's Church.

3.25 George

George Worthington, the third son of Jonathan Worthington (Article 3.11) but the eldest child of Jonathan by his second wife Elizabeth, was born in the year 1802 at Moorhill, Stourport. He was baptised on 13 December of that year at St Michael's Church, Lower Mitton.[21] He died on 7 May 1803 aged less than a year, and was buried on 11 May 1803 in the York-Worthington family tomb at St Michael's Church.

3.26 Emma Susanna

Emma Susanna Worthington, the fourth daughter of Jonathan Worthington (Article 3.11) but the eldest daughter by his second wife Elizabeth, was born in 1804 at Moorhill, Stourport, and baptised on 30 May 1804 at St Michael's Church, Lower Mitton.

On 29 May 1824 Emma married Thomas Halcomb, Emma being 19 years of age and Thomas 31. The wedding took place at St Michael's Church, Lower Mitton. A local newspaper reported:[21]

> On Monday, at Mitton Chapel, by Rev. Francis Severne, Thomas Halcomb Esq, of Marlborough, to Emma, second daughter of the late Jonathan Worthington, Esq, of Moorhill House, in this county.

Thomas born on 28 September 1792 was the fourth son of John Halcomb and Catherine Neat his wife.[14] John and Catherine lived at High Trees Farm in the Savernake Forest, south-east of Marlborough, where they were tenants of Charles Brudenell-Bruce, 1st marquess of Ailesbury, whose seat was at Luton Lye in the forest. The Brudenell-Bruces are the hereditary wardens of Savernake Forest, and have been earls of Cardigan since 1661 and earls of Ailesbury and viscounts Savernake since 1776. John Halcomb had been the farmer of High Trees since 1790, and by 1826 the farmland amounted to 650 acres, including Browns Farm. The land tax on the farm was then assessed at £32 3s. 1d.* a year.[58] John also owned the *Angel Inn* in High Street, Marlborough which was leased to the innkeepers. The Halcomb family provided horses for the coaches plying between London and Bath, Marlborough being on the route.[39] John's father was William Halcomb who had been owner and innkeeper of the *Bear* at Devizes, Wiltshire, from 1781 until he died in 1801. He had previously kept the *Kings Arms* at Devizes.[59] He came from a line of four John Halcombs extending back to John Halcomb who was buried at Devizes in 1685.[60] He had farmed at Rowde Farm, Rowde, a village about two miles north-west of Devizes.[61] Members of the Halcomb family had been members of the 'Bear Club' continuously from 1787 to 1826. The club held social meetings at the inn, collected money for charities and provided other help for unfortunates.

---

* Equivalent to 350 man-days of agricultural labour.

Thomas Halcomb's career was also farming. From 1826 to 1828 he and Emma farmed land leased from Richard Welford, but by 1829 they had moved to High Trees, presumably to support Thomas's father who was then approaching the end of his life. When his father died in 1831 Thomas succeeded to High Trees.[58] They held the farm for 20 years. The national census for 1851 for North Savernake describes Thomas, head of household, as farmer aged 58 years employing 23 labourers.[56] Also living there were his wife 'Emma Susanna', his mother-in-law 'Elizabeth Worthington', his sister-in-law 'Jane Worthington' and his nephew 'Joseph Halcomb a scholar aged 19 years'. There were three living-in servants namely, James Tucker aged 35 years, Jane Green aged 25 and Mary Chard aged 23. One of the younger farm labourers also lived there. Thomas had been elected to the corporation of Marlborough in 1827 and was mayor in 1832 and 1835. His father had been mayor in 1815, 1822 and 1828.[62] Emma's half-sister's husband John Gardner (Article 3.22) was mayor in 1830 and 1834, so these families held the mayoralty of Marlborough for seven years in the 21-year period from 1815 to 1835.

Emma and Thomas produced four sons:

Forename	Date of birth	Date of baptism	Date of burial
John Worthington		3 February 1825	3 October 1826
Charles Henry		26 January 1832	
Thomas Robert		17 June 1833	
Frederick	25 July 1836	23 August 1836	

John was baptised at St Mary's Church, Marlborough, the entry in the register being 'John Worthington son of Thomas and Emma Susan Halcomb, Gent'. John was buried at the same church aged 20 months. The other three sons were baptised at St Peter and St Paul's Church, Marlborough. Frederick, at least, was born at High Trees.[60] He in turn kept the name Worthington alive in his family by naming his son 'Guy Worthington Halcomb'.

Thomas and his brother William had inherited the *Angel Inn* at 8 High Street, Marlborough. In an 1830 trade directory this inn was described as 'commercial and coach office'. They sold it in 1833. By 18 June 1852 Thomas and Emma had left the farm, the new occupiers being A. May and W. Carter.[58] Thomas and Emma, together with Elizabeth Worthington and Jane Jukes Worthington (Articles 3.11 and 3.28), moved to The Wood House (Article 3.11) near Cheadle, Staffordshire, a house then owned by the Bills of Farley Hall, Staffordshire, to whom the Halcombs were connected by marriage. A second reason for moving there may have been that Thomas's sister, Anne Neate, was the wife of John Michael Blagg of Rosehill, Cheadle. John Blagg was a Cheadle solicitor who had met Anne while training for his profession with a Marlborough firm. Yet a third reason could have been that Emma's

11   *The Wood House, Cheadle, about 1908.*

younger brother Andrew Jukes Worthington (Article 3.30) lived at Leek, only eight miles away. Indeed, at one stage Thomas held a 50 per cent share in Andrew's silk manufacturing business – A.J. Worthington and Co of Leek. Thomas sold his holding to Andrew by deed dated 30 June 1868.[63] The partnership had been established verbally and had been in existence for 'several years'. Thomas and Emma were then living at Harewood Hall which lies on the east side of the Leek Road, about half a mile north of Cheadle.

Some time after Emma's mother Elizabeth (Article 3.11) died, Thomas and Emma moved to Cheltenham, Gloucestershire. In 1872 they were living at 28 Imperial Square, probably taking a flat or two floors. This house was one of an imposing four storey terrace of Regency houses facing the corporation gardens. Cheltenham town hall stands about 100 yards away on the opposite side of the road. They soon moved next door, and from 1873 are listed at 27 Imperial Square. Emma died at 27 Imperial Square on 23 May 1874 and was buried on 27 May 1874 at the Borough Cemetery, Cheltenham, Section R, Grave 3,339.[52] The deed issued to establish this family grave was signed by Emma's son Charles Henry Halcomb, merchant, of The Limes, Sheffield, West Yorkshire (now South Yorkshire). Thomas as a widower continued to live at 27 Imperial Square for a further year but by 1876 had further moved to

26 Imperial Square, where his sisters-in-law Jane Jukes Worthington and Marianne Cooper also lived (Articles 3.28 and 3.29). He died there on 11 July 1877 and was buried on 14 July 1877 in Emma's grave, over which a white marble cross with three bases was erected. A stone kerb was laid round the grave, but this has since been sunk level with the grass for ease of maintenance. On the front of the bases was inscribed: 'In loving memory of Emma Susan Halcomb who died May 23rd, 1874 aged 69. Also of Thomas Halcomb husband of the above who died July 11th 1877 aged 84'. Margaret Halcomb, presumably a daughter-in-law, was also buried in the grave, the following being inscribed on the right side of the bases: 'Also of Margaret Halcomb, devoted wife and mother, ob October 9, 1882, aged 45'. The cemetery records show that Margaret was a 'non-inhabitant' of the borough of Cheltenham.

In his Will dated 11 July 1874, with a codicil dated 26 June 1875, Thomas made a bequest to Emma's niece Emily Jane Goodman (Article 7.4). The remainder of his estate passed to his three surviving sons.

3.27 Eliza

Eliza Worthington, the fifth daughter of Jonathan Worthington (Article 3.11) but the second daughter by his second wife Elizabeth, was born in 1805 at Moorhill, and baptised on 3 November 1805 at St Michael's Church, Lower Mitton.

About April 1817, when Eliza was 11 years of age, she received a letter from her mother's brother, Dr Andrew Jukes, who was then the garrison surgeon at Tannah, about 24 miles from Bombay in India. The letter is as follows:

> Your letter is very well written and therefore I am sure you have been a good girl and attentive to your studies; your sister is very kind to take so much trouble with you. Tell her I very much approve of the plan she has adopted for making you write an account of what you have read each week. It will tend to impress it much upon your memory while the writing will improve your powers of composition. I am very glad you have seen Miss O'Neil in Juliet, because she is a very fine actress and it is one of her most pleasing characters. Your little cousin Andrew is a very nice little boy though he cannot yet talk much. He runs about as madly as you used to do when I was at Moorhill and calls himself a 'good baba'. His little brother is now six weeks old. You must look over your maps and find whereabouts Tannah is on the Island of Sabeth. There are some tigers upon the island and the night before last a poor boy was killed by one, but the tigers live in the woods or jungles as we call them and do not come near to any houses. I am very glad to find that you can play so well and with your sister's kind care you will improve and be able to play Duets with your aunt when she comes to England. Do not pursue too many things at once and whatever you learn be sure you do it well. As you are a fast runner, I conclude that you will be a very active dancer, but the fashion of some young ladies lately arrived from England is very unbecoming and therefore I hope you will not adopt it. Little Andrew and Mark send you many kisses

as also your Aunt Mrs Ewart. Believe me, your affectionate uncle, Andrew Jukes.

In 1820, the two Jukes children, whose full names were Andrew John Jukes and Mark Richard Jukes, were sent back to England to live for a few years with their Aunt Elizabeth and her family at Moorhill.[27] Andrew was educated at Harrow School and then became an officer in the Indian Army before settling down as an Anglican priest. As an old man he wrote on 14 February 1892 from his home in Upper Eglington Road, Woolwich, to Philip Jukes Worthington in Leek:

> I cannot tell you how much I am obliged to you for the beautiful photograph of the picture of your dear grandmother and your father and his sisters. It brings them all before me as I knew them some seventy years ago; for, if I remember, that drawing of your grandmother was taken about 1825. All the likenesses were good. I am indeed glad to have the photograph for the years my dear aunt at Moorhill was a mother to me. I used to sleep in her dressing room, immediately adjoining her bedroom, which was at the south-west corner of the house, over the dining room. It all still seems so real to me, though all who then were there, except myself, are gone. Your aunt Eliza (the figure with her hand upon the piano) was the first to go. She sung beautifully and was never tired of singing for our amusement ...

Eliza's manuscript book of songs was still kept 130 years later by Percy W. L. Adams at Woore Manor, Shropshire.[39] Most of the songs had been copied at Wribbenhall, the town about three miles north of Stourport where her great-grandparents, the Lloyds (Article 3.5), had lived.

At the age of about 19 years, Eliza left Moorhill and went with her mother to live at Malvern, Worcestershire. Alas, Eliza lived only a few months beyond her 21st birthday.[38] She died unmarried on 27 January 1827 at Malvern and was buried on 2 February 1827 at St Michael's Church, Lower Mitton.[21] She was the last member of the family to be buried in the York-Worthington family tomb there. The inscriptions on the tomb stones were completed as follows:

> Aaron York, who died March 19th, 1797, aged 55 years. Also Aaron his son, who died March 10, 1793, aged 24 years. Also Mary, wife of Aaron York who died January 29, 1817, aged 78 years.
>
> In memory of Sarah, wife of Jonathan Worthington of Stourport, who died December 22, 1796 aged 27 years. Also Jonathan Worthington, who died June 21, 1821, aged 65.
>
> In memory of: Harriet Rebecca, daughter of Jonathan and Sarah Worthington, who died February 22, 1799, aged 3 years and 11 months. Mary Anne, daughter of Jonathan and Sarah Worthington, died January 12, 1802, aged 5 years and 3 months. George, son of Jonathan and Sarah Worthington, who died March 24, 1802, aged 11 years and 6 months
>
> In memory of George, son of Jonathan and Elizabeth his second wife. He died May 7, 1803, aged 5 months and 4 days; also Eliza their daughter, who died January 27, 1827, in the 21st year of her age.

3.28 Jane Jukes

Jane Jukes Worthington, the sixth daughter of Jonathan Worthington (Article 3.11) but the third by his second wife Elizabeth, was born on 17 April 1807 at Moorhill, Stourport, and baptised on 23 June 1807 at St Michael's Church, Lower Mitton. At the age of about 17 years, Jane left Moorhill to move with her mother Elizabeth to Malvern. Sometime after Eliza's death in 1827 Jane and her mother Elizabeth moved to High Trees in the Savernake Forest, Wiltshire, near Marlborough.[39] In 1851 they both moved to The Wood House, Cheadle, Staffordshire, where they lived until Elizabeth's death in 1861. By 1876 Jane had moved to an apartment at 26 Imperial Square, Cheltenham. Her younger widowed sisiter Marianne Cooper (Article 3.29) and brother-in-law Thomas Halcomb (Article 3.26), then a widower, also lived at 26 Imperial Square, where all three spent the rest of their lives.[51] At the time of the 1881 census there were five female lodgers in the house – Jane, Marianne, a colonel's widow, and two others. There was also a 24-year-old parlour maid. Numbers 21, 23, 24 and 26 Imperial Square were then run as lodging houses by James Harris.

Jane died unmarried on 29 May 1883 at 26 Imperial Square and was buried on 2 June 1883 at Borough Cemetery, Cheltenham, in Section M, Plot 16604.[52] Marianne died at the same place within two years and was buried in the same grave. A stone cross was erected over the grave, the following being inscribed on the base:

> In loving memory of Jane Jukes Worthington, died 29th May 1883 aged 75; also of Marian Cooper, sister of the above who died at Cheltenham March 24th 1885 aged 75 years.

Since 1861 Jane had been enjoying income from property held in trust in accordance with her mother's Will. Although the property was in trust, the terms were such that Jane had the disposition of it on her death. In her Will dated 27 January 1882, Jane caused the property to remain in trust to provide income to Marianne for her life. Thereafter the property was for the benefit of five of her nephews and nieces, namely: Charles Henry Halcomb, Frederick Halcomb, Arnold Worthington Cooper, Emily Goodman (Article 7.4) and Alice Worthington (Article 7.5). The residue of Jane's estate was bequeathed in equal parts to Marianne Cooper, Emily Goodman and Alice Worthington.

3.29 Marianne

Marianne Worthington, the youngest daughter of Jonathan Worthington (Article 3.11) by his second wife Elizabeth, was born on 17 April 1809 at Moorhill, Stourport, and baptised on 19 April 1809 at St Michael's Church, Lower Mitton. Although she was entered on the register of baptisms as 'Marianne', she was more generally known as 'Marion'. An elder half-sister had been named 'Mary Anne' (Article 3.24) but had died young in 1802. A sampler made by 'Maryann' in 1819 may have been made by Marianne; if so, she would have embroidered it at the age of nine or ten years. It is now in the possession of Philip Michael Worthington (Article 8.4) having previously been in the possession of Lieutenant-Colonel Guy Jukes Worthington, who was Marianne's great-nephew. The sampler is 16 inches square and includes birds, butterflies, trees, other designs, and the words:

> Vain is the search of him that looks for bliss,
> In this vain world where nought but care is his,
> Then LORD to thee we fly, Oh let us know
> The way that leads to life and in it go.
> Contentment is a constant store
> Desire what's fit and nothing more
>
> Maryann Worthington – her work – 1819'

At the age of about 15 years, Marianne left Moorhill with her mother Elizabeth to live at Malvern. She moved again with her mother and sister Jane to High Trees in the Savernake Forest sometime in or after 1827. On 3 February 1846, at the age of 36 years, Marianne married Richard Cooper of Leek, 'son of Robert Cooper, gentleman'. They may have met during Marianne's visits to her younger brother Andrew Jukes Worthington of Leek. (Article 3.30). Richard was a widower who had been born on 6 October 1803 at Cheddleton, a village about three miles south of Leek.[64] After attending Leek Grammar School he read medicine at Guy's and St Thomas's hospitals, London, where he was a pupil of Sir Astley Cooper. He became a licentiate of the Society of Apothecaries at the age of 21 years, and the following year was elected a member of the Royal College of Surgeons. Later he became a licentiate of King's and Queen's College of Physicians (Dublin) and a licentiate in midwifery. He commenced as a general medical practitioner in Leek in 1825 and from 1837 until his death was the medical officer of the Leekfrith District. He was a trustee and class leader of the Wesleyan Methodist church in Leek and the local treasurer for the Foreign Missionary Society. His first marriage was to Mary Anne, daughter of William Birch of Leek, by whom he had one son – William Birch Cooper.

The wedding of Marianne and Richard took place at St Mary's Church, Marlborough, after which they enjoyed 26 years together in Leek. Arrangements for the marriage may not have been straightforward. The Will of Marianne's mother, Elizabeth (Article 3.11), made 12 years after the marriage, refers to a marriage settlement run by trustees to which Elizabeth had covenanted the interest on £1,000 year by year, with the £1,000* capital passing to the trustees on Elizabeth's death. Also Elizabeth referred twice in her Will to '… the husband children and kindred of my said daughter Marianne Cooper', while omitting the qualification 'husband children' in respect of the other daughters.

---

* Equivalent to 10,000 man-days of agricultural labour.

There was only one child of the marriage, namely:

Forename	Date of birth
Arnold Worthington	26 January 1852

Arnold was born at home, in Derby Street, Leek. The 1871 national census shows Marianne and Richard living at 34 Derby Street, Leek, with two living-in servants – Hannah Plant, cook, and Margaret Goodwin, housemaid.[65]

Richard died on 23 January 1872 at the age of 69 years. At about 3 a.m., Marianne woke to find him sitting up in bed. His only words were 'I am dying'. Dr Gailey was called and arrived soon, 'but life was found to be extinct' due to a rupture of a large blood vessel.[66] The Methodist Society of Leek passed the following unanimous resolution:

> That this meeting has learned of the decease of Dr Cooper, with much emotion. His steadfast Christian experience, his devout attention to divine ordinances, his unblemished reputation in the world, his untiring industry, and charity in the fulfilment of his professional duties, and his unostentatious generosity to God's cause, during a long public life, won for him the affectionate admiration of all who knew him. The meeting is consoled by the persuasion that the quiet force of his good life will long be felt in this Circuit, and desires to express its deep sympathy with the bereaved family.

He was buried in the Doctors' Corner at St Edward's churchyard, Leek.[67] His Will showed that he had inherited two shops with dwelling houses in Sheep Market, Leek, from his first wife – one in the tenancy of a printer and bookseller and the other a confectioner and baker. The properties and investments were placed in trust to provide income for his widow, the assets then passing to his two sons. He left 19 guineas* to each of his and Marianne's servants.

Soon afterwards, Marianne moved to Cheltenham, Gloucestershire, to live with her unmarried elder sister Jane Jukes Worthington (Article 3.28) in an apartment at 26 Imperial Square. They were there by 1876 and remained there for the rest of their lives.[51] By 17 March 1884 Marianne was terminally ill; she wrote that day to her nephew Philip Jukes Worthington (Article 7.8) who had proposed to visit her:

> I am afraid it must appear that I am in very dilapidated condition, when I say that I have not yet left my room ... you see then that I am not much in a condition for visitors ...

But Philip persisted, and on 23 April she relented and invited him to Cheltenham. She died on 24 March 1885 at 26 Imperial Square and was buried on 27 March 1885 at the Borough Cemetery, Cheltenham, in the same grave as her sister Jane (Article 3.28) who had died two years previously.[52]

---

* Equivalent to 18 man-days of agricultural labour.

Marianne had not written a Will, but letters of administration were granted to her nephew Ernest Andrew Worthington (Article 7.3) who was granted power of attorney by Arnold Worthington Cooper, her 'natural and lawful son and only next of kin'. Arnold had settled at Richmond in the colony of Natal, where he was a magistrate and a microscopist. He was also chairman of the board of trustees to establish and control the Natal Government's National Museum in Loop Street, Pietermaritzburg.[68]

3.30 Andrew Jukes

Andrew Jukes Worthington, the fourth son and youngest child of Jonathan Worthington (Article 3.11) but the second son by his second wife Elizabeth, was born on 22 December 1810 at Moorhill, Stourport, and baptised the next day at St Michael's Church, Lower Mitton. It is likely that his early business experience was gained with his father's interests in Manchester and with his half-brother's canal carrying business at Stourport.[39] When his mother left Moorhill in 1824, he presumably went with her to live at Malvern, Worcestershire. He was then about 14 years of age.

By the time he was 28 years of age, Andrew was in business as a silk manufacturer at Leek, Staffordshire. On 1 January 1839 Joseph Fletcher, secretary of the Hand-loom Inquiry Commission, produced a report which began:[67]

> Leek, which contains about 5,000 inhabitants, has long been the seat of the manufacture of broad silks of the best quality, and of plain ribbons by hand; upon the latter of which the manufacture by power has gradually encroached. There are about 150 broad looms and 180 engine looms in the town: but only a half of the former and a third of the latter are now fully employed ... The number of steam engine looms is about 100. Those of:
>
> | | |
> |---|---|
> | Messrs. Carr | 20 |
> | Messrs. Glendinning and Gaunt | 10 |
> | Messrs. Worthington | 10 |
> | Messrs. Wreford | 50 |
> | Messrs. Ward | 10 |
> | | 100 |
>
> There are no power looms making broad silks, though some are being erected. The power weaving of ribbons, ferrets and galloons in those looms is part of the whole system of silk manufacture in Leek factories, which embraces also the throwing and spinning of silk, and the twisting of it into sewing silk, braids, etc ...

Textile mills in which the machinery was driven by shafts and belting from central steam engines were still developing fast as part of the industrial revolution; that led to the inevitable demise of production by hand in the well-lit lofts of private houses, known as shades.

Andrew's mill was at Portland Street, Leek, and occupied part of the site of the present Portland Mills. The business had been started in 1803 under the name of 'James Goostrey and Co.' to manufacture silk thread. Several years later the business was acquired by the Turner family and renamed 'Hammond Turner and Bros'; the business was re-named 'A.J. Worthington and Co.' by 1 January 1839 when Joseph Fletcher made his report. At some stage Andrew had entered into partnership with 'James Turner of Birmingham, button manufacturer and Henry Turner, Gentleman', whereby Andrew held half the equity and the two Turners the other half. Perhaps Worthingtons supplied silk thread and braid to Turners for making silk covered buttons. This partnership lasted until 10 October 1851 when it was dissolved; Henry Turner had already died or withdrawn, and Andrew bought out James for £10,125 1s. 2d.* of which £3,000 was paid immediately, £2,000 within three months and the remainder in half-yearly instalments of £300 each.[63] The debt was secured by three life policies, but all was duly paid with interest by 10 July 1860 when a memorandum of release was signed by James Turner. An entry of 4 November 1953 in a diary kept at Portland Mills recorded the payment of a mortgage loan on the property taken out on 30 June 1839. The entry stated:

> Post cheque to Stone, King and Wardle 9th. Repayment of Mortgage. In existence since June 30th 1839 when late Andrew Jukes Worthington and others mortgaged the property to Charles Powell of Birmingham. £2,400 plus int. charges: £2,472 4s. 0d.

The small interest would have been that which had accrued since the last regular payment. The loan had existed for 114 years.

On 1 May 1839, Andrew, then aged 28 years, married a niece-in-law of James Turner: she was Sarah Booth, the eldest daughter of Thomas Pemberton of Warstone House, Warstone, near Birmingham, and his wife Mary Elizabeth, daughter of John Warwick of Birmingham.[69] James Turner had married Thomas Pemberton's sister, Ann Maria.[70] Sarah was three years younger than Andrew, having been born on 11 July 1814 and baptised on 28 July 1814 at St Philip's Church, Birmingham (later Birmingham Cathedral.) Her father was a brass-founder, continuing the business of 'Thomas Pemberton and Sons' of Livery Street. Brass-founding remained in the family from about 1680 for more than 200 years spanning seven generations. Thomas's great-great-grandfather, William Pemberton of Thringstone, Leicestershire, was a 'brazier' of Leicester. William's son, Thomas, continued the business and became a freeman of the City of Leicester; Thomas's son, another Thomas, became a brazier in Birmingham, and the remaining four generations – all called Thomas – were brass-founders of Birmingham. Sarah's father was appointed a justice of the peace for Birmingham about 1839.[71] Andrew and Sarah's wedding took place at St Martin's Church, Birmingham. For

---

* Equivalent to 111,000 man-days of agricultural labour.

12 *Andrew Jukes Worthington.*   **13** *Sarah Booth, born Pemberton.*

the first four or five years of their marriage they lived at Horton Hall, Horton, a village about five miles west of Leek, where they produced three children. They then moved to Spout Street, Leek (since 1866 re-named St Edward Street, Leek). Their house is now known as Hallscroft, 47 St Edward Street. There they produced four more children. Their children were:

Forename	Date of birth	Date of baptism	Article
Laura Eliza	6 September 1840	14 October 1840	7.2
Ernest Andrew	3 March 1842	5 June 1842	7.3
Emily Jane	29 May 1843	25 June 1843	7.4
Alice Elizabeth	11 September 1844	18 October 1844	7.5
Walter Moore	19 September 1845	30 October 1845	7.6
Rose	9 September 1847	21 October 1847	7.7
Philip Jukes	4 January 1851	19 March 1851	7.8

The baptisms of the eldest three children took place at St Michael's Church, Horton; the next three were baptised at St Edward's Church, Leek, and Philip was baptised at St Luke's Church, Leek. At the 1851 national census Andrew was away, but Sarah and all seven children were at home in Spout Street.[72] There were also four living-in servants – nurse, under-nurse, general servant and cook, all being unmarried women. At the 1861 census the family was complete and the three living-in servants were cook, parlour maid and nursery maid.

After two years of married life, Sarah wrote the following verse to Andrew for his birthday on 22 December 1842, which she gave him with a book, *Keeble's Christian Year*:

> On this thy natal day, my love,
> No splendid gift I send,
> But fervent prayers to One above,
> That He will thee befriend.
> That He will give thee through His grace,
> Those gifts that never cloy
> The holy spirit's gift of love,
> With health and peace and joy.
>
> Oh! May it be a 'Christian Year'
> This coming one to thee
> So if thy lot be weal or woe
> Thriced blessed it shall be!
> The heart's content shall light thy brow
> And humble hopes be given
> That when those early years be past
> Thou'lt live for aye in Heaven.

She wrote another, longer poem for Andrew's next birthday.

On 10 June 1845 Andrew and Sarah set off on a 10-day tour of the Lake District, travelling by train to Lancaster and then by various hired horse-drawn carriages, and occasionally a row boat. Sarah kept a diary of the event which has since been published.[73]

As the population of Leek grew, St Edward's parish church became unable to house the congregation, so some parishioners made an informal arrangement to meet for services in the upper room of the *Black Head Inn* – a half-timbered building facing the market place.[74] On 1 November 1845, a meeting was held at the National School, Leek, with the Reverend T.P.H. Heathcote in the chair. It was resolved:

> That a new District for Ecclesiastical purposes called the District of St Luke's, has, in consequence of the increasing population of the town, been formed out of the parish of Leek under the provisions of Sir R Peel's act and it is the opinion of this meeting that a new church and school are indispensable and therefore it is advisable that a church should be erected as soon as possible ... the clergy of the Town together with Mr Worthington, Mr Challinor and Mr Ward ... be authorised to obtain subscriptions and that this meeting be adjourned to Monday December 1st to receive their report.

William Challinor of Pickwood, Leek, a member of an ancient Leek family, had married Sarah's younger sister Mary Elizabeth in 1851. Andrew was much involved in the building of the church which was consecrated by the bishop of Lichfield on 19 December 1848. The Reverend B. Pidcock was appointed the first vicar. Sarah took her part

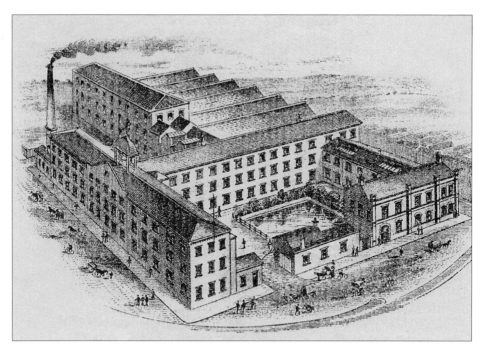

14   *Portland Mills, Leek, in 1904.*

in fundraising. For example in 1857 she was a committee member for
running the bazaar in aid of building a parsonage for the church.

At Easter 1848, Andrew was appointed the warden of Leek and
remained in that office for two years.[75] The parish of St Edward the
Confessor, Leek, is the only parish in England to have a single warden
– a custom which stems from the Saxon foundation of the parish.
Nominations are made in the vestry each Easter; if there are three
nominations or less, the vicar decides, but if there are more than three,
an election has to be held by all Leek ratepayers.

In December 1854 Andrew was elected to the committee of the
Leek district of the Staffordshire Agricultural Society. The election took
place at the 11th ordinary annual meeting of members held at the *Red
Lion Hotel*, Leek.[76]

Sometime after Andrew's business partnership with James Turner
ended on 10 October 1851, Andrew entered into partnership with his
brother-in-law, Thomas Halcomb (Article 3.26). Thomas and his wife
Emma then lived at Cheadle, about eight miles from Leek. He had
sold his share of the *Angel Inn* in 1833 so presumably had investment
money available. Perhaps he provided funds to enable the Turner interest
to be acquired. Whether Thomas was an active or passive partner of
Andrew's is not known, but the business continued to be known as

15   *Ball Haye Hall, Leek.*

'A.J. Worthington and Co, silk manufacturers'. The partnership had been established verbally and lasted for 'several years' until 30 June 1868 when Thomas, then of Harewood Hall, Cheadle, withdrew.[63] The next day, 1 July 1868, Andrew entered into partnership with his eldest son, Ernest (Article 7.3). The deed by which the partnership with Thomas was dissolved was dated 2 March 1869 when Andrew paid £7,000[*] plus interest at five percent a year for the period from 31 December 1868. The dissolution was announced in the *London Gazette* a few days later.

In 1870, after some 26 years at Hallscroft, Andrew and Sarah moved to Ball Haye Hall, Leek, A.J. Worthington & Co. having taken a lease on the property that year.[67] The hall stood splendidly in Ball Haye park. It had been re-built in 1802 and was described as 'a large stone mansion, the old seat of the Davenport family ...'.[67] It was demolished in 1972. According to the 1871 national census, Andrew and Sarah had four living-in servants including Eli Taylor, butler, and Ada M. Worthington, cook.[72] Ada had been born in Market Drayton, Shropshire. Perhaps as a house-warming, a party for all the company employees was given at Ball Haye Hall in August 1870. A marquee was erected, and according to a local newspaper of 5 August 1870:

---

[*] Equivalent to 70,000 man-days of agricultural labour.

> ... at five o'clock the party, numbering upwards of three hundred, sat down to a most excellent tea... Ample justice having been done to the good things provided, the young persons adjourned to the field where they footed it right merrily to the music of the Leek Harmonic Brass Band, whilst the older people were engaged, the men enjoying the fragrant weed and the women commenting on and discussing the merits of the respective dancers. At last the approaching shades of evening warned the party that the time for separation had arrived, and they returned to the courtyard where cake, ale and ginger beer were served out 'ad libitum' ...

Ernest Worthington made a speech, and three cheers were then given for Mr and Mrs Worthington.

Sarah's intense sense of religious discipline and public duty is revealed in her 'private' letter to her youngest child, Philip (Article 7.8), written for his 21st birthday on 4 January 1872. She was then aged 57 years. The letter begins: 'As I cannot say all I wish tomorrow, I will write a few lines, which I hope you will keep and look at sometimes, even when I am cold in my grave ...'. After congratulations, and praise for his hard work and achievements, she continues:

> ... I want you, regularly on Sunday, to make a point of going to church twice a day. The two services will be only three hours taken out of the week. That is not much to give your Maker! You have ceased to be a Sunday school teacher, about which I say nothing, but it pains me much to see so much of the day spent in idle pursuits. The example of your Father and eldest brother is not good in this respect, but if you think seriously about it, it is not right that two suitors should go alone on a winter's evening when there are three gentlemen in the house doing literally nothing, putting aside all higher motives! Then you need to be a communicant. Why have you ceased to be? If you are honestly endeavouring to do your duty, then fulfilling a sacred command will help you on and strengthen you for the battle of life! ...

The creation of St Luke's Church had been a success, and by 1873 the time had come to extend the chancel. On Ascension Day, 22 May that year, Sarah laid the foundation stone.[76] Ceremonies commenced at 8 a.m. with Holy Communion in the church, followed by a full service with Holy Communion at 10.30 a.m. At 1.30 p.m. the Leek Band, wearing their new uniforms, assembled on a platform in the churchyard near the site of the extension and played sacred music by Haydn and Rossini. The church choir assembled on another platform and areas were cordoned off for the public and about 400 schoolchildren. There were many flags, much bunting and a canvas bearing crosses. At 2 p.m. the band ceased playing while five clergymen processed to the site to the singing of Psalm 84. The vicar – the Reverend B. Pidcock who had held the office for the 25 years of the church's life – then led the outdoor service. Sarah was on the arm of her second son, Walter Worthington, who made a speech in which he referred to his mother's long association with the church. Sarah laid the stone saying: 'In the faith of Jesus Christ, we place this foundation stone, in the name of God the father, God the son, and God the Holy Ghost'. She was presented with the silver trowel and mahogany mallet, both inscribed with her name, the occasion and the date. Proceedings were completed by another service in the church at 3 p.m.

Later that year, on 22 December 1873, Andrew died at Ball Haye Hall. He was buried at St Luke's Church. A local newspaper commented:

> The family of the deceased gentleman have been distinguished by many deeds of Christian charity, and the presence in the churchyard during the burial service of many hundreds of persons testified to the general respect in which he was held.

He was the second to be buried in the family tomb there, joining his mother who had been interred in 1861 (Article 3.11). The whole churchyard had been closed to burials since 7 June 1862, possibly because of a plague present in Leek at the time. However, burials of kindred in existing family graves are expressly excluded by the Act; since the closure there have been only 18 burials at the church, of which 11 are of Worthingtons.

Andrew's Will was dated 28 February 1870 and proved on 3 April 1874 at the Principal Probate Registry. He left an income of £50 a year to each of his two unmarried daughters during the remainder of Sarah's life. All remaining income was Sarah's for her lifetime, subject to the obligation of maintaining and educating 'such of my children as being sons shall be under the age of twenty one years and being daughters shall be under that age and spinsters ...'. On Sarah's death his estate was to be divided equally among his seven children, except that Walter Worthington's share was to be £500 less than each other share 'in consequence of the expense I have already incurred and been put to on his account ...' (Article 7.6). Andrew's share in A.J. Worthington and Co. was to be included in this distribution, the executors having discretion to sell the share and distribute the proceeds.

Sarah lived as a widow for three years. She died of cardiac disease on 28 April 1877 at Ball Haye Hall, and was interred in the family tomb at St Luke's Church on 1 May 1877. She was 62 years of age.

The cohesiveness of the immediate family of Jonathan Worthington of Stourport is shown by the families' residential movements after Jonathan's early death. His seven surviving children and his second wife moved as follows after leaving Stourport:

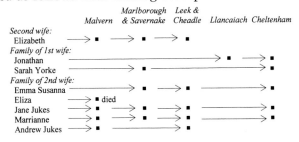

The congregation and re-congregation of the family is remarkable. Andrew's cadet line is discussed later (Chapter 7).

FIFTH GENERATION – FAMILY OF JONATHAN AND ANNE

3.31 Jonathan Yorke

Jonathan Yorke Worthington, the eldest son of Jonathan Worthington and Anne Maria his wife (Article 3.21), was born on 25 June 1827 at Moorhill, Stourport, and baptised on 27 June 1827 at St Michael's Church, Lower Mitton.[14] He lived at Moorhill throughout his childhood, as his parents did not move to Llancaiach until he was about 20 years old. He was educated by the Reverend T. Meyler at Marlborough but at Christmas 1842 transferred to King Edward VI Grammar School, Birmingham, where he remained until the end of the summer term 1844.[77] On 3 June of that year James Primner, MA, chaplain to the 7th Duke of Northumberland and fellow of Trinity College, Cambridge, wrote a reference recommending Yorke 'for admission to the East India Company's college at Addiscombe'. Addiscombe was the company's military seminary near Croydon, Surrey. After being nominated by George Lyall, MP, a director of the company, on the recommendation of Lord Ernest Bruce (heir to the earl of Elgin and Kincardine), Yorke was duly examined by the Artillery and Engineer Seminary at Addiscombe. However, a certificate dated 9 August 1844 stated that he was '... not qualified in arithmetic to be admitted ...' Accordingly, he was enlisted for three months to give him a chance to make the required standard. A further certificate dated 6 December 1844 showed that he was qualified in all respects and was duly admitted.

Yorke passed out of the seminary on 11 December 1846 when he was commissioned 2nd lieutenant. On 25 December his father Jonathan Worthington wrote to George Lyall:[77]

> Sir, we have been much gratified at the result of the late examinations at Addiscombe and in again thanking you for the appointment of my son thro' Lord Edward Bruce, I trust his future conduct thro' life will be such as to merit the approbations of his superiors and honour to the company. I was away from home when the letter of request for his appointment to either of the presidencies arrived. I returned on the 23rd late at night and read it up on the 24th and this morning I have received information thro' a private source that he has been appointed to Madras. If such should be the case may I request your interest in getting him appointed to the Bengal, for we have friends there and none at the Madras; as you must well know the advantage to a young man, entering into life, of having friends to consult in any case of difficulty. I remain, Sir, yours obliged ...

Yorke sailed in SS *Plantagenet* on 9 March 1847 arriving at Fort William (now called Calcutta) on 26 July 1847 to join the Bengal Artillery. He was posted to the foot artillery but achieved a temporary transfer to the horse artillery – 4th troop of the 1st brigade – after about 19 months; the transfer was confirmed permanently by general order dated 20 January 1852.[78]

Yorke served in the Second Sikh War of 1848 and 1849, his artillery troop being part of the army of the Punjab. He took part in the siege and capture of Multan in January 1849, the battle of Gujarat on 21 February 1849 and in the subsequent pursuit of the Sikhs and Afghans. For these actions he was awarded the campaign medal with two clasps. By March 1849 the Sikhs had been defeated and the Punjab annexed, thus extending British India to the border of Afghanistan. In August 1849, Yorke wrote home that he regretted the cessation of war, for he liked the excitement and slept soundly on the ground.[79] Yorke's horse had been shot in the battle of Gujarat; altogether two officers, one non-commissioned officer, 20 rank and file and 87 horses were killed in the battle.[80]

Yorke wrote home frequently; in a letter of late October or early November 1849 he reported that a young man who had been with him at Addiscombe had drowned in the River Indus. Yorke's younger sister, Mary Jane, relayed the information in a letter to a friend:

> ... they were bathing, a party of them Yorke amongst the number; he was not noticed at first but as soon as ever he was Yorke and another man jumped in. He, however, had sunk and notwithstanding all their endeavours was lost. It has thrown a gloom over them all ...

About March 1850 Yorke, as the senior officer of his unit, received General Sir Charles James Napier, GCB, who had been appointed commander-in-chief of the Indian Army during the second Sikh War. Yorke was then probably at Meerut and due to move to Peshawar. That year he passed the army's 'colloquial examination in Hindoostanee' and four years later he passed the complete examination in the language.

During times of peace, Yorke enjoyed six months' leave every two years. From 15 April to 15 October 1851, for example, he was granted leave to visit Murree and Kashmir. On later leaves he visited Simla, Massoorie and the 'hills north of Deyirh'.

Yorke was promoted lieutenant on 3 March 1853 at the age of 25 years. Soon after the Indian Mutiny broke out, in January 1857, Yorke was kicked by a troop horse on parade. While on sick leave in Simla he was instructed to ride with native soldiers to Phillour to order a third-class siege train to be prepared to take a contingent from Phillour to Delhi. This made his injury worse so that he was unable to take part in the siege. The rebels had taken Delhi, massacred British residents there, and proclaimed the old king of Delhi as Mogul emperor of India.

Yorke started his furlough on 21 January 1858 on medical certificate, leaving Bombay for Europe for three years according to the 'old rules'. While he was away he was moved to the 2nd company of the 6th battalion by general order dated 26 June 1858; also in 1858 he was promoted to 2nd captain. He stayed with his family at Arundel Villa in Cheltenham, Gloucestershire, during the winter of 1859-60 and took part in fox hunting with one of his brothers and an uncle. About January 1860 he 'broke a sinew in his thigh' while hunting and was brought home in a cast. He recovered in due course and had returned to the field by 14 February. Another interest of Yorke's is revealed in a letter of his younger sister, Lucy Anne, who wrote to Mary Jane Burne of Loynton Hall, near Newport, Shropshire, on 14 February 1860:

> How do you like Tennyson's last new book? It is an immense favourite of ours ... my eldest brother is a capital reader and sometimes he condescends to read for his sister's amusement ...

On 18 September 1860, towards the end of his furlough, Yorke married Henrietta Charlotte, daughter of Valentine Bryan, a barrister-at-law of County Galway, Ireland.[81] She was then aged about 26 years – a rare beauty whom Yorke had met in India. The wedding took place at the parish church, Scarborough, Yorkshire. Henrietta had married three times previously. First she had married on 20 December 1852 Captain Francis Charles Annesley, the third son of Captain the Honourable Francis Charles Annesley, RN, who in turn was the fourth son of the 2nd earl of Annesley.[82] The younger Francis was a captain in the 63rd (The West Sussex) Regiment of Foot.[8] This marriage only lasted for 17 months because Francis died on 30 May 1854. Only two months later – on 14 August 1854 – Henrietta married secondly Robert Bridgeman Wigstrom, assistant surgeon in the 14th Regiment of Light Dragoons. He had been born in County Cork, Ireland, on 14 September 1822. Like Yorke, Robert had served in the Punjab campaign of 1848 and 1849; his battles had included Ramnagar, Chillianwallah and Gujarat.[53] But Robert died at Bombay, India, on 8 September 1854 aged 31 years, less than a month after his marriage to Henrietta, which had taken place at the Dutch Church, Galle, Ceylon (now Sri Lanka). Henrietta then returned to England and was residing at 3 Western Street, Brunswick Terrace, Brighton, Sussex, on 1 December 1854 when she applied for an army widow's pension.[84] On 18 December 1856 Henrietta married thirdly Rowland Edward Cooper of Chesterfield Street, Mayfair, Middlesex (now London), son of William Henry Cooper, Esquire. Although this marriage would have extinguished Henrietta's army pension, it was probably of little significance since Rowland was wealthy. They lived at 3 Hyde Park Place, Middlesex (now London) and at Pains Hill, Cobham, Surrey. This marriage ended after 21 months by Rowland's death on 19 September 1858 at 3 Hyde Park Place. By Rowland, Henrietta had produced one daughter – Anne Constance Isabel.

Thus, after Henrietta had married Yorke on 18 September 1860, she had had four husbands in eight years. Yorke's father had died five months

16 *Jonathan Yorke Worthington.*   **17** *Henrietta, born Bryan.*

before the wedding and Henrietta's father was already dead. Yorke, and presumably Henrietta and daughter, returned to India on 28 January 1861 at the end of his three-year furlough. He went onto temporary half-pay on 11 September 1863 and retired on 31 August 1864. He was then 37 years of age and had served for 19 years.

They returned to England and lived for a while at Llancaiach House, Glamorgan, where Yorke no doubt helped his younger brother George Samuel (Article 3.32) run the colliery and estate. But by 1870 the colliery had been sold. In July 1881 when letters of administration were granted following George's death, Yorke resided at 'Saint Servan in France'. For most of their later married life they were settled at Benham Lodge on Furze Hill, Stockcross, about four miles west of Newbury, Berkshire. In 1951, Mrs Baines of 10 Wickham Road, Stockcross, gave her recollections of the household; she was the widow of Yorke's butler and mother of his under-butler (formerly buttons). A photograph of Yorke still hung in her sitting room, 49 years after his death. She said that before Yorke and Henrietta had moved to Benham Lodge, they had lived for two years at Speen Court, Speen, Berkshire, a large brick house about two miles west of Newbury, since converted into offices of the National Electricity Board. Benham Lodge was a fairly large two-storey house, to which Yorke and Henrietta added a third storey so they could accommodate grandchildren, nieces and nephews. Mrs Baines said that 'Captain Worthington kept many horses and spent much of his time in the winter fox hunting and in the summer showing horses'.

For a short time in 1895 or 1896 Yorke and Henrietta lived at Copyhold, Chievely, Berkshire, about five miles north-east of Stockcross.[85] Perhaps they had moved there while the upper storey was being added to Benham Lodge.

Henrietta's daughter, Anne Constance Isabel, married Lloyd Brinkley, an Irishman; they lived on the west coast of Ireland and had two sons and three daughters who used to stay at Benham Lodge for two to three months every year. One of the daughters, Mabel, who married C.H. Niven of The Grange, Marden, near Devizes, Wiltshire, in a letter of 18 April 1951 wrote of Yorke:

> ... He was the kindest and sweetest old gentleman, and made everyone feel that they were interesting and important – even me – his step grandchild. He and I used to hunt together with the Craven and sometimes the South Vine ...

Mabel's sister, Mrs E. Sybil Newcome, of Hale Place, Farnham, Surrey, wrote in a letter of 30 April 1951:

> ... I remember him with great affection; he was so good to us as young children. He had the most wonderful old-world manners, and made a little girl feel she was almost a Princess. I remember he and my Grandmother gave small dinners regularly to their friends, and I can see him now, watch in hand – as if any guest was two minutes late – well, dinner had to begin, as it might be spoilt. They always had a wonderful cook – no one was ever late. He was a very good horseman, and had lovely horses and hunted regularly with the Craven ... My grandmother and he were a devoted couple. I believe she was a very great beauty in her day ...

At the age of 67 years, Yorke wrote a letter dated 18 May 1895 from Benham Lodge to Ernest Andrew Worthington (Article 7.3) his half-first-cousin, in which Yorke lamented the passing of his fox-hunting days: '... time rolls on and I am an old man, have to go up to cover on wheels and make short days ...'

Henrietta died at Benham Lodge on 20 May 1896 and was buried at St John's Church, Stockcross, on 26 May 1896. Yorke continued to live at Benham Lodge but was increasingly suffering from old age. In a letter of 13 March 1901 to his half-first-cousin Philip Jukes Worthington (Article 7.8), during an exchange of letters on the family history, Yorke wrote: '... thanks much for asking me to stay with you ... but I never go out now and do not even accept dinner invitations ...' He died without issue at Benham Lodge on 3 June 1902 and was buried in Henrietta's grave at St John's Church, on 7 June 1902. On one side of the grave's headstone is inscribed 'Henrietta Charlotte Worthington died 20th May 1896 in her 63rd year'. On the other side is inscribed 'Jonathan Yorke Worthington died 3rd June 1902 in his 75th Year'.

In his Will dated 13 May 1897 with three codicils dated 21 March 1898, 6 January 1900 and 30 October 1901, Yorke made bequests to his butler

Walter Baines, and his coachman James Matthews. Half a year's wages were bequeathed to all the other servants. The main beneficiaries were his step-daughter Anne Constance Isabel Brinkley and her family. Anne also received household goods, the horses and the carriages. The other beneficiaries were Yorke's sister Lucy 'Annie' Keele (Article 3.35) and her three daughters. Lucy also received the picture of Yorke's father, Jonathan Worthington (Article 3.21), and all his family papers. One of these daughters, Ruth Helen Worthington Keele, received special treatment with a bequest of £3,000* and £300-worth of furniture of her choice. It seems that Ruth had been living with Yorke, and running the house for him in his last years. He specially designated for Ruth the 'silver medal inscribed George Worthington of Werneth' (Article 1.25). Benham Lodge was bought by the local landowner of Benham Court; he had the lodge pulled down, except for the harness room which was converted into a woodman's cottage.

3.32 George Samuel

George Samuel Worthington, the second son of Jonathan Worthington and his wife Anne Maria (Article 3.21), was baptised at St Michael's Church, Lower Mitton, on 5 March 1829.[14] He was about 15 years of age when, in 1844, his father sold Moorhill and, then or soon afterwards, the family moved to Llancaiach in South Wales.

By 1856, George was listed as proprietor of the Llancaiach Colliery.[86] In that year George was about 25 years of age; his father, Jonathan, was 62 and had probably already moved to Cheltenham. Proprietorship of the colliery actually remained firmly in Jonathan's hands until he died in 1860, having written in his Will dated 10 April 1860:

> ... I bequeath unto my said son George Samuel Worthington two fifteenths parts or shares of the clear annual profits arising from my coal and farming concerns and direct that the whole of the remainder of my property shall accumulate until the death of my dear wife ... and further direct that my said son George Samuel Worthington shall have the whole management and control of my coal and farming business and for his trouble and attention to the management thereof he shall have and be entitled to an allowance of three hundred pounds* per annum out of the said concerns in addition to the two fifteenths parts or shares of the clear annual profits before given to him ...

It is possible that George was already enjoying the salary and the two-fifteenths of the profits by unwritten understanding, and that the Will was confirming the arrangement. By that time George was living at Cardiff, Glamorgan, about 15 miles south-east of Llancaiach, but directly linked by rail. When probate was granted on his father's estate at the Principal Probate Court, London, on 13 September 1860, George was described as 'coal owner, the son and one of the executors'. George was still listed

---

* Equivalent to 24,000 man-days of agricultural labour.

18 *George Samuel Worthington.*

as owner in *Hunt's Mineral Statistics* of 1870.[86] A year later, however, the colliery had been sold to Duncan and Co who held it until 1873. From 1874 it was owned by Powell's Gellygaer Coal Company who continued to work it until 1880.

George resided at the *Royal Hotel*, Cardiff, for many years and was a member of the Country Club, Cardiff, which he visited frequently. While dining there on 30 June 1881 he died suddenly at the age of 52 years. No inquest was held, as he had been suffering from heart disease.[87] He was buried on 6 July 1881 at St Mellons, Monmouthshire, four miles north-east of Cardiff. He had died a bachelor without having written a Will. The administration of his estate was granted to his elder brother, Jonathan Yorke Worthington, who was then living in France (Article 3.31).

3.33 Mary Jane

Mary Jane Worthington, the eldest daughter of Jonathan Worthington and his wife Anne Maria (Article 3.21), was born at Moorhill, Stourport, and baptised at St Michael's Church, Lower Mitton, on 26 July 1830.[14] She was 16 or 17 years of age when she moved with her parents from Moorhill to Llancaiach House.

She was a boarder at Oakfield School, which has not yet been located. She left there at the age of about 17 years. In December 1848 she wrote from Llancaiach House to her old schoolfriend Mary Jane Burne, who lived at Loynton Hall, Newport, Shropshire:[79]

> I received your long letter last night, and was very pleased to hear that you had left school with so good a character. I thought of you much the night before you left, and wondered whether you would go to Miss Catherine. I often think of my last night at Oakfield. How miserable I was and I was so very sorry to say goodbye to Ada Fornby, I long to see her again. It is quite a different feeling when you leave school finally and does not feel like coming home for holidays. Does it to you? Remember our second half year, how miserable we were. It is so very pleasant to finish up well …

In the same letter she wrote:

> We left Marlborough, where we have been staying last month, on Monday evening, and got to Bristol that night. We slept at the White Lion Hotel, and came to Cardiff next day by the packet. I stayed on deck all the time, and the cold was really intense. We came up here by middle day train on Wednesday. The Saturday before we left Marlborough we went to a concert given by the boys of the college there; we were received in the library, and the concert was held in the dining hall. I assure you it was not at all like our concerts used to be; the boys looked so merry and happy, performers included. They commenced by singing 'The National Anthem' and finished with 'Dulci Dominee [*sic*]' …

Mary had probably been staying with her aunt Sarah (Article 3.22), whose husband, John Gardner, was the medical attendant at the college. In her next letter to Miss Burne, dated 23 May 1849, Mary wrote:

> Had we remained at dear old Moorhill it would have given me the greatest pleasure if you could have come and stayed with me, but when we make another remove I hope you will do so. At present our seclusion is so great Mama would not wish me to have any young people, as it would be impossible to make a visit pleasant to them …

Her next letter, postmarked 1 September 1849, was written from Leek where she was staying with her half-uncle Andrew Jukes Worthington (Article 3.61). She had travelled there by railway staying for 'the night at Warstone House, a nice place in Birmingham'. Warstone House, was the home of Andrew's parents-in-law, Thomas and Mary Pemberton (Article 3.30). Mary Jane asked for further mail to be addressed to her at 'A. Worthington, Esq., Leek, Staffordshire'. She wrote:

> ... Leek is a nice sociable place. On Wednesday last I dined out after tea and we danced. I had the most splendid Polka with a young man just arrived from Town, so he does it in a first rate manner, it was splendid, and I am so fond of dancing ...

Mary remained at Leek for two months, leaving about 19 October 1849 and staying with various friends and relations on the return journey. For example, she was at Stourport on 14 November 1849, presumably with her grandparent's family, the Barnetts of New Street (Article 3.31). She was certainly there two years later when the 1851 census was taken, Emma Barnett being head of the family.[47]

A glimpse of her social life in Wales is given in her letter of 13 April 1850 to Miss Burne:

> On Monday last Julian gave a concert at Merthyr; we had a few friends to dinner and drove them afterwards. I was delighted, though of course it must be very poor to anyone who has heard him in London. Julian's force was quite a study. I don't think he was still one moment, no wonder he should feel excited. Good music is the greatest treat to me. Merthyr is the most wretched place, but it is quite worth seeing at night as there are numerous iron works which are in a blaze of light; this of course has a very curious effect on the dark night. On Monday I went to an evening party at a place about six miles from here called Eglwysilan Rectory. I only returned late yesterday evening and feel extremely dull after the unusual excitement. Next week Elizabeth Leigh, one of our rector's daughters is coming to spend a week with us ...

On 20 June 1850, now aged nearly 20 years, she wrote from Llancaiach to Miss Burne:

> ... I am going this morning to call at Eglwysilan Rectory over a mountain on horseback. My cousin and Charlie will escort me. I am also going to visit an old servant of ours who is dying consumptive. It is a pleasure to see her; she is so peaceful poor girl. She said to me the other day in such a solemn manner ' Yes Miss, it's a comfort to think I had to do my duty at Llancaiach'. She was the servant who waited on me, dressed my hair etc ... and I always thought her superior ...

Her letter of 9 July 1850 to Miss Burne was impressed with the family crest – On a wreath a Goat passant holding in the mouth a Sprig of oak fructed. The envelope was sealed with a wax impressed with the same crest. She wrote:

> ... to ask if you will ask your sister Georgina if she remembered the lines relating to the parting between Hector and Andromache. We have not had the Iliad here and we are going to get up Tableaux Vivants if we can. I am Andromache and my brother Richard Hector ...

She continues later in the same letter:

> ... perhaps you would like to know our hours; get up between six and seven, go out before breakfast; first hour after breakfast practice; then read. I am now studying my Mantell's geology; to teach Carry French,

and then Lucy teaches me German the last hour, and I am doing the same for her in Italian. This brings us to one o'clock. We then walk and dine at three; afterwards we write, work or anything ... This morning we three walked to see the servant I mentioned to you in my last letter and had quite an adventure being forced completely to fly over two fields to get out of the way of a bull. I was perfectly mad with fright ...

Carry was the nick-name of her sister Sarah Caroline.

In September 1850, Mary, with her sister Lucy and their father and mother, made a week's tour westwards, travelling in their own trap with pony. The tour included the Vale of Neath, Swansea, the Mumbles and Llandeilo. In 1853 she was taking lessons in the Welsh language from one of the vicar's daughters. Mary commented in her letter: '... it is a very ugly language and difficult, only it seems so stupid not to know the language of the people you live amongst ...'

Later in the same letter she referred to their new Sunday School in which she and Lucy were teachers. The school then had 80 pupils, and Mary commented: 'The ignorance of the children here is beyond everything'. In 1853 Mary was learning to play the concertina. In September she went to stay with her aunt at Marlborough and advised Miss Burne to address future letters to her at 'J Gardner's Esq., Marlborough, Wiltshire'.

Mary fell terminally ill on 13 February 1859. It seems that she was staying in Cheltenham at the time – perhaps only months before her parents and sisters moved from Llancaiach to Arundel House, Cheltenham. She died at Cheltenham on 25 February 1859 and was buried at St Peter's Church, Leckhampton, Gloucestershire, on 1 March 1859. She was the first to be placed in the family grave there, her father following a year later and her mother 17 years later. The inscriptions on the stonework are:

> Mary Jane, daughter of Jonathan Worthington, Esquire, of Llancaiach, Glamorganshire, who died at Cheltenham 25th February 1859 aged 28 years.
> Also of Jonathan Worthington of Llancaiach, Glamorganshire, who died at Cheltenham on 12 April 1860 aged 67 years.
> Also Anne Maria relict of the above Jonathan Worthington of Llancaiach, Glamorganshire, who died at Cheltenham on 23rd March 1876 aged 79 years.

3.34 Richard Jukes

Richard Jukes Worthington, the third son of Jonathan Worthington and his wife Anne Maria (Article 3.21), was born on 10 January 1832 at Moorhill, Stourport, and baptised on 21 January 1832 at St Michael's Church, Lower Mitton.[14] Richard was a Yorke Worthington according to the custom already emerging that descendants of the first marriage of Jonathan Worthington (Article 3.11) were Yorke Worthingtons while those of the second marriage were Jukes Worthingtons. However, Richard did not take the name Jukes from his step-grandmother but from his maternal grandmother who was also a Jukes.

Richard lived with his parents at Moorhill until 1844, after which the family moved to Llancaiach House in South Wales. By May 1849, he was 'preparing for college' with a clergyman in Wiltshire – probably the Reverend T. Meyler of Marlborough who had already taught Richard's brother, Jonathan Yorke Worthington (Article 3.31). Richard's family had hoped that he would enter the Church of England for a career, but on 1 September 1849 Richard's elder sister Mary Jane (Article 3.33) wrote:[79]

> ... I'm sorry to say my brother Richard has declined entering the church. He has chosen the medical profession, so Papa will take him up to town next month and place him with a gentleman there so that he may attend hospital lectures ...

His first medical examinations took place in London in July 1850, after which he came home for vacation until 3 October 1850. On arriving at Llancaiach his elder sister, Mary, told him that 'he looked like a student ... so lanky and pale ...'.

Richard completed his medical education three years later. On 21 January 1854 he was appointed assistant surgeon in the army, joining the 34th Regiment of Foot on 24 May 1854.[83] He served with this regiment in the Crimean War, taking part in the storming and capture of the quarries and at the siege and fall of Sevastopol.[88] British losses in the campaign were huge, both from battles and diseases which took their toll during the hard winter of 1854-5. In fact 14,000 soldiers were in military hospitals there by October 1854 when the British government broke new ground by sending out 76 female nurses under Miss Stanley and Florence Nightingale, OM. Such was the size of the medical problem to which Richard, then aged 22, had to make his contribution. He was awarded the campaign medal and clasp and the equivalent medal from the Turks. The Crimean War was over by 1856 when Richard with his regiment was sent to India. He served during the Indian Mutiny of 1857 and 1858, including the Windam actions at Cawnpore from 26 to 28 November 1857, the siege and capture of Lucknow and the relief of Azimghur – for which he was awarded medal and clasp. On 29 August he transferred to the 58th Regiment of Foot. On 3 August 1860 he became staff surgeon at the headquarters of the commander-in-chief of British Forces in New Zealand.[89] He was thus involved in the Maori Wars which broke out in 1860 following a dispute of title to tribal lands. Although the war was continuing, Richard sailed for England early in 1862, perhaps on leave or perhaps because he was ill. He died at sea on 2 February 1862 at the age of 30, unmarried.

Richard made his Will on board ship three days before his death. In it he was described as 'staff assistant surgeon of the general commanding the

19 *Lucy Anne, born Worthington.*

forces in New Zealand, Esquire'. After due gratuities to those attending him, all his assets were to pass to his mother Anne Maria Worthington of Arundel Villa, Cheltenham.

3.35 Lucy Anne
Lucy Anne Worthington, the second daughter of Jonathan Worthington and Anne Maria his wife (Article 3.21), was born on 11 December 1833 at Moorhill, Stourport, and baptised on 16 December 1833 at St Michael's Church, Lower Mitton.[14] At the age of 10 years she moved with her parents from Moorhill to Llancaiach House, Glamorganshire. Her sister Mary Jane (Article 3.33) wrote on 20 April 1850 to her old school friend Mary Jane Burne:[79]

> Miss Gordon spent last Monday at Oakfield and Lucy walked about
> with her and talked of old times … Papa goes into Worcestershire in
> May, and will I expect go to see Lucy.

Oakfield, which has not yet been located, was the boarding school
which both Mary Janes had attended. Whether Lucy was also attending
or just visiting is not clear, but a boarding school was planned for her.
Mary wrote to her friend on 4 October 1850:

> Lucy is I believe going to school after Christmas, but where is not
> decided. It will be an excellent thing for, as you know, education cannot
> be carried out at home as it is in school. There are so many interruptions
> even with a regular governess, and I am not strong enough to pay Lucy
> the undivided attention I should wish to.'

Lucy was confirmed at Cardiff on 3 October 1850 at the age of 16
years. She taught at her local Sunday school, which on 13 March 1853
had about 80 pupils. Her elder sister wrote on that day '… Lucy is away
and we are in sad distress for teachers'.

After Mary's death, there was a short exchange of letters between Lucy
and Mary Jane Burne. In Lucy's first letter, postmarked 14 February 1860
and addressed to Miss Burne at Loyton Hall, Lucy described the family's
move from Llancaiach to Cheltenham:

> … We are very comfortably settled here now, and have had such a
> merry jovial circle since Christmas. In the first place my brothers and
> our uncle are down for the hunting, and we have had two cousins as
> well with us, secondly no end of balls and parties and such games,
> and tho I do not go out this minute yet I see plenty of people I know.
> The fuss and trouble of moving here quite upset me and I had to go
> to Worcestershire for some weeks to recoup and then the doctors said
> I must not dance this winter; it was a great disappointment to me at
> first – and I have only been to one ball this year, but that was the one
> of the season, and a fancy dress one. I was determined to go, and a very
> pretty sight it was. Such a blaze of uniforms and magnificent dresses,
> and no end of champagne and … it is so dreadfully cold here and I
> believe we are going this afternoon to see the gentlemen skate, as they
> say the ice will hold now. I think it is such a pretty site, though rather
> cold work for the ladies …

Lucy's letter to Mary Jane Burne, postmarked 31 May 1860, shows that
Lucy was then staying with her half-uncle and aunt – Andrew and
Sarah Worthington of Leek (Article 3.30). Sarah planned to take Lucy
to Dovedale the following day.

On 14 August 1866, Lucy married Edward Rushworth Keele, the fifth
and youngest son of John Rushworth Keele, JP, MD, and Constantia his
wife, of Southampton, Hampshire. Lucy was then aged 32 years and
Edward was 29, having been born on 30 December 1836 and baptised
at All Saints' Church, Southampton. Edward was a solicitor and lived
at Hampstead, Middlesex. His father was a surgeon and was three times
elected mayor of Southampton.[90] The families of Edward's father and

mother were naval, and Edward's grandfather, John Keele, had married Elizabeth, daughter of Captain John Rushworth, RN, the Rushworths being another naval family. Edward's uncle, Henry Keele, was a surgeon in the Royal Navy; another uncle was Admiral Charles Keele and a third uncle was Edward Keele who was killed as a midshipman on 29 December 1812 at the age of 13 years in the engagement between HMS *Java* and the United States frigate *Constitution*. Edward's mother was the daughter of Admiral Philip Paton who was the second sea lord at the time of the battle of Trafalgar having previously fought in nine naval battles. One of Edward's sisters was Lucy Henrietta who married Captain John Henry Jellicoe, commodore and a director of the Royal Mail Steam Packet Co. Their second son was John Rushworth Jellicoe who later became Admiral of the Fleet Sir John Jellicoe, Earl Jellicoe GCB, OM, GCVO, HonLLD, HonDCL, First Sea Lord from 1916 to 1918 and Governor-General of New Zealand from 1919 to 1924.[90]

The marriage of Edward and Lucy took place at St Luke's Church, Cheltenham. They had two sons and three daughters, including:

Forenames	Date of birth
Edward Yorke	20 June 1867
John Patton	26 March 1869
Lucy Constance Flora	1870 or 1871
Ruth Helen Worthington	28 February 1876

Edward and John were born at 45 Springfield Road in the sub-district of St John in the registration district of Marylebone, London, where the parents then lived. Ruth was also born at home, but the family were then living at 30 Albion Road, Hampstead. John was the only child who did not pre-decease his parents. He followed his father's career as a solicitor. He contributed to this family history by researching the business interests of Jonathan Worthington of Old Trafford, Jonathan Worthington of Moorhill and Jonathan Worthington of Llancaiach (Articles 3.5, 3.11 and 3.21).

Edward Rushworth Keele died on 18 February 1919 aged 82 years. He was buried at Hampstead Cemetery – the same grave which had been established for his two children pre-deceasing him. In his Will made on 3 April 1876 he was described as 'of No 5 Fredericks Place, Old Jewry in the City of London, and of No 30 Albion Road, South Hampstead in the County of Middlesex, Solicitor …'. He bequeathed all his real and personal estate to Lucy. Lucy died on 26 April 1922 aged 87 years and was buried in the same grave. She died intestate, letters of administration being granted to her son John Patton Keele, solicitor, who was then living at 30 Albion Road.

3.36 Charles

Charles Worthington, the third and youngest son of Jonathan Worthington and Anne Maria his wife (Article 3.21), was born on 16 July 1835 and

20   *Charles Worthington.*   **21**   *Penelope Jane Worthington, born Scott.*

baptised on 21 September 1835 at St Michael's Church, Lower Mitton.[14] He was brought up at Moorhill for the first nine years after which the family moved to Llancaiach House, Glamorganshire. He was educated in Wiltshire – presumably at the establishment of the Reverend T. Meyler of Marlborough where his eldest brother Jonathan Yorke Worthington had studied. According to a letter of his elder sister Mary Jane (Article 3.33), Charles was studying at the same place as his brother Richard Jukes Worthington.

At the age of about 21 years he had an affair with Rosana (or Rose) Andrews of Llancaiach. Their child was born on 5 November 1857 and christened 'Mary Elizabeth' at the parish church of Gelligaer on 13 November 1857: the entry in the register reads 'Mary Elizabeth, reputed daughter of Charles Worthington and Rosana Andrews, Llancaiach, gent.' Only three months later he married Penelope Jane, the second daughter of John Scott and Elizabeth his wife of Edgbaston, near Birmingham, Warwickshire. The wedding took place at the parish church of Brighton, Sussex, on 25 February 1858. Penelope was a year older than Charles, having been born at Edgbaston on 4 May 1834. She had been baptised at St Bartholomew's Church, Edgbaston, on 19 September 1837 when John Scott was recorded as 'merchant'.

Charles and Penelope moved to New Zealand where Charles was appointed a justice of the peace. Later, on 6 February 1862, the governor of New Zealand appointed 'Charles Worthington, Esq., JP, Otago', a resident magistrate.[91] In September 1862 he was appointed commissioner of the Nokomai Goldfields. He visited the location in October when an article on 'The New Zealand Goldfields' published in an Australian newspaper of 15 October 1862 included:[92]

> From the Nokomai, we received on Saturday very bad news indeed. I cannot vouch for the accuracy of the report, but it has obtained general credence in town. Mr Worthington, Commissioner of Walpori, was gazetted lately for the Nokomai field, and went there accordingly. From all accounts he found the miners in a most disorderly state. They had rushed the prospector's claim, with the cheerful result of finding not more than the colour. The gully was proclaimed an unmitigated duffer and Mr Worthington was chevied from the place altogether and riding very hard, he reached here with the doleful tidings, in three and a half days …

On returning to Nokomai, Charles wrote reports on the goldfield published on 31 October and 8 November 1862.[93] Mr Brannigan, commissioner of police, had written a glowing account of the prospect of the field, but when it became clear that Nokomai was no good it was reported that 'fearful threats of vengeance are muttered … against Mr Brannigan'. Charles was then appointed commissioner of the newly opened Wakatipu goldfield, his first report on the field being published on 17 June 1863.[93]

The first two children of Charles and Penelope were born at Wellington and baptised at Wellington Cathedral. Their third was born at Tuapeka, central Otago, not long before they returned to England. They then moved to Battersea near London, two more children being born at home – 7 St John's Hill Grove. Their sixth and youngest child was born at Wood Green, Middlesex. The complete family was:

Forenames	Date of birth	Article
Charles Henry	6 May 1861	4.2
Maude	3 December 1863	4.3
Reginald Yorke	22 August 1865	4.4
Mabel	16 May 1870 (or 1869)	4.5
Arthur George	21 August 1871	4.6
Jonathan Ernest	31 August 1873	4.7

On 29 September 1871 Charles was described as 'mercantile clerk'.

Sometime after August 1873, Charles and Penelope sailed with all six children to Durban to settle in the colony of Natal. The annual *Natal Almanac and Directory* described Charles as 'farmer, New England' in 1881 and showed that he was residing at 20 Burger Street, Pietermaritzburg, from 1881 to 1885. He was a keen cricketer and started to play for his county soon after arriving in Natal. He was still umpiring at the age of 62 years when Laurenco Marques (now called Maputo) of Mozambique played Barberton of the Transvaal in December 1897.[94]

Charles became insolvent and surrendered his estate on 29 August 1878 at the age of 43 years.[95] At the third meeting of creditors held on 27 September 1878, Charles included in his sworn statement:

… At my mother's death she left her property to myself and two other children. Her estate was never valued. I should think roughly speaking it was worth £16,000 or £17,000.* My share would be over £5,000 and I received I think £2,700 and a statement to September 1876. Since then I have had £350 without any statement … this would leave about £2,000 due to me … I have expectations that on the death of my aunt I shall have about the same amount as from my mother's estate.

His aunt was Miss Mary Barnett, then aged more than 70 years; she had a life interest in the Will trust of Charles's grandfather, Samuel Barnett (Article 3.21). 'Four gentlemen' then advanced money for Charles to proceed to England. His farm 'Hollingwood' was put up for sale, but none of the creditors offered the upset price. The Hollingwood farm, east of the centre of Pietermaritzburg, was part of the original New England estate which had been registered (Number 1462) on 1 August 1849 when J. Charles Byrne brought a large group of colonists to Natal.[96] Sometime after Charles lost Hollingwood, it was sub-divided into smaller plots for development as a housing district of Pietermaritzburg. The name Hollingwood Township was retained for a while but has since been dropped. The name New England remains. The closeness of the name Hollingwood to that of Hollinwood near Failsworth in Lancashire, England, has been noted. Charles' grandfather, Jonathan Worthington (Article 3.11), had inherited the property in Hollinwood from his aunt Rebecca Worthington (Articles 3.6 and 9.5) in 1791. Whether the link is coincidental or Charles named his farm thus, with spelling mistake, is not known. The farm had been sold by 5 September 1879 when the first liquidation and distribution of the account was filed with the office of the master of the Supreme Court at Pietermaritzburg. Oxen, a mare, a yearling bull, a cow, a gun and furniture were also sold to raise a total of £7,833 5s. 5d.,† partly used to pay the master's fees and legal, auctioneers' and other professional expenses. The second and final distribution account was not filed until 1882 following a further inheritance in Charles's favour. The creditors received a total of 95 percent payment.

His father, Jonathan (Article 3.21), had cut Charles out of his Will but had made a provision that his executors – his three other sons – could make a provision of £1,000 at their discretion. When Jonathan died, Charles had been married for two years but he and his wife had not produced a grandchild for Jonathan. The strictness of Jonathan's action, whether motivated by moral or economic principles, was not followed by Charles's mother, Anne Maria. She wrote her Will on 17 March 1864, after two grandchildren had been born. She treated Charles as one of her three residual beneficiaries.

Charles was unpopular with his family and saw little of them. His second daughter, Mabel, recalled with some bitterness at the age of

---

* Equivalent to 150,000 man-days of agricultural labour.
† Equivalent to 70,00 man-days of agricultural labour.

83 years that when he left New Zealand 'he retired from all vestige of work ... In South Africa he led a high club life and got through four or five fortunes, one after the other'. She said that he was foolish with his money and lent and gave away large amounts to his colleagues at the clubs, but 'he always gave enough to his wife and family for them to live respectably'. When Charles surrendered his estate on 29 August 1878, his six children ranged in age from four to 17 years. Presumably he was without capital for the rest of his life as he died without assets. The question thus arises as to how Charles provided for his family to 'live respectably' and continue with their education. Either he had gainful employment, contrary to Mabel's memory, or help was coming from England – perhaps his brothers, his father's Will trust (subject to beneficiaries' agreements), his mother or the Scott family. Charles's granddaughter, Betty Yorke Crosskill (Article 5.9), recalled in 1982 that:

> Charles was clever but lazy. He was a popular rogue with much charm. He was a member of the best club or clubs in South Africa and was unduly generous ...

She also recalled that Sir Frederick Moor, prime minister of Natal, once asked Charles to consider becoming a member of the Natal parliament but that he declined.

At some stage the marriage broke down and Charles and Penelope lived separately for most of their time in Natal. In supporting her six children Penelope made up for Charles's deficiencies; indeed on 2 March 1951, her grandchild Thomas Henry Yorke Worthington (Article 5.2) wrote that Penelope was a 'very wonderful old lady'.[2] She lived for a long time with her second son Reginald Yorke Worthington (Article 4.4) and his family until the late 1890s when she returned to England. She died at Highgate, Middlesex, on 20 October 1901. Her grave was damaged by enemy action during the Second World War.

Charles lived the last part of his life with his eldest son, Charles Henry Worthington and his wife (Article 4.2) at Barberton, Transvaal.[95] He was certainly in Barberton in 1895. He died on 5 February 1904 at the Sanitorium, Durban, at the age of 72 years. He was penniless, owning nothing but his clothing.

Charles had founded a cadet line, but less than two years before he died, following the deaths without issue of all three of his elder brothers, the cadet line became the senior line. Charles then represented at least five generations of the family back to Jonathan Worthington of Old Trafford (Article 1.23). Treatment of the line continues in the next chapter (Chapter 4).

3.37 Sarah Caroline

Sarah Caroline Worthington, the third daughter and youngest child of Jonathan Worthington and Anne Maria his wife (Article 3.21) was born on

22   *Sarah Caroline, born Worthington.*

30 October 1837 at Moorhill, Stourport, and baptised on 27 December 1837 at St Michael's Church, Lower Mitton.[14] She lived at Moorhill until the age of about six years and then moved with her parents to Llancaiach House, Glamorganshire.[14]

On 14 November 1849 her elder sister, Mary Jane (Article 3.33) wrote in a letter to her friend, Mary Jane Burne: 'Carry will, I think, if strong enough, go to school but not to Oakfield at present ...'.[79] Caroline was indeed at boarding school by the age of 13 years. Mary wrote from Stourport to her friend in 1850:

> ... Caroline still continues to like her school. She will not return home for the holidays, but will either remain with our aunt at Leek or come here, so in all probability I shall not see her till next Christmas. She is very fond of writing poetry, and yesterday sent me some lines on 'A Child at Prayer' which I think are pretty tolerable considering she is but thirteen.

When about 22 years of age, Caroline moved with her parents to Arundel House, Cheltenham.

On 30 March 1864, at the age of 26, she married Major-General Augustus Halifax Ferryman, CB.[52] Augustus was then 48 years of age having been born on 9 March 1816. He had married previously Jane Anne Wilhelmena, the second daughter of William Sinclair of Dunbeath Castle (or Freswick), county Caithness, Scotland, by whom he had issue. She had died on 11 November 1851. Augustus had been commissioned an ensign in the 44th Foot on 27 June 1834, promoted lieutenant on 30 June 1837, captain on 16 April 1841 and major on 22 December 1843. On 24 November 1848 he was promoted lieutenant-colonel in command of the 89th Regiment of Foot. From 15 December 1854 he served in the Crimean War, leading his battalion at the siege and fall of Sevastopol, and the attacks of 18 June and 8 September 1855.[97] He was awarded the campaign medal with clasp and the fourth-class Medjidie and Turkish medal. On 3 April 1857 he was appointed a chevalier de la Légion d'Honneur (France) and on 22 June 1857 a companion of the Order of the Bath (Military Division).[98] In that year he was sent to India to serve as brigadier-general at Bombay from 1857 to 1859 and in Bengal from 1859 to 1861. He was further promoted to major-general in 1863. Augustus was the son of John Barke Gustavus Ferryman and his first wife Frances, daughter of John Rice, Esq., of Tooting, Surrey (later in London). She died when Augustus was only eight years of age and was buried in the yard of St Peter's Church, Leckhampton, near Cheltenham. A plaque was erected to her memory on the north wall inside St Peter's Church, of which the inscription includes:

> ... It has pleased Almighty God to take her to himself, leaving an afflicted husband and three infant children to lament and to be ever deeply sensible of their irreparable loss. To those who were happy in the knowledge of her many and great virtues it will appear how almost impossible it is to give an adequate idea of the purity and excellence of her mind. To the world it may be truly said than in every duty and situation of Life she has left a perfect example of all the virtues that can adorn the moral or complete the Christian character ...

John married secondly Anna Charlotte, the daughter of the Reverend George Rhodes, vicar of Colyton, Devon, and they lived at Rhodeville,

Leckhampton, named after Anna's ancestors. The house stood in 3.5 acres of garden and paddocks on the south-east side of Shurdington Road, but is now surrounded by houses and has become the *Hallery House Hotel*. When John Ferryman died at Rhodeville on 4 June 1883, he was described in an obituary as having been one of the 'most active members of the Berkeley Hunt and having found occupation in the management of his extensive property – owning more houses in Cheltenham, than, probably, any other proprietor'.[99] The first of the five mullioned sections of the east widow of the church of St Philip and St James, Leckhampton, is 'in memoriam' to him. In his grave at St Peter's Church he is buried with both his wives and with two of his children who died as minors.

The wedding of Caroline and Augustus took place at St James's Church, Piccadilly, London. In 1865 and 1866 they were living in rooms at 1 Crescent Terrace, Royal Crescent, Cheltenham, where Mrs Ruck was the landlady.[51] Presumably this was an arrangement while their new family home 'Winterbourne' was being built. Winterbourne was in Painswick Road, Leckhampton, within a quarter of a mile of Rhodeville. They were installed there by 1867.[51] They produced two daughters, namely:

Forenames	Date of birth
Ella Frances	16 February 1865
Ada Louise	28 December 1868

Ella was born at 1 Crescent Terrace while Ada was born at Winterbourne.

A glimpse of life at Winterbourne is given in the national census return for Leckhampton, taken in 1871. The family and living-in servants were:

Augustus H Ferryman	55	Major-General, half pay
Caroline Ferryman	34	Wife
Ella Frances Ferryman	6	Daughter
Ada Ferryman	2	Daughter
Elizabeth Barnett	36	Nurse, unmarried
Elizabeth Ree	38	Cook, unmarried
Jane Meadows	27	Parlour maid, unmarried
Mary Richards	21	House maid, unmarried

At the 1881 census Augustus was on active service again; Caroline's sister and niece, Lucy Ann Keele and Lucy Constantia Flora Keele (Article 3.35) were staying there. There were still four living-in servants but the nurse had been replaced by a lady's maid.

Augustus continued to serve the army, being promoted to lieutenant-general on 19 November 1871. He was promoted general on 1 October 1877 and retired from active duty on 1 July 1881 at the age of 65 years. He was honorary colonel of the Prince of Wales's Volunteers (South Lancashire) Regiment from 23 May 1872 until 1887 and was honorary colonel of the Princess Victoria's (Royal Irish Fusiliers) Regiment from

18 September 1887 for the rest of his life.[99] He died on 10 June 1897 aged 81 years at Winterbourne and was buried at St Peter's Church, Leckhampton.[52] By his Will dated 11 November 1887 he left his estate in trust, its income being available to his widow for life. The capital then descended in equal parts to his two daughters. Caroline continued to live at Winterbourne for at least three years, but sometime later moved to Menival, 37 Crystal Palace Park Road, Sydenham, Kent, where she died on 6 May 1921 aged 83 years. Her body was taken to Leckhampton to be buried with her husband at St Peter's Church. The following inscriptions are on the four sides of the base to the stone cross surmounting the grave:

> In loving memory of Augustus Halifax Ferryman, CB, Late 89th regiment Princess Victoria's Royal Irish Fusiliers, and honorary colonel of the 87th regiment. Served in the Crimean War 1854-5, commanding the 89th regiment at the siege and fall of Sevastopol. Born March 9th 1816. Died June 10th 1987. And of Caroline his wife died May 6th 1921. Also Ada Louisa their daughter. Died August 31st 1928 aged 59. Also Ella Frances Ward-Humphreys, died October 9th 1928 aged 63, interred at Epsom parish church.

Underneath a window on the north wall inside the church is a stone plaque on which is inscribed:

> In memory of Augustus Halifax Ferryman, General, CB, and Sarah Caroline his wife. The lighting of this church was installed by the wish of their daughter Ada Louisa 1930 AD.

By her Will dated 27 June 1892, Caroline bequeathed her estate in equal parts to her two daughters.

CHAPTER 4

LINE OF CHARLES WORTHINGTON OF NATAL

4.1 Charles

Charles Worthington, the third and youngest son of Jonathan Worthington and Anne Maria his wife (Article 3.21), was born on 16 July 1835 and baptised on 21 September 1835 at St Michael's Church, Lower Mitton, Worcestershire. His life has already been discussed (Article 3.36). He and Penelope Jane his wife produced four sons and two daughters.

SECOND GENERATION – FAMILY OF
CHARLES AND PENELOPE JANE

4.2 Charles Henry

Charles Henry Worthington, the eldest child of Charles Worthington and Penelope Jane his wife (Articles 3.36 and 4.1), was born on 6 May 1861 at Wellington, New Zealand, and baptised at Wellington Cathedral.[1] Throughout his life Henry was generally called 'Harry' and appears thus in some official documents. At the age of about four years he sailed to England with his parents and two younger siblings, the family settling at Wandsworth, Surrey. (Wandsworth is now a district of Greater London.) Sometime after 1873 the family, then complete with six children, sailed to the colony of Natal to settle in Pietermaritzburg.

On 21 March 1896, at the age of 34 years, Henry married Elizabeth, daughter of Samuel Henry Fielding of Hull, Yorkshire, England. Elizabeth was then aged about 29 years and had previously married James Cooke of Hull in 1884 at Hull. The wedding of Henry Worthington and Elizabeth took place at Barberton in eastern Transvaal (now called Mpumalanga), where his younger sister, Mabel, had married six years earlier (Article 4.5). They were childless, but a few years after marriage they took in and fostered the thirteenth and youngest child of Edward Hardie Gould and his wife Florence, born Knott. The child, born on 22 August 1902, was named Charles Henry, presumably after his foster father, and his surname was changed from Gould to Worthington. Florence had died of malaria only a week after the birth, and Edward died before the child was two years and five months old, leaving the family under great strain. Edward Gould is remembered in the district, his name being given to 'Gould's Salvation Valley'. The Eastern Railway line between Pretoria and the Bay of Lourenco Marques (now called Maputo Bay) reached Kaapmuiden, 28 miles north-east of Barberton, by March 1892 and was brought into operation. A branch line was planned to link Barberton with Kaapmuiden which in the meantime would be handled by road wagons. The chosen route was mainly along the Kaap river, but infestation of tsetse fly on part of the river made it impracticable, wagons being abandoned as oxen fell in their tracks. A new route, free of the tsetse, was found and opened through the long valley by transport-rider Gould.

Thus Henry junior was reared by the Worthingtons for two decades. He took to gardening for a career, and when he was laying out the gardens of the *Palana Hotel* in Lourenco Marques he was told by one of the Goulds that he was a member of their family, and he was later introduced to his siblings. Henry had not been adopted; indeed there was no such legal status until the first Adoption Act which became law in England in 1926. In due course Henry junior elected to live with his eldest brother Sydney Gould and his wife Lily and family. Accordingly he parted from his foster parents. He became well known as a gardener, being on the staff of Durban City Parks Department for 37 years. He wrote articles on horticulture for *South African Women's Weekly* under the pen-name 'Calyx' for 33 years. He and his wife Jessica Florence, born Wood, produced three children; they and further offspring live in Natal and continue to use the surname Worthington.

Nothing is known of Henry senior's education and early career, but his niece, Betty Yorke Crosskill (Article 4.15), recalled that he fought with the Imperial Army in the Boer War. Henry would have been 38 years of age when the war started. The medals he was awarded for his services were discovered following his death in 1920. After the war, at least, Henry was in the gold-mining industry at Barberton. The first payable gold at Barberton had been discovered in 1884 when Henry was 23 years of age. There was an immediate rush of diggers and capital to the area. This led to the building of the new town which was called Barberton after three members of the Barber family discovered a reef rich in gold, which became known as Barbers' Reef.[2] Henry acquired the *Phoenix Hotel*, which he and Elizabeth ran for the rest of Henry's life. When the Barberton railway branch was opened in 1896, the hotel's horse-drawn cabs provided transport from the station to the hotel. By 1905 he was also a gold prospector on his own account. On 18 April of that year he wrote from the Atheneum Club, Johannesburg, to the district registrar of mining rights:[3]

> Sir, I have the honour to make application for a Mynpacht in extent 600 by 400 yards in terms of Act 31, Law 15 of 1898, situate on the Kaap River, Sections A and D in the mining District of Barberton as per sketch plan attached. On hearing from you to the effect that this application will be granted, I undertake to at once have the ground surveyed, 5/- stamp attached. I shall be glad to have the notices from you as soon as possible to post up on the ground. I have the honour to be, Sir, your obedient servant.

Charles Worthington, JP (New Zealand); b. 1835, m. 1858, d. 1904. *(Pedigree 3 & Arts 3.36 & 4.1)* = **Penelope Jane**, dau. of John Scott; b. 1834, d. 1901

Charles Henry Worthington; b. 1861, m. 1896, d. 1920 without issue. *(Art. 4.2)*

= **Elizabeth**, dau. of Samuel Henry Fielding; b. circa 1867, m(1) 1884 James Cook without issue, re-m 1921, d.1928

Maude; b. 1863 m. 1888 John André Masson, Inspector, and had issue; d. 1920. *(Art. 4.3)*

Mary Elizabeth Miriam, dau. of Joseph Wheeler; b. 1865, d. 1917

= **Reginald Yorke Worthington**; b. 1865, m(1) 1889, m(2) 1919, d.1947. *(Art. 4.4)*

Adelaide Lucy, dau. of Charles Ebbs Hopkins; b. 1889, d. 1973

Mabel; b. circa 1870, m(1) 1890 Alfred John Blake & had issue, m(2) 1900 Frederick Chatterton, dissolved 1906 without issue, d. 1957. *(Art. 4.5)*

Alice Maude, dau. of ... Stevens; b. circa 1868, m(1) 1891 William Henry Carney, dissolved 1896 without issue.

= **Arthur George Worthington**, Captain; b. 1871, m(1) 1896, dissolved 1911, m(2) 1911, d. 1916. *(Arts 4.6 & 5.1)*

Myra Dorothea, dau. of Jacobus George Fischer; b. 1882, re-m. circa 1951, d. 1973

Pedigree 5

Pedigree 5

Jonathan Ernest Worthington; b. 1873, m. 1897, d. 1905. *(Arts 4.7 & 6.1)*

= **Alice Constance**, dau. of Charles Hornby; b. 1875, d. 1961

Pedigree 6

Frances Louie, dau. of Henry Robson Tully; b. 1894, d. 1951

= **Thomas Henry Yorke Worthington**; b. 1890, m(1) 1915, m(2) 1953, d. 1962. *(Art. 4.8)*

= **Isabella Amelia**, dau. of James Malan Simpson; b. 1903, m(1) Gerhardus Henrie van der Merwe, dissolved without issue, d. 1973

Richard Tyrer Worthington; b. 1892, d. 1893. *(Art. 4.9)*

John Derrick Worthington; b. 1895, m. 1925, d. 1955. *(Art. 4.10)*

= **Alice May**, dau. of Joseph Johannes Wyatt; b. 1902, re-m. 1970, d. 1990

Molly; b.1904, m. 1925, Francis George Payne & had issue, d. 1944. *(Art. 4.11)*

Penelope Jane; b. 1920, m. 1943, Charles Newport Saville, Major, & had issue, d. 1990. *(Art. 4.12)*

Jill Elizabeth; b. 1922, m(1) 1942 Christiaan Botha & had issue, dissolved 1946, m(2) 1946 Victor Rafe Fountain Howes without issue, d. 1948. *(Art. 4.13)*

Alethea Nan; b. 1923, d. 1983 un-m. *(Art. 4.14)*

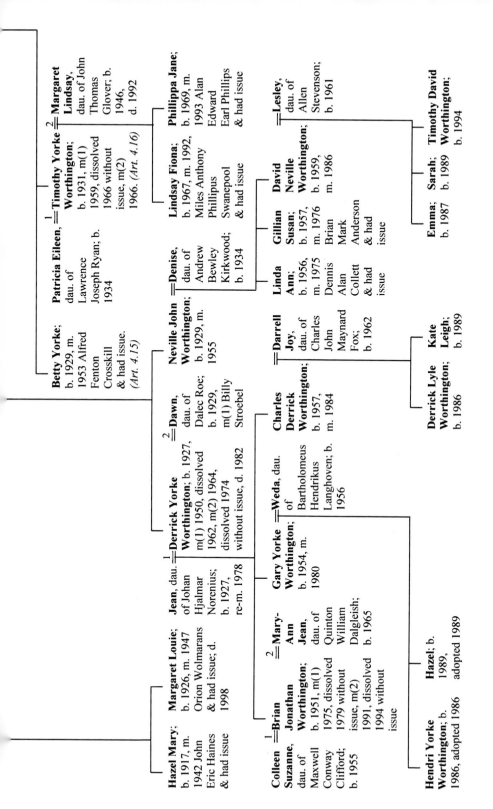

Betty Yorke; b. 1929, m. 1953 Alfred Fenton Crosskill & had issue. *(Art. 4.15)*

Patricia Eileen, dau. of Lawrence Joseph Ryan; b. 1934

Timothy Yorke ⁼¹ **Worthington;** b. 1931, m(1) 1959, dissolved 1966 without issue, m(2) 1966. *(Art. 4.16)*

² **Margaret Lindsay,** dau. of John Thomas Glover; b. 1946, d. 1992

Phillippa Jane; b. 1969, m. 1993 Alan Edward Earl Phillips & had issue

Neville John Worthington; b. 1929, m. 1955

² **Dawn,** dau. of Dalec Roe; b. 1929, m(1) Billy Stroebel

Lindsay Fiona; b. 1967, m. 1992, Miles Anthony Phillipus Swanepool & had issue

Denise, dau. of Andrew Bewley Kirkwood; b. 1934

Lesley, dau. of Allen Stevenson; b. 1961

David Neville Worthington; b. 1959, m. 1986

Timothy David Worthington; b. 1994

Gillian Susan; b. 1957, m. 1976 Brian Mark Anderson & had issue

Emma; b. 1987

Sarah; b. 1989

Linda Ann; b. 1956, m. 1975 Dennis Alan Collett & had issue

Darrell Joy, dau. of Charles John Maynard Fox; b. 1962

Kate Leigh; b. 1989

Charles Derrick Worthington; b. 1957, m. 1984

Derrick Lyle Worthington; b. 1986

Derrick Yorke Worthington; b. 1927, m(1) 1950, dissolved 1962, m(2) 1964, dissolved 1974 without issue, d. 1982

Jean, dau. ⁼¹ of Johan Hjalmar Norenius; b. 1927, re-m. 1978

Weda, dau. of Bartholomeus Hendrikus Langhoven; b. 1956

Gary Yorke Worthington; b. 1954, m. 1980

Margaret Louie; b. 1926, m. 1947 Orion Wolmarans & had issue; d. 1998

Hazel Mary; b. 1917, m. 1942 John Eric Haines & had issue

Brian Jonathan Worthington; b. 1951, m(1) 1975, dissolved 1979 without issue, m(2) 1991, dissolved 1994 without issue

Colleen Suzanne, ⁼¹ dau. of Maxwell Conway Clifford; b. 1955

² **Mary-Ann Jean,** dau. of Quinton William Dalgleish; b. 1965

Hazel; b. 1989, adopted 1989

Hendri Yorke Worthington; b. 1986, adopted 1986

23   *The old* Phoenix Hotel, *Barberton.*

The registrar duly issued a notice which called for any objections to be lodged with him within one month. On 16 March 1906 the registrar wrote to C.H. Worthington Esq. at the *Phoenix Hotel*, Barberton, to remind him that the conditions of the grant had not been fulfilled and that action was required within a few days. Presumably the periodic government fees were not paid up to date.

By 14 July 1906 Henry held a half interest in a block of 42 gold mining claims on the hill immediately to the east of the Sheba Mine, north-east of Barberton. They were on ground called Thomas West lying west of Joe's Luck Gold Mine. The other half share was held by Henry's younger brother Arthur George Worthington, a mining engineer and land surveyor (Article 4.6). It is noteworthy that Henry and Arthur's father, Charles, had been a gold commissioner in Australia (Article 3.36). The Sheba Ridge was found to be rich in gold in 1885; it became a prolific producer but is now exhausted. By 28 January 1909, Henry and Arthur had sold their rights to these claims to Bowers Randfontein Limited.

A Transvaal government document of 31 July 1907 shows that Henry was prospecting under licence 1694, which was then renewed. It appears that he then held mining rights at Kaapasche Hoop which was being worked by The Sheba Gold Mining Co. Ltd of Eureka. At that time claims and mynpachten could only be held by individual people although much of the minework was undertaken by companies and syndicates.

Henry must have been making good profits at this time, because he set about buying the freeholds of his lands. On 6 January 1909 he wrote from the *Phoenix Hotel* to the mining commissioner:[3]

Dear Sir, I beg to apply for freehold of the following stands from 1st inst.

1529, 1530, 1532, 1533	Belgravia 4
1012	Barberton 1
57, 58, 59, 60, 61, 62, 63, 64, 65	Berea 9
137, 139	Berea 2
Half of 1182 and 1181	Barberton 2
1210, 1203, 1205, 1206, 1207, 1208, 1209	Barberton 7
1228, 1229	Barberton 2

Yours faithfully

The commissioner wrote a letter dated 6 April 1910 to C.H. Worthington Esq. at the *Phoenix Hotel* to remind him that the second and third instalments on Stands 1530 and 1533 were still unpaid. On the same day the commissioner wrote to Mrs E. Worthington at the same address to remind her that the second and third instalments on Stands 1006 and 1007, which she had purchased at public auction held on 2 November 1908, were still unpaid.

On 11 December 1909 Henry pegged out, on his own account, a block of 49 claims numbered 34475 to 34523 which had been granted to him by the commissioner the previous day. The block was about 540 Cape roods long by 34 wide, making a total of about 200 acres. Near the western end were Fever Creek, the Sheba pumping station and the Walberg Store. A little further to the west lay the Ulundi Zwaart Kopjes. A letter dated 2 March 1910 from Henry's solicitors, Dumat and Davis, to the mining commissioner shows that he was then in the process of selling the block to the Zwaartkopjes Prospecting Syndicate Limited.

By 14 January 1910 Henry held 199 claims. He had sent a draft of £24 17s. 6d.[1*] to bring government fees up to date, but the sum proved insufficient because of 16 days of fines for late payment. On 30 June 1910 Henry formally applied for a mynpacht 300 yards square (about 19 acres) straddling the North Kaap River. The mynpacht was alluvial and was for the mining of precious metals. The application was heard on 6 September 1910 but the commissioner decided he could not make a grant until a deposit of £5 had been paid on account of the initial fee. Apparently the deposit was not paid within the required 14 days and the commissioner's note on minute paper stated 'regarded as withdrawn'.

Henry died without issue at Barberton Hospital on 29 August 1920 aged 59 years. He still owned the *Phoenix Hotel* which presumably either he or Elizabeth, or both, had run since 1906 or earlier. His property at the time of his death consisted of:[4]

---

* Equivalent to 176 man-days of agricultural Labour.

	£	s.	d.
Phoenix Hotel, on 7 township stands of land	4,000	0	0
Furniture, fittings and effects therein	732	18	6
Stables, on 2 stands of land	250	0	0
Brick cottage, on 1 stand of land	125	0	0
Wood and iron cottage, on 2 stands	175	0	0
12 vacant stands	90	0	0
Orange grove with buildings, on 6 stands	750	0	0
Furniture and effects therein	328	3	6
	6,451	2	0[*]

He and Elizabeth had prepared a joint Will in May 1899 – during the Boer War – and they had not replaced it during the remaining 21 years of his life. If they had had a child or children, all the assets of the deceased person would have passed to them in equal parts, but in the absence of children the assets were to pass to the surviving spouse.

Fifteen months after becoming a widow, Elizabeth married Arthur Sassum at Johannesburg. They lived in Judge Street, Barberton. She died at Barberton Hospital on 10 August 1928 and he died within a further 40 days – before 19 September 1928.[5] They had made a joint Will on 5 December 1921 by which the survivor of them would inherit all the assets of the other.[5] Seven days after Elizabeth's death Arthur made a further Will leaving the whole of his estate to his friend, James Albert Spear. Thus, Henry Worthington's assets passed to the Spear family. Spear had arrived in Barberton from England in 1901 when he enlisted in the newly-formed South African Constabulary. After retiring from the force he formed his own businesses as government and general auctioneer, general agent and undertaker. He formed the Barberton Boy Scouts in May 1910 and became commandant of the Barberton Rifle Association. Later he assisted in the formation of Botha's Natal Horse which became distinguished in the South-west African Campaign. He was mayor of Barberton from 1919 to 1922 – and again from 1948 to 1951.

4.3 Maude

Maude Worthington, the elder daughter of Charles Worthington and Penelope Jane his wife (Articles 3.36 and 4.1), was born at Wellington, New Zealand on 3 December 1863 and baptised at Wellington Cathedral.[1] She was about two years old when she sailed for England with her parents and two brothers. They lived in or near Wandsworth, Surrey, for at least eight years. Sometime after 1873 she sailed with the complete family, then including six children, to Durban to settle at Pietermaritzburg in the colony of Natal.

On 10 May 1888, at the age of 24 years, Maude married John André Masson, son of John Gustave Masson of Harrow on the Hill, Middlesex, England. John junior was often nicknamed 'Tim' probably to distinguish

---

[*] Equivalent to 18,100 man-days of English agricultural labour.

him from his father. John senior was a teacher at Harrow School. John junior had enlisted in the Natal Mounted Police on 23 May 1877 when he already had some knowledge of the Zulu language. The force of mounted police had been formed three years previously. Lieutenant-Commander D.R. Morris wrote of the force:[6]

> By 1878 they were 110 strong, well trained, self reliant and disciplined. Scattered in small posts all over the colony, they aided magistrates and caught cattle thieves and gun runners, riding patrol year in and year out.

John was described in the police records as a protestant, nearly six feet tall with light brown hair and blue eyes. The Natal Mounted Police were drafted as a unit into the Imperial Army for the Zulu War of 1879, and they fought in particular at the battle of Isandhwana. They also fought in the first Boer War, which started in 1880 (called the Freedom War by the Afrikaners). During this period of military service John was awarded the medal and clasp. He was promoted to sub-inspector on 9 January 1883.[7]

The wedding took place at St Matthew's Church, Estcourt, Natal.[8] Maude and John produced three children, namely:[9]

Forenames	Date of Birth	Date of Baptism
John Gustave	4 June 1889	3 July 1889
Eric Dartnell	10 April 1891	18 June 1891
Phyllis Janet	13 October 1894	8 December 1894

John Gustave was born at Ladysmith and baptised at All Saints' Church, Ladysmith. His grandmother Penelope Worthington and uncle Henry Worthington (Articles 3.36 and 4.2) were two of the sponsors. Eric was born at Estcourt and baptised at St Matthew's Church, Estcourt. Phyllis was born at Verulam, near the coast about 17 miles north-east of Durban. She was baptised at St Thomas's Church, Verulam.

In 1890 the family was at Himeville in the west of Natal, but sometime that year John was serving at Ladysmith, with the acting rank of inspector. By 1891 he was at Estcourt, as acting inspector. In 1893 he was posted to Verulam where he remained for about three years – first as sub-inspector and as inspector from 1894.[10] In 1896 he was again at Estcourt, as inspector, but on 9 January 1897 he retired on pension having served the police for 19 years. By 1901 he was described as 'farmer, Estcourt'. By 1907 Maude and John were living apart. In that year 'Mrs Masson' is on record as living at 185 Burger Street, Pietermaritzburg, and in 1911 John was living at 290 Retief Street, Pietermaritzburg. By 1915 Maude had moved to Durban where she lived for the rest of her life.[11] She died of 'carcinoma utori and pulmonary thrombosis' on 28 May 1920 aged 56 years at the Berea Nursing Home, Durban. She was buried at Stellawood Cemetery, Durban.[12] A letter from John concerning Maude's estate included:

> ... I would like Mr G. Masson of Miller and Masson, Attorneys, Pietermaritzburg, appointed as Executor Dative. The estate is a joint one, my marriage having been in Community. I have no assets whatever myself. The joint Estate consists of her personal effects and some money in the Bank, at value about £140.*

John had been living at Umzinto in 1912 and at Pietermartizburg again in 1916 and 1918. He was living at Hilary, Natal, when his eldest son John died on 26 March 1928. By 1930 he was living at Warner Beach, South Coast.[11]

4.4 Reginald Yorke

Reginald Yorke Worthington, the second son of Charles Worthington and Penelope Jane his wife (Articles 3.36 and 4.1), was born on 22 August 1865 and baptised in New Zealand.[1] Within a few months he sailed with his parents to England where they lived for at least eight years. Sometime after August 1873 he sailed with his parents and five siblings to Durban, to settle at Pietermaritzburg. Yorke attended Hilton College, Hilton, which lies about six miles north-west of Pietermaritzburg off the road to Johannesburg. He remained a pupil there until he matriculated at the age of about 16 years. Yorke's father had become insolvent when Yorke was only 13, so when he left school the family was in considerable financial difficulty.

He was appointed messenger to the Colonial Office, his fluency in the Zulu language and his ability as a rider probably being two of his qualifications for the post. He resigned after serving for nearly two years. This was probably the time when he and a friend rode to Barberton in the Transvaal, some 270 miles north of Pietermaritzburg. They were seeking gold, and it is said that Barney Barnato jumped their claim. They may have been following Yorke's eldest brother, Henry (Article 4.2), who was probably already established at Barberton. When their funds were exhausted, Yorke and his friend sold their horses and walked to Lourenco Marques in Mozambique – about 100 miles due east through the wild country of Swaziland. There they obtained working passages on a ship to Durban, Yorke's role being acting purser. At Durban, it is said, they won enough money to purchase horses and return to Pietermaritzburg.

On 5 November 1884, at the age of 19 years, Yorke again applied for employment in the colonial service. His letter addressed to the colonial secretary of Natal reads:[13]

> Sir, I have the honour to apply for any vacancy that you may think me capable of fulfilling, in the service of the Government. I may state that I was for nearly two years in your office. Trusting this my application will be favourably considered by you, I have the honour to be, Sir, your obedient servant.

---

* Equivalent to 390 man-days of English agricultural labour.

It appears that he returned to his former job where he served for a further year before leaving to travel to England with his father. Yorke felt guilty that he had left for a second time; after returning to Natal he wrote on 23 July 1887 to the colonial secretary:[13]

> Sir, I beg to apply for the vacancy of a Toll Keeper and Postmaster etc. at Colenso. I was in the Government Service for three years as a messenger to the Colonial Office and left to go to England with my Father. I was under age at the time or else I should not have left the service ...

His letter was endorsed by the colonial engineer: 'I am not aware that Mr Stewart has any intention of resigning his appointment'. Another endorsement states that 'there is no present vacancy ...' Yorke was not put off and wrote again on 11 February 1888 applying for the post of toll keeper and postmaster of Sundays Rivers. It is not known if he was successful, but about this time he started serious studies in accountancy and business management, and probably some engineering.

On 18 October 1889 Yorke married Mary Elizabeth Mariam, daughter of Joseph Wheeler of Estcourt and Mary his wife, daughter of John and Mary Tyrer. Joseph Wheeler was a farmer holding an estate called 'Lowlands', near the River Mooi in Weenen County.[11] At the time of his death he held property in the village of Albert in the county of Pietermaritzburg. He had a large family, the eldest child being Lydia Sarah who married John William Moor, a younger brother of Sir Frederick Robert Moor, the last prime minister of Natal, and the first minister of commerce and industries in the Union of South Africa.[14] At the time of the marriage both Mary and Yorke were 24 years of age, Mary having been born 12 days before Yorke on 10 August 1865 at Pietermaritzburg. Mary was at times given the nickname 'Polly'. The wedding took place at St Matthew's Church, Estcourt. They produced four children spaced over 14 years, namely:

Forenames	Date of birth	Date of baptism	Article
Thomas Henry Yorke	1 July 1890	3 August 1890	4.8
Richard Tyrer	4 March 1892	19 April 1892	4.9
John Derrick	10 January 1895	18 February 1895	4.10
Molly	3 October 1904	6 November 1904	4.11

The first three children were baptised at St Matthew's Church, Estcourt while Molly was baptised at St Saviour's Cathedral, Pietermaritzburg. Alas, Richard died at the age of 20 months.

At the time of Thomas's baptism, Yorke was employed by the Civil Engineering Department (CED). In 1891 he was a 'road overseer' at Estcourt. In 1893 he was styled 'overseer' with the Department and it is likely that this job continued until 1895. By 1896 Yorke and Mary were living at the *Ennersdale Hotel*, near Estcourt, which they probably owned. By 1898 they had moved to the *Plough Hotel*, Estcourt, which they did own. There were then three hotels in the town – the *Plough*

24   *Reginald Yorke Worthington.*   **25**   *Mary Elizabeth Mirian, born Wheeler.*

Hotel, the *Railway Hotel* and *Alice Bridge Hotel*.[10] Yorke appointed a manager at the *Plough*, thus being free to pursue other business interests. There is an account by his grandson Neville John Worthington, published in 1999, that Yorke:[15] '... was on his way to the coalfields when he stopped at Estcourt, where he swapped his oxen and wagons for the Plough Hotel in the town in 1895 ...'. Such an act was typical of Yorke's entrepreneurial spirit. It could fit the facts if he had by then left the Civil Engineering Department to try his hand at road transport (which for centuries had been in the family's culture). He would have known the *Plough*'s potential for profit from his earlier days at the *Ennersdale*. Yorke's ownership of a transport operation has also been told by his daughter Betty Yorke (Article 4.15). He was a friend of James Percy Fitzpatrick (later Sir Percy) who became a member of both the Transvaal and Union parliaments.[14] Percy is now best known as an author, his most popular work being *Jock of the Bushveld* first published in 1907. Percy gave a first edition copy to Yorke with a note on the fly leaf, but the book was stolen with the whole contents of a tin chest about 90 years later.

Sometime after the outbreak of the Boer War on 11 October 1899, Yorke left his wife and two surviving sons at the *Plough Hotel* and joined the Imperial Army as a civilian scout. He scouted for General Sir Redvers Henry Buller, VC, GCB, GCMG, PC, in his campaign to relieve Ladysmith from siege. Yorke was well qualified for the post, speaking the Zulu language fluently and having ridden over the country for many years. Yorke's youngest daughter, Betty Yorke (Article 4.15), recalls that Yorke considered Buller conceited and unready to listen, thus being responsible for 'many unnecessary deaths'. She added '... knowing Dad and his contempt for Buller, he rode away when the siege ended'. The siege ended on 28 February 1900.

It appears that Mary visited England in 1903. A newspaper report shows that she returned to Natal in SS *Kinfaun Castle* which docked at Cape Town on 1 September 1903.[12]

Late in 1903 or early 1904 Yorke and his family moved to Pietermaritzburg and lived at 380 Loop Street. Yorke then described himself as an 'engineer' and continued to do so until 1909.[10] He was then a contractor in his own right, being described as 'contractor' on the death notice of his father in 1904 (Article 3.36). Soon afterwards they moved to 194 Pine Street; Pine Street was given as Yorke's address in the Hilton College magazine of 1905.[16] This was described as their 'Pietermaritzburg residence' until they moved to 41 Burger Street, Pietermaritzburg, about 1912. By 1908 Yorke had purchased a farm at Stendal, Weenen on Bushmans River. The township of Weenen is 16 miles north-east of Estcourt; it has an altitude of 2,500 feet and is noted for its healthy climate. It has been claimed that Yorke was the first farmer in Natal to grow lucerne, which he sold to other farmers as winter feed for cattle. In fact he named the farm 'Nkasine Lucerne Estate'. In 1910 Yorke was a labour agent of Timber Street, Pietermaritzburg, and in 1912 and 1913 he was secretary of the White Labour Bureau.

After 1913 he ceased to be described as labour agent, farmer or engineer. His family recalled that he then made a substantial investment in the 'Natal Tanning Company' and took a leading role in its management, but no records have yet been found to confirm the link. In 1904 the tannery was listed as the second largest manufactory in the city, producing '... some capital leather' and which 'latterly has turned its attention to boots'.[10] The largest manufactory was the brewery. The tanning company, which no longer exists, owned several wattle tree plantations in Natal.

Yorke is included in a group photograph taken in 1913 of 33 'city notables' at the ceremony when R.D. Clarke, headmaster of Maritzburg College, presented his library to the school.[17] In 1915 Mary gave a collection of books to the library of Michaelhouse School, where her two surviving sons had been educated.

On 2 September 1917, Mary died at home – 41 Burger Street, Pietermaritzburg.[8] She was 52 years of age. An article in the *Natal Witness* for 7 September 1917 written on 4 September 1917 by the newspaper's Estcourt correspondent reads:[8]

> The sad news of the death of Mrs Yorke Worthington came with a sense of personal sorrow and loss to many of her life long friends in this town. Estcourt can claim her as amongst the older residents. At an early stage she arrived here with her parents, the late Mr and Mrs

Joseph Wheeler, and the greater proportion of her life was spent in the district. One of a large family, Mrs Yorke Worthington was connected by marriage with many of the residents here. The first, Mrs J W Moor, was a sister, and a brother Mr Bertie Wheeler lives here. In addition to her large circle of relatives her death is mourned by all who knew her true friendship – always staunch and true. The blow is also a very severe one, softened only by the realisation of the gain and release of suffering of one so dear and honoured.

At the time of her death she owned two parcels of land in the city of Pietermaritzburg:[11]

    (a) Subdivision of C of Erf No 4 Burger Street, having a frontage of 210 yards

    (b) Subdivision of D of Erf No 3 Burger Street, having a frontage of 44 yards.

26 *Adelaide Lucy, born Hopkins.*

Both plots extended through to the next parallel road. She had inherited them from a division of the estate of her mother Mary Wheeler who had died on 15 March 1910 aged 83 years, leaving an estate to be equally divided between two sons and Mary Worthington. Yorke had been the sole executor and administrator. Like her daughter, Mary senior had died in great pain; she had been ill for 12 months with two nurses engaged to attend her.[11]

By her Will dated 21 September 1914, Mary Elizabeth Miriam placed the whole of her estate in trust for the benefit of her daughter Molly (Article 4.11), the capital passing to her at the age of 21 years, or on marriage if earlier.[11] Mary's marriage to Yorke had been out of community of property, that is to say their marriage contract required their assets to be held separately rather than jointly.

By 1918, Yorke had become manager of Loram and Baynes, incorporated accountants and auditors, house and estate agents, general agents and agents for the Union Castle Steamship Co. His son John Derrick Worthington (Article 4.10) was then a member of his staff and living with him at 41 Burger Street. This arrangement continued in 1919 and 1920.[19]

On 30 September 1919 Yorke, described in the church records as 'widower, gentleman' of 41 Burger Street married Adelaide Lucy of 251 Prince Alfred Street, Pietermaritzburg. She was the second daughter of Charles Ebbs Hopkins of Scottville, Pietermaritzburg, and Annie Elizabeth (born Cunningham) his wife. Charles, who had been born in London the son of Henry John Hopkins, was a watchmaker and jeweller of Pietermaritzburg, and owned Subdivision 10 of Lot 494 of the town lands.[11] Yorke was then aged 54 while Adelaide (usually called 'Bobbie') was aged 30 years, having been born at Pietermaritzburg on 23 January 1889. She had been educated at St John's Anglican (Diocesan) School and taught by Anglican nuns. Her youngest daughter, Betty Yorke, wrote of her mother:

> ... Her early life at Maritzburg with her parents, three brothers, and three sisters was extremely happy – where music, books and acting were very much part of their lives. They all sang and her brother, Alfred George, produced and acted in many musicals at Maritzburg ...

The wedding took place at St Saviour's Cathedral, Pietermaritzburg.[20] This cathedral has since been dismantled and rebuilt at Irene, Transvaal.

Yorke and Adelaide produced four daughters and one son namely:

Forenames	Date of birth	Date of baptism	Article
Penelope Jane	27 August 1920	13 January 1921	4.12
Jill Elizabeth	2 January 1922	29 June 1922	4.13
Alethea Nan	1 May 1923	2 October 1923	4.14
Betty Yorke	16 September 1929	16 February 1930	4.15
Timothy Yorke	16 January 1931	17 June 1931	4.16

Penelope Jane was born at the Sanatorium, Pietermaritzburg, but baptised at St James's Church, Dundee. All the other children were born at home in Dundee and baptised at St Matthew's Church. It is on record that the arrival of the son caused great jubilation and that the servants 'danced and celebrated'. That is interesting when Timothy had two elder half-brothers. However, these brothers were then aged 36 and 40 years, so they may have appeared almost as part of a different family. Yorke himself was then 65 years of age. In keeping with her own childhood, Adelaide brought up her children with music, books, acting and religion. Her daughter Betty Yorke wrote:

> Mother was blessed with the art of listening. She enjoyed a tremendous sense of humour and being a listener was wonderful for us all and for her grandchildren. She had a very quick temper and kept us all in order! ... when Yorke went to the numerous Indabas, she always accompanied him ... During the war she helped at the local S A W L twice a week organising packing of parcels for prisoners of war in Europe and for our soldiers who were 'up north' ...

Some of the indabas mentioned were presumably the Zulu ceremonies at which transactions by Acutt and Worthington were witnessed.

About 1920, soon after their marriage, Yorke and Adelaide had moved from Pietermaritzburg to Dundee in northern Natal to join his eldest son Thomas Henry Yorke Worthington (Article 4.8) who

27   *25 Ladysmith Road, Dundee, Natal.*

had moved there about five years earlier. Thomas was practising as a solicitor, he and a schoolfriend, Benjamin Acutt, having founded the firm of Acutt and Worthington in Dundee, each having a 50 per cent interest. Yorke probably stepped into the vacuum when Benjamin died on 23 October 1918 by acquiring his share of the partnership from his executors. Yorke joined the firm ostensibly as accountant but no doubt ran much of the business side, leaving Thomas free to serve clients as the qualified lawyer. Yorke and Adelaide lived at 25 Ladysmith Road (since renamed McKenzie Street). The house has since been demolished and the garden divided into smaller plots. It stood in the vicinity of the present 85 McKenzie Street.

When Yorke retired in 1944 at the age of about 79 years, he, Adelaide and their family moved to Moodie Street, Umkomaas, on the coast of the Indian Ocean, 26 miles south-west of Durban.[19] It appears, however, that Yorke retained a business interest in Dundee for some years; he was listed as 'accountant' there in the directory of 1946 – probably he was a partner of his second son John Derrick Worthington (Article 4.10). Yorke had led an industrious and varied life. He had at different times been styled engineer, accountant, manager and gentleman, and in terms of trade he had been contractor, hotelier and farmer – and possibly, carrier and tanner. But he had also been a sportsman. An entry in a book on *Sports and Sportsmen* published by the Cape Times reads:[21]

… in the eighties and nineties Mr Worthington Sen. played a very prominent part in all branches of Natal Sport, and his work on behalf of both the Natal Cricket Association and the Natal Rugby Football Association will never be forgotten. Mr Worthington Sen. was a class horseman and in his youth a skilled polo player. He participated regularly at gymkhanas and won innumerable events. He has always been a cricket enthusiast and has often been a member of Natal cricket selection committees. Mr Worthington Sen. is an extremely popular business man of Dundee, and today he is still just as enthusiastic as he was of yore regarding sport.

He played golf to a one handicap and represented Dundee and Northern Natal for many years. He was involved in arranging the merger of the Northern and Southern Natal Golf Unions to form the Natal Golf Union. His clubs at various times were the Victoria, Zingari Cricket, Maritzburg Golf, Dundee, Dundee Golf and Umkomaas Golf. One of his hobbies was woodwork; he made furniture in his own workshop at his home in Dundee.

Adelaide was also a sporting enthusiast and a keen horsewoman. She had played hockey and tennis at school and she later played golf. She was president of the Ladies' Section of the Umkomaas Golf Club, and customarily organised the putting competitions at their annual club fetes. Bridge was one of her passions; much to the annoyance of her children she held many afternoon bridge parties at her home in Dundee.

Yorke died of angina quietly after lunch on 8 February 1947 at home in Moodie Street, Umkomaas.[11] Betty Yorke recalled that the occasion was 'very sad for us all, but more particularly for my mother as they were so happy and she was still relatively young'. The funeral service was held on 10 February 1947 at Christ Church, Umkomaas and he was buried at the General Cemetery, Umkomaas.[12]

In his Will dated 1 April 1920 (26 years before his death) he left his whole estate in trust, the income being for the maintenance of Adelaide and the education of his children.[11] If Adelaide were to die or re-marry before the youngest surviving child reached the age of 21 years, the income of his estate was for his children in equal parts, the capital of the estate passing to them when the youngest reached the age of 21 years. His marriage with Adelaide had been out of community of property.

When all the children had flown the nest, Adelaide sold the Moodie-Street house and moved to *St Andrew's Hotel*, Umkomaas, where she lived for the rest of her life. The hotel was sometimes known locally as the 'British Museum' as many retired Indian Army officers and tea planters of Ceylon (now Sri Lanka) and their wives lived there. Adelaide continued to play much bridge and fulfilled the role of family matriarch. She died at the home of her youngest daughter Betty, at 5 Hendon Road, Westville, near Durban on 14 June 1973. She was 84 years of age.[11] Her body was cremated on 15 June 1973 at Dove's Crematorium, Durban, and her ashes were placed in Yorke's grave.

By her Will dated 4 May 1973, Adelaide bequeathed all her monies invested through Acutt and Worthington to her unmarried daughter Alethea Nan. The furniture and other personal possessions were to be divided equally between her two married daughters. The remainder of her estate, including moneys invested through the Standard Bank of Africa, was to be divided equally among her six grand-daughters.

Yorke had founded a cadet line which became the senior line of Worthington's when his eldest brother, Henry (Article 4.2), died in 1920 without issue.

4.5 Mabel

Mabel Worthington, the second daughter of Charles Worthington and Penelope Jane his wife (Articles 3.36 and 4.1), was born on 16 May 1870 at Wandsworth, Surrey, England. *Visitations of England and Wales* shows her year of birth as 1869; her first marriage certificate and death certificate show the year as 1870; her second marriage certificate shows the year as 1871. At the age of four or five she sailed with her parents and five siblings to Natal, where they settled at Pietermaritzburg.[1] By the age of 19 she had moved to Barberton in the Transvaal, probably to be with her elder brother, Henry (Article 4.2), who was already involved there in the gold mining industry. On 16 January 1890 at the age of about 19 she married Alfred John Blake of Barberton, the son of John Blake. Alfred was an 'assistant collector of customs' in the Transvaal, then aged 25 years. Banns were read and Penelope gave her consent as Mabel was still a minor. The wedding took place at All Saints' Church, Barberton, Penelope Worthington and Henry Worthington signing as two of the witnesses.

At first Alfred and Mabel lived at Barberton, but later they moved to Johannesburg. They produced two sons and one daughter.[5]

Forenames	Date of birth	Date of baptism
Rodney Angus	8 December 1890	16 January 1891
Sybil May	17 August 1892	22 November 1892
Francis Boden Bertie	*c.* February 1894	

The baptisms of the first two children took place at All Saints' Church. Alfred died on 23 April 1897 aged 32 years – after only seven years of marriage. By his Will dated 16 December 1895 his estate was to be divided equally among his three children. His wife and Arthur George Blake were to be his executors.[5]

Mabel returned to England and lived for a while at 11 Rochester Square, Camden Town, about four miles north-west of the City of London. On 24 March 1899 nearly two years after Alfred's death she married Frederick Chatterton of 16 Hillmarten Road, Islington, Middlesex. Frederick was an architect then 27 years of age, the son of George Joseph Chatterton, a lead manufacturer. The wedding was held at St

Luke's Church, West Holloway in the parish of Islington, the register being signed by Edgar Chatterton and Mabel's mother, Penelope Jane. There were no children of this marriage which turned out to be unhappy. Mabel, recalling events on 17 May 1952 at the age of about 82 years, said that soon after the marriage she asked Frederick to take her to South Africa, but he refused. She then forced the move by saying 'if you don't, I'll go alone'. They sailed to Natal where he set up an architect's practice 'which prospered very well'. In 1905 they were living at, or his office was at, 5 Gray's Inn, Church Street, Pietermaritzburg.[10] Mabel recalled that he was a jealous man – even of his step-children – 'and

28   *Mabel, born Worthington.*

a separation became necessary'. She left him in February 1906 and returned to London. Proceedings commenced in the Supreme Court of the Transvaal on 22 March 1906 when Frederick obtained leave of the court to sue Mabel 'for restitution of conjugal rights or, in default, for divorce ...' for her malicious desertion.[5] The court issued a summons to Mabel giving her 10 weeks to answer the summons and pay costs, but she did not return or co-habit. On 18 April 1906, a solicitor of the Strand, London, certified that he had duly delivered the court's citation and interdict to Mabel who was then living at the *Hotel Russell*, Russell Square, Holborn, near the City of London. On 12 September 1906 Mabel confirmed through her own solicitors, Lunnor and Nixon of Pretoria, that she had no intention of returning to Frederick. On 10 October 1906 the divorce was decreed. Nothing is known of her for the next 44 years until 30 October 1950 when her address was 'care of Mrs C. Garland, 72 West Hill, Epsom, Surrey, England'.

In May 1952 Mabel was living at the *Vikta Hotel*, Clarence Parade, Southsea. There she was near one of her sons who had built a chain of four cinemas in Southsea and Portsmouth after the First World War. He managed them until about 1950 when he sold them 'to some Americans' having made his fortune. Mabel died on 28 March 1957 at 28 Victoria Road North, Southsea, the causes of death being myocardiac degeneration, coronary atheroma and carcinoma of jejunum. Her younger son, Bertie, described her as 'widow of Frederick Chatterton an architect', but she had been divorced for 50 years.

4.6 Arthur George

Arthur George Worthington, the third son of Charles Worthington and Penelope Jane his wife (Articles 3.36 and 4.1), was born on 21 August 1871 at home, 7 St John's Hill Grove, Battersea, Surrey (later in Greater London). His birth certificate gives the order of forenames as 'George Arthur'. However, a published pedigree and all other known records refer to him as Arthur George.[1] After at least a year in England he sailed to Natal with his parents and five siblings to settle at Pietermaritzburg. He trained as a mining engineer and land surveyor and set to work in the mining areas of the Transvaal.

By 1896 Arthur was in a business partnership with Ralph Wiggins, their firm being styled 'Wiggins and Worthington'. Both Ralph and Arthur, then aged about 25 years, were described as 'speculators of Barberton'. On 1 February 1896 Howard Bill, a mine manager in Barberton, brought an action against Wiggins and Worthington in the Supreme Court of the Transvaal claiming a prospect licence.[5] The case was decided on 19 June 1899 against Wiggins and Worthington who had to pay costs.

By 13 January 1897, Arthur had pegged out his first gold mining claim near Barberton, the claim being registered on that day by Claims Inspector Inzage. The claim was called 'Millicent'. Further claims called Hidden Treasure, Kimberley, Sheba West, Tyne Block, and Amsterdam Claims were also registered in Arthur's name that year. He registered a further eight claims in 1899.[5] On 24 March 1900 it appears that 'A.G. Worthington' held nine claims numbered 27813 to 27821, and had been refused a further three claims numbered 27810 to 27812.

On 23 May 1896 Arthur married Alice Maude (born Stevens), both bride and groom being described as of Pretoria. Earlier the same year Alice had obtained a divorce from William Harry Carney, a jeweller of Barberton whom she had married on 24 December 1891 at All Saints' Church, Barberton. The divorce had been granted by the Supreme Court of South Africa on the grounds that in 1895 and 1896 William had committed adultery with Lissie Cooke, Annie Smith, Ada Jones, and Maude Kew – all barmaids of Barberton.[5] Arthur had supported her at the hearing by stating that she was too poor to bear the costs of the action. His statement began:

> I the undersigned Arthur G Worthington swear and say: I am a land surveyor and resident in Barberton. I live in the neighbourhood of Alice Maude Carney (born Stevens). I know her personally and am acquainted with her financial circumstances ...

At her first marriage in 1891, Alice's age was entered as 23 years. However, at the second marriage five years later she entered an age of only 25 years. Her reason may have been to convince the priest at her first marriage that she was over 21 years of age; or it may have been to convince Arthur that she was only a little older than him. Arthur and Alice's wedding was at a Pretoria registry office. They produced one daughter, namely:

Forenames	Date of birth	Article
Penelope Maude	29 January 1898	5.2

In the summer of 1899 Arthur and Alice and their child were living in an apartment at 'Mrs Sturrock's boarding house', Marston House, Kerk Street, Johannesburg (Stand 1475). Arthur was then self-employed and styled 'mining engineer and surveyor'.

The outbreak of the Boer War caused them to move hurriedly on 5 October 1899 leaving certain furniture behind. Alice and child went to live in Cape Town while Arthur joined the British Forces, being commissioned captain, and posted as staff officer to Colonel Henry Jenner Scobell (later Major-General Sir Henry Scobell, KCVO, CB, inspector-general of cavalry). Probably Arthur was with Henry when he led a squadron of Scots Greys to reconnoitre the Boer positions at Abrahamskraal before taking part in offensives towards Bloemfontein, and on 5 September 1901 capturing Commandant Lotter's unit.[22] When Arthur returned to Johannesburg after the war, in May 1902 he found that all their private furniture had been looted, except for the piano.[5] He made a claim for losses of £42[*] and received £40. One of the investigators of his claim reported that 'the Claimant is well known, done good service in the war and his references speak most highly of him'. Another investigator reported 'The applicant is a gentleman of unquestionable integrity ...'.

After the war Arthur was in business with Henry Wilson, trading as general merchants in Pretoria and Johannesburg under the style of 'Wilson and Worthington'. On 13 May 1904 R.D. MacKenzie, a dairyman of Vitvalgron near Pretoria, brought a case against Wilson and Worthington in the Supreme Court of the Transvaal.[5] He complained that on or about 26 March 1904 he had ordered from Wilson and Worthington a bag of common salt to feed to his cattle, but that a bag of nitrate of soda had been delivered. The dairyman, thinking it was salt, administered it to his cattle of which 'nine cows died and 20 were seriously damaged'. He had had to suspend business as a dairyman for eight days and obtain veterinary treatment. He claimed £1,200 plus costs of suit. Wilson and Worthington admitted the mistake but denied the extent of the damage; they offered £250. On 21 September 1904 the court found in favour of MacKenzie, but for a sum of only £260[†] without costs.

Whether Arthur was as that time a working partner in the business is not known, but it seems unlikely because he developed many other business interests. It appears that Arthur developed the practice of entering into a separate business with each of several different people.

---

[*] Equivalent to 330 man-days of English agricultural labour.
[†] Equivalent to 1,950 man-days of English agricultural labour.

He provided capital, technical support and advice, leaving the other person to manage the business. Most of the information available on such businesses comes from legal suits. This may give a distorted impression but it is clear that Arthur was an industrious entrepreneur who built up a wide range of interests and investments.

On 30 August 1904, Wilson and Worthington petitioned the Witwatersrand High Court to place the estates of J. Liknaitsky and his business Jacob Liknaitsky and Company, produce dealers and millers, under sequestration for the benefit of their creditors.[5] J. Liknaitsky or a relation of his had on 29 August 1904 called to see Henry Wilson at the offices of Wilson and Worthington to offer a final payment at the rate of 37.5 percent for settlement of their debt of £1,246 13s. 4d.[*] to Wilson and Worthington. Henry had refused to accept.

On 15 September 1905 Frank Thomas Richards, a contractor and speculator of Pretoria, brought an action against Wilson and Worthington in the Supreme Court of the Transvaal.[5] The two parties had entered into an agreement in March 1905 whereby Richards would cede to Wilson and Worthington all rights in a contract to supply provisions to the Army in the districts of Middleburg, Barberton and Standerton, and to other authorities in the Transvaal. The provisions included oats, hay, rock salt, sulphur, animal bedding, coffee, tea, sugar, bread, mealies and pepper. Wilson and Worthington had agreed to buy, at cost, the relevant stocks at various depots and to pay for them on 30 May 1905. Richards' account for the stocks totalled £1,082 17s. 11d. of which part had been settled, but Richards claimed that £822 6s. 10d. was still due. In their defence, Wilson and Worthington claimed that certain prices and weights of goods had been incorrectly stated, but their main defence was that Richards had failed to supply the necessary customs forms for imported goods to enable the Army to obtain customs and railage rebate. The Army had therefore deducted an equivalent amount from Wilson and Worthington's bill. Judgement was given on 30 November 1905 for Richards but for a reduced sum of £688 12s. 4d.[†]

An agreement dated 14 July 1906 between Arthur, then residing in Pretoria (Post Office Box 547), and Bowers Randfontein Limited whose registered office was at 52 Queen Victoria Street, London EC, shows that Arthur had continued to build up his interests in gold mining claims. He then held a half-interest in each of four blocks in the Barberton-Lyndenburg district, about 150 miles east of Pretoria. The blocks were:[5]

> 42 claims in the name of H. Worthington situate on the Hill immediately to the East of the Sheba mines;
>
> 50 claims in the name of H. Bilski situate on the Sheba Hill;

---

[*] Equivalent to 9,400 man-days of English agricultural labour.
[†] Equivalent to 5,100 man-days of English agricultural labour.

50 claims in the name of J.G.T. Hallett situate on the Sheba Hill;

72 claims Base Metal in the name of W. Milne adjoining the claim of the Consort Gold Mine Company.

H. Worthington was, of course, Arthur's elder brother, Henry (Article 4.2). Bowers Randfontein Limited had been established in 1900 to acquire interests in South African gold. By the agreement Arthur was to sell his half-interests in the four blocks to Bowers Randfontein Limited in return for 37,000 fully-paid ordinary shares of £1 each in the company. At the same time Arthur was to subscribe £5,000[*] for a further 5,000 shares in the company. The agreement which was due for completion by 30 September 1906 was conditional on the completion of three other agreements whereby mining companies were selling their interests to Bowers Randfontein Limited. Perhaps this was the time when Arthur was appointed a director and the local agent of Bowers Randfontein Limited. He was certainly a director in January and March 1908 but was no longer a director when the company brought an action against him in the Supreme Court of the Transvaal on 25 September 1909. In the customary style of the court at the time, Arthur was summoned thus:

Edward VII, by the Grace of God, of the United Kingdom of Great Britain and Ireland and of the British Dominions beyond the seas, King, Emperor of India, Defender of the Faith, to the Sheriff of the Transvaal or his lawful deputy, Greeting! Command Arthur George Worthington of Pretoria (hereinafter named the Defendant) that within seven days …

The company's claims against Arthur were refuted and were withdrawn by the company on 23 October 1909. On the same day the company issued revised claims for a re-start of the action. It was claimed that Arthur had only subscribed £2,000 for the 5,000 shares which had been issued to him, he having failed to pay the subsequent calls for capital amounting to £3,000. The company was in the meantime retaining 37,000 shares as security for the payment of the £3,000. Whilst a director of the company on 28 January 1908, Arthur had been sent £1,000 to acquire for the company a one-fifth share of the O'Gorman Sheep Dip Syndicate then held by Wilson and Worthington, but had failed to either pass on title or return the £1,000. Again the company had sent him £500 to acquire certain shares in the Kuils River Tin Mining Company Limited but Arthur had withheld the shares. Finally, Arthur was accused of withholding the proceeds of sale of a quarter interest in the De Kapp Mines Syndicate. In his defence Arthur said that the £3,000 had been withheld because he had not received the 37,000 shares in the company. He also claimed that the agreement was null and void because it was conditional on three other agreements coming into effect, whereas one of them, that with the Swan Syndicate, had not done so. He claimed that the company had instructed him to acquire £2,000 worth of shares

---

[*] Equivalent to 37,000 man-days of English agricultural labour.

in the Kuils River Tin Mining Company Limited sending him £500 on account. They had failed to send the remaining £1,500. He claimed that the deal with Wilson and Worthington had been completed but that Bowers Randfontein Limited owed him £125, being their share of the expenses of the transaction. How the matter was settled is not known, but Bowers Randfontein Limited withdrew their court action on 2 April 1910.

It appears than in 1906 and 1907 Arthur had an interest in a further 17 claims which were then being worked on a cooperative basis by the East Rand Extension Gold Mining Co Ltd whose offices were on the second floor of Netherlands Bank Buildings, Fox Street, Johannesburg. By 19 August 1907 the company planned to buy the interests. On that day the company wrote to the district registrar of mining rights at Barberton:[5]

> With reference to the 17 claims of Moor and Worthington I have not been able to get on with the transfer of these claims to my company on account of Mr Worthington's absence in England, and my papers not being completed. Mr Worthington has just arrived here and I am getting the necessary papers for him ...

The marriage of Arthur and Alice ran into difficulty. Alice suffered alcoholism and in October 1905 Arthur sent her, their daughter and a nurse to England so that Alice could be treated at the Keeley Institute. On leaving the institute about December 1905, Alice deserted Arthur and refused to return. Five years later, on 23 February 1911, Arthur petitioned the Transvaal Provincial Division of the Supreme Court of South Africa.[5] The court's first step was to summon Alice to appear, but she confirmed in a written statement dated 25 May 1911 her refusal 'to return to Arthur George Worthington now residing in Pretoria ...'. In his statement of 27 June 1911 to the court Arthur wrote:

> ... there is a child of the marriage, a girl, aged 13 years. She is now in my custody... In 1905 the defendant went to England with my consent for treatment at the Keeley Institute. She was suffering from alcoholism. She took the child with a nurse with her. The child stayed in a different place. When my wife left for England, the understanding was that she was to remain there for six months. I made ample financial provision for her. I stipulated that she should write to me every week. Instead of staying at the Keeley Institute for six months, she stayed ... She then went to Paris. She did not take the child with her. The child stayed with my sister for two months and early in 1906 I went ... and put her to school at Brighton. She (the child) remained there until at least 18 months ago when she came out to me here. I had gone back to England again in 1906 and remained there until 1908 and saw the child frequently. Defendant only visited the child once at school at Brighton. The child is now in school in Pretoria. I saw my wife in London in 1906. She did not go back to the Keeley Institute. She has not been out to South Africa. When I last saw her in 1908 she had not been cured

29 *Arthur George Worthington.*   **30** *Myra Dorothea, born Fischer.*

of her intemperate habits. She was then living with a nurse in a small house which I bought for her there. I have always made ample provision for her. She is now in London ... I have a letter from my wife written on 12 November 1909 informing me that she had a child by another man ... the child mentioned in the letter as 'little Phipps' is not my child. That child is now dead, I believe.

On 5 September 1911 the court granted the divorce, awarded custody of the child to Arthur and ordered that Alice should forfeit the benefits which arose from the marriage being in community of property.

On 10 April 1910, an action was brought against Arthur by the Mines & Minerals Exploration Syndicate Limited in the Supreme Court of the Transvaal. The head office of the syndicate was at Bloomfield House, London Wells, London, but it was carrying on business in Barberton and elsewhere in the Transvaal. The syndicate sued Arthur for £800[*] damages sustained 'in respect of the Secret Commission paid by defendant to one Ullyett'. No more is known of the case except that the action was withdrawn on 7 April 1910.

On 9 December 1911, Arthur married Myra Dorothea, the second daughter of Jacobus George Fischer of Kimberley, Cape Colony, and Katherine Sophie Elizabeth his wife. Myra was then 29 years of age, having been born on 17 April 1882 in Cape Colony. The Fischers had been in South Africa since the 17th century when Johannes Fischer arrived, serving with the artillery of the Dutch East India Company.

---

[*] Equivalent to 5,700 man-days of English agricultural labour.

An illustrious cadet line of his family was founded by Johannes Jacobus George Fischer and Catherina Anna, born Brink, his wife. Their son Abraham Fischer born in 1850 was prime minister of Orange River Colony (later called Orange Free State) and, Abraham's son Percy Ulrich Fischer, LLB, was judge president of the Orange Free State Provincial Division. Percy's eldest son was Abram Fischer, QC, LLB, born in 1908 and a Rhodes scholar of Oxford University.[23] Abram (usually called 'Bram') supported the anti-apartheid movement and as barrister acted for Nelson Mandela (later president of South Africa) and his colleagues before being sentenced in 1966 to life imprisonment. In his autobiography, Nelson completed his account of Abram's work with:[24]

> ... Bram Fischer, the grandson of the prime minister of the Orange River Colony, had made the greatest sacrifice of all. No matter what I suffered in my pursuit of freedom, I always took strength from the fact that I was fighting with and for my own people. Bram was a free man who fought against his own people to ensure the freedom of others.

Myra's mother, Katherine, was the eldest daughter and co-heiress of Jan Daniel Bosman and his wife Catherine Sophia, born Louw. Katherine inherited the de Oude Plantage estate in Paarl, about 30 miles north-east of Cape Town. The estate had been held in the Bosman line for five generations, the first holder being Hermanus Lambertus Bosman. Hermanus had been born in Amsterdam, Holland, in 1682 and had sailed in the *de Overryp* to Cape Town in 1707. He had married Elizabeth (born Villiers) in 1708 and they settled at de Oude Plantage. After passing through Katherine to the Fischer family, the estate was sold in 1929. One of Arthur and Myra's grandchildren, Mrs Naureen Leppan, visited the estate in October 1994 and reported:

> ... The old family estate had been bought by a German industrialist and after spending eight million he had it beautifully restored. It is now called Grand Roche and is regularly listed as one of the top hotels in South Africa. He has kept it quite small and restored all the old buildings including the slave chapel. The only new addition is a conference centre building which has a wonderful painting of the original homestead in the foyer ...

Arthur and Myra's wedding was at the Presbyterian Church, Kimberley. Myra bore Arthur two more daughters:

Forenames	Date of birth	Article
Heather Myra	29 December 1912	5.3
Blanche Louise	25 December 1914	5.4

The family lived at Waterkloof, Pretoria, Transvaal where their three living-in servants comprised a Hollander nanny, a French maid and a cook. Arthur was perceived, at least by some of his relations, as 'the richest man in Pretoria' but perceptions and comparisons are often based on assets alone and ignore borrowings and other liabilities which are not in the public domain. Arthur had diverse investments through the stock exchange as well as in property, mining rights and merchanting, but they may have been financed by loans, as is often the case with the boldest of entrepreneurs. Thus it may have been that he lost most of his assets during a slump in the economy.

Arthur died suddenly aged 45 years on 6 December 1916 at the Monastery Sanatorium, Sea Point, Cape Town, Myra being with him at the time. She signed the death notice on 28 December 1916 at Paarl, presumably while staying with her parents at de Oude Plantage. His Will had been written on 5 March 1906, long before his second marriage.[25] Thus, Penelope Maude, his only child by his first marriage was the sole beneficiary. Myra and her two daughters were left without any provision. Arthur's former business partner, Henry Wilson, was one of the executors.

Myra became matron of a girl's school in the Cape, and later moved with her two daughters to Salisbury in Southern Rhodesia (now Harare in Zimbabwe), to become matron of a school there. Later still, she and her daughters returned to Pretoria where she worked for a bank and for the department of Customs and Excise. About 1951, at the age of some 69 years, Myra married at Germiston, Transvaal, John Patrick Cornwall, a retired land surveyor of Johannesburg. He had been born about March 1874 at Cape Town and had married on 14 January 1909 Alice Newton, born Soloman, by whom he had one daughter Alice Patricia Phyllis.[25] Alice Newton had died aged 65 years on 11 March 1946.[5] Myra and John, who had been family friends before their first marriages, lived at Umkomaas, on the south coast of Natal. He died on 26 June 1955 at Grey's Hospital, Pietermaritzburg, Myra being with him at the time.[11] By his Will dated 1 July 1954, he placed his estate in trust, the income and use of the house and contents being for Myra for the rest of her life. Thereafter the capital was to pass to his daughter, Alice. One of Myra's grandchildren wrote '... I well remember Jack Cornwall, he was a fine gentleman, and Gaga (my grandmother) and he were very happy ...'. She added:

> My grandmother Myra never spoke of Arthur George ... She did not speak of her life in the early days of her first marriage and we grew up being aware that she had lived in great luxury and had moved in the social circles of Kimberley and knew Oppenheimer's father ...

Myra continued to live for a further 18 years, first at their house in Umkomaas, and later at the home of her younger daughter Blanche at 409 Bulwer Street, Pietermaritzburg. (Her later burial notice recorded the address as 400 Bulwer Road.) Finally she moved to Durban. She died of cerebral thrombosis on 27 August 1973 at the Glenwood Nursing Home, Durban, aged 81 years. Her funeral service was held at Christ Church, Point Road, Durban, after which she was cremated privately.[12]

One of Myra's daughters wrote of her:

> … Her grandchildren have fond memories of her being a most gracious lady. She often played the piano and sang beautifully. She was a perfect lady with impeccable manners and had a gentle caring manner.

4.7 Jonathan Ernest

Jonathan Ernest Worthington, the fourth son and youngest child of Charles Worthington and Penelope Jane his wife (Article 3.36 and 4.1) was born at Wood Green, Middlesex, on 31 August 1873.[1] Within a year or two he sailed to Durban with his parents and siblings.

On 8 June 1895, then aged 21 years, Ernest enlisted in the Natal Mounted Police, having been recommended for the force by his brother-in-law, Inspector John André Masson (Article 4.3). The enrolment took place at Pietermaritzburg when Ernest was described as 5 feet 10 inches tall with fair hair and grey eyes. He knew the Zulu language in addition to English and he declared his religion as Protestant.[7] His police work lasted barely two years, as he was discharged by purchase on 4 May 1897. He first became a 'farmer' of Spring Valley, Beaumont, but by August 1899 he had become a 'storekeeper' of Spring Valley and was described as 'general merchant'.[10] Only two months after resigning from the police he married, on 7 July 1897, Alice Constance, a daughter of Charles Hornby and Ellen his wife of Dalton Hall, Mid Illovo, Natal. Alice was then 22 years old, having been born on 2 July 1875 at Pietermaritzburg, but she was residing at Dalton in July 1875. Charles and Ellen (born Harris) came from Dundalk in Ireland. They had sailed in the SS *Prince Alfred* with 11 children, a 12th being born on board in March 1869. Their family was completed with a further four children being born in Natal. Ten of the 16 children were surviving at the time of the marriage. Charles had purchased the Dromore estate of 999 acres at Mid Illovo from John Jardine, an original settler who had built his homestead after the grants of estate in the region had been proclaimed. But John Jardine had become insolvent in 1869 and sold the estate fraudulently as it should have remained part of the insolvent estate. For that he was committed to prison for a year. The Hornbys have been described as 'a jolly family … full of sport'.[26]

Ernest may have met Alice while at the Natal police camp at Mid Illovo, or he may have met her through his second half-cousin Arnold Worthington Cooper (Article 3.29) who was, in 1878, provisionally appointed field-cornet of Ward 6, Pietermaritzburg County, which included Dromore 'in place of C.E. Hornby'. Ernest and Alice's wedding took place at St Margaret's Church, Mid Illovo, Ernest being described in the register as a 'farmer, residing at Spring Valley, Beaumont'.[20] They produced one son, namely:

Forenames	Date of birth	Date of baptism	Article
Noel Ernest	22 July 1898	6 August 1899	6.2

Noel was born at Mid Illovo. In 1903 Alice was secretary of the Beaumont Tennis Club. Alas, Ernest died at the age of 31 years on 7 March 1905 at the Arcadia Nursing Home, Pretoria.[27] The cause was heart failure following six months of illness with hepatic abscess and malaria. He was buried at the Pretoria cemetery.

When Ernest went to the nursing home in 1904, Alice returned to Dalton Hall and stayed there at least until 1907.[10] In 1910, when Noel was 10 years of age, she was a nurse at Grey's Hospital, Prince Albert Street, Pietermaritzburg. She remained there until about 1913 when she returned to Mid Illovo. In 1917 she was living at 'The Purdah' there. She was present at the death of her niece-in-law, Phyllis Janet Masson (Article 4.3), at the Sanatorium, Durban.[11] By 1933 she was living at Machadodorp in the district of Belfast, Transvaal. In 1953 and still in 1961 she was living in a house or cottage on the farm of her son at Beach Terminus, Port Shepstone, Natal (Article 6.2). She died on 26 July 1961 at the hospital, Port Shepstone, aged 86 years, having been a widow for 56 years.[11] By her Will dated 25 April 1933 she appointed Noel as her executor and sole heir.

THIRD GENERATION – FAMILY OF
REGINALD YORKE OF NATAL

4.8 Thomas Henry Yorke

Thomas Henry Yorke Worthington, the eldest son of Reginald Yorke Worthington and Mary Elizabeth Miriam his first wife (Article 4.4) was born on 1 July 1890 at Estcourt.[1] He was baptised on 3 August 1890 at St Matthew's Church, Estcourt, his sponsors being his uncle Henry (Article 4.2) his grandmother Penelope (Article 3.36) and his uncle Herbert G. Wheeler.[20] He and his brother John (Article 4.10) spent much of their childhood on the farm of their uncle Herbert in the Weenen district of Natal. Thomas's second daughter, Margaret, wrote:

> The boys grew up with their cousins the Moor boys and young Zulu umfaans on the farm. Growing up in this manner they learnt the language and customs of the Zulu people. This was to prove useful to my Father right through his life. He was greatly esteemed by the Zulu people for his knowledge of their language and their ways.

His preparatory school was Merchiston in Pietermaritzburg. He then went to Michaelhouse School, Balgowan, Natal, where he was a boarder from 1903 to 1907. There he became a corporal in the Cadet Corps, and played for the first cricket eleven and second rugby fifteen. He won prizes for shooting, modern history and languages. His matriculation subjects included Latin, Greek, Hebrew and Zulu. On leaving school he studied law and was articled to Colonel Arthur Horace Hime of Hime and Allison, solicitors of Pietermaritzburg. Later he became an associate of that firm.

His sporting activities continued. On 13 July 1911 he sailed in RMS *Briton* for Cape Town with 25 members of the Natal Rugby Union's Currie Cup team. He was then 21 years of age. An article on him in the book *Sports and Sportsmen* published by the *Cape Times* in 1921 states:[21]

> While at Pietermaritzburg Mr Worthington played for the Zingari Cricket Club, which he captained from 1911 to 1914. He was a good batsman, and he was selected to represent Pietermaritzburg in the inter-town matches against both Durban and Northern Districts. From 1907 to 1912 Mr Worthington was a wing in the Pietermaritzburg Wanderers, which club he captained in the two years 1911 and 1912. He also represented Pietermaritzburg in the inter-town rugby matches, and in 1908 and 1911 he was honoured by selection as a member of the Natal Rugby Currie Cup Team. In 1910 he again represented Natal against Dr Smyth's British Rugby fifteen. Golf is yet another form of sport at which this versatile Natalian excels, and in 1915 he set the seal on ability when he won the Natal Golf Championship. Mr Worthington has competed at the South African Championships on three occasions, and was a member of the Natal team which won the Inter-Provincial Championships in 1928. For eleven years this popular Dundee solicitor has captained Dundee Golf Club.

Thomas's rugby was brought to an abrupt end by a serious throat injury which he suffered while playing the game. This injury also prevented him from serving with the armed forces during the two World Wars.

On one occasion when playing cricket for Northern Districts against Pietermaritzburg, Thomas hit five sixes off the first five balls of an over bowled by Saville. On the sixth ball Thomas was caught on the boundary.[8] The bowler was a relation of Thomas's future half-brother-in-law, Charles Saville (Article 4.12).

Early in 1915 Thomas was sent to Dundee to open a branch office of Hime and Allison. There he found an old school friend, Benjamin Acutt, who was a lawyer and the honorary treasurer of Dundee Golf Club. Soon afterwards, probably in 1916, they entered into partnership to form the Dundee firm of solicitors, public notaries, and conveyancers called 'Acutt and Worthington' in which each had a 50 percent interest. The *Natal Directory* lists them as the two partners in the firm in 1918. But Benjamin died aged 33 years on 23 October 1918 at his residence in Ladysmith Road (now called McKenzie Street) in the 'influenza or plague epidemic'.[11] It is thought that Thomas's father, Yorke Worthington, stepped into the vacuum by acquiring the half-share in the partnership from Benjamin's executors. Yorke would have joined the firm as accountant and office manager leaving Thomas free to serve clients as the qualified lawyer.

On 5 July 1915 Thomas married Frances Louie, daughter of Henry Robson Tully and his wife Margaret (born Whitehead) of Westoe, 16 Payn Street, Pietermaritzburg. Louie was then aged 20 years having been born

31 *Thomas Henry Yorke Worthington and Frances Louie, born Tully.*

about October 1894 at Johannesburg, the Transvaal. As Louie was still a minor and her father had died in 1913, consent for the marriage was given by her mother. Louie's father, variously described as gentleman and accountant, was a son of James Emery Tully and Eleanor his wife of Newton Hall, Northumberland, England, the Tully's being of the shipbuilding firm John Ridley, Son and Tully of Newcastle upon Tyne, England. The obituary of Robson Tully published in the *Natal Witness* in 1913 includes:[8]

> Mr Tully was born at South Shields, near Newcastle upon Tyne, in 1856, and in his early days earned a reputation of being a great sportsman. He played rugby football for the famous Westoe Club for many years, and was also among other things a keen oarsman. He was a partner in the shipbuilding firm of John Ridley Son and Tully. In the year 1878 Mr Tully came out to South Africa and has resided in various parts of the country during the last 35 years. When first he arrived in South Africa he lived for some time on the Rand, and it was after the late Boer War that he decided to settle down in Maritzburg. The deceased fought in many of the wars in this country, and has medals for the Basuto War of 1879, and the late Boer War. During the Boer War Mr Tully was with the relief column which relieved Ladysmith …

Robson had enlisted with the Natal Mounted Police at the age of 23 on 29 October 1879 and served with them for six years.[7]

Thomas and Louie's wedding took place at St Saviour's Cathedral, Pietermaritzburg.[20] A local newspaper reported:

> … The bride looked charming in a coat and skirt of ondine-faced moire antique, worn with ermine stole and muff, and velvet togue with pann mount…Mr and Mrs Tom Worthington left for Dundee that night by mail train.

Thomas and Louie produced two daughters both being baptised at St James's Church, Dundee.[20]

Forenames	Date of birth	Date of baptism
Hazel Mary	21 November 1917	3 January 1918
Margaret Louie	26 March 1926	2 May 1926

The family lived at 96 Ladysmith Road (later re-named Mckenzie Street).

Sometime after the death of Ben Acutt, Thomas took Stanley J. Hofmeyr into partnership; this lasted until sometime between 1942 and 1946 when he was succeeded by J.S. McAlistair. By 1960 Thomas had two partners, namely G. van der M. Hanekom and James Henry Preston Mallett.[19] The firm continues under the same name – Acutt and Worthington. As a lawyer, Thomas served the Indian and Zulu communities as well as the English and Afrikaans. His younger daughter, Margaret, wrote:

> … he participated in all the important African chiefs' indabas dealing with land disputes etcetera, particularly in the Nqutu and Nqudeni districts of Zululand. As young girls, my sister and I would sometimes accompany our Father to meet the Chiefs, who would arrive at the meeting place on horseback. After the greetings they would seat themselves in a circle and the customary ritual of the indabas would begin with the passing around of the 'ukhamba' of 'utshwala' (their pot of home brewed beer) … Following this ceremony the discussions were commenced.

In recognition of Thomas's services to the Dundee-Glencoe Regional Water Board, the dam and reservoir near the village of Hattingspruit,

32 *Tom Worthington Dam near Dundee, KwaZulu-Natal.*

about eight miles north of Dundee, was named 'Tom Worthington Dam'. The project was completed in February 1956. A road sign bearing the name was installed opposite the reservoir on the main road between Dundee and Newcastle. The reservoir is nearly a mile long.

On 4 December 1947 Thomas bought the Kuick Vlei Settlement farm (Number 12751) from Jan Gysbert Spies. This farm, which is about 11 miles south of Dundee, had an area of 1,385 acres, 2 roods and 6 perches.[28] He retained it for the rest of his life, after which it was sold to Petrus Johannes Eloff. He also owned two other farms: Glenlyon (Number 13396) and Morgenstand (Number 3347) which were run by farm managers. In fact Glenlyon, with 1,200 acres was managed for some years by Thomas's nephew Neville John Worthington (Article 4.10). Morgenstand, about three miles by two miles in extent lies on high ground about four miles north of Dundee and includes the hill Kwa Moongwane rising to 1,519 metres above sea level. Thomas was a lover of dogs and kept in particular Scottish terriers, spaniels and pointers which he used when shooting. He was also a keen game hunter and salt-water fisherman.

On the evening of 11 December 1951 Thomas left his home – 96 McKenzie Street, Dundee – to attend a meeting, and on his return found that his wife had died. The following May, Thomas wrote:

> … Although I was afraid that there was a possibility of her having a fatal attack, she was so full of courage and will power and seemed so well that I am afraid I got a dreadful shock when the end came … We

had been together nearly 40 years and naturally I feel very lost at times. However, I am fortunate to have my two daughters, one of whom lives next door to me, and they have been wonderful.

Louie's funeral service was held on 13 December 1951 at St James's Church, Dundee, and was followed by burial at Dundee Cemetery.[8] Her Will was dated 22 July 1915, only two weeks after her marriage, and by it she bequeathed the whole of her estate to Thomas. The estate included Erf No.8, Block 15 in the borough of Dundee, being one acre in extent. She had inherited from her mother, Margaret, a property at 8 Payn Street, Pietermaritzburg, being sub-division 9 of lot 206 of the town lands. That was described as a:[11]

> well built large house of brick under iron roof, in an elegant state of preservation, commodious, lofty and in all an attractive property with well laid out grounds and gardens.

Louie had been much respected and regarded as a 'charming lady'; she had out-dressed most and was one of the last to wear white gloves when out visiting. In the family, however, she had a cruel streak which led to 'difficult childhoods' for her two daughters.

On 5 January 1953, then aged 62 years, Thomas married Isabella Amelia of 81 Victoria Street, Dundee. She was 50 years of age, having been born on 5 January 1903 at Harrismith in the Orange Free State. She was one of the six children of James Malan Simpson, the Harrismith blacksmith, and his wife Elizabeth Geraldine, born van den Bosch. Isabella's first husband was Gerhardus Henrie van der Merwe who was the 'Atlantic representative' living at Wilson Street, Dundee, between 1933 and 1936. The Natal directories showed that the *Royal Hotel*, Dundee, was under his and Isabella's personal supervision from 1940 until sometime between 1942 and 1945. Isabella's marriage to Gerhardus had run into difficulty by 1941 when he sued for divorce on grounds of her desertion. The court reached judgement for divorce on 28 October 1941 but a restitution order was later granted.[18] Final divorce came later. At the time of her marriage to Thomas she was a 'ladies outfitter', being proprietress of a top-of-the-range dress shop which Thomas had acquired for her. The business was probably called Isabel's Ladies' Outfitters listed in the *Natal Directory* of 1952.[19] After her marriage, her attractive black-and-white timbered house, occupying a corner position in Victoria Street, was occupied by Thomas's partner at Acutt and Worthington, James Mallett and his wife. Thomas and Isabel's wedding was a civil event because of the divorce; nevertheless, it took place at St James's Church, Dundee. They had no children.

Thomas died aged 71 years on 2 April 1962 at 96 McKenzie Street, Dundee, Isabella being present.[11] The cause of death was carcinoma of the pancreas, which had been with him for about a year. The funeral was on 4 April 1962 at St James's Church, Dundee, and he was buried in Dundee Cemetery. Eulogies were given at the graveside by representatives of the English, Afrikaans, Indian and Zulu communities 'whom he had served and loved so well'. He had also been president of the Dundee Golf Club and president of the Dundee and District Club. He had been a trustee of the Dundee Building Society and was later chairman of the Dundee branch of the Natal Building Society. He had been a governor of Michaelhouse School and president of Michaelhouse Old Boys' Club. He had taken an active interest in politics and was a founder of the Dundee branch of the old Unionist Party and later vice-chairman of the executive of the Dundee branch of the South African Party. During the Second World War he had held private meetings with General Jan Christiaan Smuts, CH, PC, LLD, FRS, KC, prime minister of South Africa (later Field-Marshal, OM).

By his Will dated 3 March 1962 he made a bequest to his 'native employee Mgodoye Ndebele in consideration of the many years he has faithfully served' Thomas and his firm. All the residue of his estate was to pass in equal parts to Isabella and his two daughters. His properties then included:

(a) Holding No 37, Benon Agricultural Holdings;
(b) Lots 608, 609, 610, 611 and 612 all in Block KK of the township of Dundee;
(c) Lots 624 and 1,255 of the township;
(d) Lot 22 of the farm 'Kuick Vlei Settlement' No 12751, in the county of Klip River.

He also owned the office building of Acutt and Worthington, called the 'Acworth Buildings'. A dispute arose between the two daughters and their step-mother – the three executors. Isabella was unprepared to admit two claims made against the estate by the daughters. The daughters brought an action in the Supreme Court of South Africa – Natal Provincial Division – in Pietermaritzburg on 18 August 1965 before Mr Justice Milne, the judge president.[11] The court granted the daughters' claims on 1 December 1965, but all other legitimate claims on the estate were to be paid in priority. The daughters' solicitor for this action was Charles Saville, their half-uncle-in-law (Article 4.12).

Isabella moved away from the district; by 21 August 1964, when she wrote her last Will, she was living with her niece, Mrs A.L. Bush at 8 Arcadia Avenue, Westville, Natal. By 3 November 1970, when her mother died, she had moved to 93 Kings Lynn, St Andrew's Street, Durban, where she lived with her sister Mrs Eileen Florence Ronaldson.[11] Isabella died on 13 January 1973 at Hillcrest Hospital, Hillcrest, 12 miles north-west of Durban. Her residence was still at 93 Kings Lynn. As she had no children, her estate passed to her four sisters, her brother and her nieces and great-nieces.

4.9 Richard Tyrer

Richard Tyrer Worthington, the second son of Reginald Yorke Worthington and Mary Elizabeth Miriam, his first wife (Article 4.4), was born on 4 March 1892 and baptised at St Matthew's Church, Estcourt on 19 April 1892. His second name 'Tyrer' was the maiden name of his mother's mother. The sponsors at his baptism were his uncle Arthur George Worthington (Article 4.6), his maternal aunt Lydia Sarah Moor (Article 4.4) and her husband John William Moor.[20] Alas, Richard only lived for 20 months; he died on 18 November 1893 of inflammation of the lungs and was buried on 19 November 1893 at St Matthew's Church, Estcourt.[9]

4.10 John Derrick

John Derrick Worthington, the third son of Reginald Yorke Worthington and Mary Elizabeth Miriam, his first wife (Article 4.4), was born on 10 January 1895 at Estcourt, Natal, and baptised on 18 February 1895 at St Matthew's Church, Estcourt.[20] He was educated as a boarder at Michaelhouse School, Balgowan, Natal, from 1907 to 1911, where he became a member of the 1st XI cricket team. At the age of 16 years he started work as a 'junior clerk' and continued in various clerking roles for the next three years.

On 18 August 1914, only two weeks after the British declaration of war on Germany, John joined the Natal Field Artillery as a gunner and served with the Citizen Battery through the German South-West Africa campaign.[29] The Citizen Battery was formed in 1914 for immediate action; it had six 13-pounder QF guns, each drawn by eight to 12 mules depending on the type of terrain, most of which was roadless. All soldiers other than the wagon drivers were mounted on horses. German South-West Africa was successfully conquered and administered by South Africa after the war; for his service John was awarded the 1914-15 Star.

On completing his war service on 13 August 1915, he returned to live with his parents at 41 Burger Street, Pietermaritzburg. Both father and son then worked for Loram and Baynes, Yorke Worthington becoming the manager in or before 1918. Loram and Baynes were 'incorporated accountants and auditors, house and estate agents, general agents and agents for Union Castle Steamship Co'. From 1922 to 1925 the *Natal Directory* lists John's residence as Hardy's Chambers in Printing Office Street, Pietermaritzburg; there was a John Hardy, builder and contractor, with an office in the building.[19] John had presumably moved residence following his father's remarriage in 1919 and departure to Dundee.

On 1 July 1925 John, then described as an accountant aged 30 years, married Alice May who was then residing at Whitby Lodge, Longmarket Street, Pietermaritzburg. Banns having been read, the wedding took place at St Peter's Cathedral, Pietermaritzburg.[20] May was then aged 22 years having been born on 7 September 1902 at Pietermaritzburg,

33 *John Derrik Worthington.*   **34** *Alice May, born Wyatt.*

and baptised on 2 November 1902 at St Peter's Cathedral. She was the daughter of Joseph Johannes Wyatt and Charlotte Elizabeth his wife, who then lived at 32 Zeederberg Road, Pietermaritzburg. From 1898 to 1900 Joseph had been described as 'superintendent of Roads, Stanger' in the Civil Engineering Department. Joseph was the eldest son of Richard Fortner Wyatt and Sarah Elizabeth his wife, farmers of Pietermaritzburg.[11]

John and May produced two children, both born in Pietermaritzburg:

Forenames	Date of birth	Date of baptism
Derrick Yorke	12 March 1927	15 May 1927
Neville John	20 May 1929	15 September 1929

Derrick was baptised at St Peter's Cathedral, Pietermaritzburg, and Neville at St James's Church, Dundee. The family were then living at 98 New England Road, Pietermaritzburg. They were certainly there from 1928 to 1936.[19]

Soon after his marriage, and while still aged 30 years, John established his own business as a stock and share broker with an office at 5 and 6

Green's Chambers, Chancery Lane, Pietermaritzburg. He was assisted in this work by his wife's brother, Norman Wyatt. John became a member of the Johannesburg Stock Exchange and had agents there. Although John had no previous experience as a stock broker, the business was successful at first, as described in a report published in the *Natal Witness* of 13 June 1936.[8] '... For six years he carried on steady business, working a comfortable living, conditions being normal. Then there set in a period of acute depression ...' His annual turnover had peaked at £5,000,000,* but he was caught in the slump of the 1930s – the worst slump of the 20th century. Some of his clients also fell on hard times and could not pay for their shares, while the value of the shares fell. In desperation, John brought actions against certain clients in 1935. For example, he was plaintiff in an action against A. Kaplan on 27 September 1935 when judgement was given in John's favour.[30] Whether the money was recovered is not clear. Only three months later civil actions started against John; the first was an action on 20 December 1935 brought by L.C. French who claimed 'delivery of a share certificate or market value'. Judgement was given on 6 February 1936 against John who was ordered by the court to deliver the shares by noon on 5 February 1936 or failing such delivery to pay £554 0s. 4d.† being the value of the shares and cost.

A criminal action followed against John in the Supreme Court of South Africa, Natal Provincial Division, before Mr Justice Matthews, acting judge-president. The case was heard in Court C starting on 4 June 1936 and lasting for a week.[8] He was charged on 36 counts of theft consisting of misappropriation of £16,000 from clients. John pleaded guilty on all counts and was sentenced to three and a half years of hard labour. According to the report in the *Natal Witness*:[8]

> ... Worthington found himself with a contingent liability of £130,000.‡ That money represented the amount of share dealings outstanding in respect of which Worthington was liable in Johannesburg. If those shares realised nothing he would have had to pay his agents £130,000. This was the mistake the accused had made. He entered into the transactions and rendered himself personally liable to his agents in Johannesburg without having adequate security from his friends and clients ... He was in the unfortunate position of having debtors who would not pay and creditors who would not wait ... There was no evidence in the case that Worthington was in the position of the scheming man who misappropriated large sums of money, kept them hidden, served his sentence and enjoyed his ill gotten gains. His position was accounted for entirely by the failure of his clients to pay the money they owed him ...

---

* Equivalent to 16,000,000 man-days of English agricultural labour.
† Equivalent to 1,770 man-days of English agricultural labour.
‡ Equivalent to 42,000 man-days of English agricultural labour.

It is said by members of the family that John's elder brother Thomas Henry Yorke Worthington (Article 4.8) helped repay all debts. During the trial it emerged that John had been betting to a great extent on the racecourse, but that 'his racing money had been kept scrupulously apart from his business money'. The judge, in summing up, said that there was no excuse for the 36 offences. Points in favour of Worthington, however, were that he had exhausted his personal resources in order to minimise his obligations and that before his arrest did everything he could to assist those to whom he owed money. The judge said that he would have proposed to sentence John to five years' hard labour, but in view of the circumstances he would reduce the sentence to three and a half years.

Soon after his discharge from prison, the family moved to Dundee where his elder brother Thomas Worthington (Article 4.8) and his father Yorke Worthington (Article 4.4) were already established. At first the family lived with Mr Bertie Langley on his farm near Danhouser, 14 miles north-west of Dundee, until they made their own home at 51 Bulmer Street, Dundee. John became an accountant with Greenhough and Methardy, auditors. Later he transferred to Acutt and Worthington to run their accounts section, where he remained until 1950 or later.[19] By 1952 John was manager of Dundee Tattersalls, the local branch of the nationwide racecourse betting service. Meanwhile May had become book keeper at the Union Glass Limited factory at Talana, which lies about 1.5 miles north of Dundee. The factory made 64 million bottles and other glass containers a year and then employed 100 Europeans and 700 non-Europeans. In 1952 the family was living at Victoria Street, Dundee, but three years later they were living at 8a Grey Street, Dundee.

John died aged 60 years on 1 May 1955 at Government Hospital, Dundee. The cause of death was cirrhosis of the liver. His funeral service took place the following day at St James's Church, Dundee, and he was buried in the Dundee Cemetery.[18] By his Will dated 27 August 1954, his wife May was to receive the income of his estate until her death or re-marriage. The capital was then to pass in equal parts to their two sons Derrick and Neville Worthington.[11] According to one of his nephews, John had been 'a very humorous and kind man, but rather withdrawn at times'. He had been a keen sportsman, having captained the Zingari cricket team, Pietermaritzburg, and having played rugby football for the Wasp Wanderers. He had been a fine golfer with a handicap of two.

May remained a widow for 15 years until on 3 February 1970, at the age of 67 years, she married James McPherson Fleming, a retired bank messenger. He had previously been married to Gladys Ivy, born Preston, who had died on 9 September 1966 leaving him two sons. The wedding took place at the Old Fort, Durban, May being given away by her elder son Derrick Yorke Worthington. May and James lived in Durban. The marriage lasted for only 18 months, as James died on 21 August 1971 at Durban.[11] By his Will dated 6 May 1971 he bequeathed the whole of his estate to May. May lived for a further 19 years, during which time she returned to Dundee to live at Emoyeni Farm, Dundee, which was owned and run by her younger son Neville John Worthington. She died on 27 November 1990 aged 88 years at Dundee, the cause being cancer of the oesophagus. By her Will dated 18 August 1982, the residue after certain bequests to her grandchildren was divided into two equal parts, one passing to her younger son, Neville Worthington, and the other in three equal sub-parts to the three sons of her elder son, Derrick Worthington, who had pre-deceased her.[11]

John Derrick Worthington's line continues. On the death of Thomas Henry Yorke Worthington (Article 4.8) in 1962, John's elder son Derrick Yorke Worthington became the head of the family, representing at least seven previous generations back to Jonathan Worthington of Old Trafford, Lancashire, England. (Article 1.24). Derrick's line continues; so does the cadet line founded by Derrick's younger brother Neville John Worthington.

4.11 Molly

Molly Worthington, the eldest daughter of Reginald Yorke Worthington (Article 4.4) and the youngest child by Mary Elizabeth Miriam, his first wife, was born at Pietermaritzburg, on 3 October 1904. She was baptised on 6 November 1904 at St Saviour's Cathedral, Pietermaritzburg.[1] She was educated at Wykeham School, Pietermaritzburg, where she matriculated. Her mother died when Molly was 13 years of age, after which she spent the school holidays at Dundee with her eldest brother Thomas Worthington and Louie his wife (Article 4.8). Indeed, Molly lived there after her schooling was complete. Horse-riding was then one of her principal and most loved sports.

On 30 September 1925 Molly married Francis George Payne. Francis was seven years older than Molly, having been born on 29 August 1897 at Glencoe Farm, Glencoe Junction, a village about six miles west of Dundee. (Since 1927 the name has been shortened to 'Glencoe'.) He attended school at Dundee and later Hilton College. He was the only son of Francis John Payne and his wife Louisa, daughter of Charles Matthews of Hex River Valley, Cape Province. Francis senior was 'one of the earliest settlers at Glencoe' and became one of the leading businessmen in the area.[8] When he died in 1920 his estate included the *Glencoe Hotel*, the *Helpmekaar Hotel*, the Glencoe store, and the mill at Glencoe. He owned several farms including 'Glencoe', 'Sweetwaters' and 'Droogmynkee' in the division of Dundee, 'Fairbreeze' in the division of Newcastle, and 'Sterling' in the division of Helpmekaar. He also owned other properties in Glencoe township.[11]

Molly and Francis's wedding took place at St James's Church, Dundee.[20] The consent of Yorke Worthington had been duly given as Molly was three weeks under 21 years of age. Molly bore Francis three sons, namely:

Forenames	Date of birth	Date of baptism
Francis Michael	30 April 1927	29 May 1927
John Terrence	29 May 1929	15 September 1929
Bruce	17 January 1938	

The first two children were baptised at St James's Church, Dundee. No baptism has ever been traced for Bruce, and it was certainly not recorded at St James's Church. A suggestion has been made that the baptism was overlooked because of his father's death when Bruce was aged only eight months.

Molly's husband, being the only son, was in a very privileged position and much was expected of him. Indeed, on his father's death on 4 January 1920 he inherited the 'Glencoe Junction store business' and the 'Helpmekaar property and business', Helpmekaar lying 24 miles south of Dundee. An advertisement of 1923 describes the store as having been established in 1893; it sold 'up to date stocks of draperies, outfits, boots and shoes, stationery, groceries, provisions, general merchandise, wines and spirits'. Louisa retained the remainder of the estate, it being understood in their joint Will that she would 'undertake the care, responsibility and maintenance of our daughters'. Alas, Molly's husband was not as successful in business as had been her father-in-law. One of Molly's half-siblings wrote:

35 *Molly, born Worthington.*

> Frank and Molly were extremely extravagant, ... he didn't do much work and left business to others to manage and was done down.

A brief obituary in the *Natal Witness* said that '... he finally retired from active participation in commercial life'.[8] From 1920 to 1922 he had been described as 'hotel and storekeeper', from 1923 to 1927 as 'general merchant and direct importer', from 1928 to 1931 as 'house and general agent', in 1932 and 1933 as 'general merchant' and from 1933 to 1935 as 'general agent'.[11] There are no further listings of him in the Natal directories. After losing his fortune, Francis worked for a time as a bookkeeper at the glassworks at Talana. At this time he and his family lived at Cornhill Street, Dundee, but later he took a job as weighbridge clerk at The Natal Cambrian Collieries at Dannhauser, living in company accommodation while Molly and the two sons remained in Dundee.[11]

Meanwhile Molly's mother-in-law, Louisa, continued to run her part of the businesses. From 1921 to 1924 she was listed as proprietress of the *Glencoe Hotel*. About 1925 she placed the hotel under other management, but she still held the freehold of the hotel when she wrote her last Will 28 March 1953. In that Will she provided well for her three married daughters, but also made provision for her grandchildren, including the three sons of Molly.[11]

Francis died on 10 October 1938, aged 41 years, at Dundee Government Hospital, the cause being essential hypertension and myocardial degeneration. His residence was then recorded as Cambrian Colliery Boarding House at Dannhauser. The funeral was the following day at St James's Church, Dundee when the pall bearers included Molly's elder brothers Thomas and John Worthington. Members of Toc H took part and recited the Toc H prayer.[8] Acutt and Worthington, solicitors, reported that 'there are no assets whatever in the estate but there will be an amount of approximately £20 representing a gratuitous payment by the Natal Cambrian Collieries ... in lieu of holidays'. However, on 3 December 1958 (20 years after Francis's death), Acutt and Worthington wrote to the master of the Supreme Court to say that 100 shares in African Film Productions Limited had come to light. These shares were transferred to his three sons.

Molly continued to live for a further five years. From 1940 to 1942 she was listed in the directory as a 'boarding-house keeper'. However, she was, at about that time, matron of the Girls Hostel of the Government School at Dundee. Perhaps 'boarding-house keeper' was referring to her role as matron. She died aged 39 years on 16 February 1944 at the Government Hospital.[11] Death came suddenly of 'cardiac failure and hyperpiesis', although the disease had been with her for three years.[9] At the time of her death her residence was listed as in Ladysmith Road. Her funeral service was held the following day at St James's Church, Dundee, after which she was buried at the Dundee cemetery. Her three sons were then aged 16, 14 and six years; their uncle Thomas Worthington became their guardian. Molly had had a short and unhappy life but 'was much loved by her sons and us all ...'.

4.12 Penelope Jane

Penelope Jane Worthington, the second daughter of Reginald Yorke Worthington (Article 4.4) and the eldest child by Adelaide Lucy his second wife, was born on 27 August 1920 at the Sanatorium, Pietermaritzburg, and baptised on 13 January 1921 at St James's Church, Dundee. Her elder half-brother Thomas Worthington and his wife Louie (Article 4.8) were two of the three sponsors. The family was then living at 125 Ladysmith Road, Dundee. Penelope, usually called 'Pen' throughout her life, was confirmed at St James's Church on 7 May 1936.

Penelope was educated at the Holy Rosary Convent, Dundee. This school was founded in 1898 as the first offshoot of the Newcastle Congregation of Dominicans which had been founded in 1896. The school was successful and expanded. In 1909 it acquired the former hotel near the Dundee railway station; in 1922 a new

36 *Penelope Jane, born Worthington.*

house for 100 boarders was added and in 1948 a new three-storey block was built. Seven Worthingtons attended the school – the two daughters of Thomas Henry Yorke Worthington (Article 4.8) and their four contemporary half-aunts and one half-uncle, being the children of Reginald Yorke Worthington by his second marriage. Mrs Ethne Eland, born Williams, wrote in a letter of October or November 1999: 'Pen took the part of the Admiral, was very good and highly amusing in her part … The part suited Pen particularly well …'. Ethne was, of course, referring to Gilbert and Sullivan's light opera *HMS Pinafore*. Ethne had been at school with the Worthington girls, being about three years senior to Penelope; she later returned to teach, and played the piano for the opera. She described Penelope the schoolgirl as plump and vivacious, and said that she and all her sisters 'spoke with pronounced English accents – undoubtedly their mother's'. She and her younger sister Jill (Article 4.13) had the good fortune to be taught music by Sister de Sailes, a French nun. Penelope was a member of the percussion section of the school orchestra, a member of the choir of St James's Church from 1935 and a member of the Amateur Dramatic Society of Dundee from 1937. On leaving the convent she took a course at the Girls' Collegiate School, Pietermaritzburg, a private school which has since amalgamated with the Wykeham to form the Wykeham Collegiate. While at the college she lived with her mother's sister, Beatrice Lawler, in Pietermaritzburg.

Penelope's first job was with Acutt and Worthington, the Dundee firm of solicitors.

At the age of 21 years she joined the South African Women's Auxiliary Air Force to take part in the Second World War. She made an oath of her allegiance to King George VI on 7 August 1942 at Voortrekkerhoogte and served as airwoman, first as staff at the Vathalla WAAF Camp and from 15 June 1943 at the Air Force Headquarters Station at Pretoria. She took her discharge on 18 October 1943 following marriage. She was awarded the War Medal (1939-45) and the Africa Service Medal. In the service records she was described as fair with blue eyes, 5 feet 3 inches tall.[31]

On 17 March 1943 Penelope married Captain Charles Newport Saville, by special licence, while he was on leave from the 46th South African Armoured Car Regiment of the Union Defence Force. The marriage took place at St James's Church, Dundee, when Penelope's home was recorded as 85 Ladysmith Road, Dundee, and Charles's as Ashdene Farm, Dundee.[8] Charles had been born on 12 December 1916, the second son of Edgar Cowley Saville and his wife Florence Ophelia, daughter of Alfred Walter Simms. Edgar and Florence farmed at 'Ashdene' about 10 miles south-west of Dundee on the Wasbank road – the name 'Ashdene' having been taken from the home of the Simms family in England where Florence had been reared. The Savilles were the first sugar planters in the north of KwaZulu where the family are still farming. Percy Saville, a brother of Edgar, founded the Illovo Sugar mill. Edgar Cowley Saville was the sixth son of Joshua Saville and his wife Helen, daughter of Isaac Cowley. Helen's brother Alfred Sandlings Cowley (later Sir Alfred Cowley, Kt, OBE, speaker of the Legislative Assembly of Queensland, Australia) had, as a young man, also been a sugar planter in Natal.[32] Joshua Saville had been born on 29 March 1833 at Birstall, West Yorkshire, England, his ancestors having resided in West Yorkshire for several generations.

Charles had chosen law for his career and served his articles with Acutt and Worthington where he probably first met Penelope. In 1935 at the age of 18 years he joined, on a part time basis, B Squadron of the 2nd Regiment Natal Carbineers – a mounted regiment carrying short rifles. He was promoted to sergeant soon afterwards and in 1938, at the age of 22 years, received his commission as second-lieutenant. Charles was promoted lieutenant in 1940 after attending the qualifying course at Roberts Heights (later renamed Voortrekkerhoogte). Roberts Heights is near Pretoria and is the headquarters of the Union Defence Force. Mobilisation notices were issued on 9 September 1940 and the regiment was converted to an armoured car unit as part of the South African Tank Corps. He was then sent for further training at Kaffirs Krall, near Sonderwater, north of Pretoria, the Transvaal. In March 1941 the unit moved to Rhodesia and then proceeded in convoy to

Kenya where they integrated with the Imperial Light Horse to form the 6th Armoured Car Regiment. On 3 June 1941 they moved by rail to Mombasa from where they sailed by cargo ship to the Suez Canal. On 21 August 1941 he was promoted temporary captain and placed second-in-command of the Headquarters Squadron stationed at Melfa. In November 1941 Charles's unit went into action for the relief of Tobruk, Libya, and then proceeded to penetrate the German lines as far as El Agheila. In June 1942 Charles was moved to be second-in-command of C squadron which was then attached to the 50th British Division. He saw action again in the tank battles at Cauldron, east of the Gazala Line. While in battle, the 150th Brigade, of which C Squadron was part, was surrounded by the enemy and was eventually obliged to surrender. However, on orders from Headquarters, C Squadron was part of the force which broke out in what became known as the 'Gazala Gallop' just before the enemy closed the gap. Later that year Charles was placed in command of C Squadron.

In July 1942 General Bernard Law Montgomery (later Field-Marshal, Viscount Montogmery, KG, GCB, DSO, Hon DCL, HonLLD, DL) was placed in command of the Eighth Army. This was one of a number of changes aimed at stepping up action and achieving victory in the Middle East. While preparing for the Battle of El Alamein, C Squadron's role was to patrol the southern flank and reconnoitre no man's land. The battle commenced on 22 October 1942 and brought final victory for the allies south of the Mediterranean. Charles then returned to South Africa for a few months' leave, during which time he married Penelope. On 1 September 1943 he was promoted to war-substantive captain and later that month embarked for Khatatba, Egypt, and in April 1944 proceeded to Italy with the 12th Brigade to take up a sector of the Gustav Line (the German line then held across Italy). Battle commenced on 11 May 1944 when 2,000 allied guns opened fire, followed by the advance on Rome which was successfully taken on 4 June 1944. The following day Charles was promoted to temporary major on taking command of a company. In October 1944 he took part in three attempts to take Monte Stanco, Italy, the third being successful. In respect of one of the earlier attempts it was written:[33]

> Major Saville – in pulling back his men of D'Coy had managed to link up on the night. Enemy pressure was too strong, however, and when fierce hand-to-hand fighting led to such confusion that supporting weapons could no longer engage the enemy with safety, a D Coy platoon was overrun …

Charles was released from service on 25 October 1945 and awarded five medals: Africa Star, Italy Star, Defence Medal (British), War Medal 1939-1945 and Africa Service Medal.

In 1946 Penelope and Charles moved to 10 Paterson Street, Newcastle, about 34 miles north-west of Dundee. Charles entered into partnership with

Edward Jubal Edmonds in Anderson and Edmonds – an old established firm of solicitors described as 'attorneys, notaries public and conveyancers'.[19] Penelope and Charles produced five children, namely:

Forenames	Date of birth	Date of baptism
Jeffrey Charles	5 February 1947	21 September 1947
Stuart Worthington	2 February 1949	16 July 1950
Mark	22 April 1952	25 January 1953
Ann Penelope	16 April 1953	20 December 1953
Sally Diana	8 April 1957	2 November 1958

All five baptisms were at Holy Trinity Church, Newcastle.[20]

Penelope joined the Newcastle Amateur Dramatics Society and the Newcastle Golf Club. She was ladies' champion of the golf club in 1950, 1954, 1961 and 1964, having also been ladies' captain in 1950. One year she became Northern Natal Ladies' Golf Champion. Penelope was also involved in politics with the United Party. In 1951 they moved to a larger house with 48 acres of land off Victoria Street, about four miles out of Newcastle, where they lived for the next 30 years. Again, they renamed the house 'Ashdene'. The land had been part of a farm called The Anchorage which had been divided into 20-acre plots ready for sale. Charles had purchased one of them and promptly sold the old house standing on it with part of the land; he then purchased two more plots on which stood Ashdene.

Edward Edmonds had left the partnership by 1960, when the firm's address was 88 Scott Street, Newcastle.[19] Charles was then the senior partner with W.M. Crook as his partner. By 1974 there were three solicitors in the firm – Charles, T.J.I. Botha and L. du Toit. Charles remained with Anderson and Edmonds until he retired on 31 August 1981. Described as the 'doyen of Newcastle's practising legal profession' he was given a retirement lunch by the Standard Bank and there presented with a pair of gold cufflinks to mark his long association with the bank; the firm had served the bank as solicitors for 91 years.[34] Penelope was then beginning to suffer from motor neurone disease. On retirement they moved to 5 Matapan Drive, Westville, Natal, where they lived for the rest of Penelope's life. Their son, Stuart Worthington Saville, solicitor of Stuart Saville and Company Inc. of Newcastle took over Ashdene and six acres of land. Charles sold part of the remainder and used the proceeds to add roads and services to the other part which he then sold in half-acre plots as residential building sites.

Penelope died on 14 July 1990 at Durban, the cause being the motor neurone disease coupled with chronic active hepatitis.[11] Her funeral service was at St Elizabeth's Church, Westville, and she was cremated the same day.[35] Her ashes and a memorial plaque were placed in the Garden of Remembrance at St Elizabeth's Church. She had been 'reserved and gentle and loved by all'. Mrs Ethne Eland, her old school colleague, recalled that Penelope was a good raconteur; 'she could tell a story like no one I know'.

Charles returned to Newcastle in November 1993 to be nearer to members of his family. He lived with his daughter Mrs Ann Penelope Poulton at 19 Mercurius Street – one of the half-acre plots from Ashdene. He died on 29 January 2001 at the age of 84 years.[8] His funeral service was held on 3 February 2001 at Holy Trinity Church, Newcastle.

4.13 Jill Elizabeth

Jill Elizabeth Worthington, the third daughter of Reginald Yorke Worthington (Article 4.4) and the second child by his second wife Adelaide Lucy, was born on 2 January 1922 at home in Dundee, and baptised on 29 June 1922 at St James's Church, Dundee. She was confirmed on 7 May 1936 at St James's Church, with her elder sister Penelope. She was educated at the Holy Rosary Convent, Dundee, where she played all the sports and excelled as a swimmer. In fact she won the Girls' Inter-School Diving competition when competing for the convent at the Newcastle High School Annual Swimming Gala in 1938. She took the part of the hero in the convent's production of *HMS Pinafore* which later toured Natal. Her elder sister Penelope took the part of the admiral (Article 4.12). After leaving school she became a typist while continuing to live with her parents at 85 Ladysmith Road, Dundee. Later she worked for Maurice Alexander, accountants of Durban.

On 5 December 1942, at the age of 20 years and with her father's consent, Jill married Christiaan Botha. He was then aged 23 years having been born on 28 April 1918 at Vryheid, about 27 miles north-east of Dundee. His home was nearby at 91 Ladysmith Road, but he was then serving with the South African Air Force as a ground engineer. He was the eldest son of Louis Botha, insurance agent of Dundee, and his wife Maria daughter of William Matthew Friend, a farmer of Stryfontein near Utrecht.[11] Louis was in turn the son of Christiaan Botha and nephew of General Louis Botha, commandant-general of the Transvaal forces during the Boer War, later first prime minister of the Transvaal and later still the first prime minister of the Union of South Africa. The wedding took place at St James's Church, Dundee.

37 *Jill Elizabeth, born Worthington.*

Jill and Christiaan produced one daughter who was born at Dundee and baptised at St James's Church:

Forenames	Date of birth	Date of baptism
Patricia Ann	9 September 1943	2 January 1944

The marriage did not last long; it is said that they did not live together after the honeymoon. Jill and her daughter went to live at Moodie Street, Umkomaas, presumably with her parents who by then had retired and were living at Moodie Street. Christiaan went his way and in due course managed the family farm at Vryheid which he and his sister had inherited from their father. Divorce proceedings started in the Supreme Court of South Africa, Natal Provincial Division, on 29 March 1945 when Christiaan declared that Jill had deserted him in January 1944. By then Christiaan was serving in the Middle East as an air-sergeant in the Royal Air Force. The divorce was granted on 8 August 1946 or later, Jill having custody of the child subject to reasonable access by Christiaan. Christiaan was to pay £5* a month until the child reached the age of 18 years.

On 5 October of the same year, Jill married Victor Rafe Fountain Howes at the Presbyterian church, Commercial Road, Durban. The wedding was heralded in the press without reference to the name Botha, the caption to the entry being 'Howes – Worthington'. Rafe was an accountant of Durban. He had on 9 June 1940 joined the 1st Battalion of the Mounted Rifles to fight in the Second World War.[36] After initial training he embarked at Durban on 4 October 1940 on SS *Llangibby Castle*. He was declared missing on 17 June 1942 and confirmed a prisoner of war on 19 November 1942. After nearly three years as a prisoner in Italy and Germany he was released on 12 April 1945 to rejoin his unit for six months before being discharged on 6 September 1945. He was awarded four medals – the 1939-45 Star, the Africa Star, the 1939-45 War Medal and the Africa Service Medal.[37] Rafe had been born at Durban on 18 September 1920, the elder of two sons of Walter Fountain Howes and his wife Florence Natalie Roe, born Scott, who had been married at St James's Church, Dundee. Walter's mother, Florence, had lived for 100 years, having been born on 30 September 1892 and died on 17 October 1992.[11] Walter was a journalist who had been born in Northampton, England.

Jill and Rafe lived at 155 Hartley Road, Durban, where Rafe's father also lived, but their marriage was short-lived and childless. Jill died aged 26 years on 27 June 1948, the cause being carcinoma of the pancreas. She had been cared for at the Berea Nursing Home, Durban, and Rafe was with her when the time came. The funeral took place the following day at the Crematorium, Stellawood, when she was the first known descendant of the Worthingtons of Failsworth to be cremated.[12] By her

---

* Equivalent to 15 man-days of English agricultural labour.

Will dated 10 April 1948 she bequeathed the whole of her estate to Rafe and appointed him guardian of Patricia Ann Botha – then only four years of age.[11]

Rafe later married Florence Maude, born Todd, by whom he had two daughters. When he retired, he and Florence moved to 39 Westville Road, Westville, Natal. She died on 30 November 1995. Rafe had been an underwriting member of Lloyd's of London during the disastrous years of that institution. Jill's younger sister, Betty (Article 4.15), wrote on 31 May 1996 of Rafe:

> ... his second wife has just died and he has come back to us all. The poor chap has lost everything; he was a name at Lloyd's.

He died aged 79 years on 12 March 1999. By his Will dated 2 June 1992, he bequeathed his estate to his wife, but as she pre-deceased him the estate was divided between his two daughters equally. He made a provision that no beneficiary should succeed to his or her share of the capital until reaching the age of 28 years.

4.14 Alethea Nan

Alethea Nan Worthington, the fourth daughter of Reginald Yorke Worthington (Article 4.4) and the third child by Adelaide Lucy his second wife, was born on 1 May 1923 at home in Dundee and baptised on 2 October 1923 at St James's Church, Dundee. She was confirmed on 5 June 1939 at St James's Church. Nan suffered an accident while on holiday with her family in Umkomass when she was aged six years. She was jumping on her bed when she fell onto a cracked china jug and washbasin which broke and lacerated her face from her left eye to the top of her lip. The scar caused her to be self-conscious while she was young but it became less noticeable in her adult years. Nan was educated at the Holy Rosary Convent, Dundee, where she excelled at all sports.

On 29 April 1941, at the age of 18 years, Nan enrolled for service in the South African Women's Auxiliary Air Force (SAWAAF), and served for the remainder of the Second World War.[36] After training in Pretoria she served at the Air Force station near Pretoria, being described in the records as 'WADC full time volunteer'. During that time she represented Southern Transvaal at hockey and athletics. She received her demobilisation papers on 26 November 1945 at which time she had the rank of corporal. She was discharged on 2 March and awarded the War Medal (1939-45) and the Africa Service Medal.

In 1946 Nan moved to Southern Rhodesia (now called Zimbabwe), joined the Women's Army, and played hockey with the national team. This military service came to an end when in 1963 the federation of Southern Rhodesia, Northern Rhodesia and Nyasaland failed and the Women's Army was disbanded. She then moved to Gosport, Hampshire, England. She and

38 *Alethea Nan Worthington.*

her friend Mavis, whose husband was studying to be an Anglican priest, bought a village shop there and lived above it. However, after Rhodesia made its Unilateral Declaration of Independence (UDI) on 11 November 1965, Nan hastened to Salisbury to work for Ian Douglas Smith's government, and was attached as a civilian to the Rhodesian Regiment, F Company, as the public relations representative. Thus she continued throughout the post-UDI conflicts. When Ian Smith's regime succumbed and Robert Gabriel Mugabe (later President Mugabe) became prime minister in 1980, Nan had to leave the country. She returned to South Africa that year and worked as a civilian clerk for the South African Defence Force in Durban until the end of 1982 when she retired because of ill health.

Nan died on 7 January 1983 of lung carcinoma at the age of 59 years, having been a heavy cigarette smoker.[11] She was then living at the home of her younger brother Timothy Yorke Worthington (Article 4.16), at 31 Lansdowne Drive, Westville, Natal. She died there in the presence of Charles and Penelope Saville (Article 4.12) and Betty Crosskill (Article 4.15). Her funeral service was held on 10 January 1983 at the South Chapel, First Avenue, Durban, followed by cremation at the Stellawood Crematorium, Durban. She had remained unmarried, her fiancé having been killed during the Second World War. One of her siblings described her as tall, graceful, well groomed, an excellent sportswoman, a tomboy and secretive.

4.15 Betty Yorke

Betty Yorke Worthington, the fifth and youngest daughter of Reginald Yorke Worthington (Article 4.4) and the fourth child by Adelaide Lucy his second wife, was born on 16 September 1929 at home in Dundee, Natal. She was baptised on 16 February 1930 at St James's Church, Dundee, and was confirmed there on 14 May 1944.[20] Also being confirmed at the same ceremony were Betty's younger brother Timothy (Article 4.16) and her half-nephews Michael and John Payne (Article 4.11).

She was educated at the Holy Rosary Convent, Dundee, from 1934 to 1946, boarding for the last year as her parents had moved to Umkomass.

On leaving the convent at the age of 16 years she took a book-keeping course for a year at the Durban Business School. For that she travelled daily from her parents' home in Umkomass, some 25 miles south-west of Durban. Her main sports were tennis, swimming, hockey and golf, and she played for the Southern Natal hockey team in the 1949-50 season.

At the age of 20 years she had a serious car accident at Clansthall, near Umkomass, receiving severe head injuries. She was an invalid for a year at home, under the care of her mother. She then became a bookkeeper at the Umkomass estate agency.

On 14 March 1953, at the age of 23, Betty married Alfred Fenton Crosskill (normally known as 'Bill'). He was a coffee planter of Sharok

39   *Betty Yorke, born Worthington.*

Estate, about 15 miles form Arusha in Tanganyika Territory (now part of Tanzania). They had met in Natal when he was on leave there in 1951. Alfred was 22 years older than Betty, having been born on 23 March 1907 at Beverley, East Yorkshire, England. He was educated as a boarder at the Old College, Windermere, Cumbria. He then proceeded for naval training on HMS *Conway* because his grandfather Edwin Fenton planned that Alfred should join Edwin's shipping company, Brown and Atkinson, at Hull, East Yorkshire. Although Alfred spent two years at sea, he chose farming as his career. After attending a business college, he and his brother William Edmund Crosskill went to Tanganyika in 1928 to serve as pupils on the 'Ndurama', the coffee estate of Sir Milsom Rees, then managed by Sir Milsom's son. This estate consisted of 500 acres of land on the slopes of Mount Meru, the extinct volcano 4,565 metres high, about 40 miles west of Kilimanjaro. Sir Milsom Rees, KCVO, DSc(Hon), FRCS, was laryngologist to King George V and had several interests in East Africa.[38] In 1936 Alfred, with the aid of two partners in England, purchased his own estate called 'Sharok' 15 miles east of Arusha in Tanganyika. Sharok consisted of 350 acres bordered by the River Usa in the south, its tributary the River Tengeau in the north and forest elsewhere. Coffee was the main crop but 100 acres were arable for crops such as seed beans; also 70 acres were devoted to pawpaw for the production of latex which was kiln dried on the estate.

Alfred succeeded in buying out his financial partners after about two years. He won the 1951-2 Challenge Cup awarded by the Tanganyika Coffee Growers' Association Limited for the best coffee of the year. Alfred had previously married Molly Bruce Steele on 31 August 1936 in Nairobi, Kenya, and they had produced two sons, namely William Bruce Crosskill and James Fenton Crosskill. That marriage was unsuccessful and was dissolved in 1951 at Dar-es-Salaam because of incompatibility and alcohol. Alfred retained custody of the children but they boarded at St Peter's School, York, for much of their schooldays. Alfred's father was William M. Crosskill, an agricultural engineer and director and co-founder of The Star Brush Co. of Holloway, London. His father was Edmund Crosskill, mayor of Beverley from 1880 to 1882. Edmund's father was William Crosskill, the town's mayor in 1848: his bust still stands in the Guildhall at Beverley. Edmund's brother Alfred Crosskill was mayor in 1876. These brothers Edmund and Alfred have been described as 'the dictators of Beverley'.[39] The family had owned and managed the metal-working and machinery manufacturing business known since 1863 as 'William Crosskill and Sons'.[40] William had built the Beverley Ironworks in Mill Lane by 1825 and by 1853 employed 800 men on a seven-acre site, mainly manufacturing agricultural machinery. One of their contracts was to supply horse-drawn ambulance wagons for the Crimean War. The company was sold to the Yorkshire Cart and Waggon Co. Ltd in the 20th century.

Betty and Alfred's wedding took place at the District Office, Dar-es-Salaam. They lived at the Sharok Estate for a year, but by 1954 the political situation was in turmoil because of Mau Mau terrorism in neighbouring Kenya. They sold the farm and sailed from Dar-es-Salaam on the MV *Africa* of the Lloyd Tristino Line. The ship was anchored off-shore for security, and passengers boarded by rope ladder from a lighter. Thus they returned to Natal, landing at Durban and settling at Umkomaas. Betty and Alfred produced two children:

Forenames	Date of birth	Date of baptism
Jeremy Yorke	3 September 1954	February 1955
Jane Philippa	8 April 1956	

Jeremy was born at Scottburgh and baptised at Christ Church, Umkomass, but Jane was born in New Zealand and baptised at Hamilton, New Zealand. The family had moved there in June 1955, sailing on SS *Ceramic* of the Shaw Saville Line from Cape Town. They encountered the tail end of a cyclone on the way and had to disembark at Melbourne, Australia. They then had to travel to Sydney by rail because the dockers at Sydney were on strike. From Sydney they sailed to the north island of New Zealand on the ship *Wanganella*. After a month of searching there they bought 'The Lake Farm' at Whiteku, 20 miles north of Hamilton. The farm had 400 acres of land surrounding a central lake. It produced dairy products, beef and sheep. Alfred and Betty owned the farm for three years, during which time output doubled. They sold the farm and returned to Natal on the SS *Dominion Monarch* in October 1958, settling at 3 Hendon Road, Westville, near Pietermaritzburg. About 1960, Alfred ('Bill') entered into partnership with Donald ('Don') to form Bildon Products (Pty) Limited – a business which supplies aluminium sections and fabricates aluminium building components such as windows, balustrades and shower cubicles. The firm established agencies in the larger cities of South Africa. Alfred was the design partner for a year, after which he bought out his partner and became the sole owner. Many of the designs were patented and the business grew successfully.

The Crosskills lived at Westville for 15 years during which time they were much involved with local sport. Betty played golf at the Royal Durban Golf Club and tennis at the Westville Country Club. Alfred was president of the tennis section of the Westville Country Club from May 1964 until 1967. He also served on the general executive committee from 28 July 1964 until 28 June 1965 and was a member of the planning and development committee. Although the club had existed since 1960, it was formally opened by the mayor on 15 October 1965, by which time all four members of the Crosskill family were members. Alfred and Betty remained members until 1977.

Betty was also involved in politics, being treasurer of the Westville branch of the United Party for many years until they left the district in 1977. She took the turn as chairman for a year. The family escaped the hot and humid season at Westville by spending weekends and holidays on the Mbona Mountain Estate – a private reserve, 17 miles from Howick, Natal, on the Reit Vlei Road, and 5,100 feet above sea level. There they built 'The Cottage, 1 Pine Lodge' for which they generated their own electricity. The whole estate, over which they had free access, comprised 2,000 acres of grassland and forest with two tennis courts, a bowling green and seven reservoirs stocked with trout. The rich variety of wildlife included zebra, wildebeest, bles-bok, reedbuck, bushbuck and monkeys. The Crosskills themselves kept horses.

Alfred retired in 1975 at the age of 68 years, handing over control of Bildon Products to his son Jeremy. Alfred and Betty then sold their Westville house and retired to the principality of Andorra in the Pyrenean mountains, between Spain and France – a tax haven. There they joined Alfred's brother William and Elizabeth his wife who had already retired from farming in Kenya. He had been a member of Kenya's Legislative Council and minister of tourism. Society in Andorra was dominated by retired British civil servants, military officers, farmers and others from the colonies. Betty considered that they drank too much, and she wrote: '... It seems to me that everyone wanted to party, so I never settled and after four months we left and motored through France and ferried to England where we stayed for four months – too cold'.

Thus they returned to Natal once more, sailing on the SS *Windsor Castle* of the Union Castle Line. They then resided at their cottage on Mbona Mountain Estate for the next '15 wonderful years'. By 1990, however, Alfred was suffering ill health, so they moved to 15 Duncan Drive, Westville, to be nearer to the leading hospitals. This house had a swimming pool and half an acre of garden.

Alfred died of cardiac failure on 19 November 1991 at Pietermaritzburg.[11] He was cremated at Dove's Crematorium, Pietermaritzburg, and his ashes were spread on Mbona Mountain Estate. By his Will dated 3 November 1988, the whole of his estate passed to Betty.[11] However, he expressed the wish that Betty should in turn leave all his residential property to their daughter Jane to compensate for the fact that all his shares in Bildon Products (Pty) Limited had already passed to Jeremy. He drew to the attention of his executor the fact that all four of his children were capital beneficiaries of the Will trust of his father, William Crosskill.

In 1992 Betty moved to a cottage standing in the grounds of the home of her daughter Jane (now Mrs Moffat) at 66 Methuen Road, Westville. In the spring of 2001 she moved again to join her younger brother Timothy Yorke Worthington, a widower (Article 4.16) at 1 Milner Street, Umkomaas. Their house is kept by two daytime servants. As the last living woman of her generation of the Worthingtons of Natal, she is fulfilling the matriarchal role and has researched much South African information for this history.

4.16 Timothy Yorke

Timothy Yorke Worthington, the fourth son and youngest child of Reginald Yorke Worthington (Article 4.4), being the only son by Reginald Yorke's second wife Adelaide Lucy, was born on 16 January 1931 at home in Dundee, Natal. He was baptised on 7 June 1931 at St James's Church, Dundee, and confirmed on 14 May 1944 at the same church. He attended the kindergarten of the Holy Rosary Convent at Dundee. Although the convent was a girls' school, the junior section was open to boys. From there he moved to Kearsney College at Botha's Hill, about 17 miles north-west of Durban on the main road to Pietermaritzburg, where he boarded in Finningly House. He was a member of the school's first cricket team.

On leaving school in 1947 Timothy studied accountancy for two years, being articled to du Plessis and Fairbury and studying at the Durban Business College. Although accountancy turned out not to be the discipline he wished to follow, the course provided a base of financial knowledge which proved invaluable throughout his career. In 1949 or 1950 Timothy started his career by joining the staff of St Bernard's farm at Swartburg in East Griqualand. The farm had about 2,000 acres of land producing mainly dairy products, sheep and potatoes. However, the farm was sold about a year later, bringing Timothy's work there to an end. He then joined his half-nephew Neville John Worthington (Article 4.10) at Glenlyon Farm, Wasbank, about 11 miles south-west of Dundee. Neville had leased Glenlyon from his uncle Thomas Henry Yorke Worthington (Article 4.8) for £500* a year. The farm had about 1,200 acres and concentrated mainly on dairy products. Thomas, who was then 40 years older than Timothy, wrote on 31 October 1951:

> ... I have my half-brother with me, Timothy, ... I have not seen him for a few years and he has become interested in farming, but the place where he was ... was sold and I now have him at my farm. I'm afraid he was rather spoilt by his parents and four sisters and takes his life rather easily. So far I find his greatest interest in life is golf which he plays off a handicap of two. However, he is a good active youngster and not difficult to handle.

Timothy and Neville working together was an interesting experiment; Timothy was senior by being Neville's half-uncle while Neville was senior in age by two years. The relationship did not work well and they soon went their separate ways. One report says Timothy remained for five months while another report recorded two years.

From 1953 to 1956 Timothy managed Victor Joshua Samuel Crookes' 600-acre sugar farm near Umzinto on the coast, about 36 miles south west of Durban. Victor had other interests in cane sugar production in Natal, being part owner of Crookes Brothers Limited, C.C. Smith Limited and Natal Cane By-Products Limited.[11] The cut cane was sent to the sugar mill at Sezela about nine miles further south-west along the coast. Timothy was known for being hard on his farm workers, and occasionally lost his temper with them. On one occasion the labourers turned on him, causing a severe head injury before he saw them off with the help of the induna. The injury caused epileptic fits for some years, and migraines for life. One of his siblings said that Timothy was in a number of fights, as he 'always defended the underdog'.

In 1956 Timothy was invited by a friend, Max Charney, to join him in the glass distribution business. Thus Timothy left farming and joined the Natal Glass Works at Durban as a sales representative. The company imported, processed and distributed flat glass. He loved the work and thrived in the business, remaining there for about eight years. In 1964, at the age of 33 years, he and a golfing friend started their own business known as Worthington Biggs, each holding 50 percent. The business distributed glass and entered into glazing contracts.

On 7 February 1959 Timothy married Patricia Eileen, the only child of Lawrence Joseph Ryan and his wife May, born Holding, of 1006 Arnleigh Esplanade, Durban. Lawrence was a fire engineer who had been born at Hollinwood near Failsworth, Lancashire, England, and had married May on 10 June 1933 at Oldham, Lancashire. Patricia was three years younger than Timothy, having been born on 13 March 1934. The wedding

---

* Equivalent to 500 man-days of English agricultural labour.

40 *Timothy Yorke Worthington in 1961. Leyden's cartoon, by courtesy of his son, Mr Murry Leyden.*

took place at Durban. There were no children of the marriage which lasted for only six years. They were divorced on 14 January 1966 having separated in May or June 1962 while living at Westville. At the court hearing each claimed that the other had deserted.[41] Timothy was then described as company director, and Patricia as clerk.

Throughout, Timothy had been a sportsman. He started playing golf at the age of seven years, and 10 years later was the champion of the Umkomaas Golf Club. While at Kearnsey College he played cricket and Rugby football. Later he played cricket for the Umkomass team, and later still for the Natal Southern District team. In 1951, aged 20 years, he won the Northern Natal golf championship and later won the Southern Natal and Zululand championships. He was a member of the Natal golf team for many years, being the youngest ever to be appointed. His greatest golfing achievement came in 1963 when he won the Natal Amateur Championship. While playing the final for this at the Royal Durban Golf Course, he was watched with anxious approval by his eldest half-brother Thomas, who had won the same championship in 1915 (Article 4.8). The international-prize-winning cartoonist John Leyden (generally known as Jock Leyden) published the following lines after the style of Sir Noel Coward's lyric 'Mrs Worthington' written in 1931:[42]

> Don't put your daughter on the stage Mrs Worthington,
> Don't put your son on the links;
> He will age Mrs Worthington, sage Mrs Worthington,
> Waiting for the putt that never sinks.

It is thought that the daughter of the stage was Timothy's third half-cousin, Margaret Elizabeth Valentine Worthington (Article 8.3).

On 9 July 1966, at the age of 35, Timothy married Margaret Lindsay, only daughter of John Thomas Glover, electrician, and his wife Margaret, born Eden. Margaret junior was 15 years younger than Timothy, having been born on 22 May 1946 at home, 2 Hillside, 348 Carrie Road, Durban. She had been educated at the Gordon Road Primary School,

Durban, followed by Our Lady of Fatima Convent, Durban North. She matriculated in 1965 at the Durban Technical College. Being a minor, Margaret married with her parents' consent. The wedding was by civil ceremony at the Methodist Church, Durban North. Their nuptial home was 31 Lansdowne Drive, Westville, where their first daughter was born; but they had moved to 12 Furndale Avenue, Westville by the time the second daughter was born:

Forenames	Date of birth	Date of baptism
Lindsay Fiona	16 August 1967	24 October 1967
Phillippa Jane	15 August 1969	23 November 1969

Both daughters were baptised at the Methodist Church, Westville.

Margaret was good at many sports, excelling at tennis, squash and horse riding. She was captain of the Technical College's first tennis team for three years and was the first person to be awarded the college colours. In 1975 she joined the Westville Defence Club which specialised in armed and unarmed combat. By April 1976 she had been selected as one of the club's team of six practical shots, concerned with moving targets and shooting while on the move and running an assault course.

All members of the team made their own ammunition. She was selected a member of the 1979 South African Team at the World Practical Shooting Championships held at Roodepoort, Transvaal. She came second shooting with a colt 45, and was awarded her Springbok colours.[43]

41 *Margaret Lindsay, born Glover.*

Timothy continued to run Worthington Biggs for about five years until, in 1969, he sold the firm to Plate Glass Co., plate glass distributors whose head office was in Johannesburg. Timothy was appointed managing director – Natal – of the enlarged business. After six years he left Plate Glass to be appointed, on 2 November 1975, managing director of Durban Glass and Timber Merchants of Sydney Road, Durban. This distribution company, with the nickname 'Home of 1001 Things' catered for a wide range of customers, from large building contractors to DIY

42 *Elgin Glass, Durban, in 1985, and Timothy Worthington by courtesy of the Mercury, Durban.*

enthusiasts. The company had a sales turnover of R.6,000,000 a year. In January 1985 the company was acquired by the Elgin Merchandising Group, and was accordingly re-named Elgin Glass, Natal. Elgin Merchandising was, in turn, part of the Murray & Roberts Group.[44] Timothy remained managing director of Elgin Glass, but soon afterwards he left to form a specialist glass company called Saf-T-Lite to develop and produce security, bullet proof and sound resisting glass in which layers of toughened glass are bonded together by the meniscus process with polyester resin. Such glass was later sold by the company in thicknesses ranging from 4.5 to 100mm.[44] On 11 March 1986, only a year after the birth of Saf-T-Lite, the company was acquired by Africa Glass and Timothy was appointed managing director – Natal. He was still responsible, amongst other duties, for the development of Saf-T-Lite, which was successful and, in time, exported to many other countries. In due course, Timothy was appointed managing director of the whole of Africa Glass which had branches in Cape Town, Port Elizabeth, Bloemfontein, Rustenburg, East London, Johannesburg, Pretoria, Newcastle and Durban. There were also overseas subsidiary companies in the USA, United Kingdom and Germany. As Africa Glass dominated the South African glass sector, Timothy was given the nickname 'Mr Glass of South Africa'.

In 1988 Timothy became a founder member of the Selborne Country Club at Pennington, near the coast 42 miles south-west of Durban. He proposed that Hole 10 on the 18-hole course should be designed for Par 5; the suggestion was adopted and the hole has since been known as the

'Tim Worthington'. On one occasion Timothy dismissively remarked to Margaret that she would never play golf. She proved him wrong by taking lessons and practising at the Club. Indeed, one of her long shots scored a direct hit on him.

In 1991, Timothy and Margaret left their nuptial home, moving to 3 Cedar Close, Cedar Ridge, 37 Jan Hofmeyer Road, Westville. In August 1992, they and two other couples set out to tour the British Isles, one object being to play golf on the principal courses. Alas, on 30 August 1992 Margaret, aged only 47 years, died suddenly from a brain haemorrhage while staying at *The County Lodge Hotel*, Beauly, Inverness-shire, Scotland. Timothy found her body in the bathroom and brought her home by air. Many messages of condolence were published in the *Natal Daily News* including one from the directors and staff of the Africa Glass group:[42]

> We are deeply shocked and sorrowed by the sudden death in Scotland of Margaret, beloved wife of our close colleague, Tim. Over the years we have admired and loved her for her special qualities that made her unique in our Natal operation, and indeed throughout the Group. Our deepest sympathy and condolences to Tim and his daughters at this time of their deep sorrow and tragic loss.

She was cremated on 7 September 1992 and her ashes were spread at the Selborne Country Club. Her memorial service was held on 9 September 1992 at the Westville Methodist Church. Their friend Richard Watt, in delivering the eulogy, said:

> ... Margaret lived every day to the full. She was vibrant, vital, caring, loyal friend, unselfish, wise ... Margaret was perhaps the most complete person I have ever known ... Every life she touched, she enriched. We thank God for her.

Timothy continued to live at Cedar Ridge, Westville, until 1994 when he moved to Scottburgh. In 1995 he returned to Westville, moving first to Albergie Place and then to 6 Canel Drive – a plot attached to the home of Phillippa Jane Phillips, his younger daughter. Finally he moved to 1 Milner Street, Umkomaas, where he was joined in the spring of 2001 by his widowed sister, Betty Yorke Crosskill. He had retired from full-time duties by 2002, but continued to serve Africa Glass as vice-chairman.

CHAPTER 5

FAMILY OF ARTHUR GEORGE WORTHINGTON OF THE TRANSVAAL

5.1 Arthur George

Arthur George Worthington, the third son of Charles Worthington and Penelope Jane his wife (Article 3.36) was born on 21 August 1872 at 7 St John's Grove, Battersea, London, England. His life has already been discussed (Article 4.6). He had one daughter by Alice Maude his first wife and two further daughters by Myra Dorothea his second wife.

SECOND GENERATION – DAUGHTERS OF ARTHUR GEORGE

5.2 Penelope Maude

Penelope Maude Worthington, the eldest daughter of Arthur George Worthington (Articles 4.6 and 5.1) by Alice Maude his first wife, was born on 29 January 1898 in South Africa.[1] For the first 18 months of her childhood she lived with her parents in an apartment at Marston House, Kerk Street, Johannesburg, the Transvaal. On 5 October 1899, following the outbreak of the Boer War, she and her mother hurriedly moved to Cape Town while her father joined the British Forces.

In October 1905, at the age of seven years, Penelope was sent to England with her mother and a nurse so that the mother could receive treatment for alcoholism at the Keeley Institute. Alas, the mother was not cured and soon deserted the family, being divorced six years later. It appears that Penelope stayed with her Aunt Mabel (Article 4.5) in England for about two months in 1905 or 1906 after which Penelope's father visited and placed her in boarding school in Brighton. She was there for the next five years, during which time her mother visited her only once. Her father visited frequently during the period 1906 to 1908 while he was living in England. At the age of nearly 12 years, Penelope left the school and returned to Natal to live with her father.

Penelope married in Cape Town William Vallancy Simkins, the fourth son and youngest child of another William Vallancy Simkins, stockbroker, and Dora Helen Adelaide (born Ford) his wife.[2] In turn William senior had been born in England the son of Anthony Lacam (or Lacarn) Simkins and Belinda Isabella his wife. William junior and Penelope produced two children, namely:[3]

Forenames	Date of birth
William Vallancy	Before 1939
Daphne Valerie Worthington	Before 1940

PEDIGREE 5 – FAMILY OF ARTHUR GEORGE WORTHINGTON OF THE TRANSVAAL

Alice Maude, dau. of ... Stevens; b. circa 1868, m(1) 1891 William Henry Carney, dissolved 1896 without issue

$\stackrel{1}{=}$

Arthur George Worthington, Captain; b. 1871, m(1) 1896, dissolved 1911, m(2) 1911, d. 1916. *(Pedigree 4 & Arts 4.6 & 5.1)*

$\stackrel{2}{=}$

Myra Dorothea, dau. of Jacobus George Fischer; b. 1882, re-m. circa 1951, d. 1973

Penelope Maude; b. 1898, m. William Vallancy Simkins & had issue, d. 1959. *(Art. 5.2)*

Heather Myra; b. 1912, m. 1945 Roger Leonard Smith & had issue, dissolved 1971, d. 1979. *(Art. 5.3)*

Blanche Louise; b. 1914, m(1) 1937 Ludwig Willem John Hartman & had issue, dissolved 1944, m(2) 1953 Daniel McCallum & had issue, d. 1990. *(Art. 5.4)*

Thus, the names William Vallancy were retained for the third generation. Penelope's husband died on 9 May 1939 but she lived for a further 20 years. During that time she served as a 'casual lady clerk in the Expenditure Section of the Systems Manager's office of South African Railways at Pretoria', Transvaal. On 22 December 1955 she was admitted to Wes-Koppies Mental Hospital, Pretoria. On 4 January 1956 a court order was made to further detain her there as she was incapable of managing her own affairs.[4] She died at the hospital on 9 June 1959. By her Will dated 2 September 1952 she bequeathed all her assets, other than a coral ring, to her daughter Daphne Valerie Worthington Hamman.

5.3 Heather Myra

Heather Myra Worthington, the second daughter of Arthur George Worthington (Article 4.6) and the elder child by Myra Dorothea his second wife was born on 29 December 1912 at Pretoria.[1] Her father died suddenly three weeks before her fourth birthday, and as he had not rewritten his Will since his second marriage the whole of his estate descended to Heather's elder half-sister, Penelope (Article 5.2). Heather, her younger sister Blanche and their mother were therefore destitute and became dependant on the care of relatives.

Heather's early education was at the Star of the Sea Convent in the Paarl area of Cape Province. The convent was not far from de Oude Plantage – the vineyard of her maternal grandparents, the Fischers. Indeed, Heather and several cousins had many memorable holidays there. Later, the family moved to Salisbury, Southern Rhodesia (now called Harare,

43   *Heather Myra, born Worthington.*

Zimbabwe), where she completed her education at Salisbury High School. Later she returned to Pretoria, lived at 206 Union Park Gate, Church Street, Pretoria, and joined the staff of Customs and Excise. She became engaged to be married to Leztnew Wentzel, a son of family friends, but he died before the planned wedding.

On 22 August 1945 Heather, then aged 32 years, married Roger Leonard Smith. He was six years younger than Heather, having been born on 25 March 1919 at Benoni in the Transvaal. Roger was the son of William Smith who had been born at Washington, County Durham, England, and Martha, born Ferreira, who had been born at Klerksdorp,

Transvaal. William had worked at the gold mines until 1927 when the family moved to Southern Rhodesia – living at Bulawayo for the first year, then at Shabani for two years and finally at Selukwe. In September 1939, following the outbreak of the Second World War, Roger joined the 2nd Battalion Rhodesia Regiment. He was one of the first troops to leave Rhodesia, being seconded to the 1st Battalion Cheshire Regiment to serve in the Sahara Desert under General Archibald Percival Wavell (later Field-Marshal Earl, GCB, CMG, MC, PC, LLD). The battalion was sent on to Malta where they lived on starvation rations for a time when the island was under siege. He met Heather first at Margate, Natal, while on 28 days' home leave in 1943. Following the leave he was seconded to the 1st/11th Anti-Tank Force, serving in Italy until the end of the war. For most of the war he was in the front lines, and was awarded seven medals. In 1945 he returned to Selukwe where he became a diamond driller at the Wanderer Mine. Roger had played Rugby football for Southern Rhodesia, he had won the Selukwe area golf championship and played water polo for the Midlands.

Heather and Roger's wedding took place at St Michael and All Angels' Church, Sunnyside, Pretoria.[5] They produced two children, namely:

Forenames	*Date of birth*
Beverley Dawn	12 July 1947
David Roger	12 September 1949

The family's home was first at Selukwe, about 160 miles south-west of Salisbury, where Roger was employed at the Globe and Phoenix mining company at Que Que. Later they lived at Turk Mine and Matapos. Dawn, as Mrs Dawn Palmer, recalled those happy days in Southern Rhodesia saying that Heather was a talented homemaker, gardener and dressmaker, and that Sundays were the customary baking days. In 1958 the family moved to Salisbury, Roger working for the Irrigation Department. However, the political situation in Rhodesia was then becoming intense so in 1962 they moved to Durban, Natal. Roger took a position with the Durban Municipality, but at only half the salary he earned in Rhodesia. Later he became estates manager of the Durban Country Club.

In 1967 Heather joined Christ Church, Addington, an area near the sea front of Durban and 'committed her life to Christ'. She spent much time working for the church, the younger of the children having reached the age of 18 years. Alas, her marriage broke up and on 26 March 1971 the final order of divorce was issued by the Durban and Coast Local Division of the Supreme Court of South Africa.[5] Heather had been plaintiff in the suit, so thereafter Roger had to pay maintenance and reasonable medical expenses to Heather. Later that year Roger married Dorothy Welthagen and they lived at 88 Feilden Drive, Carrington Heights, Durban, until 1990 when Roger retired. They then moved to Aberdeen in the Karroo, Cape Province.[6]

After the divorce Heather worked at Addington's Community Development for three years before retiring. Her retirement was devoted to the church, classical music and her family – especially her grandchildren. In 1978 Heather suffered an inoperable cancer. For the last month of her life she was nursed at the home of her son David and his wife Diane at 1 Swales Crescent, Pinetown, 10 miles west of Durban. She died on 6 March 1979.[7] The funeral service was held on 9 March 1979 at 125 Old Main Road, Pinetown, followed by a private cremation.[8]

5.4 Blanche Louise

Blanche Louise Worthington, the third daughter of Arthur George Worthington (Articles 4.6 and 5.1) and the younger child by Myra Dorothea his second wife, was born on 26 December 1914 at Waterkloof, Pretoria, Transvaal, and baptised on 7 September 1915 at Christ Church, Arcadia, in the diocese of Pretoria. Throughout her life Blanche was known as 'Blarney' by her family and close friends. Her father died before she reached the age of two years, and as her mother did not remarry until late in life, Blanche virtually grew up without a father. During her second year the family moved to Cape Town where she started her education. Later they moved to Salisbury, Southern Rhodesia, where she attended Salisbury High School. Later they returned to Pretoria where Blanche completed her education at the Pretoria Girls' High School. She then commenced work at the Reserve Bank at Pretoria, while living at 1268 Park Street, Pretoria.

On 28 April 1937, at the age of 22 years, she married Ludwig Willem John Hartman, a 'newspaper representative' of 52 Twelfth Street, Orange Grove, Johannesburg. In his father's death notice, the name Willem was written Wilhelm, but he was usually known as Wim. He was then 28 years of age, having been born in Holland about 1909. He was the elder son of John Philip Hartman, a farmer, and Emile Mathilde Sophie (born Rabe) his wife.[7] Blanche and Willem's wedding took place at St Luke's church, Orchards, Johannesburg, after which they lived at 3 Louisweg, Orchards, Johannesburg, Willem being a journalist on the Afrikaans newspaper *Die Faderland*. They produced four daughters, namely:

Forenames	Date of birth
Deanne Myra	3 August 1938
Naurene June	9 February 1941
Patricia Worthington	23 June 1942
Pamela Worthington	23 June 1942

Deanne was born at home and Naurene's birth was registered at Johannesburg. The twins were identical.

The marriage did not last long. On 22 August 1943, when the twins were less than 14 months of age, Willem left home. Blanche started proceedings in the Supreme Court of South Africa, Witwatersrand Local Division, accusing Willem of 'unlawfully and maliciously' deserting her. The divorce was granted on 11 April 1944. Blanche had custody of the children and Willem was ordered to pay £10* for the maintenance of each child until such child married or reached the age of 21 years. Willem then married Helen Mary, usually called 'Peggy', and they lived in Cape Town. There he was a freelance journalist, writing and holding interviews for *Die Huisegeneot, Sarie Marie* and other local newspapers. His second daughter, Mrs Naurene Leppan, has said that: 'he also wrote romantic novels which brought in a good financial return, but that he wrote many of these novels under a series of pseudonyms such as 'Ferona Bosman', 'Louwrens de Kock' and 'Selma le Roux'.[9] The name 'Bosman' was, of course, that of

44 *Blanche Louise, born Worthington.*

an illustrious line of Blanche's ancestors (Article 4.6). Peggy was a dress designer; she had a dress shop in Cape Town where two seamstresses were employed.

Following the divorce, Blanche and her four daughters moved to Moodie Street, Umkomaas, Natal. Her daughter Naurene remembers a 'lovely large house across the road from Bissett Park'. Blanche became the receptionist at the *McCallum's Golf Course Hotel*, Umkomaas, owned and operated by Daniel and Mary McCallum, Daniel being a member of the town board.[10] An advertisement for the hotel described it as:

> The most popular and up-to-date hotel in the district... Music daily and Dances every Saturday night with the Hotel Orchestra ...

The McCallums sold the hotel about 1945 and acquired *St Bernard's Peak Hotel* at Elange, Swartberg, Griqualand East, Cape Province, 80 miles south-west of Pietermaritzburg. Blanche and her family remained in Umkomaas for two years; in 1949 and 1950 she was operating a taxi service there. However, in about 1952 they moved to join the McCallums. Naurene recalled the 'idyllic years on the farm surrounding the hotel where they all learnt to ride horses and came and went as they pleased'. Mary McCallum died about 1949, and on 12 June 1953 Blanche and Daniel were married at the Magistrates' Office, Peitermaritzburg. Daniel was 11 years older than Blanche, having been born on 1 May 1903 at

---

* Equivalent to 24 man-days of English agricultural labour.

Charlestown, Natal. The surnames of Blanche's four children were informally changed from Hartman to McCallum, but following Daniel's death in 1982 the surnames of the twins reverted to Hartman, as they moved to live with Willem until their respective marriages. Soon after their marriage Daniel, Blanche and family moved to Carge's Post Guest Farm outside Kokstad, Griqualand East, where Blanche ran a market garden. During that period, Blanche sang in Gilbert and Sullivan operettas and Daniel played the clarinet in the Kokstad Orchestra. After nearly five years or marriage, Blanche and Daniel produced a son, namely:

Forename	Date of birth
Angus John	4 April 1958

While Daniel's three hotels had provided a handsome way of living, none was successful financially. Daniel had been trained and had started his career as a teacher but had diverted into hotel management, probably with the encouragement of his first wife Mary, who had endless energy and resourcefulness. Thus it was that, in about December 1953, the family moved to Pietermartizburg and Daniel returned to teaching. But he and Blanche retained their tastes for business; Daniel had a 'business of duplication of examination papers for the National Education Department' while Blanche grew strawberries for the market.[7]

In 1965, Blanche, Daniel and Angus then aged seven years sailed by Union Castle Line to the United Kingdom for a five-month tour of the British Isles and continent of Europe. They purchased a car in England and Angus was placed as a boarder at Fancourt School, Weymouth, for a term. After the tour they returned with the car by Union Castle Line. Daniel played the clarinet again in the regimental band of Royal Natal Carbineers and the orchestra of the Pietermaritzburg Philharmonic Society. In 1973 the McCallums were living at 409 Bulwer Street, Pietermaritzburg.

Daniel died on 17 August 1982 after residing for some time at Victoria Memorial Homes, Retief Street, Pietermaritzburg. His last Will was dated 23 November 1978, but there remains on record a codicil to an earlier Will.[7] This codicil shows that he bequeathed the duplicating business to Margaret Mary, his daughter by his first wife Mary.

Blanche lived as a widow for a further seven years. In 1985, at the age of 71 years, she toured Scandinavia and made another brief visit to England. In 1988 she was living at 3 Lorraine Road, Pelham, Pietermartizburg, and later she moved to The Gables, New England Road, Pietermartizburg. She died on 14 February 1990 of a cardiac arrest at the home of Angus her son and Heather his wife. Her funeral service was held at the Presbyterian Church, Pietermaritzburg, which was filled to capacity. During the service a tribute was paid to her work for the community. She was buried at the Mountain Rise Cemetery, Pietermaritzburg. By her Will dated 2 August 1985, she made bequests to the Leprosy Mission and Tape-Aids for the Blind.[7] After certain family bequests, the residue of her estate was to pass in equal parts to her children, Deanne, Naureen and Angus. The twins Patricia and Pamela were not beneficiaries, perhaps because they had moved to live with their septuagenarian father, and reverted to their original surname.

CHAPTER 6

LINE OF JONATHAN ERNEST
WORTHINGTON OF BEAUMONT

6.1 Jonathan Ernest

Jonathan Ernest Worthington, the fourth son and youngest child of
Charles Worthington and Penelope Jane his wife (Articles 3.36 and 4.1)
was born at Wood Green, London, England, on 31 August 1873. His
life has already been discussed (Article 4.7). He had one son by Alice
Constance his wife.

SECOND GENERATION –
SON OF JONATHAN ERNEST AND ALICE CONSTANCE

6.2 Noel Ernest

Noel Ernest Worthington, the only son of Jonathan Ernest Worthington
and Alice Constance (Articles 4.7 and 6.1), was born on 22 July 1898 at
Inginga, Eston, Mid Illovo, Natal.[1] He was baptised on 6 August 1899
at St Margaret's Church, Mid Illovo.[2] 'Inginga', meaning 'rich man' in
Zulu, was probably the name of the house or farm; it has not yet been
traced. Noel's father died on 7 March 1905, when Noel was under seven
years of age, after which he and his mother moved to Dalton Hall,
her family's home – where they lived for a few years. When Noel was
aged 10 years, his mother went to Grey's Hospital, Pietermaritzburg,
to pursue a nursing career for three years. It was probably during this
period that Noel went to live with one of his mother's sisters at Eshowe
in Zululand. He was educated at Eshowe Junior School and later at
Weston Agricultural College, Mooirivier, Natal. The college had been
founded in 1914 by John William Moor, brother of Sir Frederick Moor,
the prime minister of Natal, and brother-in-law of Mary Elizabeth Miriam
Worthington (Article 4.4), Noel's aunt-in-law.[3] Noel must have been one
of the earliest pupils there, leaving at the age of 17 or 18 years. Records
exist only from 1916 and there is no mention of him.

After a period of farming, Noel joined the Natal Veterinary Department
as a dipping inspector and was stationed at Incevati, near Pietermaritzburg.
By 1928 he had been posted to Impendhle during which time he lived
at Furth. It may have been then that he met his future wife. At the
age of 30 years, on 19 December 1928, Noel married Amy Kathleen
the eldest of the nine children of William Root and his wife Catherine
Regina, born Els.[2] Amy was then 26 years of age, having been born on
11 April 1902 at Alicedale, Impendhle. William Root's was one of the

176

PEDIGREE 6 – LINE OF JONATHAN ERNEST ERNEST WORTHINGTON OF BEAUMONT, NATAL

Jonathan Ernest Worthington; b. 1873, m. 1897, d. 1905. *(Pedigree 4 & Arts 4.7 & 6.1)* ╤ **Alice Constance**, dau. of Charles Hornby; b. 1875, d. 1961

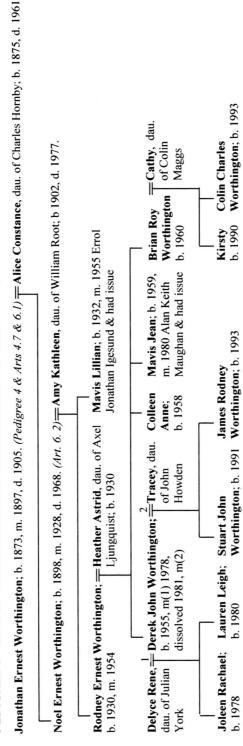

Noel Ernest Worthington; b. 1898, m. 1928, d. 1968. *(Art. 6.2)* ╤ **Amy Kathleen**, dau. of William Root; b 1902, d. 1977.

Rodney Ernest Worthington; ╤ **Heather Astrid**, dau. of Axel
b. 1930, m. 1954   Ljungquist; b. 1930

Mavis Lillian; b. 1932, m. 1955 Errol
Jonathan Igesund & had issue

Delyce Rene, ╤¹ **Derek John Worthington;** ╤² **Tracey,** dau.
dau. of Julian   b. 1955, m(1) 1978,   of John
York   dissolved 1981, m(2)   Howden

**Colleen
Anne;**
b. 1958

Mavis Jean; b. 1959,
m. 1980 Alan Keith
Maughan & had issue

**Brian Roy
Worthington**
b. 1960

╤ **Cathy,** dau.
of Colin
Maggs

Joleen Rachael;
b. 1978

Lauren Leigh;
b. 1980

**Stuart John
Worthington;** b. 1991

**James Rodney
Worthington;** b. 1993

Kirsty
b. 1990

**Colin Charles
Worthington;** b. 1993

pioneer families of Natal whose farm was at Loteni in the Impendhle District in the west of Natal at the foot of the Drakensberg Mountains.[4] The farmhouse still stands but the farm is now the Loteni nature reserve under the National Parks Board. Amy's grandfather, John Root, had travelled about 1844 from Dagenham in Kent, England, to settle at Boston in the Mpendhle District of Natal, where he was granted 10,000 acres of land. Amy's mother, Catherine, was the daughter of a neighbouring farmer in the Impendhle District. Noel and Amy were married at the Magistrates' Office, Pietermaritzburg.[5] According to the Social and Personal column of the *Natal Witness* the honeymoon was spent at Durban.[6] They produced two children, namely:

Forenames	Date of birth
Rodney Ernest	17 July 1930
Mavis Lillian	29 July 1932

On 25 April 1933, Noel's address was given as 'Private Bag, Wilberfoss', but in 1934, at the age of about 36 years, he acquired a smallholding of 27 acres at Beach Terminus, near Port Shepstone. He and Amy lived there for the remaining 34 years of his life. He continued to serve the Natal Veterinary Department and, at the time of his death, was described as 'assistant stock inspector (smear examiner)'. He died on 22 September 1968 at Addington Hospital, Durban, aged 70 years, the cause of death being terminal pneumonia and carcinoma of the prostate. He was buried at the Marburg Cemetery, about 10 miles west of Port Shepstone. He had played golf and cricket, and his main hobby was woodwork – especially furniture-making. Examples of his stinkwood tables remain with his descendants.

Amy continued to live as a widow for a further eight years, during which time she moved to 48 Droten Park, Port Shepstone. She died on 16 February 1977 at Pzotea Park, Port Shepstone, and was buried at the Marburg Cemetery.

Noel and Amy, who had been married in community of property, had made a joint Will dated 12 May 1953. After both deaths, their estate was to be divided equally between their two children. There was a provision, however, that Noel's mother, Alice Worthington, should be provided with a house for the remainder of her life 'in the building wherein she has hitherto resided' or in a cottage which was planned to be built on an acre of land. In the event, this provision was not needed as Alice had died in 1961 – before either Noel or Amy.

Noel's cadet line continues and has multiplied to form another cadet line (Pedigree 6). Both grandsons of Noel – Derek John Worthington and Brian Roy Worthington – have sons.

CHAPTER 7

LINE OF ANDREW JUKES WORTHINGTON OF LEEK

7.1 Andrew Jukes

Andrew Jukes Worthington, the fourth son and youngest child of Jonathan Worthington (Article 3.11) but the only son of Jonathan by Elizabeth his second wife, was born on 22 December 1810 at Moorhill, Stourport, and baptised the next day at St Michael's Church, Lower Mitton. His life has already been discussed (Article 3.30). He and Sarah Booth, his wife, produced three daughters and three sons.

SECOND GENERATION – FAMILY OF ANDREW JUKES AND SARAH BOOTH

7.2 Laura Eliza

Laura Eliza Worthington, the eldest child of Andrew Jukes Worthington and Sarah Booth his wife (Articles 3.30 and 7.1), was born on 6 September 1840 at Horton Hall, Horton, Staffordshire. She was baptised on 14 October 1840 at St Michael's Church, Horton.[1] When she was three years of age, the family moved from Horton Hall to Hallscroft, Spout Street (now called St Edward Street), Leek, Staffordshire, where she resided for the rest of her childhood.

On 26 May 1864, at the age of 23 years, Laura married Major William Adams of The Oakes, Wolstanton, Staffordshire.[2] William, then 30 years of age, belonged to an ancient family of North Staffordshire potters. His father, of The Hall, Greenfield, Tunstall, was the senior partner of the Adams pottery at Greenfield. His mother was the elder of two co-heiresses of Jesse Breeze, proprietor of Greengates pottery at Tunstall.[3] His uncle, Edward Adams of Basford Hall, near Stoke-on-Trent, Staffordshire, married the other co-heiress. William's grandfather, another William Adams, of Fenton Hall, Staffordshire, was proprietor of potteries in Stoke-on-Trent. The family had been pottery manufacturers continuously for 10 generations and there is evidence of potters in earlier generations.[4] Indeed, William's ancestor, William Adams of Sneyd, Staffordshire, and his elder brother Richard were potters in 1448.[2]

Besides his principal career as a potter, William had other business interests. In 1862, he and his brother Thomas with five others formed a company to build retorts at Bradwell Wood, near Newcastle-under-Lyme, for the purpose of making crude oil from cannel coal and shale

PEDIGREE 7 – LINE OF ANDREW JUKES WORTHINGTON OF LEEK, STAFFORDSHIRE

Andrew Jukes Worthington; b. 1810, m. 1839, = **Sarah Booth**, dau. of Thomas Pemberton, JP; b. 1814, d. 1873. *(Pedigree 3 & Arts 3.30 & 7.1)* | d. 1877

Philip Jukes Worthington, Major; b. 1851, m. 1889, d. 1902. *(Arts 7.8 & 8.1)* == **Margaret Elizabeth**, dau. of Sir Thomas Wardle, Kt, JP, chevalier de la Légion d'Honneur (France), officier dans l'Ordre des Palmes Académique (France); b. 1869, re-m. 1904, d. 1949

Pedigree 8

Laura Eliza; b. 1840, m. 1864 William Adams, Lieut-Colonel, JP, & had issue, d. 1914. *(Art. 7.2)*

Ernest Andrew Worthington, JP; b. 1842, m. 1880, d. 1896. *(Art. 7.3)* == **Margaret Maude**, dau. of Thomas Pearson, Captain; b. 1859, re-m. 1898, d. 1927

Emily Jane; b. 1843, m. 1867 Thomas Davenport Goodman & had issue, d. 1913. *(Art. 7.4)*

Alice Elizabeth; b. 1844, d. 1916 un-m. *(Art. 7.5)*

Walter Moore Worthington; b. 1845, d. 1885 un-m. *(Art. 7.6)*

Rose; b. 1847, m. 1874 Augustus Theodore Wirgman, Archdeacon, Lieut.-Colonel, VD, DD, MA, DCL (USA), Hon. Chaplain to King Edward VII, d. 1926 without issue. *(Art. 7.7)*

Sybil; b. 1884, d. 1959 un-m. *(Art. 7.9)*

Guy Jukes Worthington, Lieut-Colonel, MA; b. 1886, m. 1933, d. 1978 without issue. *(Art. 7.10)* == **Kathleen St. Claire**, dau. of Thomas McClure, MD (Belgium), FRCSI; b. 1904, d. 1980.

Gwenyth, MBE; b. 1888, d. 1955 un-m. *(Art. 7.11)*

Roger Ernest Worthington, Rear-Admiral, CB, DSC, ADC to King George VI; b. 1889, m. 1926, d. 1967. *(Art. 7.12)* == **Primrose**, dau. of Henry Edgar Grace, Admiral, CB, commander of the Order of St Anne (Russia), commander of the Order of Redeemer (Greece), Croix de Guerre (France); b. 1905, d.1999

Freda Margaret; b. 1891, d. 1966 un-m. *(Art. 7.13)*

Andrew Yorke Worthington, Major; b. 1895, d. 1950 un-m. *(Art. 7.14)*

Margaret Rose; b. 1927, d. 1996 un-m. *(Art. 7.15)*

Sybil Rosemary; b. 1930, m. 1965 Arthur Allen Douglass & had issue. *(Art. 7.16)*

Patricia Grace; b. 1934, m. 1969 Donald Rae Ward, MSc (USA), & had issue. *(Art. 7.17)*

and then converting the oil into paraffin and other hydro-carbon products. The company was a financial success until 1869 when petroleum oil wells were opened up in America. William rode to hounds with the North Staffordshire Hunt. On 4 January 1860 he had been appointed captain in the newly formed 9th Company, Staffordshire Rifle Volunteers, and with other officers was presented to Queen Victoria at St James's Palace on 7 March 1863. He was promoted major on 28 November 1863.

45   *Laura Eliza, born Worthington.*

The wedding took place at St Luke's Church, Leek. A newspaper reported:

> Early in the morning gay flags were to be seen flying on the towers of both the parish and St Luke's Church, and hanging from the upper windows of many houses in the principal streets. Opposite Mr Worthington's house in Spout Street, a fine triumphal arch, composed of evergreens and flowers, had been erected, while the road, footpath and all the windows of the neighbouring houses were crowded with hundreds of inhabitants of 'the metropolis of the moorlands', anxious to see and be seen. Near the principal entrance of St Luke's Church, in which the marriage ceremony was performed, a similar arch might be seen surrounded by a crowd of people, who, by their manner and conversation, seemed to be deeply interested in the coming event ... an arch of the same materials with a beautiful crown on each side placed at the entrance to the chancel ...

After describing the arrivals of 12 carriages, and the wedding service, the newspaper continues:

> ... On each side of the carpeted way between the church doors and the gates, upwards of twenty girls dressed in white (scholars in the bride's Sunday school class) had previously arranged themselves and, as the happy couple passed to their carriage, sprinkled their path with roses, tulips and fuchsias and other flowers from small ornamental baskets which they held in their hands ... Miss Worthington, by the kind of liberality and deep interest which she had always manifested in the affairs of St Luke's Church and Schools, and in religious and educational matters generally, had secured the affection and regard of a large number of persons both rich and poor. Of Major Adams it can with truth be said that in Tunstall he is looked upon as a model gentleman, being loved and respected by his work people, and possessing the devoted

attachment of the company of rifle volunteers, of which he was, until recently, the captain ... We understand that the wedding party spent a portion of that afternoon and evening at Rudyard Lake, where dancing, boating and other amusements were carried on with a great spirit. A considerable number of Mr Worthington's workpeople, who had been allowed a day's holiday with a day's wages into the bargain, also visited Rudyard Lake and spent a very enjoyable evening.

On return from their wedding tour, Laura and William were met at Longport railway station by the Tunstall Rifle Volunteers with band, who escorted the couple to their newly acquired home at Porthill, in the parish of Wolstanton, near Tunstall. Beer was served and William addressed the company before it marched off. There was also a peal of bells at the parish church. Laura and William produced four sons and two daughters, namely:

Forenames	Date of birth	Date of baptism
Laura Mildred	5 May 1865	1 June 1865
Cecily Janet	24 September 1866	15 November 1866
William	12 August 1868	30 September 1868
Hugh Worthington	12 February 1870	10 April 1870
Frank Pemberton	3 April 1872	26 May 1872
Percy Walter Lewis	24 January 1875	4 April 1875

All the children were born at Wolstanton and baptised at St Margaret's church, Wolstanton.

On 27 June 1867 William was promoted lieutenant-colonel to command the 1st Battalion, Staffordshire Rifle Volunteers. He was the chief bailiff of Tunstall in 1872, in which year he was appointed a justice of the peace for Staffordshire. On 27 May 1879 he was appointed a commissioner of taxes. He was a member of the Wolstanton and Burslem Board of Guardians and a Conservative county councillor. He was a warden of St Margaret's Church, Wolstanton for more than 20 years, and chairman of the building committee of the new St Andrew's Church at Porthill.

William died on 5 March 1905 and was buried at St Margaret's Church. A clock tower was built to his memory in Tunstall Park by subscription of 'the workpeople and firm of William Adams and Co of Greenfield'.[2] Laura lived as a widow for nine years, and died aged 73 years on 27 April 1914 at Moreton House. Moreton House, formerly called Wolstanton Hall, had been the home of Laura and William for many years – at least since 1902. She was buried beside her husband at St Margaret's Church. In the church is a memorial inscription to her and a stained glass window to the memory of 'William and Laura Eliza Adams'. Another stained glass window to their memory is in the chancel of St Leonard's Church, Woore, Shropshire. She had been a committee member of the North Staffordshire Nurses' Institution, an executive committee member of the Wolstanton Nursing Association, and president, until her death, of the North Staffordshire (Potteries) division of the Soldiers' and Sailors' Families' Association.[5] The Reverend C.J. Winn wrote of her in the *Wolstanton Parish Magazine*:[6]

> ... She was a devout and consistent church-woman, with a keen sense of duty. If work wanted doing she took her share in it at once and as a matter of course. She was never a grumbler, and never in opposition, but was always the firm and loyal supporter of the five vicars of Wolstanton she has known. She never missed attendance at God's house and was regular and devout in the receiving of Holy Communion and all other religious duties. She set a consistent example in her own home, and endeavoured to make her household all that a Christian home should be. She was a friend of the poor, and not only freely gave to them, but worked for them and spent many long hours patiently and industriously stitching and sewing for them ... She was a beautiful example of solid English piety at its best ...

By her Will, Laura placed her assets in trust for the benefit of her two unmarried daughters for their lives. The assets were then to pass in equal parts to her six children or their families.

7.3 Ernest Andrew

Ernest Andrew Worthington, the eldest son of Andrew Jukes Worthington and Sarah Booth his wife (Articles 3.30 and 7.1), was born on 3 March 1842 at Horton Hall and baptised on 5 June 1842 at St Michael's Church, Horton.[1] In 1843 or 1844 he moved with his parents and two sisters to Hallscroft, Spout Street, Leek. Ernest was educated at the Macclesfield Grammar School, Cheshire about 12 miles north-west of Leek.

On 18 August 1859, at the age of 17 years, he was commissioned cornet in the Queen's Own Royal Staffordshire Yeomanry, then under the command of Lieutenant-Colonel Sir William Bagot, Bt, 3rd baron Bagot (later honorary colonel of the regiment). Ernest was promoted to lieutenant on 6 October 1862. His position as second-in-command of the Leek Troop is shown by a record of the regiment's eight-day annual camp at Lichfield, Staffordshire in June 1867. At the review taken on Whittington Heath by Lieutenant-Colonel Macnaghten of the 8th Hussars, the Leek Troop consisted of Captain Sergisson Smith in command, Lieutenant Worthington, Cornet Davenport and 37 other ranks; Lord Bagot had a total of 672 on parade. Ernest served the regiment for 13 years, retiring in 1875. According to F.A. Crisp in his *Visitation of England and Wales* published in 1917, Ernest achieved the rank of captain.[1] The same statement is made in the pedigree given in *Burke's Landed Gentry* published in 1952, though this would have drawn on 1917 sources. However, no corroborative evidence of the rank has come to light. Perhaps he retired with the substantive rank of captain, or perhaps he was then acting captain. Acting rank would be compatible with a statement made in his obituary notice of 1896 that, at the time of his retirement, he had been practically in command of the company.

On 1 July 1868, Ernest entered into partnership with his father, Andrew Jukes Worthington, as a silk manufacturer in A.J. Worthington and Co. He was then aged 26 years and had, no doubt, already been a trainee and manager in the business for several years.[7] In the partnership, Andrew retained the whole freehold of the property, the steam engine and the gearing, while the business itself and the profits therefrom were allocated 75 per cent to Andrew and 25 per cent to Ernest. The agreement provided that Ernest should draw no more than £300* a year and that all the remainder of his part of the profits be placed to Ernest's capital account in the business.

Andrew died on 21 December 1873, only five years after the partnership had been established – Andrew then being 63 years and Ernest 31 years of age. Ernest was then in complete control of the business but owed Andrew's executors and trustees £12,002 6s. 2d.† being the value of Andrew's stake. As empowered by the terms of Andrew's Will, the executors agreed to leave their capital in the business in return for a mortgage on the property, boiler, steam engine and other principle plant – the agreement between Ernest and the other three executors being recorded in a deed dated 30 December 1874.[7] Ernest had to pay interest on the loan at 10 per cent per year, pre-tax. However, after three months' notice by the executors, the principal sum would become payable by eight equal half-yearly instalments, during which period the interest rate would be reduced to five per cent a year on the outstanding amount. In fact, the principal sum was not called for some years, and still stood at £12,002 6s. 2d. in 1888.

Later – certainly by 1875 – Ernest took his younger brother Philip into partnership (Article 7.8). By an indenture of 29 September 1875, Ernest and Philip agreed that Henry Russell of London, a silk agent, should be taken into the partnership from 30 June 1876 – the end of the financial year.[7] The event was celebrated at Ballhaye Park, as reported in a local newspaper of 28 August 1876:

> The occasion was the entrance of Mr Henry Russell, of London, into the firm of Messrs A.J. Worthington and Co, and right well was the event celebrated. The workpeople numbered more than 200, and a large number of personal friends shared in the pleasures of the day. In a spacious marquee, refreshments of a substantial character were provided, while in the Park the materials for recreation were various and ample. The band of the Rifle Corps, in compliance to Captain Worthington, was present and discoursed sweet music at intervals, guiding the feet of the many who preferred dancing to swinging and other recreative means offered in such profusion. The ladies of the party and Messrs E.A. and P.J. Worthington and Mr Russell contributed much to the comfort of the guests by the kindly fashion in which they put them at their ease, sharing in the sports with the greatest heartiness. The weather was of

---

* Equivalent to 3,000 man-days of agricultural labour.
† Equivalent to 120,000 man-days of agricultural labour.

a most favourable kind, until dusk, when a warning shower made the party disperse. This, however, was not done before Mr E.A. Worthington and Mr Russell had addressed a few words of advice and encouragement to the workpeople, on whose behalf Mr Richard Clowes made a suitable reply; and the party separated with ringing cheers for those who had provided and arranged the pleasantest afternoon's entertainment that ever took place at Ballhaye Park.

Henry may have already been the London sales agent for the company. Two trademarks for the partnership were registered in the names of himself, Ernest and Philip.[8] One was *upon a wreath a Goat passant holding in its mouth a sprig of oak fructed* – the crest then in use by the family. The other was the Prince of Wales' Feathers with the prince's motto 'Ich Dien', which was granted for 'sewing silk, machine twist, silk twist and legee twist'. It has been highly prized ever since and is still in use. The circumstances in which the prince gave his consent – or whether such consent was sought – are not known. However, Philip Worthington was then commanding officer of 1 Company (the Leek Company) the 1st Volunteer Battalion (Prince of Wales's) North Staffordshire Regiment (Article 7.8). The inclusion of Henry in the partnership lasted until he died about nine years later. By an indenture of 8 June 1886 Henry's widow assigned his share of the partnership to Ernest and Philip.[2] Henry's capital in the partnership was then £2,963 3s. 8d.; interest was paid to his successors for 13 years – until the last of the capital had been repaid in 1899. A deed of 27 March 1888 confirms that Ernest and Philip were then the only partners, and that, with effect from 30 June 1888, Ernest would enjoy nine-fifteenths of the profits and Philip six-fifteenths.[7]

In 1874 Ernest had been elected churchwarden of St Luke's Church, Leek, at the annual vestry meeting. However, when Thorncliffe church was built, about two miles north-east of Leek, Ernest transferred part of his loyalties there, and became its first treasurer. The communion rails at Thorncliffe were given in his honour, after his death, by his eldest son Guy Jukes Worthington (Article 7.10).

On 30 September 1880, aged 38 years, Ernest married Margaret Maude, the second daughter of Thomas Pearson and Mary Lucy his wife, the youngest daughter of George Robert Clover of Lingdale, Birkenhead, Cheshire (now in Merseyside). Maude was 22 years of age having been born on 23 July 1858 at the Pearson's home, Hillesdon in Torquay, Devon, and baptised on 22 September 1858 at St Mary's Church, Birkenhead. When young she often visited her mother's relations, Mr and Mrs John Ward of Leek, thus meeting Ernest. Thomas Pearson, a businessman, had on 23 November 1854 been appointed a captain in the Exeter and South Devon Volunteer Rifle Battalion. Later, the Pearson family moved to Birkenhead and finally to Northumberland Avenue, Putney, London. The wedding took place at St Mary's Church, Barnes, Surrey.[9]

46 *Ernest Andrew Worthington.*

47 *Margaret Maude, born Pearson.*

On return from their wedding tour, Ernest and Maude were greeted at the mill by 'an interesting and novel spectacle': a local newspaper described 'elaborate decorations of the various workrooms'. In the weaving room a marionette theatre had been fitted above a loom, many miniature actors being moved by the strings of the machine in 'ludicrous and amusing' dances. The Worthington family crest appeared in the braid room. Mottoes were displayed and company trademarks were featured in the decorations, and all the employees wore artificial flowers. The following New Year's Eve, Ernest and Maude returned the compliment with a 'tea party and ball at the mill, to which all employees were invited'. A knife and fork tea was provided in the skeining room after which there was dancing until 2.00 a.m. to music provided by the Leek Volunteer Rifle Band. Ernest's sisters, Alice Worthington and Emily Goodman, were present (Articles 7.5 and 7.4 respectively); so also was Philip Worthington (Article 7.8) and some friends of the family. Ernest and Maude's first married home was Ball Haye Hall. Ernest had retained it as his home after the deaths of his parents. The national census of 1881 shows Ernest and Maude living there with four living-in servants; Henry Russell and his wife Eileen were guests at the time.[10]

48   *The servants at Haregate Hall, Leek.*

The following year, Ernest and Maude moved to Haregate (sometimes called Haregate Hall) which lies in Tittesworth, adjacent to the north of Leek. They produced three sons and three daughters, namely:

Forenames	Date of birth	Date of baptism	Article
Sybil	19 March 1884	25 April 1884	7.9
Guy Jukes	26 February 1886	4 April 1886	7.10
Gwenyth	2 June 1888	1 July 1888	7.11
Roger Ernest	19 November 1889	12 January 1890	7.12
Freda Margaret	11 September 1891	18 October 1891	7.13
Andrew Yorke	29 April 1895	2 June 1895	7.14

All the children were born at Haregate and all were baptised at St Luke's Church, Leek.

On 1 January 1883 Ernest took the oath of allegiance and the judicial oath as a justice of the peace for the county of Stafford. The ceremony took place at the Staffordshire Quarter Sessions held at Shire Hall, Stafford. He served on the Leek bench for the rest of his life.

A Grand Fancy Bazaar was held at the Town Hall, Leek from 13 to 15 October 1885 to raise money for the development of St Luke's Church, three schools – at the church, at Ball Haye Green and at Thorncliffe.

49   *Hillesdon, Leek, in 1913.*

These schools had a total of 600 pupils. Ernest and his cousin William Challinor were the treasurers while Maude and Mrs Berrisford (the parson's wife) were the secretaries of the ladies' committee. Maude, Mrs Beresford and Mrs Bradley also ran one of the six stalls. Entertainments included an orchestral band, Punch and Judy, ventriloquism and a performing giraffe. Philip Worthington (Article 7.8) was a member of the general committee.

In 1885 or 1886 Maude took her part in the making of the Leek replica of the Bayeux Tapestry (Article 7.8). She, Miss Elizabeth Eaton of Etwall, Derbyshire, and Miss Emily Parker (later Mrs Campion) together produced Panel 11.[11]

After 14 years at Haregate, the family moved in 1896 to their new home. They had acquired nine acres, three roods and 13 perches of land adjacent to Mount Pleasant and Buxton Road, Leek, and built their house which they called Hillesdon after the old Pearson home in Torquay. The drive to the house leads off Mount Road.

Sometime after 1886, the Leek Conservatives bought the *Crown Inn* in Church Street, Leek, demolished it, and built in its place a new Conservative Club building. When the foundation stone was laid by Mrs Cruso, Ernest, as president of the club, handed her the silver mallet. Ernest's first cousin Edward Challinor was secretary of the club and was praised for the work he had done for the project. Later that evening there was a Conservative dinner for about 250 people in the Town Hall when Ernest's brother, Philip, gave one of the three responses to the toast to 'The Army, Navy and Reserve Forces'. It was announced that night that Maude had consented to be the first president of the new Leek branch of the Primrose League.

Ernest was a keen educationalist, being one of the original promoters of the Leek High School. He was a manager of the three St Luke's Church schools and treasurer of those at Ball Haye Green and Thorncliffe. He was also a member of the Board of Improvement Commissioners. He had been a trustee of the Leek United Permanent Benefit Building Society (now called the Leek United Building Society) for 29 years and was a member of its management committee. He was also a commissioner of Inland Revenue.

On 7 October 1896, at the age of 54 years, and only a few weeks after moving from Haregate, Ernest died at Hillesdon. His health had been waning for four or five years. His six children then ranged in age from one to 12 years. An obituary notice in a local newspaper reported:

> ... In private life he was a keen sportsman, riding to hounds when young, and always fond of a gun. It has indeed been thought that some twenty years ago he met with a slight accident while hunting, which laid the seeds, in an otherwise vigorous constitution, of the weakness from which he died ...

The funeral service was held at St Luke's Church, Leek. The route from Hillesdon to the church was '... lined by crowds of persons anxious to pay their respects to the deceased ...'. The local newspaper continued 'there has seldom been a funeral in Leek at which there was such a large and sincere sign of sorrow'. The bells of St Edward's Church rang a muffled peal on the Friday and a half-muffled peal on the Sunday. Ernest's body was interred in the family vault at St Luke's Church.

At the regular service held at St Luke's Church the following Sunday morning, the Reverend William Berrisford took his text from 1 Corinthians vii, 7: 'Every man hath his proper gift in God, one after this manner and another after that'. He said that:

> ... The late Mr Worthington was singularly reticent in speaking of religion but ever ready to obey it. No work was ever suggested as being important in connection with the church which he did not unhesitatingly support, even though it demanded a sacrifice of substance and an expense of time and trouble ...

The parson referred to the love and trust which existed between him and his fellow labourers in A.J. Worthington and Co:

> The workmen and workwomen grew old in that firm because they believed in their employers and their employers believed in them. The masters treated their workpeople rather as hearts than as hands ... His

gentle and dignified, ever genial and courteous manner made him an influence for good ...

At the end of the service the organist played *The Dead March* from *Saul* while the congregation stood.

Ernest had made a simple Will on 9 March 1886 – 10 years before his death. The only bequest was to his son Guy Jukes Worthington (Article 7.10), consisting of three heirlooms which had descended from Ernest's great-uncle Richard Jukes of Stourport (Article 3.11). One was a life-size head and shoulders portrait of Richard in oil, another an inscribed silver tankard or loving cup and the third a china bowl inscribed with Richard's initials. All the remainder of Ernest's estate was devised to Maude.

Ernest's younger brother, Philip, was now in effective control of A.J. Worthington and Co, although £11,596,[*] being more than half the capital of the business, belonged to Maude. According to her eldest son Guy Worthington, Maude's father – 'a business man of considerable means and decided views' – told Maude to withdraw the capital for re-investment, adding that he would only support her family if she did. Maude did so 'against her natural wishes' (Article 7.8). A deal was struck in a deed poll of 6 April 1897, by which Philip would pay just half of this amount to Maude by eight equal half-yearly instalments, plus interest, in return for which Maude would release Philip from any further claim. The release was granted by an indenture of 15 October 1900.[7]

On 11 October 1898, two years after Ernest's death, Maude married John Wilson at St Mary Abbots Church, Kensington, London. John was then aged 51 years having been born on 17 March 1847. He was a London businessman whom she had met on a cruise to Norway.[12] Maude protected her family's interests by arranging a marriage settlement which was completed the day before the wedding. Various investments of both John and Maude were put into trust, the trustees being William James Brooks and Ernest's nephews, Frank Pemberton Adams (Article 7.2) and Arthur Worthington Goodman, BD, MA, FSA, rector of St Botolph's, Cambridge (later honorary canon and librarian at Winchester Cathedral). The income of the trust was to be paid to John during his and Maude's joint lives and to the survivor thereafter. On the second death the capital was to be paid in equal parts to the six children of Ernest and Maude. Hillesdon was not put in the trust, being for the inheritance of Guy as son and heir; nor were certain of John's real and leasehold properties in Melbourne, Australia, which were for the inheritance of John's son, George Wilson. When Maude died in 1927 the value of the trust was £15,830 10s. 11d.[†] made up as follows:

---

[*] Equivalent to 93,000 man-days of agricultural labour.
[†] Equivalent to 52,000 man-days of agricultural labour.

Wife's fund (A)	£4,754	12s.	8d.
Husband's fund (B)	11,075	18s.	3d.
	£15,830	10s.	11d.

John Wilson died at Hillesdon on 24 August 1920, and was buried in the Leek Cemetery. After bequeathing his Melbourne properties to George Wilson, all the remainder of his estate was devised in equal parts to Maude and George.

On 19 January 1905 Maude mortgaged Hillesdon in favour of Arthur Frederick Pearson of Claygate Lodge, Claygate, Surrey, and Frances Issette Jessie Pearson (Maude's sister) of 10 Northumberland Avenue, Barnes, Surrey. This was as security for a loan of £2,600[*] at an interest rate of four per cent a year. The reason for the loan is not known, but this was, perhaps, the most costly period for the education of her six children who then ranged in age from nine to 20 years.

Maude was co-founder, with Mrs Cruso, of the 'Cruso Habitation of the Primrose League'. The habitation (or branch), which covered the area of the Leek parliamentary division, held its inaugural meeting in the Town Hall, Leek on 16 October 1886.[13] Maude was elected the ruling councillor and her first-cousin-in-law Godfrey Davenport Goodman was elected secretary (Article 7.4). Maude was a member of the Leek Unionist Association executive. On formation of the Leek Women's Unionist Association she was elected chairman – a post she held for the rest of her life. For many years she attended the annual national Conservative Party conferences. She was founder and first president of the St Luke's Ladies' Working Party. She took a keen interest in the Mothers' Union, being the enrolling member for the Alstonfield and Leek deaneries. For many years she was the rural deanery presiding member and was instrumental in forming several new branches. When she retired from active involvement with the Union, the Countess of Harrowby, on behalf of members, presented Maude with an illuminated address of thanks. During the latter part of the First World War, Maude undertook the placing of young boys on farms in Staffordshire and Cheshire for the Boys' Country Work Society. She was also vice-president of the Girl Guides for the county of Stafford.

Maude died at Hillesdon on 4 May 1927 aged 68 years. A local newspaper of 14 May 1927 reported that the immediate cause of death had been heart failure following 'indifferent health during January and February'. She had had her breakfast and was in bed writing letters, calling a meeting of the Leek Women's Unionist Association of which she was president. She was found dead by Guy Worthington, her pen still in her hand. Her funeral service was held at St Luke's Church, Leek, at which 60 members of the Leek Company of Girl Guides were present. The Countess of Dartmouth and the Staffordshire Guides were

---

[*] Equivalent to 19,200 man-days of agricultural Labour.

represented by the county commissioner Elizabeth Wardle, sister of Lady Gaunt who had been Ernest's sister-in-law (Article 7.8). Maude was buried in the Leek Cemetery, where on 26 September 1922 she had reserved a piece of ground next to the grave of John Wilson.[14]

By her Will dated 21 September 1821 and proved on 29 October 1927 she bequeathed Hillesdon to her eldest son Guy Worthington and the residue to the six children in equal parts.

7.4 Emily Jane

Emily Jane Worthington, the second daughter of Andrew Jukes Worthington and Sarah Booth his wife (Articles 3.11 and 7.1) was born on 29 May 1843 at Horton Hall and baptised on 25 June 1843 at St Michael's Church, Horton. The following year, she moved with her parents, brother and sister to Hallscroft, Spout Street, Leek. A bazaar was held in Leek in aid of the Leek Company of the Staffordshire Rifle Volunteers in 1861 when Emily was 18 years of age. An exhibition there included a 'handsome and valuable banner screen, worked by Miss E. Worthington' and the refreshment stall 'presided over by Miss Russell and Miss Emily Worthington'. Another glimpse of Emily's life before marriage is given in a newspaper account of her wedding when she was 24 years of age:

50   *Emily Jane, born Worthington, with her children.*

… The well known devotedness and unwearied exertion of the young lady in promoting the education of the children in the day and Sunday schools of St Luke's Church, her kind and winning manner to the poor, and her exemplary Christian conduct, created a very widespread interest in an event in which her future happiness is so involved.

Her marriage was to Thomas Davenport Goodman, of Eccles House, Chapel-en-le-Frith, Derbyshire. Thomas was a solicitor practising on his own in Chapel-en-le-Frith, having been admitted to the roll by The Law Society in 1863. Gregory and Rowliffes were his London agents. Thomas was also a lieutenant in the 7th Volunteer Corps of the Territorial Force. The Goodman family had lived at Eccles House and held land there for three previous generations, having acquired the estate by the marriage on 2 December 1765 of George Goodman to Sarah, the heiress of Thomas Moult.[15] The Moult family had held Eccles at least since 1509. Thomas, born on 28 July 1839, was the only surviving son of Davenport Goodman who had attended Manchester Grammar School where the following note was entered in the school register on 6 August 1821:[16]

> Davenport, son of Thomas Goodman, gentleman, Chapel-en-le-Frith. This family is of Welsh origin, lineally descended from Edward Goodman of Nantglyn, in the county of Denbigh, High Sheriff in 1528, whose second son Gabriel was Dean of Westminster 1561-1601, and whose grandson Godfrey was Bishop of Gloucester 1625-1640 ...

Emily and Thomas's wedding took place on 29 October 1867 at St Luke's Church, Leek. Their home was Cromwell House, Chapel-en-le-Frith, and they produced two sons and three daughters, namely:

Forenames	Date of birth	Date of baptism
Godfrey Davenport	4 October 1868	17 November 1868
Winifred	3 May 1870	17 June 1871
Arthur Worthington	26 October 1871	30 November 1871
Dorothy	14 May 1873	19 June 1873
Alice Katherine	30 November 1874	31 December 1874

All five baptisms took place at St Thomas à Becket's Church, Chapel-en-le-Frith.

Alas, Emily only enjoyed seven years of married life; Thomas died 'somewhat suddenly' on 4 June 1875 at the age of 35 years. The 7th Volunteer Corps asked for a military funeral, but the family decided to keep it civilian. A local newspaper recorded:[17]

> The solemn procession started from the deceased's residence. Sergt Wm Frith, Corpl Platt, Corpl Ford and Pvt J Creed of the 7th Volunteers bore the coffin, which was of polished oak, to the church gate. In addition to the relatives and friends, a detachment of the Volunteer Corps, the Sunday scholars, a representative of the Church of England Young Men's Society and the trustees of the savings bank followed their departed friend to the church, after which the corpse was carried to the grave ... As a mark of respect the shops in the town were closed and the blinds of the principal houses were drawn during the ceremony.

An obituary notice recorded that:

> Mr Goodman was an advocate of no mean ability, and the assiduous manner with which he always pleaded the cause of his clients will be fresh in the memory.

He had been a superintendent of Sunday schools, a trustee of the savings bank, a member of the Young Men's Church Association and organist at the church. Thomas had pre-deceased his father, so in due course the Eccles estate passed directly from Thomas's father to Thomas's elder son Godfrey (later Brigadier-General Sir Godfrey Goodman, KCB, CMG, DSO, VD, TD, JP, DL, ADC to King George V).

After rearing her children, Emily moved to Hillside in the city of Lichfield, Staffordshire, but at the end of her life she was living at 31 Manchester Road, Buxton, Derbyshire, five miles south of Chapel-en-le-Frith. She died aged 70 years on 13 August 1913, and was buried on 18 August 1913 at St Thomas à Becket's Church, Chapel-en-le-Frith. An obituary notice recorded:[17]

> ... A lady of kindly disposition, many local organisations have lost by her death a generous supporter. She performed many acts of kindness amongst the poor in an unostentatious manner ... Like her late husband, the deceased was held in high esteem and regard by all who had the pleasure of her acquaintance. The church has lost a staunch supporter, and no request to her was made in vain for assistance in any movement which had for its object the benefit of the town and its inhabitants.

By her Will, dated 20 February 1905 and proved on 2 October 1913, she made a bequest to her servant Hannah Robinson, established annuities for any daughters still unmarried, and divided the remainder among her five children.

7.5 Alice Elizabeth

Alice Elizabeth Worthington, the third daughter of Andrew Jukes Worthington and Sarah Booth his wife (Articles 3.30 and 7.1) was born on 11 September 1844 at Leek. She was baptised on 18 October 1844 at St Edward's Church, Leek.[1]

She lived with her parents at Hallscroft, Spout Street, Leek, until 1870 when the family moved to Ball Haye Hall, Leek. After the death of both her parents she moved to Regent Cottage, Regent Street, Leek, where she lived the rest of her life with two resident maids. Regent Cottage is a double-fronted brick house only 130 yards from A.J. Worthington & Co.'s mill and 200 yards from St Luke's Church. According to her nephew and godson Guy Worthington (Article 7.10), her main interests were St Luke's Church and her health; she was haughty but amusing. It is said that she disapproved of the remarriage of her sister-in-law Maude (Article 7.3) and was thus always cool towards John Wilson. Her nephew Godfrey Goodman (Article 7.4) lodged with her while he was articled to Challinors and Shaw, solicitors of Leek. Two more nephews, Frank Adams (Article 7.2) and Lancelot Worthington (Article 8.2), lodged with her for some years while working at A.J. Worthington and Co. She was a Sunday school teacher in her younger days. She was one of the founders of the Ladies' Working Party of St Luke's Church and took part in almost all their fund-raising activities. She was a manager of the church's schools, and for many years was secretary of St Luke's branch of the Society for the Propagation of the Gospel.

For some years up to 1909, Alice held £1,000[*] of the capital in A.J. Worthington & Co., and received interest on the sum at the rate of seven per cent a year. Having no children, she converted the sum into a life annuity by means of an indenture dated 27 July 1909 with her former sister-in-law, Margaret Elizabeth Gaunt. Thereafter Margaret was to pay Alice £110[†] a year for the remainder of her life. In return Alice passed the £1,000 capital to trustees to hold as security for Alice's life after which the capital would pass to Margaret. The trustees were Godfrey Goodman, then of Buxton, and Margaret's second husband Captain Guy Gaunt, RN (Article 7.8) of the United Services' Club, Pall Mall, London. When A.J. Worthington was converted into a limited company, the £1,000 capital was converted into 200 preference shares of £5 each.

51 *Alice Elizabeth Worthington.*

Alice died unmarried on 24 January 1916 at Regent Cottage. The funeral service took place at St Luke's Church and her body was interred in the family tomb there. Her Will was dated 23 December 1913 with a codicil dated 29 October 1915. Amongst various bequests, the watercolour of her grandmother Elizabeth Worthington (born Jukes) passed to Lancelot Worthington (Article 8.2). Each servant in her service at the time of her death who had lived at Regent Cottage for at least two years was to receive a year's wages. A bequest was also made to St Luke's Church and its schools. All the residue of her estate was divided equally among her three sisters or their families – the Adams, Goodmans and Wirgmans (Articles 7.2, 7.4 and 7.7).

7.6 Walter Moore

Walter Moore Worthington, the second son of Andrew Jukes Worthington and Sarah Booth his wife (Articles 3.30 and 7.1), was born on 19 September 1845 at Leek and baptised on 30 October 1845 at St Edward's Church, Leek.[1]

---

[*] Equivalent to 7,200 man-days of agricultural labour.
[†] Equivalent to 790 man-days of agricultural labour.

52 *Walter Moore Worthington.*

Walter's father directed in his Will dated 28 February 1870 that the residue of his estate be divided equally among his six children (Article 3.30):

> ... Provided nevertheless that the share of my son Walter in the said moneys stocks funds and securities shall be Five hundred pounds* less than the shares of my other sons and daughters therein in consequence of the expense I have already incurred and been put to on his account.

The cause of the expense was still continuing four years later, after Andrew's death, when Walter's elder brother Ernest considered that he might take on the responsibility (Article 6.3). Their mother, Sarah, wrote from Ball Haye Hall to Ernest Worthington on 26 January 1874:

> The message Laura brought from William was that, in his opinion, you ought not make yourself liable in any way for Walter's expenses ... it should come out of the estate ...

In his Will dated 21 August 1881 when aged 36 years, Walter described himself as 'Walter Moore Worthington of Shaftesbury, in the county of Dorset, Surgeon ...' He does not appear in the national medical directories of the period, but there was then no legal requirement for a surgeon to belong to a regulatory body. In his Will he bequeathed his 'library of medical books and instruments' to Dr Edgar Gailey of Leek. After certain other bequests to relations, he left the residue of his estate in trust for the benefit of his sister Emily Goodman, widow (Article 7.4).

Walter was ill at Boscombe Infirmary, Dorset, on 7 January 1885. He died aged 39 years on 21 January 1885 at Boscombe and was buried at St Clement's Church there. A memorial service was held at St Luke's Church, Leek, on 1 February 1885 which his eldest brother Ernest was unable to attend, being ill at Haregate (Article 6.3). *The Dead March* was played following the service. Thomas Harris, a pathologist, wrote to Walter's youngest brother Philip Worthington (Article 7.8) on 4 February 1885 from the Radcliffe Infirmary, Oxford:

---

* Equivalent to 4,500 man-days of agricultural labour.

I can hardly tell you how grieved I was to hear of poor Walter's early death. I certainly had hoped for a better result, but consumption is so liable to be complicated with other ailments that our calculations are but too often upset. In Walter's death we lose a man of exceedingly kind disposition and one who I always regarded as possessed of great ability and one who, had he not been so unfortunate, would have been most useful in this life; for my own part I feel that I have lost a sincere true friend whom it will be impossible to replace. I am sure that at Brewood his death will be deeply regretted for I never knew any medical man win the esteem of his patients so readily and come to be so universally respected …

53   *Rose, born Worthington.*

Thomas Harris was soon to become pathologist to the Royal Infirmary, Manchester, and assistant lecturer and demonstrator of pathology at Owens College. Brewood is about 12 miles south of Stafford, and it seems that Walter must have lived or served there at some stage. After various bequests by his Will dated 21 August 1881, Walter left the residue of his estate to his widowed sister Emily Goodman (Article 7.4).

7.7 Rose

Rose Worthington, the fourth and youngest daughter of Andrew Jukes Worthington and Sarah Booth his wife (Articles 3.30 and 7.1) was born on 9 September 1847 at Leek, and baptised on 21 October 1847 at St Edward's Church, Leek.[1] She lived with her parents at Hallscroft, Spout Street, Leek, until 1870 when the family moved to Ball Haye Hall, Leek.

As a young woman Rose taught in the Sunday school of St Luke's Church, Leek. In this respect she followed her elder sister Emily (Article 7.4). On Rose's retirement as teacher, soon before her marriage, her pupils presented her with a framed illuminated address and framed photograph of themselves. The address read:

> This address was presented to Miss Rose Worthington, together with the accompanying photograph, by members of the Sunday school class, as a token of gratitude for the loving and unwearied manner in which she has ever fulfilled her sacred trust; and they earnestly pray that a merciful Providence will follow her to her new home and that every blessing both here and hereafter may be graciously vouchsafed for her.

In reply, Rose said that she had always experienced great pleasure in teaching them and was sorry that circumstances would not permit of her still remaining amongst them. These were early days in the development of education of the working classes – a development in which the Church of England took a leading part. Sunday schools were then a means of providing education for people who were at work throughout the week.

Rose was a member of the Leek Embroidering Society, founded and managed by Elizabeth Wardle (Article 7.8). She participated in many of the society's earlier projects.

On 13 January 1874, at the age of 26 years, Rose married the Reverend Augustus Theodore Wirgman who had just been appointed vice-principal of St Andrew's College, Grahamstown, South Africa. He was then 27 years of age, having been born on 22 September 1846. Theodore had been educated at Rossall School, Fleetwood, Lancashire, and at Magdalene College, Cambridge. He attained a BA (classical tripos) degree followed by a second-class honours theological tripos and an MA degree. He had been curate to his father the Reverend Augustus Wirgman, MA, vicar of Hartington, Derbyshire, in 1870 and 1871, curate at Alton Towers, Staffordshire, in 1871 and 1872, and curate at Handsworth, Staffordshire, from 1872. His mother was Jane Elizabeth, fifth daughter of Thomas Pearson of South Wingfield, Derbyshire. (18) The Wirgmans were direct descendants of Peter Virgunder who had been born in 1624 at Biorkeroes in Smaland, Sweden, and was ordained priest following his education at the University of Uppsala.[3] His youngest son, Abraham, changed his surname to Wirgman on entering into commerce, and later became an alderman of Gothenberg. His son, Gabriel, settled in London, thus giving rise to the English Wirgmans. Theodore's grandfather Thomas Wirgman had, in 1814, been appointed a Chevalier of the Order of the Fleur de Lys by King Louis XVIII of France in recognition of aid and services while the king was in exile in England, prior to the Bourbon restoration.

Theodore had been an occasional visitor to Leek for some years before the marriage. For example, he was in Leek in February 1871 for the laying of the foundation stone of St Luke's New Boys' School to provide additional capacity for the growing population. Fifteen clergymen were present including 'Rev. A.T. Wirgman (Hartington)'. The order of procession from the school to the church was the architect (Mr W. Sugden), the builders, Harry T. Davenport, Esq., the choir and the clergy.

The wedding took place at St Luke's Church, Leek, but alas, Rose's father had died only three weeks earlier (Article 3.30). Three days after the wedding, Rose and Theodore visited Hartington where they were greeted by a peal of church bells. That evening a deputation visited the vicarage to present the bride and groom with a silver tea and coffee service, the coffee pot being inscribed with the event and date of presentation.

There was also a gift to the bride of six silver napkin rings. These gifts had been subscribed for by 60 parishioners. Speeches were made, and in his reply Theodore said that he was 'taking to a far and distant land the greatest treasure in the person of his wife' and he entreated their prayers that they might be blessed in their work there.

A few days later Rose and Theodore sailed to Cape Town on the SS *Edinburgh Castle*, the voyage taking about 24 days. After a short stay there they proceeded in the same ship to Port Elizabeth where they had to transfer to a smaller sailing vessel to land. They were met by Archdeacon White with whom they stayed for two days before proceeding to Grahamstown by Cobb's coach, drawn by four horses – a journey which lasted 11 hours.

They lived in Grahamstown for a year only; in 1875 Theodore was appointed rector of St Mary's Collegiate Church in Port Elizabeth.[19] For the next 42 years until Theodore's death, they lived at St Mary's Rectory in St Mary's Terrace – a two-storey house situated just over the road from the church. A first-floor balcony stretched the whole length of the house, one end of which was used by Theodore as his open-air sanctum where he wrote his books and received visitors. Theodore's deputy, the Reverend Cuthbert Edward Mayo, resided with the Wirgman's at the rectory for some 30 years, starting a few years after his ordination which was in 1883. This old rectory has since been demolished.

Theodore took the lead in building a new church at the south end of Port Elizabeth, called the Mission Church of St Peter. In due course the bishop came to lay the foundation stone, returning on 29 July 1876 to open and consecrate the church.

Rose and Theodore made their first return visit to England in 1882, during which Theodore attended and spoke at the Derby Church Congress. He was promoted to rural dean in 1884 and vice-provost of the collegiate church in 1888. In 1893 they made their second visit to England 'for rest and change', sailing on the SS *Pretoria* and arriving to 'see the fresh beauties of an English spring'. During the visit Theodore took his BD degree at Cambridge, based on his work on *The Constitutions and Canons of the Anglican Communion*.[20]

At midnight on 9 March 1895, the rectory household was aroused by cries of 'fire'; St Mary's Collegiate Church was ablaze.[21] By the time Theodore arrived at the scene, the church roof was alight and nothing could be done to save the building. The roof fell in at 3 a.m. and the flames were not subdued until 6 a.m. Theodore reported:

> The fire brigade was very active – too active in my own case, for I got deluged by the hose of a zealous fireman, an experience which very nearly made me lose my temper ...

Theodore immediately set about rebuilding to a new plan. At an early stage he showed drawings to his friend Cecil John Rhodes, PC, MA, Hon

DCL, prime minister of Cape Colony, who gave £250.[*] This generous contribution made a good start to Theodore's fund-raising tour which included Bloemfontein and Johannesburg, and a personal visit to President Stephanus Johannes Paulus Kruger, president of the Transvaal.

Theodore had been appointed a chaplain of the Colonial Forces in 1875 and promoted major in 1886. He received the South African General Service Medal in 1880, probably in connection with the Zulu war of 1879. He also received the Volunteer Officer's Decoration (VD) in 1896. He was called into active service for the Boer War of 1899 and 1900, and in 1900 was promoted to principal chaplain of the Cape Colonial Forces with the rank of honorary lieutenant-colonel.

In January 1902 Rose and Theodore made their third visit to England, sailing on the P&O steamer *Plassey*. After Easter that year they visited the continent, crossing the sea to Flushing, travelling down the Rhine to Lucerne and thence through the St Gothard tunnel to Milan, Florence, Pisa, Ravenna, Rome, Venice, Innsbruck, Strasbourg and Cologne before returning to England via Flushing.

In 1905, Theodore was appointed honorary chaplain to King Edward VII. In 1907 he was promoted archdeacon of Port Elizabeth while remaining rector of the collegiate church and in 1911 he was appointed select preacher at Cambridge. He had been awarded an honorary DCL degree in the University of the South, USA, in 1877, having been a frequent contributor to American journals on African church affairs. He had also attained, in 1899, the DD degree in the University of Cambridge. In that year he had also been appointed a canon of Grahamstown Cathedral.

A glimpse of Theodore's character is given by an event published under the heading 'Muscular Humanity' in the *Port Elizabeth Chronicle*. The date is not known as the newspaper cutting was detached from the rest of the page. The author wrote:

> To show the stamp of clergymen we have in Port Elizabeth, allow me to mention the following of this day's occurrence: A fellow was brutally ill-treating a cab horse on the Hill; two clergymen, of whom one was the Rev A.T. Wirgman, MA, rector of St Mary's ... and the other was his newly appointed curate, saw the event and remonstrated, but without avail. They went to collar him, but he sprang on the box and drove off. Nothing daunted, the two gentlemen – doubtless remembering their old athletic feats at University – went after him, and were not the men to give up chase until they had the fellow in custody. They prosecuted, too, and got him heavily fined. I need hardly say that this generous, humane act has won for the two gentlemen golden opinions. Said one of the unwashed – and the unwashed admire pluck and blood whenever it is exhibited – referring to Mr Wirgman – 'He may be Eye Church; he may be a parson; he may be fond of purcessions and all that sort of thing; but let one of you say he ain't a man and I'll fight him on the spot for whets round ...

---

[*] Equivalent to 2,000 man-days of agricultural labour.

Theodore died on 15 October 1917; his body was buried before the altar of St Mary's Church, where a marble memorial is laid in the floor bearing a full-length front view of him together with the words:

> Augustus Theodore Wirgman Doctor of Divinity Cambridge Priest of the Catholic Church Archdeacon of Port Elizabeth 42 years Rector and Vice Provost of St Mary's Collegiate Church, Nat Sep XXII MDCCCXLVI ob Oct XV MCMXVII Jesu Mercy

Rose returned to England as a widow about 1919, aged about 72 years. She had served St Mary's for 44 years and had founded the Mothers' Union branch in the town. For the rest of her life she lived with her niece, Cecily Janet Adams of The Little Croft, The Marsh, Wolstanton, Staffordshire. She died there without issue on 24 January 1926 and was buried at St Margaret's Church, Wolstanton. By her Will dated 12 January 1921 she made bequests to Canon Cuthbert Mayo, who had succeeded Theodore as rector and vice-provost, and to 17 nephews and nieces including Sybil, Guy, Gwenyth, Freda, Yorke and Lancelot Worthington (Articles 7.9 to 7.11, 7.13 and 7.14 and 8.2). The residue of her estate was devised to her nephew and godson, Roger Ernest Worthington (Article 7.12).

'H.L.G.E.' wrote of Rose in his *Biographical Sketch* appended to Theodore's book *Storm and Sunshine in South Africa*:[21]

> ... Here in this quiet Rectory, for over forty years, she made his welfare and happiness, his efforts and his ambitions, her own supreme charge. In his successes and failures (not a few), in peace and storm (and there were heavy storms), she was always the staunch comrade, ever at hand with ready intuition and watchful sympathy, with encouragement and counsel ... Nor must we omit to recall the unaffected and unfailing hospitality so long associated with St Mary's Rectory. Numberless are those who have experienced it, and who will ever remember the camaraderie of their genial host (who, by the way, was an amazing raconteur), and the thoughtful care and kindness of their hostess ... Nor did Mrs Wirgman confine herself to the duties of the home, for she was an indefatigable worker in all that pertained to the church and parish, and was the personal friend of the members of its large and varied congregation in all the joys and sorrows; and when, after the death of the Archdeacon, Mrs Wirgman finally left the home of her adoption for the land of her birth, it was with the respect and affection of a people who will never forget her nobility of character, her dignity of manner and her long and loving service.

A posthumous tribute was paid to Rose at Port Elizabeth. An arch, in 13th-century gothic style, was built facing Market Square to complete a walled enclosure at St Mary's.[22] The arch, built by public subscription following news of her death, is in local ironstone with dressings of imitation stone. The arms of the diocese of Grahamstown are carved in stone on one side of the arch and the arms of St Mary's on the other. A bronze figure of the archangel Gabriel stands on the corbel and

54 *The Rose Wirgman gateway at Port Elizabeth.*

there are two bronze memorial plaques – one bearing the initials RW with two roses and the other bearing the Wirgman and Worthington arms impaled.[23] There is an inscription: 'This gateway is erected in the memory of Rose Wirgman, AD 1926. RIP'. The unveiling ceremony held on 23 December 1926 was followed by a memorial service when Canon Mayo said of the monument:

> ... Its solid character, too, is especially appropriate to the one in whose honour it has been erected, for the venerated late archdeacon's wife, most unobtrusive of workers, built on solid foundations indeed, and those who as girls were brought into contact with her learned principles and thoughts which have guided them for the better throughout their lives ...

Rose had been instrumental in procuring from the Leek Embroidery Society several altar frontals and supers for St Mary's; they were red, white, green and violet – doves being one of the motifs.[11] Replacements were provided by the society following the fire of 1895. A Leek frontal was also made for Grahamstown Cathedral in 1892 – white with peacocks. It was still in use 100 years later (Article 7.8).

7.8 Philip Jukes

Philip Jukes Worthington, the third son and youngest child of Andrew Jukes Worthington and Sarah Booth his wife (Articles 3.30 and 7.1), was born on 4 January 1851 at Spout Street, Leek.[1] He was baptised on 19 March 1851 at St Luke's Church, Leek. In 1870 he moved with his parents to Ball Haye Hall, Leek.

Philip joined A.J. Worthington & Co., probably working first in production departments, but it is known that he was on the road as a traveller for a time. His father was senior partner and his eldest brother, Ernest, the junior partner; but his father died on 21 December 1873, leaving Ernest in charge. By 1875, at the age of 24 years, Philip was taken into partnership with a share of two-fifteenths of the equity. From 30 June 1876 Henry Russell of London, the silk agent, became a third partner (Article 7.3).

55   *Philip Jukes Worthington.*

Henry died about nine years later leaving Ernest and Philip as the only partners. Philip was not content with his comparatively small share of the equity, and by negotiation coupled with years of patience he had his share raised to six-fifteenths from 30 June 1888 with an undertaking that it would be seven-fifteenths from 30 June 1892. These changes were confirmed by a deed of 27 March 1888.[7] The capital on interest in the business was then £21,526 0s. 11d.[*] made up as follows:

Partners' capital	£	s.	d.
Ernest Andrew Worthington	4,112	11	5
Philip Jukes Worthington	2,813	3	4
Estate of Andrew Jukes Worthington (deceased)	12,200	6	2
Mortgage loan, against the property	2,400	0	0
	21,526	0	11

Philip was also a member of the volunteer forces, having been commissioned an ensign in the 28th Rifle Volunteer Corps on 7 October 1870 – at the age of 19 years. There was a ceremonial parade on 23 August 1872 when Princess Mary Adelaide, Duchess of Teck (first cousin of Queen Victoria) and the Duke of Teck passed through Leek on a visit to Rock

---

[*] Equivalent to 19,400 man-days of agricultural labour.

Hall, Swythamley, near Leek. They had been staying at Alton Towers, home of the Earl and Countess of Shrewsbury, from where they came by special train. Philip's uncle-in-law, William Challinor (Article 3.30), gave the address of welcome. A newspaper report continues:[24]

> ... The procession, which consisted of nine carriages, then started from the station. It was headed by Lord Shrewsbury's brass band, under the superintendence of Mr Forester, and followed by the Leek Rifles, under the command of Lieutenant Sleigh and Ensign Worthington, and also by the fine band of the corps ...

On 18 November 1871 Philip was promoted lieutenant. He was 'Lieut. Commanding 28th Company SRV' by 25 July 1874 when his letter from the armoury in Ford Street, Leek, to the editor of the *Leek Times* was published:[25]

> Sir, noticing that in the police report in the Leek Times, under the heading 'Mad Drunk', George Bainbridge, a private in my company, is described as in the Rifle Corps, and also as behaving very badly, I have to request that in your next issue you will mention that on Thursday last, 23rd inst. I dismissed him, before the company, for his ill-conduct, and also fined him 30s. By so doing you will oblige.

On 8 January 1875 Philip was promoted captain '28th (Leek) Staffordshire Rifle Volunteers' (then known briefly as 'the Leek Volunteers'). A week later, on 15 January 1875, he presided at the annual dinner and ball held jointly by the Leek Troop of the Queens Own Royal Yeomanry and the 28th Staffordshire Rifle Volunteers, held at the *Swan Hotel*, Leek. After dinner and speeches the room was cleared for the ball which continued until 2a.m. to music by the Volunteers' band.

There were annual camps of the whole of the 1st battalion at such places as Newcastle-under-Lyme, Lichfield and Cannock Chase, and the Leek company's band with a strength of about 18 was often appointed as battalion band for the purpose.[25] The camp in June 1876 was held at the Newcastle Butts on the Seabridge Road where 160 tents had been erected. The numbers present on review day were 32 officers and 896 other ranks, including the Leek company of 73 led by Captain Worthington and Lieutenant Watson.

When the company was inspected by Captain Pope, battalion adjutant, in 1878, it mustered the captain, the surgeon (Mr E. Gailey), the chaplain (the Reverend E. Belcher), six sergeants, and 67 rank and file. Preceded by its band it marched from the Armoury Yard, Leek to Ball Haye Hall where it was inspected for drill, arms, firing, bayonet exercises and knowledge of the manual before the march past.

Presumably Philip and his unmarried sister, Alice (Article 7.5), continued to live at Ball Haye Hall with their mother until after her death there in 1877 (Article 3.30). By 1883 both of them were living at Regent Cottage, Regent Street, Leek. During the late 1870s and the 1880s Philip and F.J. Milner often took the roles of joint stage managers for various productions of the Leek Amateur Dramatic Society. For some time, Philip was also a churchwarden of St Luke's Church, Leek. He was certainly so in 1882 when the Reverend Benjamin Pidcock retired as the first vicar of the church. Philip read the address at the retiring ceremony, and he and Joshua Andrew signed the document as churchwardens.

Shortly before his marriage Philip retired from active duty with the Volunteers – by then renamed '1 Company 1st Volunteer Battalion, (Prince of Wales's) North Staffordshire Regiment'. He was then aged 37 years, had served the force for 18 years and been leader of the Leek company for 16 years. In recognition he was promoted honorary major. A dinner was given in his honour at the *Quiet Woman Inn*, Leek, on 24 January 1889 by the officers and sergeants of the

56 *Margaret Elizabeth, born Wardle, on the occasion of presentation at court.*

company. Philip responded to the toasts to the guests, and Philip's nephew, Lieutenant Godfrey Goodman (Article 7.4) proposed the toast to the sergeants.

On 26 September 1889 Philip married Margaret Elizabeth, the third daughter of 'Mr Thomas Wardle, FGS, FCS, silk dyer' (later Sir Thomas Wardle, Kt, JP, chevalier de la Légion d'Honneur (France), officier dans l'Ordre des Palmes Académique (France), honorary freeman of the Worshipful Company of Weavers and freeman of the City of London). Thomas's father, Joshua Wardle, had founded a dyeworks at Cheddleton, three miles south of Leek, in 1830 (the business later being known as Joshua Wardle and Sons and from 1929 as Joshua Wardle Limited).[26] In 1885, Thomas had been appointed consultant to the British government and to Major-General Sir Pratap Singh, GCSI, maharajah of Jammu and Kashmir, to advise on the development of the silk industry of the region. Thomas was the first president of the Silk Association of Great Britain and Ireland. Margaret's mother, Elizabeth Wardle (born Wardle), had founded the Leek Embroidery Society and School of Embroidery in 1879. The society became well known for their ecclesiastical embroidery, but the most famous of their products was the full-sized replica of the Bayeux Tapestry, 230 feet long, now kept at the Reading Museum.[27] At the time of Philip and Margaret's marriage Philip was aged 38 years – twice the age of Margaret who had been born on 12 October 1869. The wedding took place at St Edward's Church, Leek.[25] The choir sang the processional hymn, the psalm and another hymn specially composed for the occasion by the bride's father. The music was dedicated to the vicar, the Reverend C.B. Maude, MA and published by Novello Ewer and Co. of London and New York. On leaving the church, the married couple were greeted with '... many a shower of rice by the assembled work people from Messrs Worthington's silk mills who had been granted a half day in honour of the occasion ...'. The wedding breakfast was at the Wardles' home in St Edward Street. The bellringers' records at St Edward's Church show that the bells rang for three hours 30 minutes, for which the ringers received a dinner at the *Swan Hotel*. At 2.30p.m. the bride and bridegroom left by carriage to Macclesfield, en route to Harrogate in Yorkshire where they spent their honeymoon.

Philip and Margaret's nuptial home was in Hugo Street; letters to Philip from 1891 to 1894 were addressed simply to 'Hugo Street, Leek'. At the 1891 census, Philip and Margaret were living there with two servants – cook and housemaid.[10] Here Philip and Margaret produced their only child:

Forenames	Date of birth	Date of baptism	Article
Lancelot Jukes	28 May 1891	28 June 1891	8.2

He was born at home and baptised at All Saint's Church, Leek. In 1894 the family moved to Stockwell House, Stockwell Street, Leek. On 13 January of that year Philip entered into an indenture with Arthur Nicholson (later Sir Arthur Nicholson Kt, JP) whereby Philip leased the house,

> with the outoffices, stables, coachhouse, (with dwelling rooms over the same), vinery, conservatories and other buildings and appurtenances and the yard and gardens, pleasure grounds and close of land ...

The land amounted to 2 acres, 3 roods, 15 perches. The lease was for seven years starting from 1 February 1894 for an annual rent of £90,[*] but Philip reserved the right to extend the lease for a second period of seven years at the same rent. In fact he extended it for three years – until 31 January 1904 – by letter dated 31 July 1900. On the east side of the house stood the Nicholson Institute.

On 1 March 1895 Princess Mary, Duchess of Teck, visited Leek again and was entertained by Philip and Margaret at Stockwell House, a group photograph being taken in the gardens. The Duke and Duchess of Schleswig-Holstein (he being a grandson of Queen Victoria) and the Duke and Duchess of Sutherland were present. Their tour included Portland Mills.

---

[*] Equivalent to 650 man-days of agricultural labour.

57 *The royal party leaving Stockwell House, Leek.*

Margaret was seriously ill in the autumn of 1896. Philip's uncle, Dr Oliver Pemberton, FRCS, a Birmingham surgeon and the city coroner, wrote to Alice Worthington on 3 October 1896 'poor Philip, it is so hard – so loveable a wife and woman. The malady should be recoverable where there are no complications ...'

When Philip's eldest brother, Ernest (Article 7.3) died on 7 October 1896, his widow Maude sought the advice of her father, Thomas Pearson, on what should be done with the business. Thomas then dealt directly with Philip. Thomas's demands included re-drafting of the Articles of Partnership, which Philip refused, and acrimony ensued. Thomas finally withdrew his family from the business and demanded rapid repayment of Ernest's capital. Sir Thomas Wardle came to the rescue with a loan enabling Philip to complete the deal, thus becoming sole proprietor. The resulting debts of Philip and his business to his brothers and sisters and Sir Thomas were considerable, but the business thrived. Maude, with three sons requiring careers, saw the new situation with bitterness. Acrimony broke out again when John Wilson wrote on 8 January 1901 to Philip claiming that Philip had become a partner incorrectly and that Ernest had never understood any partnership agreement then drawn up. The business, he claimed, had always been Ernest's private concern. In his reply of 10 January 1901, Philip recalled:

> ... Unfortunately, afterwards I had to deal with her father, who acted for, and in, her behalf. By the course he took he spoiled everything of

> a friendly nature, and caused me trouble upon trouble and the deepest anxiety; holding over my head the threat of Chancery proceedings, his daughter, my sister in law approving ...

He added that he resented the slight on his brother's memory. Philip obtained evidence from Challinors and Shaw that agreements had been correctly drawn up and that Ernest had understood his actions. However, Philip provided in his Will, drawn up the following year, for Ernest and Maude's youngest son, Yorke (Article 7.14) then aged only six years to take a quarter of the equity in due course. Presumably Yorke, being three years younger than Philip's son, Lancelot, was considered the most suitable as Lancelot's future junior partner.

Margaret and Lancelot, then aged nine years, went on a cruise in August 1900, which included a visit to South Africa. Perhaps Philip's reason for not joining them was that business was difficult. He wrote to Thomas Mellor, his principal traveller, on 26 February 1901, '... I hope that for my sake as well as yours, from 1st July next profits will mend. I have serious sums of borrowed capital in the business.'

In January 1901, Philip and Margaret gave a dinner at the Town Hall, Leek, to celebrate Philip's jubilee. About 200 employees of A.J. Worthington & Co. and 60 relations and friends were present, including the parsons of St Edward's, St Luke's and Sandon churches. In his speech, Philip noted that there were one or two still at the mill who were there before his father came to Leek in 1837, '... a period of service which cannot be matched'. He referred especially to William Simpson who had been with the firm for 63 years and Richard Clowes for 58 years; it was said that 20 employees had been with the firm for more than 50 years. Philip hoped that his son would inherit the same kindly feelings that had been shown to his father, his brother and himself. After dinner there was a Punch and Judy show, conjuring, ventriloquism and humorous songs and sketches. Finally there was dancing until the early hours of the morning.

In May 1902, Philip subscribed for 20 £1 shares in the Leek and Manifold Valley Light Railway Company, formed to build a narrow-gauge railway from Waterhouses to Hulme End. His father-in-law was one of the initial directors.[28]

By the spring of 1902, Philip became terminally ill. On 11 March 1902 he wrote to his son, then aged 10 years and boarding at Aysgarth School, North Yorkshire:

> It seems quite a time since I wrote to you, but I have been poorly, not felt I had much to say and one or two of your letters seem to have been a good deal on stamps etc, not much in my line to reply to. Dr Harris of Manchester came to see me ...

He wrote again on 16 May 1902 referring to a lift being installed at the mill to get him up to his office, instead of being carried on a chair. In a further letter, Philip wrote:

> I have not been to the mill for perhaps a month, but I see the letters, and Mr Bagley etc come as I want. I believe the new lift is most useful for business goods.

Philip died of consumption on 20 July 1902 at Stockwell House, and was buried in the family vault at St Luke's Church. When the vault was opened, the umbrella which Philip had lost at Ernest's funeral, five years previously, was found! By his long and complex Will dated 17 January 1902, A.J. Worthington & Co. was to be held in trust by his widow and Edward Challinor (solicitor and first cousin) and then to pass to Lancelot on his reaching the age of 21 years. £2,000* of the capital of the business was earmarked to provide an income to his widow for life and further income of £900 a year was to be paid to her for life out of the residue of his estate. Edward Challinor died sometime around 1908, whereafter Margaret was the sole trustee. In an undated letter 'To the Trustees of my Will', Philip expressed the hope that the business could be 'successfully carried on for Lance to succeed to'. He described how a mortgage loan should be obtained if necessary and advised on future management including promotion of Thomas Mellor to be general manager and Herbert Trafford to take a leading sales role. He also suggested pensions for previous managers. Finally he wrote:

> If the business has to be sold, I should like an offer to be made for one or more of my brother Ernest's children to buy it, even if somewhat more could be got in the open market, from loving regard for my brother, knowing that he looked forward to one or more of his sons going into the Business.

Amongst the letters of condolence is one dated 17 September 1902 to Margaret from Frederick Halcomb, MA (Article 3.26), Philip's first cousin, written from 'Parliament, South Australia, Adelaide'. Frederick was then clerk of the parliaments and the Legislative Assembly of South Australia, and a member of the Senate of the University of Adelaide.[29] He recalled Philip in the Spout Street days of about 1859 as '... very fair and rather delicate looking and fragile and not giving indications of the fine well grown man that he became'. The letter from Thomas Shaw, clerk to the justices, at the request of the magistrates sitting in petty sessions at the Town Hall, shows that Philip had been placed on the Commission of the Peace for the county of Stafford, but had been prevented by his illness from taking the oath.

On 23 November 1904 Margaret married Commander Guy Reginald Archer Gaunt of the Royal Navy (later Admiral Sir Guy Gaunt, KCMG, CB, MP, ADC to King George V). The Gaunts were an ancient Leek family whose pedigree is published in Sleigh's *History of Leek*.[30] Guy was well known to Philip and Margaret and had been present at the

---

* Equivalent to 15,300 man-days of agricultural labour.

celebration of Philip's 50th birthday in 1901. The marriage took place at the Cathedral Church of St John, Victoria, Hong Kong. Both of them were then 35 years of age. Margaret, who had borne the nicknames 'Maggie' and 'Mag', henceforth also bore the name 'Meg' after her new initials.

Lady Wardle had died in 1902 and Sir Thomas died in 1909. Margaret and Guy between them enjoyed incomes from the Wardle and Worthington Will trusts in addition to his naval salary. When on 7 July 1909 Sir Thomas's properties were put up for auction at the Town Hall, Leek, Margaret acquired his country residence – Swainsley, near Leek, Staffordshire – described in the sale brochure as 'a charming residence ... beautifully situated on the banks of the River Manifold, containing altogether about 37.5 acres'. Guy and Margaret renamed the property 'Gaunt's Wood', and they proceeded with major developments. A new three-storey servants' wing with separate staircase was added at the back of the house. The previous servants' quarters on the top floor of the old house were up-graded for use by the family, two dormer windows being added to the south face. A ballroom – convertible for use as a billiards room – with a stage at the north end was completed in 1912. From the south-east corner of the room a turret provided a circular staircase leading to the flat roof which they called 'the quarter-deck'. A squash-racquets court with viewing gallery was built adjacent to Swainsley farm. About 700 acres of adjacent land were purchased from Victor William Cavendish, 9th Duke of Devonshire, KG, GCMG, GCVO, PC, LLD. Also three glasshouses, each 50 feet by 10 feet, with a boiler house, were built near the river. For much of the period, from their marriage until the First World War, Guy served at sea, while Lancelot (Article 8.20) was at boarding school, so Margaret remained to supervise much of the development work.

From 1914 until early 1918 – most of the duration of the First World War – Margaret and Guy lived in Washington, USA, while he was naval attaché at the British Embassy. Many years later it was also learnt that he had been Britain's senior intelligence officer in the USA and had, in particular, monitored various Irish republicans there. After a short period commanding convoys later in 1918, he was transferred to naval intelligence at the Admiralty, London. He retired towards the end of 1918, having been knighted that year. On returning from Washington in 1918, Lady Gaunt became chairman of A.J. Worthington & Co. Limited and put great energy into preparing the company for her son's return after the war.

Following Sir Guy's retirement, gracious living at Gaunt's Wood blossomed and there was much fine entertaining. Margaret was undoubtedly an excellent hostess. Her nephew, the Very Reverend Michael Leake Underhill, CBE, dean emeritus of Christchurch, New Zealand, wrote at Christmas 1991 – 72 years after the event:

58   *Swainsley, Butterton, Staffordshire.*

> ... My first visit there was in 1919 when Uncle Guy and Aunt Meg arrived from the USA with an electric car and two stand-up motor scooters. We had several holidays there after that ...

At Christmas 1992 he wrote '... I love that place; I don't quite know why'. Margaret's granddaughter, Valentine, recalled her memories of the period about 1927, when she was three years of age:

> The first holidays I remember were at Swainsley – or Gaunt's Wood as it was called – ... Gran provided us with a complete wing, two double bedrooms, sitting room/nursery and bathroom. Nanny had a bedroom in the servants' quarters. In those days it was very grand and well staffed. I recall being thrilled to be allowed to have lunch in the servants' hall where I sat between cook and butler ... There was a staff of about six or so then in the house ...

Margaret acquired for the winter seasons Villa Trianon, Rue Grimaldi, Monaco, being the garden flat at the top of a building overlooking Monte Carlo harbour. There she kept two Italian maids.

Alas, this potentially idyllic life was based on insecure foundations. Debts grew. The admiral formed a liaison with Sybil, daughter of A. Grant-White of Worthing, Sussex, and wife or widow of W.O. Joseph. Margaret divorced Guy, the decree absolute being granted by the Family Division of the High Court of Justice on 2 July 1928. He married Sybil in 1932. The name 'Gaunt's Wood' reverted to 'Swainsley', but financially the day of reckoning had come. The servants had to be dismissed except for a caretaker to look after the glasshouses and one maid. The estate was put up for auction at the *Swan Hotel*, Leek, on 12 August 1931 and divided into 22 lots. The 'valuable antique and modern furniture', running to about 800 lots, was auctioned there on each of the following three days. The estate for sale consisted of 722 acres made up as follows:

	Acres	Roods	Poles
Swainsley hall, grounds, outbuildings, squash racquet court, home-farm, cottage and farm buildings and all fishing rights	22	1	27
Ecton Lee – a stone built house	3	1	5
Dale Farm, with stone farmhouse	80	1	28
Wetton Mill Farm with stone farmhouse	57	1	13
A stone cottage	0	1	34
The Ecton Quarries yielding roadstone	16	1	18
Market Garden, cottage and glasshouses	2	3	11
Cheese factory, stone built	2	0	0
Hill land, plantation, meadow and pasture	537	2	11
	722	2	27

The sale was disastrous, coming in the eye of the worst slump of the century. The contents of the house were sold at low prices, but the house and virtually all the land remained unsold as prices were not sufficient to satisfy the bank. Margaret moved with her remaining maid to the home farm cottage, which she renamed 'Swainsley Cottage'. Her debt to the bank was £13,000,[*] so she continued to look for opportunities to sell parts of the estate. On 6 January 1939, for example, she completed the sale of Dale Farm and Wetton Mill Farm, together with some of the pasture and meadowland, to the National Trust.

The garden flat at Monaco was also sold in due course, but the temptations of the principality remained; Margaret continued to winter there with the hope that the casino would reinstate her fortune. Her last visit was in 1947. Her granddaughter, Valentine Worthington (Article 8.3), due to be married on 22 March that year, wrote in her memoirs:

> ... everything was in top gear when on 4th March Daddy had a phone call from Monte Carlo saying his mother was ill and would he go and fetch her home immediately. So I was left to look after Rochemount, Stuart, Rosalie, the nurse maid Phoebe and the cook general, plus all the last minute wedding arrangements and presents coming in etc ...

---

[*] Equivalent to 40,000 man-days of agricultural labour.

Stuart and Rosalie, Valentine's half-brother and half-sister (Articles 8.6 and 8.7), were then aged six and two respectively. Lancelot (Article 8.2) took with him Marjorie, his second wife, and they returned with Lady Gaunt on Sunday 16 March. Valentine wryly continues: '... I wonder why they were so long? ... Gran was able to attend the wedding'.

The hall remained empty for 14 years, but in 1945 Margaret sold it to Mr J.W. Blackhurst, who opened it as the *Manifold Valley Hotel*. By the time she was 78 years of age she had taken up residence at the hotel, her room being the old wooden pipe loft to her father's organ – the loft having long since been converted to a bedroom. Alas, at 11 o'clock on the night of 8 February 1949, a fire started in her room, probably because she had pulled her bed closer to the unguarded coal fire to keep herself warm.[31] Mr Blackhurst had gone to collect his wife from a whist drive at ten and when they returned soon after 11 o'clock they '... noticed that Lady Gaunt's room and the one beneath were blazing inside'. Her son, Lancelot, having been telephoned, arrived from Leek at 2 a.m. to find the fire brigade at work, but by that time the bedroom floor and Margaret's body had fallen into the dining room bay where the organ used to be.[32] She was cremated on 14 February 1949 at Carmountside Crematorium, Milton, Staffordshire, and her ashes were scattered at Swainsley by Lancelot.

There was no funeral service by Margaret's own request. She had written to her son, Lancelot (Article 8.2), on 5 April 1943 to say:

> PLEASE no funeral whatever, no sadness whatever, but gladness that my Promotion came along. NO flowers, no black or any sign of old-fashioned Death, no Church Service whatever. I have left the English Church long ago. I shall not be dead but very much alive, so just have my body, that I have worn all these years, cremated and my ashes scattered over the Crematorium garden. You have not to see this done: they will attend to it all. Nor have you to see the cremation; ...

In her letter of condolence, Mrs Beryl Johnson of Abbotsfield, Buxton Road, Leek, referred to 'Lady Gaunt's gaiety and originality – very refreshing in an age of stamped-out personalities'. Freda, la Comtesse des Garets, of 8 Passage Barriera, Monte Carlo, wrote: 'I cannot bear to think that I will never see Tassets again.'

By her Will dated 7 May 1946, with codicil dated 19 July 1946, Margaret bequeathed all her real and personal estate to Lancelot.

THIRD GENERATION – FAMILY OF ERNEST ANDREW AND MARGARET MAUDE

7.9 Sybil

Sybil Worthington, the eldest daughter of Ernest Andrew Worthington and Margaret Maude his wife (Article 7.3), was born on 19 March 1884 at Haregate Hall, Leek, and baptised on 25 April 1884 at St Luke's

59 *Sybil Worthington.*

Church, Leek.[1] Her early education was by governess at home and later she attended a boarding school at Worthing, Sussex. On leaving school she returned to Hillesdon, Leek, to live with her mother.

In 1919 she became the housekeeper of Moorhill Preparatory School, Leek, which was owned and run by her brother Guy Jukes Worthington (Article 7.10). She held that post until 1933 when Guy married. One autumn during this period she took time off for a long visit to her cousins, the Coopers, in Richmond, Natal. Arnold Worthington Cooper, JP (Article 3.29), was Sybil's first cousin who had been born in Leek but had emigrated to Natal where he practised as an advocate, solicitor and notary public; he became solicitor to the Bank of South Africa Limited and to the London and Lancashire Fire Insurance Company. He also became the first chairman of the board of trustees of the new government museum built in 1924 in Loop Street, Pietermaritzburg.[33] Sybil maintained a life-long link with Arnold's family; he mentioned her in a memorandum attached to his Will of 28 February 1927.[34]

Sybil devoted much of her life to the Girl Guides, joining as captain of St Luke's Girl Guides when the unit was formed soon after the First World War. One of the highlights for her unit was the visit to Leek of the world chief scout Lieutenant-General Sir Robert Stephenson Smyth Baden-Powell, Bt (later 1st Baron Baden-Powell, OM, GCMG, GCVO, KCB, LLD) and his wife the world chief guide Lady Olave St Clair Baden-Powell (later Dame Olave Baden-Powell, GBE). The date of the visit is unknown, but it was on a Sunday afternoon before 1925. Five or six thousand people assembled at Beggar's Lane cricket ground to attend a drumhead service supported by Foden's brass band. A local newspaper reported:

> There was a capital turnout of Boy Scouts and Girl Guides, their appearance being very smart and highly creditable. The 1st Leek Girl Guides and Brownies were commanded by Capt. Miss Worthington, Moorhill, Leek, and Lieut. Miss Baggs ...

Sir Robert and Lady Baden-Powell had lunched with Mr and Mrs Horace Wardle at Ladydale, Leek, Mrs Wardle being the county commissioner of the Girl Guides. Admiral Sir Guy Gaunt, Mrs Wardle's brother-in-law (Article 7.8) and Major Lancelot Jukes Worthington, Mrs Wardle's nephew (Article 8.2), were amongst those supporting Mr W.A. Furmston, JP, chairman of the Leek Urban District Council. Later, Sybil was promoted district commissioner of Leek and later still divisional commissioner. On retiring from active service with the Guides she was appointed divisional president, an appointment she held for the rest of her life.

At some stage, following the sale of the contents of Hillesdon, probably in 1934, she rented and lived in a bungalow called Windycote in Cheddleton, three miles south of Leek. By the early 1940s she had moved to Stella Maris, a cottage at Nanquido, St Just, Cornwall, which she shared with Miss E. Patchett who had at one time been matron at the Moorhill Preparatory School. On Miss Patchett's death, Sybil moved to Daneor, Mossley, Congleton, Cheshire, to live with her younger sister Gwenyth Worthington (Article 7.11). On Gwenyth's death, Sybil moved to Brierley, a nearby bungalow.

According to Sybil's brother, Guy Jukes Worthington (Article 7.10), 'she was one of the most unselfish women, very interested in people, especially relatives, and was particularly devoted to cats'. She died, unmarried, of a heart attack on 26 November 1959 at Brierley. The funeral service was held on 30 November 1959 at Mossley church, followed by cremation at Carmountside Crematorium, Milton, Staffordshire. In her Will dated 10 October 1955 she declared:

> ... in the event of my death away from the town of Leek in the county of Stafford there is no need to have my body brought back there for burial and I hereby express my wish that everything should be done to give as little trouble as possible ...

However, she asked for her ashes to be placed in the Worthington family tomb in St Luke's churchyard, Leek, and the request was fulfilled. After making 10 bequests, the residue of her estate was to be divided into three equal parts – one for her brother Guy Jukes Worthington, one for her sister Freda Margaret Worthington (Article 7.13) and one to be divided equally between her three nieces Margaret Rose, Sybil Rosemary and Patrica Grace (Articles 7.15 to 7.17).

7.10 Guy Jukes

Guy Jukes Worthington, the eldest son of Ernest Andrew Worthington and Margaret Maude his wife (Article 7.3), was born on 26 February 1886 at Haregate Hall, Leek, and baptised on 4 April 1886 at St Luke's Church, Leek.[1] From 1895 to 1899 he was a boarder at Arden House Preparatory School, Henley-in-Arden, near Birmingham – a school owned and run by Mary Bracknell (born Pemberton) who was a first cousin of Guy's father. Guy transferred to Shrewsbury School for the Michaelmas

60 *Moorhill, Leek, with the gymnasium.*

term 1899 and stayed there for five years where he excelled in sports and athletics.[35] His father died during this period, after which Maude sold Ernest's share in the textile business to his brother Philip (Articles 7.8 and 8.1). Thus it soon became clear that Guy would not be able to enter the family business. On leaving Shrewsbury, therefore, he had to choose a career and decided on teaching. He entered Lincoln College, Oxford, where he attained a BA degree in 1907 and an MA in 1911.[12]

Guy was an assistant master at a preparatory school in the south of England from 1907 to 1913. By 1913 he had decided to establish his own preparatory school, and with a mortgage loan provided by the Leek and Moorlands Building Society, he built a school in the grounds of Hillesdon. He named it 'Moorhill' after the Worcestershire home of his great-grandfather, Jonathan Worthington (Article 3.11). Although the building was completed in 1914, the First World War intervened, the building was temporarily let and the 'Moorhill Preparatory School' did not open until 1919.

Guy took part in the movement for establishing a World language – Esperanto. On 16 April 1914 he was awarded the diploma of the Brita Esperantista Asocio.

He had already joined the Territorial Army, being commissioned on 3 March 1909 as a second-lieutenant in the 5th battalion (The Prince of Wales's) North Staffordshire Regiment. War was declared on 4 August 1914 and within a fortnight the Stone Company of the 5th battalion, of which he was second-in-command, was mobilised for service in France. A local wartime postcard shows the 120-strong company marching out of Stone, Staffordshire, in column of fours led by Guy, then a lieutenant, preceded by a 16-strong band. The caption read 'The Stone Territorials off to the front, August 1914'. On 22 August 1914, he was appointed temporary captain.

On 13 October 1915, Guy was slightly wounded in the Battle of Loos. This battle consisted of a British assault on the German defences in the neighbourhood of Loos-en-Gohelle, about 50 miles south-west of Calais. The assault was a failure, the British casualties being 50,000 against the German 20,000. The 5th North Staffordshire battalion was to attack the Hohenzollern redoubt and mining village near Loos. The battalion joined other units at the village of Drouvain, near Béthune, where there were lectures and other preparations. Then at night the brigade band played them off to the trenches which had been dug by the Germans some 1,000 yards from the redoubt. At noon next day British artillery started bombarding the enemy lines, and in the evening the brigade went over the top for the attack. In Guy's own words, taken from his report now kept at the *Imperial War Museum*:[36]

> ... At two minutes to zero I led my company over the top and we lay down according to orders in front of our own wire to wait for the moment for advance. This was, I believe, accomplished almost, if not quite, without casualties. I could see the 6th South acting in similar fashion on our right. At 2-5pm exactly I jumped up and waved my cane and the whole line rose and commenced a steady advance. We were met by a hail of bullets and men fell fast but we kept on. I myself was struck on the side of the thigh and knocked over, but got up and went on again only to find I had only four or five men with me. We struck a trench running diagonally which we crossed, and lay down on the other side. Then as there was no one else in sight we made a dash for the trench and jumped down into it – at least one or two of us were successful. The others were shot down ...

Alas, 19 officers and 488 men of the 5th battalion were killed – most within the first 10 minutes by machine guns. At daybreak Guy found that a bullet had passed lengthways through the New Testament bible which he kept in the left breast pocket of his tunic. He reckoned that it had saved his life. The bible is now kept at the Prince of Wales's Regimental Museum at Whittington Barracks, Lichfield, Staffordshire. On 30 April 1916 Guy was mentioned in a despatch from General Sir Douglas Haig, GCB, KCIE, ADC to King George V (later Field-Marshal, 1st Earl Haig, KT, OM, GCVO), the citation being 'for gallant and distinguished services in the field'. Guy also fought in the Battle of the Somme. On 1 July 1916, 13 British divisions went over the top in regular waves from their trenches, but the attack was another failure – 19,000 British soldiers being killed and a further 57,000 wounded. This is the greatest loss which had ever been sustained by a British army in a single day.

Guy served in Egypt as well as France, but in February 1918 he was appointed chief instructor of the Lewis Gun School at General Headquarters, Le Touquet-Paris-Plage, about 30 miles south-south-west of Calais, where he served for the rest of the war. There he earned the reputation of being more exact in drill than any other instructor in

61   *Guy Jakes Worthington and Kathleen St Clair, born McClure.*

France. He was demobilised as from 9 January 1919 with the substantive rank of captain.

Later that year Guy was appointed commanding officer of the Leek battery in the Territorial Army, with the rank of major. However, the demands of the Moorhill Preparatory School, of which he was proprietor and head master, were too great and he resigned in 1920. On 18 March 1923 he attended the unveiling of the War Memorial at St Luke's Church, Leek, by his first cousin Colonel Godfrey Davenport Goodman (Article 7.4). Guy read out the names of 87 parishioners who had died on active service. He was probably already a churchwarden; he certainly was in 1925.

On 19 April 1933 Guy married Kathleen St Clair, the youngest daughter of Dr Thomas McClure and his wife Minnie Maude of Lower Addiscombe Road, Croydon, Surrey. Thomas was a graduate of Trinity College, Dublin, a fellow of the Royal College of Surgeons in Ireland and had attained an MD degree in the University of Belgium in 1876. Prior to the wedding Kathleen was living at The Cottage, The Parsonage, Manchester, but she had previously been a teacher at the Moorhill Preparatory School.[32] Indeed, it was customary for jesters to say that 'Guy married his mistress'. Kathleen had been born on 9 November 1904 at Whittington Moor, Derbyshire, and baptised on 19 December 1904 at St Mary's and All Saints' Church, Chesterfield, Derbyshire. She attended Metfield School, Southport, Lancashire as a boarder. The school magazine for the autumn term 1921 shows that she was one of the five prefects and one of the committee of three responsible for *The Metfield Magazine*.[37]

The marriage took place at St Ann's Church, Manchester. As her father had died previously she was given away by her brother, Dr Walter St Clair McClure, MRCS, DPH, assistant medical officer of health for Manchester. Yorke Worthington was best man, Valentine Worthington one of the four bridesmaids and Philip Worthington a page (Articles 7.14, 8.3 and 8.4 respectively). Asked by the parson 'Do you take this man to be your lawful wedded husband?', Kathleen replied 'No'. She was taken to the vestry by the parson and one or two members of the congregation;

Guy remained but was summoned to the vestry later. After some 20 minutes' delay the service was resumed, this time with the affirmative answer. After the ceremony there was a reception for 80 guests at the *Midland Hotel*, Manchester. In the weeks that followed there was much gossip and speculation as to why Kathleen had said 'no'; one possibility was that she had been dared to by Miss French, a cousin.

In 1928 Guy was nominated a director of the Leek and Moorlands Building Society.[38] His first cousin's step-father, Admiral Sir Guy Gaunt, had been vice-president of the society from 1918 to 1924 (Article 7.8). The society had been established on 30 May 1856 with its head office at 1 Stockwell Street, Leek, and later at 15 Stockwell Street, next door to Stockwell House – the home of Philip Jukes Worthington and his wife Margaret Elizabeth (Article 7.8). Later the society bought and demolished Stockwell House and built its new head office in its place.[39] 'New Stockwell House' was opened in 1937 by Sir Enoch Hill, Kt, JP, FCIS, a native of Leek who was president of the Halifax Building Society, then the largest building society in the world. Guy introduced Sir Enoch who was given the golden key to enter. The ceremony was followed by luncheon at the *North Stafford Hotel*, Stoke-on-Trent, where Guy presided and replied to Sir Enoch's toast to the society.[39] Guy was deputising for the chairman who was absent through illness, but a year later, in September 1938, Guy was unanimously elected chairman.

The society appointed its first agent in 1920, opened its first branch in 1930 and made its first acquisition – the Longton Permanent Benefit Building Society – in 1937. By that time the society had 80 branches and was the largest in Staffordshire. The progress of growth then accelerated; the society changed its name to the Leek and Westbourne Building Society, later to the Leek Westbourne and Eastern Counties Building Society and finally to the Britannia Building Society, a much larger head office having been built on the outskirts of Leek. Guy remained chairman for seven years until 1945 and then continued to serve as deputy chairman. The 10th congress of the International Union of Building Societies and Savings' Associations was held at *The London Hilton Hotel* from 4 to 8 October 1965. Hubert Newton (later Sir Hubert Newton, Kt, HonMA), then chairman of the Leek and Moorlands Building Society, was president of the Union for the year. The Leek and Moorlands had that year created a Presidential Badge and Collar to be worn by the successive presidents of the Union. It fell to Guy, as deputy chairman of the Leek and Moorlands, to invest Hubert with the insignia by placing it over his head. Guy ended his speech with:[40] '... Although I have been closely associated with Mr Newton for more than 30 years, I have never been so keen to ring his neck'. Guy retired in 1970 at the age of 84 years, having been a director of the society for 42 years. He was still attending the annual luncheons of the society at the *North Stafford Hotel* at the age of 90 years.[32]

By 1934 Guy had reached a decision to sell Hillesdon, the house in Leek which had been built by his parents (Article 7.3). Presumably he had hoped that the school would have expanded enough to use Hillesdon as an additional boarding house, but England was then in the worst slump of the century. The contents of the house were valued by Chinneck, Gardner and Corbet Ltd of London on 17 February 1934, the following being a summary:

	£	s	d
Furniture and general contents	252	6	0
Linen	10	0	0
Silver	129	14	0
Plated items and cutlery	27	5	0
China, glass and ornaments	42	0	0
Books	10	10	0
Pictures	24	15	0
Motor mower	7	0	0
	503	10	0*

It is not known when the contents were sold, but the inventory is marked to show which items were retained by Guy himself and his five brothers and sisters. The house was not sold until about 1936.

On 13 May 1937 Guy appealed to the minister of transport against a local authority plan to build a road through the playing fields of his school and encroaching on the 'garage attached to the school gymnasium'. The minister did not uphold the appeal. In 1940, following the outbreak of the Second World War, the school was closed and the main building sold after the war to the Staffordshire County Council for use as an old people's home. Guy and Kathleen retained the gymnasium which they converted into their new home with the name 'Moorhill'. The old people's home was renamed 'Moorview'. Although the school, which had run for the 21-year period between the two world wars, had not enjoyed economic growth, it had been academically successful and had a long list of pupils who had followed through to university.

During the early months of the Second World War, declared on 3 September 1939, there was a small auxiliary force known as the Local Defence Volunteers, but early in 1940 the government decided to rename the force the 'Home Guard' and expand it greatly in view of the increasing fear of a German invasion. Over 1,000,000 men enrolled by the summer of 1940. On 27 May 1940 Guy was appointed lieutenant-colonel commanding the 5th Staffordshire (Leek) battalion, Home Guard, which was built up to a strength of 1,400 men. The battalion continued in service until December 1944 – when the fear of an invasion had passed. The stand down parade was held early in December, 710 officers and men being present, supported by a Royal Air Force band. A service was held at St Edward's Church, Leek, and afterwards Guy took the

---

* Equivalent to 1,660 man-days of English agricultural labour.

salute and addressed the battalion.[32] On 28 February 1945, the officers gathered at the old battalion headquarters to present Guy with a silver salver inscribed with the battalion's insignia and the words 'Presented to Lt.-Col. G.J. Worthington, CO 5th Staffs (Leek) Battalion Home Guard 1940-1944 by his officers'. A musical evening followed.[32]

By 1956 Guy had become president of the Fifth North Staffordshire (1914-1919) Reunion Association which met each April for their annual dinner. There were traditionally five toasts and one response, Guy as president always proposing 'Absent comrades' and sometimes proposing 'the Guests'. These reunion dinners continued until 1976, the golden jubilee of the association. Guy was then 90 years of age and the average age of the surviving members was eighty.

At a ceremony held on 12 June 1971, Guy laid the foundation stone of the new church and community centre at Novi Lane, Leek.[32] The church is a branch of St Luke's Church. He used the silver trowel and mallet which had been used by his grandmother, Sarah Booth Worthington, when laying the foundation stone of the chancel to St Luke's a century earlier in 1873 (Article 3.30). Kathleen placed a purse containing a set of the recently minted decimal coins within the stone.[41]

Earlier in life, Guy had been an actor with the Moorland Players; his sports were cricket, soccer, hockey, tennis, golf and shooting. For many years he was president of the Leek Choral Society and president of the Leek British Legion Band. He was also chairman of the trustees of the Carr Charity.

He died without issue at Moorhill on 16 December 1978 aged 93 years.[32] The funeral service was on 21 December 1978 at St Luke's Church, Leek, and afterwards he was cremated at Carmountside Crematorium, Milton, Staffordshire.[31]

Kathleen continued to live at Moorhill for the remainder of her life. One of her interests was the Royal Society for the Prevention of Cruelty to Animals. For over 40 years she was secretary of the Leek Auxiliary of the North Staffordshire Branch of the society. About two years after her retirement as secretary she was awarded the society's Queen Victoria bronze medal and presented with a Staffordshire china figure depicting a shepherdess. She also took part in the work of the Leek Dogs' Home.

She died at Moorhill on 13 April 1980 aged 75 years. The funeral service held at St Luke's Church, Leek, on 18 April 1980 was followed by cremation at Carmountside Crematorium. Her ashes were spread over the grave of her mother, Minnie Maude McClure, in Leek Cemetery.

Guy and Kathleen had made a pair of similar Wills on 12 April 1973 so that whichever died first the other would inherit for life, the estate then passing in an agreed way regardless of who died first. Bequests were made to Guy's three nieces, Margaret, Rosemary and Patricia (Articles 7.15 to 7.17). Bequests of family pictures, silver and china were made to the

62 *Gwenyth Worthington.*

five children of Guy's first cousin, Lancelot Worthington. (Articles 8.3 to 8.7) Other beneficiaries included the RSPCA and the Leek Dogs' Home. The residue of the estate passed to Kathleen's niece, Mrs Patricia Bell, of 73 Lower High Street, Thame, Oxfordshire.

7.11 Gwenyth

Gwenyth Worthington, the second daughter of Ernest Andrew Worthington and Margaret Maude his wife (Article 7.3), was born on 2 June 1888 at Haregate Hall, Leek, and baptised on 1 July 1888 at St Luke's Church, Leek.[1] She was known throughout her life as 'Gwen'. Her early education was by governess at home. Later she attended the Leek High School for Girls, followed by a year at a finishing school at Saint-Maur-des-Fosses, near Paris, France. When she returned home she did much voluntary work for the Red Cross in Leek. When the First World War broke out in 1914, then aged 26 years, she was appointed commandant of the Red Cross Hospital, Foxlowe, Leek, which was a convalescent home for servicemen. Foxlowe had been the house of Mrs Cruso (sometimes known as the Queen of Leek) and stands in a dominant position overlooking Leek market square. Gwenyth held that post from December 1914 to March 1919 for which she was appointed a member of the Order of the British Empire.[42] She led a contingent of 15 members of the Voluntary Aid Detachment in the Leek peace celebration procession held in July 1919 when her cousins Colonel W.F. Challinor DSO and Major L.J. Worthington (Article 8.2) were marshals.[13]

In 1920 Gwenyth was at St Thomas's Hospital, London SE1, being trained as a nurse; on qualifying she duly received the badge of the 'Florence Nightingale School of Nursing'. She then attended a midwifery course, probably in Newcastle upon Tyne. Her first delivery after qualifying was her first cousin once removed, Philip Michael Worthington (Article 8.4); she often called him 'my first baby'. That event on 24 April 1926 prevented her from attending the wedding of her brother Roger Ernest Worthington (Article 7.12) three days later. At about that time, Gwenyth was appointed matron of the Shamrock Hospital in Durham. She held that post until 1926 when she was appointed matron of the

War Memorial Hospital at Congleton, Cheshire, which had been opened by the Duke of York (later King George VI) in 1924. She was given a month's leave to be midwife at the birth of the first baby of her sister-in-law, Primrose Worthington (Article 7.12) at Hillesdon, Leek. Although living at Congleton, Gwenyth retained her interest in the Red Cross at Leek. For some years, certainly including 1936 and 1937, she was 'lady superintendent' of the Leek Detachment, Red Cross. In that capacity she had a consulting or advisory role. During her tenure as matron, the hospital was extended: 15 beds were increased to 33, a nurses' home was built, and x-ray and outpatients' departments were added.

At the hospital's annual general meeting held in April 1948 she was presented with a cheque for £333[*] in recognition of 21 years' service as matron, the sum having been subscribed by staff and townsfolk. That was the last annual general meeting as an independent hospital, as it became part of the National Health Service on 5 July 1948. On her retirement in 1952 at the age of 64 years, the medical and nursing staff presented Gwenyth with a silver salver, on the reverse of which was inscribed:

> Presented to Miss G. Worthington, MBE, by the Medical and Nursing Staff at the War Memorial Hospital, Congleton, on her retirement after 26 years as matron, November 27th 1952.

The presentation was made at a ceremony at the hospital.[43] Within the next few days there were further presentations by the female patients the male patients and the domestic staff of the hospital.

For her retirement Gwenyth purchased the house called 'Daneor' in Biddulph Road, Mossley, Congleton, where she lived with her sister Sybil (Article 7.9) for the rest of her life. Gwenyth was a member of the Lady Golfers' Club and the Tailwaggers' Club.[44] She died unmarried on 10 September 1955 at the Stoke-on-Trent City General Hospital. The funeral service was held at Astbury church after which she was cremated at the Carmountside Crematorium, Milton, Staffordshire. Her ashes were placed in the family vault at St Luke's Church, Leek. By her Will, dated 8 January 1948, she bequeathed her silver salver to her godson Philip Michael Worthington. After making 16 other bequests, the residue of her estate was divided into two equal parts for her sisters Sybil and Freda (Articles 7.9 and 7.13).

7.12 Roger Ernest

Roger Ernest Worthington, the second son of Ernest Andrew Worthington and Margaret Maude his wife (Article 7.3), was born on 19 November 1889 at Haregate Hall, Leek, and baptised on 12 January 1890 at St Luke's Church, Leek.[1] He was educated at Shrewsbury School from the Lent term of 1902 until the end of the summer term of 1904.[35] His

---

[*] Equivalent to 470 man-days of agricultural labour.

ambition was to pursue a naval career, so it was a disappointment to learn in 1904 that his vision was not to the standard required for deck duties. He then visited France and Germany to learn their languages, and he studied accountancy and passed the entrance examination for the Accountancy Branch of the Royal Navy. He enrolled on 15 July 1907 and was posted to the Royal Naval Barracks at Chatham, Kent, on 27 August 1907. At all stages of his training he received first-class certificates. His final paymaster examination was taken on 19 November 1910, having served in HMS *Prince of Wales* – the flagship of Admiral Prince Louis Alexander of Battenberg (later Admiral of the Fleet Sir Louis Mountbatten, GCB, GCVO, KCMG, PC, LLD, DL, ADC to King George V, 1st marquess of Milford Haven), commander-in-chief of the Atlantic Fleet.

Roger was commissioned assistant paymaster on 6 December 1910, and on 31 December 1910 he became additional assistant paymaster on HMS *Powerful* as secretary's clerk to Vice-Admiral George F. King-Hall (later Admiral Sir George King-Hall, KCB, CVO) commander-in-chief – Australia. Sir George was the last of the English naval commanders of the Australian fleet, as the Royal Australian Navy took over in October 1913.

On 3 September 1913 Roger transferred to HMS *Psyche* and was appointed senior officer's clerk and the official German interpreter of the New Zealand Division. He was there when the First World War was declared on 4 August 1914, and took part in the New Zealand Expeditionary Force to Samoa in the Pacific Ocean – then a German possession. The force, consisting of six warships and two troop transports, steamed in line ahead to the port of Apia, led by HMS *Psyche*, on 29 August 1914. While the force stood offshore, a power boat was lowered to take Roger, two other officers and a contingent of sailors to the harbour under a flag of truce. The officers (Roger as interpreter) delivered the summons to surrender. Roger noted that the governor had '… we were told, gone to a meeting with some high chiefs …', but a position was reached with the deputy governor, and the troops disembarked.

While on leave at Hillesdon, Roger received a letter dated 9 June 1915 appointing him assistant paymaster to HMS *Princess Margaret* for duty with the captain in charge of the mine-layer squadron and as interpreter in German. He was involved in 19 night operations in such areas as the Heligoland Bight and off the Belgian coast, and 11 of these were in enemy waters. For this he was awarded the Distinguished Service Cross on 1 October 1917.[44] On 7 March 1917 he joined HMS *Victory* to become assistant paymaster to Admiral the Honourable Sir Stanley C.J. Colville, GCVO, KCB. On 13 June 1918, promoted to paymaster lieutenant, Roger re-joined Vice-Admiral Sir George King-Hall who was then commanding Orkneys and Shetland, and he was present at the surrender of the German Fleet.[45]

A letter dated 4 April 1919 addressed to 'Paymaster Lieutenant Roger E. Worthington, DSC, RN, care of the Dardanelles Committee, Annexe 2, Admiralty, London SW1' confirmed his appointment as secretary to the committee, set up to report on the attacks on the Dardanelles which commenced on 19 February 1915. This was part of a mixed services' commission visiting the Gallipoli battlefields to learn lessons from the failure.

In November 1919 he took a staff position at the Boys' Training Establishment – HMS *Ganges* at Shotley, near Ipswich, Suffolk but this post lasted for two months only. From 1 January 1920 he attended the first-secretary's course at Portsmouth which he passed with 80 per cent marking. His subjects were naval, military, criminal and international law, naval prize law, commercial law, the *Merchant Shipping Act*, lecture and précis. A few months later he was promoted paymaster lieutenant-commander. On 19 November 1920 he was appointed a member of the Inter-Allied Naval Control Sub-commission at Berlin, presided over by his future father-in-law, Captain Henry Edgar Grace, RN (later Admiral Grace, CB, commander of the Order of St Anne (Russia), Croix de Guerre avec Palme (France), commander of the Order of the Redeemer (Greece), ADC to King George V).[45] This assignment lasted 18 months. On 22 April 1922 Roger became secretary to Edgar, who was then taking up duties as commodore, Hong Kong.[46] Commodore and Mrs Grace, their three daughters and Roger set sail on SS *Kashmir* of the P. & O. line on 28 April 1922 arriving in Hong Kong on 3 June 1922. The Grace family lived on board HMS *Tamar*, a 320-foot troopship converted for the use of the Hong Kong commodore and moored in the dockyard there. Roger, as commodore's secretary, had a cabin on board, separate from the commodore's family, but he ate with them. This appointment lasted until December 1924 when they sailed from Hong Kong in SS *Mantua* of the P. & O. line, calling at Singapore. The passenger list from Singapore to England shows that Commodore Grace, Miss G. Grace, Miss P. Grace, and Lieutenant-Commander Worthington were on board. In 1925 Roger attended a victualling course at Deptford, London, and on 1 November of that year he became assistant to the drafting commander at the Royal Naval Barracks, Chatham.

On 27 April 1926 Roger married Primrose, the third and youngest daughter of Edgar (then rear-admiral) and his wife Alice Catherine (born Slaughter) of Nortons, The Avenue, Sherborne, Dorset.[9] Primrose was then 21 years of age, having been born on 19 April 1905 at 25 York Crescent, Clifton, Bristol, and educated at Sherborne School for Girls for eight years until 1922. Edgar and Alice's three daughters were nicknamed 'Miss Grace, Disgrace, and Misdemeanour', of whom Primrose was the last. Primrose's grandfather was William Gilbert Grace, MRCS, the famous cricketer.[47] W.G. Grace took after his father, Dr Henry Mills Grace, who was also a medical practitioner and cricketer; but so were four of

63   *Roger Ernest Worthington and Primrose, born Grace.*

W.G.'s brothers, making six Dr Graces in all. W.G. had a fifth brother, but he died shortly before completing his medical studies. Roger and Primrose's wedding took place at Sherborne Abbey and was followed by a reception for 250 guests at the *Digby Hotel*, Sherborne.[48]

Roger and Primrose produced three daughters, namely:

Forenames	Date of birth	Date of baptism	Article
Margaret Rose	22 March 1927	22 May 1927	7.15
Sybil Rosemary	16 March 1930	19 April 1930	7.16
Patricia Grace	12 September 1934	4 October 1934	7.17

Margaret was born at Hillesdon, Leek, while Rosemary and Patricia were born at the War Memorial Hospital, Congleton.

During the years of peace between the two world wars there was much time for sport, and Roger and Primrose took their part. In March 1920 Roger played centre-half for the Royal Navy in a hockey match against the Rifle Brigade. The Royal Navy won nine nil and a London newspaper noted:[49] '... Paymaster Lieutenant Worthington, the centre-half, gave a sterling display of endurance and, alike in defence and attack, he was the most outstanding player on the field ...'. On 9 and 10 July 1920 he played in the first Inter-Services Lawn Tennis

Championship at Queen's Club. There, Wing-Commander The Duke of York (later King George VI) and his comptroller, Wing-Commander Louis Greig (later Group-Captain, KBE, CVO, MB, ChB, DL), playing doubles for the Royal Air Force, beat Roger and the naval historian Paymaster Lieutenant-Commander Archibald Colquhoun Bell, FRHistS, playing for the Royal Navy.[49] In 1924 Primrose won the ladies' tennis championship of Hong Kong. Roger held the singles championship of the Royal Navy and the Royal Marines for three consecutive years – 1925, 1926 and 1927 – for which he won the Earl Beattie Challenge Cup. His fame in doubles was such that the Worthington brewery launched an advertisment claiming that 'Worthington is a perfect partner'. When once he played Hennessy in singles, a cartoon was published with the caption, 'Where are the doubles?'

On 1 September 1927, Edgar Grace was appointed head of the Submarine Branch, his headquarters being the shore station HMS *Dolphin* at Gosport, Hampshire. Roger became his secretary on the same day and they worked together for the third time in two years. On 5 September 1929 Roger was promoted paymaster commander and posted to HMS *Furious*. In April 1930 he returned to the barracks at Chatham as secretary to Commodore Arthur Lionel Snagge (later Vice-Admiral, CB).

Tragedy came to the Grace family on 20 July 1930 when Primrose's elder sister, Mary Gladys Grace, was killed. Gladys and Lieutenant S.E.H. Spencer, who was serving at the submarine headquarters, had visited Roger and Primrose for lunch at their home – The Bungalow, Gillingham Green, Gillingham, Kent. Roger's sister, Gwenyth (Article 7.11), was staying there at the time. Roger, Primrose, their three-year-old daughter Margaret Rose (Article 7.15) and Gwenyth drove their guests to Detling aerodrome, near Maidstone, in Kent, and watched them take off in Lieutenant Spencer's two-seater aeroplane. Primrose later said to a newspaper reporter:

> ... They had just risen from the aerodrome, which is really an emergency landing ground. They circled round once, looped the loop, and were looping for a second time when the machine suddenly dived to the ground. They were not very high at the time. There was a terrific crash, and huge sheets of flame burst from the wrecked machine ...

Roger and Gwyneth ran forward, but the flames kept them away. In a few minutes it had burnt out. Although Gladys had not been at the controls on this occasion, she was known as a daring pilot, being a member of the Hampshire Light Aeroplane Club at Hamble, near Southampton. The previous March she had been flying alone in one of the club's machines when, following a number of stunts, she stalled at the top of a loop at 2,000 feet, entered a spiral dive and crashed at Bursledon, near Southampton. Although the machine was wrecked, she was found unconscious in the cockpit.

From 1932 to 1934 Roger served on HMS *Sussex* of the Mediterranean Fleet while his family lived in Malta. In 1935 he became secretary to Vice-Admiral (later Admiral) the Honourable Sir Reginald Aylmer Ranfurly Plunkett-Ernle-Erle-Drax, commander-in-chief, Plymouth – a post which continued for three years. Roger and his family lived at Mount Wise House, Devonport, Plymouth, Devon – an official residence facing Admiralty House, across the parade ground. On leaving Plymouth he served at the Royal Naval Hospital at Chatham, Kent. On 1 July 1939 he was promoted to paymaster captain. In December 1939 Sir Reginald became commander-in-chief, the Nore, to establish defences against a possible German invasion early in the Second World War. Roger was posted to support him until April 1941 when it was considered that the danger of invasion had receded. For the next three years of the Second World War, Roger was deputy paymaster-director-general at the Admiralty, London. On 13 January 1944 he was appointed aide-de-camp to King George VI.[50] In the king's birthday honours of June of the same year Roger was appointed a companion of the Order of the Bath (Military Division).[51] During this period, Roger and Primrose lived at Ridgeway, Claygate, Surrey.

He left the Admiralty at normal retiring age on his 55th birthday – 19 November 1944, but continued to serve in the Royal Navy as paymaster captain of HMS *Collingwood*, the on-shore naval training establishment near Fareham, Hampshire. He finally retired in January 1947 with the rank of rear-admiral.

On 26 March 1953 Primrose was presented at court to Queen Elizabeth II. The presentation was made by Adelaide, the wife of Primrose's brother, Commander Edgar William Grace, OBE. In turn, Primrose presented her three daughters, Margaret, Rosemary and Patricia; Roger was present.

After Roger left the Admiralty, he and Primrose lived at Tamar, 15 Beech Grove, Alverstoke, where they lived until 1947. They then moved to a larger house at Fort Road, Alverstoke, taking the name 'Tamar' with them. They lived there for four years, but Roger then suffered from osteo-arthritis in one hip and could not maintain the garden, so they moved again to a seven-bedroomed house at 10 Beech Grove. Again they took the name 'Tamar' with them, the house in Fort Road being renamed 'Gramsholme'. Tamar, 10 Beech Grove, where they lived for 16 years, later became an Abbeyfield Nursing Home. From 1943 to 1958 Roger was the honorary secretary of the Alverstoke Lawn Tennis Club. In 1948 he became a warden of St Mary's Church, Alverstoke. After serving the church for 14 years, he resigned at the annual general meeting held at Easter 1962 when, to his surprise, he was elected churchwarden emeritus, a post he held for life.[52] In 1949 he and two other retired naval officers established an Officers' Advice Bureau to provide confidential advice to young naval officers. From

1950 to 1956 he was Gosport's Poppy Day organiser for the British Legion. Also from 1950 he was a committee member of the Royal Naval Benevolent Society. He was one of the managers of the Alverstoke and Leesland Church of England schools, and was a non-playing member of the Wimbledon Lawn Tennis Club. Primrose took her part in most of Roger's local activities, and for many years she was the honorary secretary of the Stoke Road Infant Welfare Centre.

Roger died on 20 October 1967 at Tamar. His funeral service took place on 24 October 1967 at St Mary's Church, after which he was cremated at Portchester Crematorium, Hampshire.[32] In his Will dated 2 September 1966, with codicil dated 14 August 1967, he made a bequest to his married daughter, Sybil Rosemary Douglass (Article 7.16). All the remainder he left in trust, the income to be paid to Primrose for life, and then the capital passing in equal parts to his three daughters.

In March 1968 Primrose sold Tamar and moved to 2 Little Green, Alverstoke, where she lived for a further 29 years. About November 1997 she sold 2 Little Green and moved to the Alverstoke House Nursing Home. On 29 May 1998, aged 93 years, she opened an exhibition at Lord's Cricket Ground, London, to commemorate the 150th anniversary of the birth of W.G. Grace.[9] She had previously, on 21 October 1995, broadcast on Radio Four's 'Sport on 4' to celebrate the 80th anniversary of W.G.'s death.

Primrose died on 23 January 1999 at Alverstoke and was cremated on 1 February 1999 at the Portchester Crematorium. A service of thanksgiving was held the next day at St Mary's church, Alverstoke.

7.13 Freda Margaret

Freda Margaret Worthington, the third and youngest daughter of Ernest Andrew Worthington and Margaret Maude his wife (Article 7.3), was born on 11 September 1891 at Haregate Hall, Leek, and baptised on 18 October 1891 at St Luke's Church, Leek. In her early years she was educated by governesses at home, but she later attended the Leek High School for Girls followed by the Oxford High School for Girls. While boarding at Oxford she became seriously ill, probably with pneumonia. Later she took a secretarial course in London.

She visited France for a year with her elder sister Gwenyth (Article 7.11), and later visited Germany with her younger brother Andrew Yorke (Article 7.14) with the intention of learning the German language. When the First World War was declared on 4 August 1914, Freda was allowed to return to England while Yorke was held as a civilian prisoner. She then joined the government's Censorship in London for the duration of the war, after which she returned to Germany to work with the British Army of the Rhine. Later, she returned home to live with her mother at Hillesdon.

64   *Freda Margaret Worthington.*

Freda was a member of the Moorland Players, an amateur dramatic society which produced plays at the Grand Theatre, Leek, and the Church Hall, Cheddleton.[53] On one occasion she played the part of the Honourable Monica Flane in *The Lilies of the Field* by J.H. Turner. Of the cast of 12, four were Worthingtons, namely: Freda, Phyllis (Article 8.2), Guy (Article 7.10) and Yorke (Article 7.14). A fifth member, Andrew Gawen Goodman (later major, MBE, TD, DL) was a close relation, being a grandson of Emily Jane Goodman, born Worthington (Article 7.4). A surviving poster shows that the play was staged at Leek on 19, 20 and 21 March, but the year is not given: however it would have been in the early 1930s.

Although her mother died in 1927 and Hillesdon became the property of Guy Worthington, Freda and Yorke continued to live there until it was sold in about 1936. Freda then rented Altenahr, 13 Milner Terrace, Leek, about 600 yards west of Hillesdon and Moorhill.

She took a keen interest in politics and, following her mother's example, became a member of the Leek Women's Unionist Association (later called the Women's Advisory Committee of the Leek Division of the Conservative and Unionist Association). She also worked for the British Red Cross Society.

On the outbreak of the Second World War in 1939, Freda re-joined the Censorship, then in Liverpool, Lancashire, and served there until the end of hostilities in 1945. Her work included censoring letters written by German prisoners of war. The heavy bombardment of Liverpool caused her to spend nights in a damp air-raid shelter which may have accounted for her poor state of health in later life. She then returned to Altenahr at the age of 54 years where, as Guy Worthington described, she '... became concerned with her health ...' She was a regular worshipper at All Saints' Church, Leek, was a member of the parochial church council, and took a leading part in its management. All Saints' was the high church of the town. According to Guy, she was clever and at times amusing. In character, she resembled her aunt Alice Elizabeth, and was given to making frequent contentious statements. An instance, recounted many times since, illustrates Freda's character or sense of humour (or perhaps a combination of the two): when Primrose Worthington (Article 7.12) was leaving Altenahr after a few days' visit, Primrose dutifully gave Mabel the maid a tip. Freda later said to Primrose, 'You shouldn't have tipped Mabel; I'll take it out of her next week's wages'.

Freda died unmarried on 27 January 1966 at the Orthopaedic Hospital, Hartshill, Staffordshire. The funeral service was held on 31 January 1966 at All Saints' Church, Leek and she was buried at the cemetery at Leek, in the grave of her mother and stepfather. In a note dated 15 May 1956 to her executors, she declared:

> I wish to place on record that on my death I desire that my body be buried at the Leek Cemetery – preferably on a high piece of ground. I wish to make it absolutely clear that I do not desire my body to be cremated and I do not desire that my body be placed in the Family Vault in St Luke's Churchyard.

In her last Will dated 5 June 1961, she made bequests to All Saints' Church, St Luke's Church, the Society of the Holy Trinity of Ascot and her maid Phyllis Mabel Wood. Half of the residue of her estate was placed in trust to provide income for life for her eldest brother Guy, and later his widow, the capital then descending to her three nieces, Margaret Rose, Sybil Rosemary, and Patricia Grace (Articles 7.15 to 7.17 respectively).

7.14 Andrew Yorke

Andrew Yorke Worthington, the third son and youngest child of Ernest Andrew Worthington and Margaret Maude his wife (Article 7.3), was born on 29 April 1895 at Haregate Hall, Leek, and baptised on 2 June 1895 at St Luke's Church, Leek. Although strictly a Jukes Worthington, Yorke took his second name from his half-cousin once removed, Jonathan Yorke Worthington (Article 3.31). Ernest wrote to Jonathan for permission to use the name and received a reply dated 18 May 1895:

> I do not see why you should not call your boy Yorke if you fancy it. It comes through my grandmother from the Yorkes of Beverley ...

The Yorke Worthingtons had already made a counter-exception, Jonathan Yorke's younger brother being baptised Richard Jukes Worthington (Article 3.34).

Yorke was educated at Shrewsbury School, after which he attended a course in silk textiles at Owen's College, Manchester (later known as the Victoria University of Manchester). Then he visited Germany to learn the language. He was on his second visit, this time with his elder sister Freda (Article 7.13), when, on 4 August 1914, the United Kingdom declared war on Germany. Freda was allowed to return home but Yorke, being of military age, was interned for the duration of the hostilities. He was placed in a local prison for two days, then transferred to Berlin for

65   *Andrew Yorke Worthington.*

three weeks and finally taken to the Ruhleben racecourse, near Berlin. While there he was responsible for the camp library, and at times had to sleep in a horse box.

Aged 23 years, he returned home in 1918 ready to take up a full-time career with A.J. Worthington & Co. Limited. Such a career had been offered to him at the age of seven years by his uncle, Philip Jukes Worthington (Article 7.8). Philip had stated in his Will dated 17 January 1902:

> ... I also authorise my Trustees to allow my nephew Yorke Worthington in case he shall choose to come into the business on finishing his education a yearly salary not exceeding one hundred pounds* per annum for his services until he shall attain the age of twenty one years ...

The Will provided that, on attaining the age of 21 years, Yorke could contribute £2000[†] to the capital of the company on which he would receive interest in addition to a salary not exceeding £200 a year until he reached the age of 24 years. On attaining that age he would be entitled to a quarter of the profits of the business in lieu of salary.

Philip had died on 20 July 1902 soon after making his Will, and his widow Margaret Elizabeth had since become the wife of Sir Guy Gaunt (Article 7.8). When Yorke returned from Germany Lady Gaunt was chairman of the company, holding that position while her son, Lancelot Jukes Worthington (Article 8.2), was abroad on military service. She did not wish to accept Yorke into the business, partly because it would later involve Lancelot in the loss of a quarter of the profits and partly because she had been vexed by the hurt Philip had suffered when York's mother had withdrawn her family from the business (Article 7.3). Her first attempts to extinguish Yorke's rights had been made when Yorke was aged 13 years. She had argued that Philip's Will only had legal force in respect of Yorke so long as the business continued to be held by the family in its old form as a proprietorship or partnership. The requirement to honour Philip's Will, she held, would not transfer

---

* Equivalent to 770 man-days of agricultural labour.
† Equivalent to 15,400 man-days of agricultural labour.

into a new limited company formed for the purpose of acquiring the business. She obtained counsel's opinion on the subject from Howard Wright, KC, of Lincoln's Inn, London. In his report of 13 July 1908 he warned that:

> ... the point is not free from doubt and I think that Mr Yorke Worthington would have a stronger case if the sale took place after he had attained 21 and complied with the conditions of the Will.

Accordingly, when the business was transferred to a company in 1909, its articles of association contained the former provisions relating to Yorke. On Yorke's return, Lady Gaunt again tried to keep him out. She entered into extensive correspondence with Morley Shireff & Co., solicitors of 53 Gresham House, Old Broad Street, London EC2. The solicitors were worried that the company had already implied acceptance of Yorke by advising him on his training programmes. Mrs Wilson, Yorke's mother, had written to the company on the subject as early as 14 May 1912 and the company secretary had replied on 31 May 1912. Starting on 1 January 1913 Yorke had then undergone an ordinary course for three months and a special course for six months, obtaining a second-class certificate in silk throwing and spinning. Because of this background a swift and clear refusal of Yorke was not possible, so prevarication set in on both sides and negotiations became deadlocked. Yorke kept asking for advice on which course of training he should take, perhaps with an object of getting the company to further imply commitment. Lady Gaunt and the company avoided giving advice lest they should further commit themselves. Lady Gaunt obtained a second opinion from her brother Frederick Darlington Wardle, a solicitor of Bath, Somerset. He wrote from the *Bath Spa Hotel* in late May 1919:

> I don't feel comfortable after reading the correspondence. There is so much artificiality about it and you could easily be manoeuvred into a false position ... I would sooner grasp the nettle and say 'we will take you in if you do qualify. We shall not be able to judge this till you have had the training ...' I feel that the correspondence on present lines has too much risk for you and if they get a chance they will have material for saying ' they never really meant anything and kept us at arms length all the time without saying what the poor lad was to do to get what his uncle wanted him to have!

More letters were exchanged between Lady Gaunt and Yorke which showed both parties were frustrated and in deadlock. Meanwhile, Yorke was obtaining information from technical colleges in Leicester on available courses in knitting. On 12 June 1919 Lady Gaunt wrote to Morley Shireff & Co.:

> Here is Yorke's answer. We still get no forrader. What we want before we advise him is a decided answer. He is either holding back purposely, or is just a fool; I am beginning to think the latter ... his two chief friends

> are Frank Adams and a Mr Trafford, keen competitors of ours; in fact
> both left us to start for themselves taking some (as many as they could
> get) of our customers. Mr Trafford is sending his two boys in September
> to Guy Worthington's school which opens at Hillesdon then ...

Frank Adams (Article 7.2) was Yorke's first cousin. Herbert Trafford
became a well-known Leek businessman, having been born at Nelson
Street, Tittesworth, Leek, on 1 February 1870. He started his career
as an errand boy in A.J. Worthington & Co. and worked his way up
in the company to sales representative before joining Frank Adams in
George Davenport, Adams and Co. of Hope Mills, Leek. Later he was
a co-founder of Trafford and White, knitwear manufacturers of Leek.
By 1934 he was living at Portland House, Portland Street, Leek, and
was chairman of the Leek Division Unionist Association.

Correspondence with Yorke continued apace until 27 June 1919
when the company admitted that a course in Leicester would be more
suitable, but they re-stated that they '... in no way bind themselves to
take you into this business ...'. On 8 July 1919 Yorke wrote to Lady
Gaunt, addressing her 'Dear Aunt Maggie':

> I have written to the Board to say that I am arranging to take the course
> in Leicester and to thank them for their advice. I want to thank you
> also as a Trustee of Uncle Philip's Will for what you have done for me
> in laying before the Board the wishes expressed in the Will. I think the
> course should be very useful to me and, I hope, also to the Firm, if they
> take me into their employment when I apply to them again.

Yorke was then allowed to join the knitting department for a month's
experience before the course began. The Articles of Association were
duly amended at an extraordinary general meeting of the company
held on 7 October 1919 to enable Yorke to postpone taking up his
400 ordinary shares of £5 each until any time up to 31 December
1923. The 400 shares constituted the promised 25 per cent of the
ordinary capital – the capital of the company then consisted of 1,600
ordinary shares and 6,000 preference shares of £1 each. At least 17
letters on the subject had been written by Lady Gaunt, 17 by Morley
Shireff & Co., eight by Yorke, two by Frederick Wardle and two by
A.J. Worthington & Co.

Yorke eventually joined the company, became head of the knitting
department, took up his 400 shares, was elected a director and earned
a reputation as a disciplinarian. Thus he continued until the great
recession of the early 1930s brought down the company. When the
new company – A.J. Worthington & Co. (Leek) Limited – was formed
out of the ashes of the old, Yorke lost his directorship, but entered
into an agreement dated 6 November 1936 to 'serve the company as
Manager ...' for an initial term of three-and-a-half years, after which the
employment could be terminated by either party giving three months'
notice. He held 4,000 shares of £1 each in this new company, being

two per cent of the ordinary capital. His full-time employment by the company came to an end during 1940 to enable him to take up war-time duties, but another agreement dated 21 March 1941 appointed him a consultant to the company for three calendar years 1941 to 1943 at a salary of £600[*] a year, less any dividends he might receive on his shares. This deed shows that he had already been reinstated as a director and confirmed that he should continue as such through the three-year period. A further deed of 1 January 1944 extended the arrangement for a further three years – to 31 December 1946. A final agreement dated 2 April 1946 appointed him as consultant for a further five years, the fee being £500 a year, payable monthly.

When Hillesdon was sold about 1936, Yorke moved to 42 Newcastle Road, Leek, where he lived for the rest of his life. In 1937 he served on the Entertainments' Committee for the celebrations in Leek to mark the coronation of King George VI and Queen Elizabeth. In 1940 Yorke was appointed civil administrator of the 5th Staffordshire Battalion of the Home Guard of which his elder brother, Guy, was the commanding officer (Article 7.10). Subsequently he was commissioned as the intelligence officer in addition to his civil role, and accordingly was promoted captain. These appointments he held until the Home Guard was disbanded on 31 December 1944. He was later appointed commanding officer of the Leek Battery, Army Cadet Corps, with the rank of major.

As a young man Yorke had been captain of the Leek Hockey Club for 10 years.[54] He belonged to the Leek Golf Club, and for many years was an actor with the Moorland Players. He was a fellow of the Royal Meteorological Society and sent to their headquarters daily local rainfall and other information. He assisted Miss Eleanor Wardle in running the local branch of the Primrose League. For many years he was treasurer of the Leek Board of Guardians; he was also treasurer of the Leek Conservative and Unionist Association and chairman of its North Ward Committee.

He was elected a member of the Leek Rural District Council in 1925, and in due course became chairman of their Sanitary and Hospitals Committee. In 1934, the parish of Lowe, which he represented, was absorbed into the Leek Urban District Council, which Yorke continued to serve. He was vice-chairman in 1941 and 1943 and chairman in 1942.[55] He continued as a councillor until 1947, thus having served the councils for 22 years.

He was chairman of the Youth Employment Committee and the Food Control Committee. He was also chairman of the Leek Disablement Advisory Committee from its formation in 1945. Sometime prior to 1942 he was appointed a commissioner of Inland Revenue. Yorke was also a warden of St Luke's Church, Leek, for three years.

---

[*] Equivalent to 1,680 man-days of agricultural labour.

Yorke died unmarried on 11 February 1950 at the North Staffordshire Royal Infirmary, Hartshill. The funeral service, held on 14 February 1950 at St Luke's Church, Leek, was conducted by five priests – the rural dean, the vicars of St Luke's and All Saints' in Leek, the vicar of St Edward the Confessor's in Cheddleton, and the curate of St Edward's, Leek. Non-commissioned officers and cadets of the Leek Battery, Army Cadet Corps, formed a guard of honour while four lieutenants of the battery carried the coffin which was draped with the Union Jack. Yorke's body was cremated at the Carmountside Crematorium, Milton, Staffordshire, and the ashes were placed in the family vault at St Luke's Church.

In his Will dated 11 March 1941, Yorke made two bequests – one to St Luke's Church and one to his godson, Andrew Ralph Worthington (Article 8.5). The residue of his estate he left in equal parts to his five brothers and sisters.

FOURTH GENERATION – FAMILY OF ROGER ERNEST AND PRIMROSE

7.15 Margaret Rose

Margaret Rose Worthington, the eldest daughter of Roger Ernest Worthington and Primrose his wife (Article 7.12), was born on 22 March 1927 at Hillesdon, Leek, the home of her paternal grandmother Margaret Maude, then Wilson (Article 7.3). Margaret Rose's aunt Gwenyth Worthington (Article 7.11) was the midwife and nurse, having taken a month's leave as matron of the War Memorial Hospital at Congleton for the purpose. Margaret was baptised on 22 May 1927 at the naval church at the Royal Navy Barracks, Chatham, Kent.

She attended day schools in Malta and in Plymouth, Devon, before boarding at Copplestone Preparatory School, Budleigh Salterton, Devon, in 1938. From 1940 to 1944 she boarded at Eversley Girls' School at Lymington, Hampshire, but the school moved away from Lymington for part of the time during the Second World War because of the possibility of air raids. Margaret's home had changed frequently and her father had spent much of his time at sea with the Royal Navy, but in 1941 life became more settled when she, her parents and her two sisters lived at Ridgeway, Claygate, Surrey, while her father was deputy paymaster-general at the Admiralty, London. While living there, Margaret commuted daily in 1944 and 1945 to a Pitman's shorthand and typing course at Wimbledon, Surrey. Later she attended a domestic science course at Portsmouth Technical School.

She became under-matron, firstly at Boundary Oak Preparatory School at Purbrook, Hampshire, and later at Byculla Girls' School near Petersfield, Hampshire. In December 1966, at the age of 39 years, she joined the Civil Service, starting work in HMS *President* which was moored on the River Thames at The Embankment, London. Later she transferred to the Board of Trade in London as a clerical assistant. She never took part in the Civil Service strikes which occurred in the 1960s and 1970s, and was noted for entering and leaving the offices daily through the picket lines. By 22 June 1987 she was working at Companies House, Department of Trade and Industry, City Road, London, when she noted:

> ... We seem to get more and more work with less and less staff, especially at this time of year – the holiday season. I hope to retire before the end of the year. I will have completed 21 years' service in December ...

She did in fact retire then, at the age of 60 years.

Margaret was then living at 41 Highstone Mansions, 84 Camden Road, London NW1 – a flat which

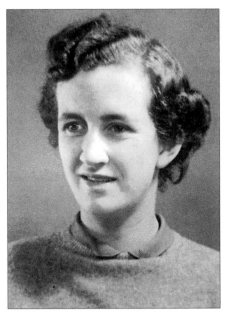

66   *Margaret Rose Worthington.*

she owned – and she continued to live there for the rest of her life. She had always been a keen member of the Anglican Church. Having passed an examination in the theory and practice of evangelism, she was commissioned on 20 February 1958 by the bishop of Willesden to serve as a parish visitor of All Souls' Church, Langham Place, London W1. Later she attended St John's Church, Hampstead, London NW3, and later still St Saviour's Church, Chalk Farm. She did much work with stroke victims. She often spent her annual leave at Christian house parties and events. For the other holidays she visited her sisters, nephews and nieces in the USA.

Early in 1995 Margaret developed an inoperable tumour of the brain, but it was not diagnosed until she was admitted to the Middlesex Hospital towards the end of November. She was later transferred to the War Memorial Hospital at Gosport, Hampshire, to be near her mother. She died there, unmarried, on 30 December 1995 and was cremated on 11 January 1996 at Portchester Crematorium, Hampshire. A thanksgiving service was held at St Mary's Church, Alverstoke, Hampshire, the following day. In his address the Reverend William Haydn Price, formerly of the Royal Navy, said:

> ... From all these tributes, it is so apparent that Margaret was a person who held out a hand of friendship to all around her. She always gave great support to the work of the church and was a keen evangelist as a parish visitor. In moments of crisis, Margaret always maintained a

67 *Sybil Rosemary, born Worthington.*

sense of calm and control. She had her own unique brand of humour that endeared her to everyone. One of her great delights was visiting places of Christian fellowship and she was particularly fond of the Fellowship of Leigh Abbey ...

7.16 Sybil Rosemary

Sybil Rosemary Worthington, the second daughter of Roger Ernest Worthington and Primrose his wife (Article 7.12), was born on 16 March 1930 at the War Memorial Hospital, Congleton. Her aunt, Gwenyth Worthington, matron of the hospital, was present at the birth. Rosemary was baptised on 19 April 1930 at St Luke's Church, Leek. As the daughter of a naval officer, she travelled much when young; her early years were spent at Chatham, Alverstoke, Plymouth and Malta. Her early education was provided by governesses at home. Then followed periods at schools in Alverstoke and Chatham. At the age of nine years, following the outbreak of the Second World War, she attended Copplestone House School at Budleigh Salterton, Devon, where her elder sister, Margaret (Article 7.15) was already a boarder. From January 1942 until 1948 she attended Sherborne School for Girls, boarding in Thurstan House. She matriculated with five credits. She was keen on sports, especially tennis, playing in tennis tournaments at school and at Alverstoke, where her father was secretary of the lawn tennis club.

After leaving school, Rosemary spent two years at the Norland Nursery Training College at Chislehurst, Kent. She qualified there despite absences for mumps and measles and closure of the school for several weeks because of an epidemic of poliomyelitis. One of her first jobs as a Norland nurse was with a family in Halifax, Yorkshire, who took her with them when they moved to Norwich in Norfolk. Then she worked for several years in London before serving abroad in Denmark, Greece and Gibraltar. Her work brought her into contact with many interesting families. For example, after returning from Greece, she worked for Major Carol Matther (later Lieutenant-Colonel Sir Carol Matther, Kt, MC, MP, and a lord commissioner of the Treasury and comptroller of the household of Queen Elizabeth II), who had been the assistant military attaché at the British Embassy in Athens. His wife was Philippa, daughter of Major Robert Godfrey Wolsley Berwicke-Copley, DSO, MC, JP, DL, KStJ, the 5th baron Cromwell.

While embarking on the Union Castle Line for her return journey from Gibraltar, a great storm caused the ship to drag anchor. She was delayed for two days while divers examined the hull. While at sea, the ship was hove-to for a further 24 hours because of a second storm. It seems that Rosemary was unlucky at sea; whilst crossing the North Sea to Denmark in the Danish packet ship *Kronprinsesse Ingrid*, she was again hove-to because of 40-foot waves. In August 1960 she flew with John Adam Thompson (later Sir John Thompson, KCMG), his pregnant wife Elizabeth and their three children to New York. John was taking up his position as first secretary at the British Embassy in Washington. He later became high commissioner to India and later still United Kingdom permanent representative at the United Nations Organisation and the Security Council. Rosemary worked for them in Washington for two years, after which she returned with the family and stayed with John's father Professor Sir George Thompson, Kt, DSc, HonLLD, FRS, master of Corpus Christi College, Cambridge and a Nobel prize winner for physics. In 1962 Rosemary returned to the USA to become secretary to the director of the Florence Crittenton Home for Unwed Mothers in Washington.

On 6 October 1964 Rosemary's engagement to Arthur Allen Douglass was announced.[9] On 16 January 1965 they were married, during a blizzard, at St Alban's Church, Washington.[55] Alas, her father could not be present because of failing health, including chronic arthritis. He deputed the duty of giving away Rosemary to Captain John D. Mason of the United States Navy. John and Peggy his wife had previously been neighbours of Roger and Primrose Worthington while John was serving with the North Atlantic Treaty Organisation at the shore station HMS *Dolphin* in Gosport, Hampshire. The wedding reception followed at Satterlee Hall, an adjunct of St Alban's Church.

'Arthur Allen Douglass Jr', as he was often styled, was seven weeks older than Rosemary, having been born on 30 January 1930 at Georgetown Hospital, Washington, the only son of Arthur Allen Douglass and Maybelle his wife. Arthur Allen junior had been reared at Arlington, Virginia, where he studied the piano from the age of 10 years. He studied the organ between the ages of 17 and 21 years, being a pupil of Dr Paul Calloway, organist at Washington Cathedral, and David Pew, organist at St John's Cathedral, Denver. Arthur Allen had sung soprano for three years in the junior choir at the Cathedral Church of St Peter and St Paul, Washington (now the National Cathedral). In 1948, at the age of 18 years, he became apprenticed to Lewis and Hitchcock, pipe organ builders at Washington. In 1951, during the Korean War, he joined the United States Air Force. After basic training at Geneva, New York

State, he served at Denver, Colorado, where he trained as a gunsight mechanic in Aircraft Instrument Control. He was then assigned to Portland, Oregon. In 1952 he took the chaplain's assistants' course and worked in the chaplain's offices and as organist. Later he was assigned to Cheyenne, Wyoming, where he passed a supply records' course and later taught the subject. There he was also able to renew his organ studies. In 1955 he returned to Lewis and Hitchcock but continued with his chaplaincy administration, in the air force reserves, at Andrew's Air Force Base, Maryland.

Arthur Allen's father had graduated in general surgery in the University of Pittsburgh, Pennsylvania, in 1912 but he never practised; instead he returned to his father's farm near Pittsburg and continued a farming career for some years before moving to Arlington, Virginia. His grandfather, Robert Douglass (1778 to 1846), had moved to the United States from Newcastle upon Tyne, England, where the family were said to be kinsmen of Sir Nicholas Douglass, whose family had been settled at Blaydon, near Newcastle since the 13th century. Sir Nicholas's son was Sir James Nicholas Douglass, FRS, engineer-in-chief of Trinity House, known mainly for building the Eddystone Lighthouse in 1882. Arthur Allen junior's mother was Mabel Beverly, born Harris. Her mother was Lucy Beverly, a direct descendant of Major Robert Beverly (1641 to 1687) of Beverley in Yorkshire, who settled in Jamestown, Virginia.[57] He fought in the Bacon Rebellion in Virginia in 1676 and later became clerk to the House of Burgesses.

Rosemary and Arthur Allen's first home was an apartment at 3801 39th Street North-West, Washington, where they lived for a year. Rosemary had lived at 3760 in the same street before their marriage. From December 1965 until July 1969 they lived at 4113 Horseshoe Drive, Annandale, a suburb about 15 miles south-west of Washington. Then they moved to 2525 Buckelew Drive, Falls Church, Virginia, just over the River Potomac immediately west of Washington, where they lived until July 1978. While there they produced their family of two daughters and one son, namely:

Forenames	Date of birth	Date of baptism
Mary Rose	5 March 1966	1 May 1966
Lucy Patricia	29 August 1968	17 November 1968
Charles Berkeley Worthington	17 January 1970	28 March 1970

Mary Rose was baptised at St Alban's Church, Washington while Lucy and Charles were baptised at St Barnabas's Episcopal Church, Annandale.

In 1978 Arthur Allen decided to set up his own business and accordingly left Lewis and Hitchcock after 30 years of service. Rosemary wrote in a letter of 10 December 1978:

> ... Arthur Allen took the plunge – gave up his job. We found a house
> 130 miles south west of Washington with three acres. We are in the

Shenandoah Valley, with mountains all around us and just a mile outside the city of Harrisonburg. It is a small university town and we feel it is a good place to raise the children ... Arthur Allen has had to convert a large barn to the needs of a workshop ...

In December 1979 she added:

... We love being in the country and Mary Rose has a chance to ride regularly. We feel we made the right decision for Arthur Allen to start off on his own. He has spent most of the past six months working in Washington, DC, and commuting home for weekends. It hasn't been easy with the large garden (three and a half acres) but we manage ...

The business was indeed successful. An article in *The Washington Post – The District Weekly –* describes a project to refurbish a 50-year-old Skinner organ at the Presbyterian Church of the Pilgrims in north-west Washington.[57] Three thousand man hours of time were spent by 375 members of the congregation working on the organ under the direction of Arthur Allen. By this arrangement the church saved about $55,000. The minister, the Reverend William Thompson, described Arthur Allen as 'a very loving, pasturing kind of person' who attracted some of the church's elderly members who had come to feel disfranchised by the new younger members. Later, Arthur Allen progressively developed a clientele nearer home.[58]

In 1976 and 1977 Rosemary was treasurer of the Parent-Teacher Association of the Timber Lane Elementary School at Falls Church, Virginia. From 1983 to 1985 she was treasurer of the Episcopal Churchwomen at Emmanuel Church, Harrisonburg, and from 1985 to 1986 she was president. She had been a member of the Altar Guild since 1982. She was also a leader with the Brownies and the Girl Scouts there, and a member of Extension Homemakers. Her interest in sport remained and she played tennis for the Poplar Heights team in Falls Church. From 1986 to 1995 Rosemary was a departmental manager in Watson's Departmental Store, Harrisonburg. Her responsibilities included accessories, jewellery, lingerie and sleepwear. After retiring in 1995 at the age of 65 years she did voluntary work at Sunnyside Retirement Community – a Presbyterian nursing home – mainly helping with Alzheimer patients. She became a United States citizen on 4 July 1995, the ceremony taking place at Monticello, near Charlotteville, at the old home of Thomas Jefferson.

Railways were a consuming hobby of Arthur Allen from childhood onwards. He joined the Shenandoah Valley Railroad Club and participated in several steam train excursions in the United States and United Kingdom. He was vice-president of the club in 1988 and president in 1989. He continued as director until 1991.

7.17 Patricia Grace

Patricia Grace Worthington, the third and youngest daughter of Roger Ernest Worthington and Primrose his wife (Article 7.12), was born

68   *Patricia Grace, born Worthington.*

on 12 September 1934 at the War Memorial Hospital, Congleton. She was baptised on 4 October 1934 at St Mary's Church, Alverstoke, by Ernest Neville Lovett, CBE, DD, bishop of Portsmouth (later bishop of Salisbury), who was said to be a relation of the family. When the bishop noted her good behaviour during the service, he said that he hoped she would be equally well behaved for the rest of her life. Roger interjected 'Heaven forbid!' Throughout her life she was generally known as 'Tricha' or 'Trich'.

As the daughter of a naval officer, Patricia's domestic life was highly mobile; by the age of eight years she had lived at Plymouth in Devon, Chatham in Kent, Budleigh Salterton in Devon, Hatch End in Hertfordshire, and Claygate in Surrey. From about 1942 to 1945 she was educated at Rowan Brae and Rowan Hill schools at Claygate. She then boarded at Rookesbury Park preparatory school at Wickham, Hampshire. From September 1947 until 1951 she attended Sherborne School for Girls at Sherborne, Dorset, being a boarder at Thurstan House and house captain for her last term. In 1951 and 1952, aged 17 years, she attended Harcombe House School of Domestic Science at Lyme Regis, Dorset. Then in 1953 and 1954 she worked for a Danish family in Denmark. From 1954 to 1955 she attended St James's Secretarial College in London, living at the Queensbury Club in Egerton Gardens.

Appropriately, Patricia's first job as a secretary was at The Missions to Seamen, London. She held that post for a year, moving on in 1957 to the King Edward VII Sanatorium at Midhurst, Sussex. In 1960 and 1961 she held a secretarial post in the Commercial Export Department at Nestle Chocolate (Africa) SA at Vevey in Switzerland. In 1961 she moved to Washington, District of Columbia, USA, where she became a secretary at the British Embassy. She remained there for three years, the latter part of which she assisted the private secretary to the ambassador, Sir William David Ormsby Gore, KCMG, PC (later 5th baron Harlech). In 1965, Patricia became secretary to the communications director of Washington Cathedral, where she remained until 1969. While in Washington, Patricia lived at an apartment in Idaho Avenue, within walking distance of both the cathedral and the embassy.

Following in the footsteps of both her parents, Patricia's main sport was tennis. She started serious play at the age of 11 at the Alverstoke tennis club and is still playing. At the age of 24 years she also took to gliding, having her first flight on 3 May 1959 at the Portsmouth Royal Naval Gliding Club at Lee-on-the-Solent, Hampshire. She pursued the sport in the USA, flying at Westminster and Frederick in Maryland and later at Leesburg and Warrenton in Virginia. In 1968 she took five one-hour lessons in a power plane; her interests in aviation followed that of her aunts Gladys and Bessie Grace (Article 7.12).

At the Capital Area Soaring School, Leesburg, Patricia met Donald Rae Ward whom she married on 3 May 1969 – 10 years to the day since her first flight. The wedding took place at Mount Rainier Christian Church (Disciples of Christ), Maryland, USA. Alas, Patricia's father had died 18 months earlier, so she was given away by her father's old friend, Captain John D. Mason of the United States Navy – as her sister Rosemary had been previously (Article 7.16).

Donald was six years older than Patricia, having been born on 28 February 1928 at Washington – the son of Calvert Orlea Ward of the District Water Department, Washington, and his wife Gladys, born Talcott. Donald was educated at Eliot Junior High School in Washington. He joined the United States Army and, on 18 October 1946, was awarded the certificate of proficiency as a special diesel mechanic at the Ordnance School, Aberdeen Proving Ground, Maryland. From December 1946 to October 1947 he served with the Army of Occupation in Japan. He received an honourable discharge on 29 October 1947 and later took a course of study in refrigeration and air-conditioning at the National Institute of Commerce and Technology in Washington. He received their certificate of merit on 21 December 1949. On 5 June 1954, at the age of 26 years, he attained a bachelor of science degree in finance of the University of Maryland, having studied at the College of Business and Public Administration. His interests then turned to banking; the American Institute of Banking awarded him a pre-standard certificate on 20 December 1956, a standard certificate on 30 April 1957, and a major in commercial banking on 18 April 1960.

Donald was a member of the Capital Area Soaring Association having started to fly gliders in 1966. He was later accredited as 'flying instructor – gliders'.

The first home of Patricia and Donald was 1804 Metzerott Road, Apartment 57, Adelphi, Maryland. From 1971 until 1979 they lived at 728 Gormley Drive, Rockville, Maryland, where they produced their only child:

Forenames	Date of birth	Date of baptism
Peter Worthington	29 April 1974	3 November 1974

His baptism took place at St James's Church, Potomac, Maryland. When Peter was three years of age, Patricia and Donald fostered a girl

– Danielle Lewis – as a companion for Peter, but after a further three years Danielle was reclaimed by her mother and later adopted by her mother's sister.

On 2 August 1969, Donald flew in the North American 1-26 Soaring Championships at Richmond, Indiana, USA. In the early 1970s he was a member of the Montgomery County Savoyards, performing in operettas including Gilbert and Sullivan's *The Mikado, Pirates of Penzance* and *HMS Pinafore*, and Victor Herbert's *The Red Mill*. In 1973 he joined the Warranty Department of Rolls-Royce Inc, where he remained for 20 years until he retired in 1993, having been their warranty administrator for airplane engines. While at Rolls-Royce he continued studies at The American University and took part in the Summer programme of 1981 aimed at '… creating a climate that fosters better understanding of business and political conditions on both sides of the Atlantic between the United States and EC member countries'. A tour took place in Europe – mainly the Netherlands, Belgium, France, Luxembourg and East Germany – from 7 to 27 June 1971, packed with lectures, discussions and visits. On 6 May 1982 the university conferred on Donald the degree of Master of Science in international business studies.

In April 1979, Patricia and Donald moved to 227 North Street North East, Leesburg, to be nearer to Donald's office at Rolls-Royce. Patricia re-opened her career as a secretary in 1981 when Peter was about seven years of age, first becoming secretary to the administrator of Loudoun Memorial Hospital, Leesburg. This was a job-share post in which she worked two days a week. She left the hospital early in the summer of 1986 and three months later became full-time secretary at the law office of Woodrow W. Turner Jr. (later known as Turner Carrothers and Parks) of Leesburg. From 1992 she was office manager and secretary at Bench Title Inc. who were considered to be one of the foremost examiners of real estate titles in the state of Virginia. Bench Title Inc. were acquired by Lawyers Title Insurance Corporation in November 1997, Patricia continuing in her post until June 1999 when she retired.

In 1987 Patricia was a member of the Giant Food Consumer Board which met four times a year to put consumers' points of view and to make proposals and suggestions to Giant Food – a group of supermarkets in the District of Columbia, Maryland and Virginia.

Soon after Donald retired from Rolls-Royce in 1993 – at the age of 65 years – he became a founder member of the Advisory Commission of the Thomas Balch Library, Leesburg. He held the post for the remainder of his life, and served as secretary to the commission. Donald died of a heart condition on 6 June 1996 at Reston Hospital Centre, Reston, Virginia, after several months of failing health. His funeral service was held on 10 June 1996 at the Church of our Saviour, Oatlands, Virginia, where he is buried.[60] His many interests had included membership of the International Group for Historic Aircraft Recovery and membership of the Academy of Model Aeronautics. He had built his own radio-controlled model aeroplanes and gliders and participated in the national championships in Virginia in 1988.

Patricia continued to live at 227 North Street North East until 9 May 2000. She then moved to 305 Patterson Court North West, Leesburg – a newly-built house where she developed the garden from a field. Her interest in tennis persisted through life; in the USA national competion for Super Seniors in the Summer of 2003, at the age of 68 years, her team won the first round and was placed third in the second round.

CHAPTER 8

LINE OF PHILIP JUKES WORTHINGTON OF LEEK

8.1 Philip Jukes

Philip Jukes Worthington, the third son and youngest child of Andrew Jukes Worthington and Sarah Booth his wife (Articles 3.30 and 7.1), was born on 4 January 1851 at Spout Street (later called St Edward Street), Leek, Staffordshire, and baptised on 19 March 1851 at St Luke's Church, Leek. His life has already been treated (Article 7.8). He and his wife Margaret Elizabeth produced one son.[1]

SECOND GENERATION – SON OF PHILIP JUKES AND MARGARET ELIZABETH

8.2 Lancelot Jukes

Lancelot Jukes Worthington, the only child of Philip Jukes Worthington and Margaret Elizabeth his wife (Articles 7.8 and 8.1), was born on 28 May 1891 at Hugo Street, Leek, and baptised on 28 June 1891 at All Saints' Church, Leek.[2] The vicar of All Saints', the Reverend W. Benson Wright, became one of Lancelot's godfathers. Throughout his life, Lancelot was called 'Lance'. His early education was at the Leek Church High School Kindergarten, where, initially, he was the only boy. He excelled in mathematics which remained a hobby throughout his life.

On 25 July 1900, the Duke and Duchess of York (later King George V and Queen Mary) visited Leek to open the Leek Technical Schools and to lay the foundation stone of the Carr Gymnasium. Lancelot's grandfather, Sir Thomas Wardle (Article 7.8), officiated and Lancelot, then aged nine years, presented a bouquet of flowers to the duchess. After the ceremony the duchess called on Lady Wardle who was too infirm to leave home. From September 1901 Lancelot boarded at Aysgarth Preparatory School in North Yorkshire. Whilst there he won five prizes and was head boy for his last year, ending in July 1905. His main sport was boxing. From September 1905 to 22 December 1908 he attended Winchester College, Hampshire, boarding at Morshead's. He was a cadet in the Officer Training Corps (Junior Division) where he was twice reported as 'efficient'.

Soon after leaving the school at the age of 17 years, he sailed to Hong Kong, on a cruiser, as a guest of his stepfather Guy Gaunt (Article 7.8), who was taking a relief crew there. This was probably

Philip Jukes Worthington, Major; b. 1851, m.=**Margaret Elizabeth**, dau. of Sir Thomas Wardle, Kt, JP, chevalier de la Légion d'Honneur 1889, d. 1902. *(Pedigree 7 & Art. 7.8 & 8.1)* (France), officier dans l'Ordre des Palmes Académique (France); b. 1869, re-m. 1904, d. 1949

Phyllis Mary, dau. of Ernest =1 **Lancelot Jukes Worthington**, Colonel, TD, JP, 2= **Marjorie Brown**, dau. of
Alfred Sadler, MD, MRCS; Order of the Nile (Egypt); b. 1891, m(1) 1923, Charles Edward Gibson,
b. 1899, re-m. 1947, d. 1981 dissolved 1937, m(2) 1939, d. 1975. *(Art. 8.2)* Captain; b. 1908, d. 1981

Margaret Elizabeth Valentine, JP; b. 1924, m. 1947 Norman Dowse Gibson, Captain, chevalier de l'Ordre de Léopold II (Belgium), Croix de Guerre 1940 (Belgium), & had issue. *(Art. 8.3)*

1= **Philip Michael Worthington**, BSc(Eng), CEng, CBIM; b. 1926, m(1) 1955, dissolved 1980, m(2) 1983. *(Art. 8.4)*

Gillian Hazel, dau. of Sir William Sidney Albert Atkins, Kt, CBE, BSc, CEng; b. 1935, re-m. 1986

2= **Judith Sonia May**, BSc, JP, dau. of Henry Peter Robson Hamlin, Captain; b. 1942 m(1) 1963 Ian Anthony Donald Gale, PhD, BSc, & had issue, dissolved 1982

Andrew Ralph Worthington, Brigadier, OStJ, MB, ChB, MFCM, MBIM; b. 1928, m. 1961. *(Art. 8.5)*

1= **Tessa Helen**, dau. of Wilfrid Ernest Thorowgood, MA, AMICE, MIStructE; b. 1935

Stuart Gibson Worthington, JP, FBIM; b. 1940, m. 1972. *(Art. 8.6)*

2= **Geraldine Judith**, dau. of Lieut-Colonel John James Seth, MBE, MBIM; b. 1943, m(1) 1965 Murray Roger Malcolm Snowball & had issue

Rosalie Frances; b. 1944, m. 1973 Michael John Courage & had issue. *(Art. 8.7)*

Nicholas Robert Worthington, BSc, MBA; b. 1960, adopted 1961, m. 1990, dissolved 1998 =**Henrietta Mary**, dau. of Alexander Bennett Gosling, MA; b. 1966

Catherine Clare; b. 1962, adopted 1963, m. 1988 Mark Thomas Dacres Butler, Lieut-Colonel, & had issue

Miranda Elizabeth; b. 1985

Rupert Lancelot Worthington; b. 1962, m. 1983, d. 2000 without issue =**Bernadette Christine**, dau. of Sidney Fisher; b. 1946

Charlotte Helen; b. 1965

Victoria Louise Emma; b. 1973, m. 2004 Kevin Neve Coventry, BSc (USA)

Victoria Mary; b. 1994

69   *Lancelot Jukes Worthington.*

the visit referred to by Thomas Mellor, the director and general manager of A.J. Worthington & Co., when he wrote to Lancelot's mother on 20 January 1909: 'When Lance arrived at the mill last Saturday morning, I could not broach the subject re trip to him as I had not received Capt. Gaunt's reply ...'. On returning from Hong Kong Lancelot attended for several months the weaving school at Krefeld, near Essen, Germany; he had been entered into the company's books as an employee from 1 January 1909. During the next five years he worked in various production departments and travelled for the company. In July 1912, for example, he returned from a visit to Australia, New Zealand and South Africa.

Lancelot had joined the Territorial Force in January 1909, being commissioned temporary 2nd-lieutenant in the Leek Battery of the Royal Field Artillery (later called the Royal Artillery). In March 1910 he transferred to the Derbyshire Yeomanry with the substantive rank as 2nd-lieutenant, and took charge of the regimental signal troop. Communications had long been one of his hobbies. It was said that he was the first person in the Leek area to receive radio signals, having done so with a home-made crystal receiver taken to a barn two-thirds of the way up Ecton Hill, near Swainsley, where he was then living; on another occasion he received the news transmitted in morse code from Poldew that the SS *Titanic* had been sunk by an iceberg.

Within a few days of the proclamation of war against Germany, made on 4 August 1914, the Derbyshire Yeomanry, the South Nottinghamshire Hussars and the Sherwood Rangers were mobilised as the Nottinghamshire and Derbyshire Mounted Brigade under the command of Acting Brigadier-General (substantive Colonel) Paul Aloysius Kenna, VC, DSO, ADC to King Edward VII and King George V. Lancelot was promoted lieutenant on 17 September 1914.[3] He and his troop were re-constituted as the brigade signal troop with an initial strength of about twenty-two. Lancelot took with him two chargers from Swainsley, Peter being his own and Rotax being on loan by Captain Gaunt for war service. The troop's equipment included heliograph, semaphore, telephone, radio, horses, and motorcycles, and there was a horse-drawn limber wagon for the transport and laying of telephone cables.

In April 1915, the brigade proceeded by rail to Avonmouth near Bristol and embarked on two ships for Alexandria, Egypt. Lancelot duly placed his groom and two chargers on the ship on which the brigade headquarters were to sail, but when the brigadier-general found insufficient space for his two grooms and three chargers he instructed Lancelot to remove his groom and chargers to the second ship. Alas, the second ship was torpedoed off southern Spain. All personnel were saved, but all the horses, Peter and Rotax included, were drowned and all signals equipment lost. In May 1915 the brigade proceeded by rail to Cairo, where Lancelot received two Australian chargers – Dick and Bob. He was quartered with the brigade headquarters at the *Continental Hotel* in Ezbekiah Square. The brigadier-general arranged the dining table plan at the hotel and henceforth Lance was seated with the Marquess of Hartington (later 10th duke of Devonshire, KG, MBE, TD) and Lieutenant Thomas Edward Lawrence (later Colonel 'Lawrence of Arabia'). Hartington, four years younger than Lancelot, was aide-de-camp to the brigadier-general, and Lawrence, two years older, had duties in the map room at the nearby *Savoy Hotel*.[4]

Early in August 1915 Lancelot's signals work was temporarily over; he was appointed acting staff captain of the brigade. Later that month the brigade proceeded, without horses, to join the Gallipoli campaign – first by train to Alexandria and then by ship across the Mediterranean Sea to Suvla Bay in the Gallipoli Peninsula of Turkey.[5] They landed there on 9 August 1915. Lancelot was left at the jetty to supervise the off-loading of stores while the brigade moved across the salt lake – then dry – to positions on the adjacent ravine.[6] He followed later, finding headquarters settled in a cave facing north-east on high ground. Within a few minutes a bullet lodged in one of his ankles. The brigade medical officer, who was in the cave, had Lancelot taken on a stretcher to a hospital ship in the port which returned with many other casualties to Alexandria. There the bullet was removed. Brigadier-General Kenna was killed at Suvla Bay later that month. The Gallipoli campaign continued for four more months, after which the British withdrew having suffered huge casualties.

In September 1915 Lancelot returned to the *Continental Hotel* in Cairo for duties with the Western Frontier Force office at the *Savoy Hotel*. This office was planning for the anticipated attack by the Senussites from the Libyan Desert west of Egypt. Hostilities started on

15 November 1915 when the Senussi occupied the port of Sollum in the extreme north-west of Egypt.[7] The Western Frontier Force, consisting of a composite brigade of cavalry styled 'Imperial Yeomanry Brigade' and a composite brigade of infantry, assembled at Mersa Matruh (later called Matruh). Lancelot was in charge of signals for the cavalry, for which he had raised a mounted brigade signals troop at Mena Camp, Cairo. The Senussi were defeated and Sollum was re-occupied by the British on 14 March 1916. Lancelot then returned with his troop to Mena Camp. All efforts were now devoted to advance eastwards against the Turks. The Egyptian Expeditionary Force was formed for the purpose, and Lancelot and his troop were enrolled on 19 March 1916. By this time Lancelot was seconded to the Royal Engineers Signal Service (which was separated in 1922 to form the Royal Corps of Signals). In April 1916 he took a small working party to lay cable by means of a camel-drawn cable barrow to link El Maghrah to a wireless transmitter at El Alamein.

On 10 March 1917, Lancelot's rank as acting captain was made substantive, with precedence as from 21 March 1916.[8] While at Cairo on 28 May 1917 – his 26th birthday – he was presented with the Order of the Nile, 4th class (officer), the appointment to the order having been made by Sultan Husayn Kamil on 9 December 1916.[9]

In May 1917 he went to Ismailia on the Suez Canal, 73 miles north-east of Cairo, for signal and reconnaissance duties with the Camel Corps led by Edward Turnour (later 5th Earl Winterton, JP, DL, Order of the Nile, Order of Nahada). In July 1917 Lancelot was attached to the newly formed 75th Divisional Signal Company, Royal Engineers, as second-in-command. The company was being assembled at Moascar, near Ismailia, but later that month they proceeded by rail to El Arish, 90 miles east of the Suez Canal, on the Mediterranean coast. In August 1917 he and Lord Hartington were promoted major on the same day, and Lancelot was temporarily given command of the 20th Corps Signal Company then at Rafah, 50 miles south-west of Gaza. He provided signals support for the Battle of Beersheba on 31 October 1917 and the Third Battle of Gaza from 1 to 6 November 1917 – both being successful. The Turks were now in flight, and Lancelot took part in the pursuit. Jerusalem fell to British forces on 9 December 1917, and Lancelot entered the city in January 1918. He was posted in charge of the 20th Corps Signal Company at the Kaiser's Hospice (later called 'Empress Victoria Hospice') on the Mount of Olives, Jerusalem – the headquarters of General Sir Philip Walhouse Chetwode (later Field-Marshal, 1st Baron Chetwode, 7th Bt, GCB, OM, GCSI, KCMG, DSO, GCStJ, DCL). By October 1918 the Turkish army had been driven north in confusion, so the 20th Corps headquarters moved by road to Haifa.

In January 1919 Lancelot and Lord Hartington, who was then aide-de-camp to Chetwode, were granted leave; they returned to the

Continental Hotel, Cairo for a few days before visiting Upper Egypt. The Territorials in the region were disembodied as from 21 February 1919, and Lancelot returned to civilian life at Leek. He lived at Swainsley with his mother and step-father (Article 7.8), but he also rented a small property in Osborne Street, Leek, about 150 yards from the mill. At the peace celebrations held in Leek towards the end of July 1919, Lancelot and his cousin Lieutenant-Colonel William F. Challinor, DSO, were two of the four marshals of the procession which marched to the band of the 3rd Staffordshire Battery, Royal Field Artillery.[10]

Lancelot took on the day-to-day management of A.J. Worthington & Co. Limited, having been nominally managing director since 1912. Thomas Mellor had been the general manager since Philip Worthington's death in 1902, but he had died in February 1918. Lancelot had then sent a cable from Palestine on 28 February 1918 to Thomas Valentine Clowes 'to assume managership pending Mrs Gaunt's arrival'.

On 6 June 1920 Lancelot was appointed to re-constitute and command the 46th (North Midland) Divisional Signals in the Territorial Force (from 1 October 1921 re-named the Territorial Army).[6] He had companies at Derby, Nottingham and Chesterfield, with his headquarters and cable-laying section at Phoenix Street, Derby. Lord Hartington was second-in-command until he became a member of parliament, and later under-secretary of state for dominion affairs.[11] Lancelot continued to be in command of the unit until 11 February 1929, having been promoted brevet lieutenant-colonel on 31 December 1924 and lieutenant-colonel on 11 February 1925.[12] He was awarded the Territorial Decoration on 29 July 1924, and later the Territorial Efficiency Decoration with two clasps.[8] After handing over command to Lieutenant-Colonel Foreman on 11 February 1929, Lancelot was promoted colonel and placed on the unattached list. When Foreman was killed in April 1930, Lancelot accepted a request that he should return to the command for a further two years. This caused a problem, as he would then be reporting to the chief signal officer of Northern Command who only held the rank of lieutenant-colonel. Although Lancelot accepted a temporary reduction in rank to brevet colonel from 1 May 1930, an impasse developed between them. The chief signal officer sent an adverse report on Lancelot to the divisional commander, who promptly dismissed the chief signal officer. Lancelot retired from command again on 13 November 1931, resuming the rank of colonel the following day.[8] The strength of the unit was then 17 officers and 308 other ranks. From 18 February 1940 until 10 July 1947 he was honorary colonel of the 21st Corps Signal Regiment (TA), this regiment being the successor to the 46th (North Midland) Divisional Signals. He had been a member of the Territorial Army Association for the County of Derby from its inception in the mid-1920s, and his membership continued until his resignation on 31 December 1941.[13]

On 6 February 1923, Lancelot married Phyllis Mary, daughter of Dr Ernest Alfried Sadler, MD, MRCS, and his wife Elizabeth of The Mansion, Ashbourne, Derbyshire. Phyllis was then 23 years of age, having been born at The Mansion on 14 December 1899 and baptised at St Oswald's church, Ashbourne, on 9 February 1900. After leaving school, she devoted her time to public work in Ashbourne, her main interest being the 1st Ashbourne Company of Girl Guides and Rangers. This company, of which she was second-in-command, was stationed at the old coach house at the lower end of The Mansion garden. Phyllis's father Ernest was the senior partner of a general medical practice in Ashbourne and a district medical officer of health of Derbyshire and

70   *Phillis Mary, born Sadler.*

Staffordshire County Councils. He was an associate of the University of Birmingham and author of books and papers on medical, historical and archaeological subjects.[14] Ernest's father and grandfather – Alfred and Frederick Sadler respectively – had held properties and been land and coal owners in Tamworth, Staffordshire, where both in their times had been justices of the peace and mayors.

Phyllis's mother, Elizabeth, was the second daughter of William Richard Holland of Holland House, Barton-under-Needwood, Staffordshire, founder of the firm of Holland, Rigby and Williams, solicitors of Ashbourne. The Hollands had held land near Barton since 1314 when Richard de Holland was granted rights in the Forest of Needwood.[15] In 1313 he had been appointed 'instaurario de Pecco' to Thomas, 2nd earl of Lancaster, earl of Leicester, earl of Derby and High Steward of England. Instaurario de pecco almost certainly meant instaurator of the Peak. The honour of Peak (sometimes called High Peak) extended from North Staffordshire through part of Derbyshire to the border of Nottinghamshire. Elizabeth taught at St Oswald's Sunday school, Ashbourne, for over 60 years; she was superintendent of the boys' school until she was over 80 years of age. She also ran the Ashbourne group of Young Britons – a youth organisation of the Conservative Party.[16]

The wedding took place at St Oswald's Church, Ashbourne. As the churchyard gates are only 70 yards from The Mansion, the processions both ways were on foot. A guard of honour at the church entrance was formed by nine officers of the 46th (North Midland) Divisional Signals and a guard of honour for the recession was formed by the 1st Ashbourne Company of Girl Guides. Lord Hartington was Lancelot's best man. There were 203 guests, plus members and officials of the Leek Urban District Council and managers and employees of A.J. Worthington & Co. Limited. A special train was arranged to take the guests from Leek to Ashbourne and back. The main reception was at The Mansion, while the employees were entertained to lunch at the Town Hall.[17] Amongst the guests was Ernest's second cousin Sir Michael Ernest Sadler, KCSI, CB, MA, vice-chancellor of Leeds University (later master of University College, Oxford).[18] Lancelot and Phyllis spent the first few days of their honeymoon in London followed by three or four days in Paris and several weeks at Lady Gaunt's villa in Monte Carlo (Article 7.8). Lady Gaunt had travelled to England for the wedding and then returned to the villa to receive the couple. They then went to live at Rochemount, 22 Weston Street, Leek, which Lancelot had acquired as his Leek home some years previously. They produced three children:

Forenames	Date of birth	Date of baptism	Article
Margaret Elizabeth Valentine	14 February 1924	25 March 1924	8.3
Philip Michael	24 April 1926	19 May 1926	8.4
Andrew Ralph	31 May 1928	5 July 1928	8.5

Lancelot had been elected to the Leek Urban District Council in 1913 and, although abroad for war service between 1914 and 1919, he remained a councillor. He became chairman of the Health Committee of the council about 1921 and chairman of the Maternity and Child Welfare Committee in 1929. He was chairman of the council itself for the 1929-30 year. He had been appointed one of the five trustees of the Leek United and Midlands Building Society in 1922 and a justice of the peace for the county of Stafford in 1925.

One of Lancelot's consuming interests was postage stamps. His interest started at the age of 10 years, but from 1919 to 1929 he built up a valuable collection of unused stamps of the British Empire. He became a member of the Royal Philatelic Society on 1 January 1925 and had a paper on *The Postage Stamps of South West Africa* published in April that year in *Stamp Collecting*.[20] The paper discusses misprints, other faults and type-set overprinting in considerable detail. He was promoted a fellow of the Society on 28 April 1927. It may have been the publication of the paper which caused King George V to invite Lancelot to some three private meetings with him at Buckingham Palace to discuss stamps – one of the meetings being devoted to stamps of South West Africa. The king was then developing a collection, later acknowledged to be pre-eminent worldwide.

Phyllis was presented to King George V at court soon after her marriage and again about 1929. She was president of the Leek Division of Girl Guides, a member of the Child Welfare Voluntary Committee, and from April 1929 vice-president of the Leek Division of the Red Cross Society – following the retirement of Brevet-Colonel Arthur Falkner Nicholson, TD, DL, high sheriff of Staffordshire (later CBE).

Alas, Lancelot's trail of success during the first 40 years of his life crumbled during the 1930s. Phyllis left him in 1935; A.J. Worthington & Co. Limited was liquidated in 1936; he had acute personal financial difficulties and he failed to be re-elected to the Leek Urban District Council in 1939.

Phyllis encountered another member of the Leek Amateur Dramatic Society – the Reverend Samuel Clifford Stevens, associate of King's College, London.[19] He had been vicar of St Edward's Church, Leek, since 8 November 1933.[21] Phyllis left Rochemount for London about 23 March 1935 using a nervous complaint and need for quietness as an excuse, but she later admitted that Clifford had 'come into her life' early in 1934, and in a letter to Lancelot of 3 April 1935 she wrote that '... it couldn't be helped, it had to happen, and we belong to each other in mind, soul and spirit ...'. She lived in lodgings at 51 Edith Grove, Chelsea. Clifford was slow in deciding what to do, but on 8 October 1935 he placed his resignation in the hands of the bishop of Lichfield, and left his wife to join Phyllis. Phyllis's landlady would not allow Clifford to live there, so he and Phyllis lived for some time at 63 Richmond Road, Kingston upon Thames, Surrey.

Lancelot divorced Phyllis on the grounds of adultery at Kingston.[21] The decree nisi was granted on 29 June 1936 and the decree absolute on 11 January 1937 by the High Court of Justice, Family Division. Custody of the three children – Valentine, Philip, and Andrew – was granted to Lancelot. Phyllis had tried to bargain for limited access to the children but Lancelot had opposed it and had been supported in the matter by Dr and Mrs Sadler. Indeed they made an affidavit against their daughter's access. Whilst living at 63 Richmond Road, Clifford and Phyllis produced a son, Edward Jeremy, who was born on 23 March 1937 at home. On the birth certificate Clifford is described as 'journalist'. Later, Phyllis changed her surname to 'Stevens' by deed poll but she did not marry Clifford then because his wife had refused a divorce. But they did marry on 25 August 1947 following the death of Clifford's wife. The wedding was at the Registry Office, Chelsea, London. He was then described as 'law clerk' and his father as a 'wool broker'. Phyllis and Clifford were then at 30 Elm Park Mansions, Chelsea, where they lived for many years.

Phyllis worked for a long time in the motor vehicle licensing department of London County Council at County Hall, Lambeth. Sometime after the Second World War, Clifford and Phyllis moved to Cornerways, Robertsbridge, Sussex, which Phyllis acquired. Finally they moved to Gateway Cottage, Whydown, Bexhill-on-Sea, Sussex, also owned by

Phyllis. Their interest in amateur dramatics continued and they were active members of various societies in Sussex. Clifford died in 1960. In 1976 Phyllis left Gateway Cottage and returned as a widow to Ashbourne to live at 1 Coachman's (the old coachhouse to The Mansion), then owned by her younger brother, Michael Sadler. Finally she had a flat at the home of her son, Jeremy – Chesterfield House, Wall, Staffordshire. She died there on 14 March 1981, the funeral service being held at Wall parish church on 20 March 1981. By her Will dated 4 June 1968, with a codicil dated 8 April 1971, she made small bequests to her three children by her first marriage and bequeathed the remainder of her estate to Jeremy.

Phyllis's departure from Rochemount was compounded by financial problems as A.J. Worthington & Co. Limited headed for bankruptcy. Relations rallied; Lancelot's mother-in-law, Elizabeth Sadler, took Philip and Andrew to live at The Mansion, Ashbourne, while Lancelot's aunt, Elizabeth Wardle, took him and Valentine to live at her home, Ladydale, Fynney Street, Leek. Rochemount was closed and its tennis court and garden were fenced off so that sheep could graze there.

The Great Depression commenced about October 1929; it lasted for three or four years before a slow recovery was underway. It was the western world's worst depression of the century and had a profound effect on manufacturing industry. About half of the textile companies of Leek and Macclesfield were brought to their knees, some being liquidated entirely, and some being merged with larger firms. A.J. Worthington & Co. Limited survived most of the period with difficulty but went into liquidation in 1936. At that time 75 per cent of the ordinary shares were held by Lancelot and 25 per cent by Andrew Yorke Worthington (Article 7.14). These investments were lost. However, the on-going business was considered to be viable so a new company called A.J. Worthington & Co. (Leek) Limited was incorporated on 26 October 1936 which purchased the trade, machinery and premises from the liquidator. The three owners of this new company were:

William Read Wadsworth	Chairman	20%
Lancelot Jukes Worthington	Joint-managing	40%
Harry Newall	Joint-managing	40%

William Wadsworth, OBE, JP, was a textile mill owner in Macclesfield, Cheshire, and visited Worthington's mill at monthly intervals. Harry Newall had been a successful traveller with A.J. Worthington & Co. Limited for some years; he was commercially minded and hard headed, and in many ways a good partner for Lancelot. Henceforth, Lancelot concentrated on technical and production aspects of the business, and looked after Government customers such as the Ministry of War and their parachute manufacturers. The business prospered once more.

To enable Lancelot to subscribe for his shares in the new company, his aunt Elizabeth Wardle lent him a substantial sum, and his father-in-law Ernest Sadler lent him £2,000* using the main part of Lancelot's stamp collection as collateral. Half the stamp collection was sold by auction through Harmer's of 131 New Bond Street, London, in a two-day devoted sale held on 15 and 16 September 1937. On the title page of the sale catalogue appears:

> A Mint Collection of Queen Victoria, King Edward VII and King George V Postage Stamps (Offered by order of Colonel L.J. Worthington, TD, JP, of Leek). The collection, which is almost entirely in horizontal pairs with Control numbers, is replete with varieties, dies, shades, papers etc and represents one of the most specialised studies of mint British Colonials.

The other half was sold in another two-day devoted sale held on 27 and 28 September 1937.

Lancelot was one of the progressive members of the Leek Urban District Council. For example, he led the construction of a new sewage scheme and on 11 May 1934 presided at its public opening while Phyllis opened some of the valves. He upgraded the ambulance service and the refuse disposal service and argued for a re-organisation of the hospitals.[23] The expense of such developments was not liked by some sections of the ratepayers, especially during the recession; public attitudes hardened and there was much discussion on the subject in the local press. For Lancelot the matter came to a head when in 1936 and again in 1938 he championed the construction of new swimming baths. Such baths had been proposed as early as 1911 but had repeatedly been postponed on grounds of cost. On 25 October 1938 the Leek Combined Butchers', Licensed Victuallers' & Traders' Associations wrote to the chairman of the Leek Urban District Council:

> At a joint meeting of the four Trading Associations held on the 12th inst. it was decided that an opportunity be given to the Ratepayers of Leek to register their disapproval of the Scheme for the erection of new baths as proposed by the Urban District Council, by signing a petition. This has been done with the result that 3,486 dissenters have objected to the scheme ...

Lancelot stood for re-election on 3 April 1939 but lost, after serving the council for 26 years.

When Phyllis resigned her vice-presidency of the Leek Division of the British Red Cross Society, in November 1935, Lady Dorothy Meynell (later OBE, JP), president of the Staffordshire Branch of the society, asked Lancelot to take over the duty. He was reluctant and delayed a decision for some months, but was appointed on 9 April 1936. After holding the office for three years, he resigned on 3 September 1939

---

* Equivalent to 6,400 man-days of agricultural labour.

71 *Marjorie Brown, born Gibson.*

– the day the Second World War was declared.

Lancelot and his family returned to Rochemount in the summer of 1939. In 1938 Lancelot had taken a short holiday at the *Raven Hall Hotel*, Ravenscar, North Yorkshire, where he rode each day. At a dinner dance there he met Marjorie Brown Gibson in a Paul Jones. They were married at the Registry Office, Bridlington, East Yorkshire, on 4 November 1939. Marjorie was then 31 years of age having been born at Cottingham, East Yorkshire, on 6 August 1908 and baptised at St Mary's Church, Cottingham, on 28 August 1908. She had been a secretary at Reckitt and Coleman Limited in Hull for some years. She was the eldest daughter of Charles Edward Gibson and his wife Lilian of Tenter Close, Beverley Road, Great Driffield, East Yorkshire.

Charles was then a provisions merchant. He had, on 1 April 1909, been commissioned a 2nd-lieutenant in the 5th (Cyclist) Battalion, the East Yorkshire Regiment – the 5th being a Territorial Force battalion with headquarters at Hull. He was promoted lieutenant on 2 October 1910 and captain on 29 August 1914. The battalion was mobilised in December 1914 for coastal defence duties in Lincolnshire and Yorkshire, and later formed part of the Humber Garrison. Charles resigned in 1922 and the battalion was disbanded soon afterwards when all the cyclist battalions were abolished.

Marjorie's mother, Lilian, was the daughter of Captain Thomas Davidson Dowse, an elder brother of Hull Trinity House, a member of the board of the House from 1902, warden of the House for four years and, at times, chairman of the pilotage committee. He was also a governor of Hymers College, a member of the Humber Conservancy Board, a director of St Andrew's Steam Fishing Company and chairman of the Trinity Provident Society.

Lancelot and Marjorie lived at Rochemount for 12 years, producing two children:

Forenames	Date of birth	Date of baptism	Article
Stuart Gibson	30 October 1940	8 December 1940	8.6
Rosalie Frances	10 September 1944	28 October 1944	8.7

Both were born at Rochemount and baptised at St Edward the Confessor's Church, Cheddleton, Staffordshire. On 24 July 1953 Lancelot, Marjorie and their two children moved to Swainsley Cottage which he had inherited from his mother (Article 7.8). Rochemount was sold and became a kindergarten school. They then purchased and renovated Swainsley, the hall which Lady Gaunt had sold in 1945 for use as a hotel. Major repairs and re-decoration took more than a year to complete, but the family were back in residence by October 1955.[23] Swainsley still had some 140 acres of hill land and five miles of fishing rights on the River Manifold.

Marjorie had, since her marriage, taken part in local affairs; she was joint secretary of the Women's Advisory Committee of the Leek Division of the Conservative and Unionist Association; she was secretary and one-time president of the Leek branch of King George's Fund for Sailors, and she was a member of the Leek Arts' Club.[19] Various charitable garden parties were held at Rochemount. Later, when living at Swainsley, she became a governor of Warslow School.

During the Second World War, A.J. Worthington & Co. (Leek) Limited were required by the government to concentrate on the manufacture of braided cord, periphery tape and sewing threads for parachutes and other military supplies. Lancelot devoted his attention to raising production by acquiring more machinery and running it for 24 hours a day, and to refining quality control and testing procedures. He liaised with the supply ministries and the armed services as well as the manufacturers concerned with assembly. Such was the demand on his time, that he transferred to the supplementary list as a justice of the peace. He was president of the Leek Silk Manufacturers' and Dyers' Association (later called The Leek and District Manufacturers' and Dyers' Association) from 1942 to 1944 and was still a member of the executive committee in 1963. He was the United Kingdom's delegate for sewing threads on the International Silk Association, founded in Zurich, Switzerland, in 1949, and he represented the narrow fabrics industry on the national Silk and Man-made Fibre Users' Association.[24]

In 1953, Lancelot and the other two owners of A.J. Worthington & Co. (Leek) Limited agreed that the company should be floated on the market by selling the majority of their shares to the public. By this time the three owners had acquired three other Leek textile companies, namely Heavers & Pace Limited (crochet trimmings and fringe manufacturers), William Swindells & Co. Limited (textile braids and wooden bobbin manufacturers) and William Gallimore & Co. Limited (factors of sewing threads). A new holding company, A.J. Worthington (Holdings) Limited, was incorporated for the purpose of acquiring all four of these companies, which it did on 23 December 1953. Lancelot remained one of the two joint-managing directors of the Group until he retired on 31 August 1971 at the age of 80 years. He was Group chairman from 1963 to 1968, following William Wadsworth's death. When the Group became quoted on the London Stock Exchange on 30 December 1953, Lancelot's holding of shares fell from 40 per cent to 12.5 per cent. The proceeds of the remainder he used mainly for the renovation of Swainsley.

Lancelot and Marjorie lived at Swainsley for the remainder of their lives, but, alas, Marjorie's activities were severely curtailed by multiple sclerosis. The disease developed through the 1960s and confined her to a wheelchair from the 1970s. Lancelot died at the Lismore Nursing Home, Buxton, Derbyshire on 3 June 1975 at the age of 84 years.[19] The funeral service was held at St Luke's Church on 6 June 1975, after which his body was interred in the family.

By Lancelot's Will dated 14 February 1974, the whole of his estate passed to Marjorie who in turn bequeathed it to her two children. Nearly five years earlier, on 21 December 1970, Lancelot had created a settlement of some of his ordinary shares in A.J. Worthington (Holdings) Limited, the income of which accumulated as capital during his lifetime but was paid to Marjorie during her widowhood. On her death, the capital was divided equally among his five children.

Marjorie died at the Portland Nursing Home, Buxton, on 11 December 1981 at the age of 73 years.[19] Her body was also interred in the family tomb following a funeral service at St Luke's Church, Leek.[25]

THIRD GENERATION – FAMILY OF LANCELOT JUKES OF LEEK

8.3 Margaret Elizabeth Valentine

Margaret Elizabeth Valentine Worthington, the eldest child of Lancelot Jukes Worthington and Phyllis Mary his first wife (Article 8.2), was born on 14 February 1924 at Rochemount, Leek, Staffordshire, and baptised on 25 March 1924 at St Luke's Church, Leek. The names Margaret and Elizabeth were those of her paternal and maternal grandmothers respectively (Articles 7.8 and 8.2), and the name Valentine was that of the saint on whose day she was born. She was known throughout her life as 'Tally' because, when young, she mispronounced Valentine as Tallytine.

Noel Coward (later Sir Noel Coward, Kt, Hon DLitt, FRSL) composed his comic lyric *Mrs Worthington* about 1931.[26] It begins with chorus:

> Don't put your daughter on the stage Missis Worthington;
> Don't put your daughter on the stage ...

The verse opens with 'Regarding yours, dear Mrs Worthington, of Wednesday 23rd ...' Noel was two days younger than Valentine's mother, Phyllis, having been born on 16 December 1899. Phyllis claimed that this link, and her keen interest in amateur dramatics and light musicals, led to an exchange of letters.[27] However, confusion has been caused because there have been other claimants, especially Angela Fox, born Worthington. In her autobiography she claimed to be the 'daughter' of the song. She was the wife of Edward Fox and the mother of Robert, James and Edward Fox – all of whom have had successful careers on the stage. Angela's obituary, published in the *Daily Telegraph* of 9 December 1999, states:[25] 'It was Angela who inspired Noel Coward to write "Don't put your daughter on the stage Mrs Worthington" ...'. The Fox claim was undermined a few days later when Angela's sister, Yvonne Crichton of Hartley Wintney, Hampshire, responded with a letter to the editor of the *Daily Telegraph* to say: 'It is time the record was put straight regarding my sister Angela Fox's claim ...' Yvonne wrote that her sister never met Noel Coward and that Noel did not know of Angela, who was inclined to creative notions which she came to believe.[25] However, Emilia Fox, a member of the third generation of the Fox drama family, still made the claim in March 2000.[28]

Until the summer of 1929, Valentine was educated privately at home, Rochemount, with a small group of other children. Her mother then arranged for the group to move to separate accommodation at Moorfields, Leek; thus the Moorfields School and Kindergarten was founded 'for sons and daughters of professional people', which Valentine attended from 1929 to 1935.[29] She was at Westwood Hall High School from 1935 to 1937 and then became a boarder at Meynell House, at the School of St Mary and St Anne, Abbots Bromley, Staffordshire, until 1941. After gaining her school certificate in 1940, her final year was spent on a pre-nursing course, as a school prefect and as second-head of Meynell House. She played hockey for the school's first team and was captain of her house hockey and cricket teams. She was also in the school's second teams for tennis and cricket. In a letter of 24 June 1941 her grandfather, Dr E.A. Sadler (Article 8.2), advised her not to pursue a nursing career but to consider the many other careers then open to young women. On leaving school in the summer of 1941 she took a 12-week Pitman shorthand and typewriting course at the Underwood Secretarial College, Hanley, Staffordshire, to fill the time until she reached the age of 18 years and could join the armed forces.

Her mother had left home when Valentine was 11 years of age, and soon afterwards she and her father went to live with her great-aunt Elizabeth Wardle at Ladydale, Fynney Street, Leek. She was there for four years before the family was reunited at Rochemount. During that period she had the opportunity to ride and she occasionally hunted with the North Staffordshire foxhounds as a member of the Pony Club.

The Second World War had been in progress for two years when, on 22 June 1942, Valentine joined the Women's Auxiliary Air Force as a radar operator. Her initial training was at RAF Innsworth Lane, near Gloucester, and her radar training started in July 1942 at RAF Yatesbury, near Calne, Wiltshire. In September 1942 she was posted to RAF West Beckham in Norfolk – the radio direction-finding station. While there she plotted an enemy aircraft in to zero distance, at which time the station was bombed! The following month she was posted to RAF Great Bromley, near Colchester, Essex, the monitor station of the eastern chain of aircraft navigational aid stations. There she received training in the new Gee system by which bombers were guided to their targets by radio pulses sent simultaneously from three stations spaced well apart across England. In 1942 the whole station moved to RAF Barkway near Royston, Hertfordshire, where she was promoted to leading aircraftwoman and later to corporal. She was billeted at Newsells Park, a large country house owned by Captain Sir Humphrey Edmund de Trafford, 4th Bt, MC, JP, DL, who was the lineal descendant of the de Traffords from whom Valentine's great-great-great-grandfather, Jonathan

72 *Margaret Elizabeth Valentine, born Worthington.*

Worthington, had leased the Old Trafford demesne (Article 3.5). On 14 September 1943, she began a week's leave in Leek, but that night Newsells was gutted by fire. All her possessions there were destroyed and henceforth she lived in huts closer to the radar station.

At 11 pm on 13 February 1945 – one hour before the start of her 21st birthday – she started the night-duty shift, during which she and a colleague guided the heavy air raids on Dresden, Germany. On completion of the watch at 7 a.m., she hitch-hiked home, arriving in Leek in time for her coming-of-age ball at the Town Hall.

On 9 April 1945 she was posted to RAF West Prawle, Devon, a slave station for the southern chain, and on 8 May she was sent on a training course for senior non-commissioned officers at Cherry Orchard, near Cheltenham, Gloucester, in which she qualified. She was also interviewed at RAF Mountbatten, Plymouth, for commissioned rank in photographic interpretation. However, Victory in Europe was celebrated on 8 May 1945 and from that day plans for demobilisation took shape. She was demobilised on 4 February 1946 when she returned to Rochemount. In her release papers she was described as '... quick and efficient in her own work, and a good NCO'. This reference also described her as, '... popular amongst her fellow workers. She took a keen interest in station activities & camp entertainments & is a very good all-round sportswoman'.

On 22 March 1947 Valentine married Captain Norman Dowse Gibson, the only son of Captain Charles Edward Gibson and his wife Lilian Brown, borne Dowse. Norman was, thus, the only brother of Valentine's step-mother, Marjorie. Norman was nine years older than Valentine having been born on 2 October 1914. He was educated at Hymers College, Hull, for nine years leaving in 1932. He then worked for E.B. Bradshaw and Sons Limited, corn millers of Great Driffield, East Yorkshire. At the same time he studied flour milling and science at the Hull Municipal Technical College, obtaining in 1938 a second-class certificate of the City and Guilds of London Institute. On 1 April 1940 he enlisted in the Royal Army Pay Corps, Territorial Army. He received a Regular Army emergency commission on 18 October 1941 with the rank of 2nd-lieutenant and then transferred to the 61st Field Regiment, Royal Artillery, which had been part of the 59th (Staffordshire) Infantry Division for about two years. (30) This division consisted of nine infantry battalions (mainly 'Staffords') arranged in three brigades and supported by units from the usual corps including artillery, engineers, signals and medical services. Norman arrived in time to go with the division to Northern Ireland where IRA aggression was increasing. Norman's personal role was liaison officer, to prepare for the arrival there of the first contingent of the US Army. He was promoted substantive lieutenant on 1 October 1942. In February 1943 the division moved to Kent to 'defeat enemy raids and invasion'. But the fear of invasion was then receding fast and the division soon became part of the plans for the invasion of France. Norman was promoted acting captain on 14 July 1943 and temporary captain on 14 October 1943. Starting on 17 June 1944 the infantry brigades concentrated at Newhaven on the south coast of East Sussex, while the artillery and other units concentrated on the north bank of the River Thames. Sailings for Normandy, France, started on 25 June 1944 (being D-Day plus 19) and were completed by 1 July. On 8 July the division engaged with the enemy at the Battle of Caen (known as Operation Charnwood). They then took part in the Battle of Noyers (called Operation Pomegranate) which lasted from 15 to 18 July 1944. After a bridgehead across the River Orne had successfully been established, Norman's division was disbanded for break-up and transfers to other divisions which were under strength. Norman, with the 61st Field Regiment, Royal Artillery, moved to Dunkirk to support the Czech brigade, but on 5 February 1945 they returned to England for three weeks' re-training at Welbeck Abbey, Nottinghamshire, as the '61 Super Heavy Regiment, Royal Artillery'. Towards the end of February embarkation of the regiment with its new heavy equipment began at Tilbury, Essex, to join the British Army of the Rhine. By this time Norman was the regiment's adjutant. In March 1945 they fired in support of the Rhine crossing at Emmerich, Rees and Wesel, Germany, near the Dutch border but because of the size of its equipment the regiment was left behind in the hurried pursuit of the enemy into the heart of the Reich. On 15 April 1945 the regiment moved north to fire in support of advancing troops at Emden on the German side of the mouth of the River Ems.

Norman was demobilised on 2 March 1946 and released from active service on 17 May 1946. He was granted the honorary rank of captain on 1 July 1959. On 11 March Prince Charles, the Regent of Belgium, had appointed him chevalier de l'Ordre de Leopold II avec palme, '... pour le courage et la bravoure dont il a fait preuvé dans les glorieuses batailles qui ont amené la libération de la Belgique'.

He had also been awarded the Belgian Croix de Guerre 1940 avec palme. He returned to work at E.B. Bradshaw and Sons Limited as their grain buyer.[31]

Valentine and Norman's wedding took place at St Edward's Church, Leek, followed by a reception for 200 guests at the Town Hall, Leek. A local newspaper gave an account of the wedding under the headline 'Large crowds greet the Bride of the Year'.[32] Their honeymoon was planned for Paris but was changed to London, staying at the *Dorchester Hotel*, because deep snow and floods prevented travel. Their first home was Rosegarth Cottage, St John's Road, Great Driffield, where they lived for two years. In December 1949 they moved to Tenter Close, Beverley Road, Driffield, a much larger house owned and occupied by Norman's widowed mother. In October 1954 they purchased and moved into a house called 'Cartref' in St John's Road; they renamed the house 'Ladydale' after the house Valentine had lived in for four years with her father and great-aunt in Leek. The children of the marriage were:

Forenames	Date of birth	Date of baptism
Martin Charles	18 December 1947	18 January 1948
Timothy Lancelot	27 February 1951	17 July 1951

Martin was baptised at All Saints' Church, Nafferton, and Timothy at St Edward's Church, Leek. At their baptisms, both wore a robe made from embroidered Decca muslin which had been brought from India in 1886 by their great-great-grandfather, Sir Thomas Wardle (Article 7.8). This robe, first worn by Valentine herself and still in her possession, has been worn for the baptisms of seven Worthingtons and four Gibsons.

From 1957 to 1962, Valentine was Driffield branch secretary of the Institute for the Blind and later she took over the chairmanship from her mother-in-law. She was also the secretary of the Driffield branch of the Royal Society for the Prevention of Cruelty to Children. She was twice president of the Driffield Ladies' Luncheon Club, the first year being 1967-8. She was appointed a justice of the peace for the County of York (East Riding) on 4 May 1965.[33] About 10 years later she became deputy chairman of the Bainton Beacon Bench, which covered the Driffield area. She was chairman of the Juvenile Bench, chairman of the Probation Committee and bench representative on the Humberside Probation and Aftercare Committee.

For their 1964 summer holiday the family visited Northern Ireland, where Norman had been stationed as liaison officer during the Second World War. When they visited the *Kilmorey Arms Hotel* in Kilkeel, Norman pointed out a bullet hole in the panelling of the hall which had been made in his presence when an American army officer had fired the shot in 1942 or 1943. This caused great excitement amongst the local people and there was much telephoning. As a result Valentine and Norman were invited to a party the following night; the mayor attended and much Irish Mist whiskey was consumed.

In February 1969, Valentine was a member of the panel of five answering topical questions from the public at an 'Any Questions?' meeting organised by the British Legion Women's Section in the Cass Hall at Driffield. She was noted for her outspokenness when speaking in public and did not shrink from berating sections of society who fell short of their public duties.

In March 1971 the family moved to Meadow Cottage, Applegarth Lane, Bainton, a village lying about five miles south-west of Driffield. Alas, on 26 February 1974, Norman died at Chapel Allerton Hospital, Leeds, the cause being lymph cancer from which he had suffered for about two years. He was cremated on 1 March 1974 at Scarborough, East Yorkshire, and his ashes were spread in the sea off Flamborough Head.

In June that year, Valentine started working for two days a week at The Dormouse, a new children's clothing shop in Beverley, East Yorkshire. This lasted about three years until the shop was sold. For the next four years she undertook in-depth interviews for National Opinion Poll Research Group Limited for 15 hours a week – her area being Spurn Point to Filey, East Yorkshire. She also conducted agricultural surveys for Field Search Surveys. She was appointed a non-executive director of A.J. Worthington (Holdings) plc (later called Worthington Group Plc) on 1 July 1978.[34] After a serious heart attack in July 1981 and another in June 1982 she decided to resign her directorship on 31 March 1983.

In December 1983 she moved to The Old Cottage, Letcombe Regis, near Wantage, Oxfordshire, to be nearer to her two sons and four grandchildren. The cottage had been built in 1680. When she resigned as a magistrate for East Yorkshire she was presented with an engraved silver coaster by her colleagues. As a justice of the peace she was placed on the supplementary list and transferred, on 19 March 1984, to the Oxfordshire commission. On 20 April 1983 she flew to Johannesburg, South Africa, to stay with a school friend; she then proceeded by the

Blue Train to Cape Town to stay with a WAAF colleague. Finally she flew to Natal to stay with her half-fourth cousin, Betty Yorke Crosskill, and her husband (Article 4.15). She met several members of the Natal branch of the Worthington family who entertained her splendidly.

In the summer of 1990 Valentine toured the south of France. On the evening of 21 September, she and a friend, Millicent Eskell, were returning to Millicent's home when they witnessed the great forest fire on the hills above Cavalaire, Var. Valentine wrote:

> ... the lights of Cavalaire across the bay were non-existent. Only the lighthouse was flashing on the Iles d'Hyères. We all collected our money, passports and most important items into hand luggage. George (our host) made a ramp to enable him to get the new Volvo out of the drive, upon which work was in progress, and Sheila armed herself with the Opel keys. We stood on the terrace appalled at what we were witnessing. Flames flaring into the sky as they rushed up trees, deeper glows where more substantial things blazed, racing along the crests of the hills and in great swathes down the hills and into the valley behind our nearest hill, smoke filling the sky and billowing out to sea joining up with that from Ste. Maxime to the east, thank goodness blowing away from us. Should the wind change we would be in deep trouble ...

In the early hours of the morning it became clear that their house was safe.

8.4 Philip Michael

Philip Michael Worthington, the eldest son of Lancelot Jukes Worthington and Phyllis Mary his first wife (Article 8.2), was born on 24 April 1926 at Rochemount, Leek, and baptised on 19 May 1926 at St Luke's Church, Leek. From September 1930 to July 1934 he was educated at Moorfields School and Kindergarten, Leek. For the next two years he attended Moorhill Preparatory School, Leek, being a day boy for the first year and a boarder for the second. From September 1936 he boarded at the Boys' Grammar School, Ashby-de-la-Zouch, Leicestershire. In his letter of 14 October 1936 to the headmaster, Thomas Arnold Woodcock, MA (later OBE, JP), Lancelot wrote: 'Philip is rather a dreamer, and has reached the age of being a little wayward, so I am glad to hear that you have made him toe the line in discipline ...'. He was a keen swimmer, and in the summer of 1939 was awarded the intermediate certificate of the Royal Life Saving Society.[35] Having developed an interest in military signalling from his father, Philip formed the 'ABGS Signalling Club' on 8 January 1941, the opening membership being 18 boarders; but the spirit in the Second World War was such that day boys joined and membership grew to 71 by September 1941. Signalling was by means of semaphore and Morse code, using flags, light and telegraphy. As money was in short supply, most of the equipment had to be made by members; it included a home-made heliograph which could be used in sunny weather. A.J. Worthington & Co. (Leek) Limited made a pair of blue and white arm bands for each member. The club enjoyed the support of the headmaster, who excused boys from compulsory sport when attending club meetings and field work. Drill was a feature and the club, led by Philip, took part in the Warships' Week parade at Ashby on 14 March 1942. By the summer term of 1942 the club became too ambitious for its own good and for the comfort of the school. It changed its name to 'Ashby Signalling Corps'; it set up a workshop with power lathe and other tools; it booked the town hall for a concert to be staged on 23 October 1942, and it formed an eight-strong recorder and drum band, of which Andrew Ralph Worthington (Article 8.5) was the band sergeant. The club lost the headmaster's support and was stood down.

In Philip's school report for the summer term 1943, the headmaster remarked: 'The disparity in his progress in different subjects is too marked. His enthusiasm for some things is excellent but needs restraint …'. The housemaster, Geoffrey V.S. Bucknall added, 'He has done some foolish things and his main cause seems to be egotism and a conviction of his own right judgement …'.

Meanwhile, Philip had joined the Air Training Corps on 20 October 1941 and later became the senior flight sergeant of 648 Squadron. He left the service on 21 July 1944 with Flight Lieutenant Addison's commendation: 'An exceptional NCO. He has proved himself as a leader, well able to handle a difficult flight. His worth in drill and signals has been of very high quality'.

He was awarded a state bursary and attended University College, Nottingham, (now the University of Nottingham) until July 1946 when he attained the BSc (Engineering) external degree in the University of London, with second-class honours. He joined W.S. Atkins and Partners, consulting engineers of Sutton House, 57 Victoria Street, London SW1, on 16 September 1946. The firm had a staff of about 200 and was expanding. He was attached to the Statics Squad which was concerned with the analysis of stresses in complex structures and with research generally into structural problems.[36] Early in August 1948 he was sent to lead the Concrete Control Section at Abbey Works, Port Talbot, South Wales – a major new steelworks for which W.S. Atkins and Partners were the consulting civil and structural engineers.

During the two years he had worked in London, his sport had been sailing; he had owned an 18-foot quarter-decked gaff-rigged sloop at Sunbury-on-Thames, and he was lent for a season a 30-foot 10-ton Bermudan cutter based at Birdham Pool, near Chichester, Sussex. On moving to South Wales he gave up sailing and took to riding – hunting occasionally with the Llangeinor foxhounds. On 2 April 1951, he gave a lecture and paper on 'The Design of Economical Concrete Mixes' to the South Wales and Monmouthshire Association of the Institution of Civil

Engineers. The paper was forwarded to the institution's headquarters, for which he was awarded the institution's Miller prize. Philip returned to head office in September 1951 to concentrate on structural engineering and the design of buildings. During that year he wrote a paper on 'The Elastic Stability of I-Beams Subject to Complex Load Systems'. The paper, with written discussion, was published by the Institution of Civil Engineers. It was the second of nine published papers by him on technical, economic and organisational subjects.[37] On 30 June 1952 he was posted as the resident engineer for the reconstruction of the BSA motorcycle works at Small Heath, near Birmingham, which had been destroyed by German bombing during the war. For this purpose, Philip and his horse moved to Hillfield Farm, Solihull, Warwickshire. On 22 July 1953, Philip left Warwickshire to return to Abbey Works where a major expansion was starting. This time his role was head of South Wales Research and Development Department which embraced concrete control at Abbey Works and at the tin-plate works being built at Velindre, near Swansea. During this period he received the Sir Lister Lister Kaye prize of the Midland Counties Branch of the Institution of Structural Engineers for his paper and lecture on 'The Design of Crane Gantries and the Action of Wheels on their Tracks'. While in South Wales, Philip lived with old friends, Mr and Mrs Raymond Rees, at Mount Pleasant Farm, Stormy Down. They kept and bred horses as well as producing milk. He was recalled to head office on 15 January 1955.

On 19 February 1954 it was announced that Philip was engaged to be married to Gillian Hazel, the younger daughter and co-heiress of William Sydney Albert Atkins and Elsie Jessie (born Foreman) his wife, of Kingswood Manor, Lower Kingswood, Surrey.[25] Gillian was eight years younger than Philip, having been born on 21 February 1935 at 14 Gyllyngdune Gardens, Ilford, Essex, and baptised on 9 June 1935 at All Saints' Church, Goodmayes, near Ilford. She was educated at Sherborne School for Girls, Dorset, boarding at Aldhamstead East House. Later she attended the Constance Spry Flower School which was then at St John's Road, London. Her father, William (later Sir William Atkins, Kt, CBE, BSc (Eng), FEng, CEng, FICE, FIStruct E, fellow of University College, London), was a son of Edward Atkins and Martha his wife. William was founder, senior partner and 75 per cent owner of W.S. Atkins and Partners. Before the war he had acquired a firm of contractors which he re-named London Ferro-Concrete Limited.[36] This firm had a workforce of about 2,000 and during the war was awarded a parcel of the Mulberry Harbour contract for the Normandy landings. He formed W.S. Atkins and Partners in 1938 as a consulting firm in structural steelwork to run in parallel with his contracting interests, but after the war it was W.S. Atkins and Partners which prospered more and to which William devoted his whole time.[38]

Philip and Gillian's wedding took place on 25 June 1955 at St Andrew's Church, Kingswood, followed by a reception at Kingswood Manor. Their first home was Hazelworth, Downs Way Close, Tadworth, Surrey – a newly built house. After five years without children, they adopted:

Forenames	Date of birth	Date of adoption	Date of baptism
Nicholas Robert	10 October 1960	13 June 1961	9 July 1961
Catherine Clare	3 July 1962	18 December 1962	2 June 1963

Both were born at Lambeth, London; both were adopted by orders of the Guildford County Court, Surrey, and both were baptised at St Lawrence's Church, Chobham, Surrey. By then the family had moved to Chobham Place, Chobham, Surrey, which had been acquired by the Atkins and extended and divided to accommodate six families. The Atkins took the centre house, the Worthingtons took the attached house to the east and the Micklethwaites (Gillian's sister's family) took the attached house to the west. Mrs Atkins' mother and stepfather lived in a nearby cottage and the Atkins' chauffeur and gardener in two more. The Worthingtons managed the 150 acres of parkland and fields, grazing beef cattle on behalf of the Atkins. The Worthingtons also kept and bred hunters for themselves and ponies for the children. Hunting was with the Bisley and Sandhurst foxhounds.

Meanwhile, W.S. Atkins and Partners were expanding their scope from civil and structural engineering and architecture to encompass all aspects of industrial technology. From 1955 to 1959 Philip had been a project manager, and from 1959 he headed the Plant Engineering Department. From October to December 1961 he attended Session 42 of the Administrative Staff College at Henley-on-Thames, Oxfordshire. About this time, all the London departments moved to the firm's new premises at Woodcote Grove, Epsom, Surrey.

In 1962 Philip formed and led a new department initially called 'Economics and Industrial Planning' but later simply 'Strategic Planning'. It grew to a strength of about 60 staff including market researchers, process and production planners, business economists and manpower planners. Strategic studies were undertaken in many countries including Argentina, Canada, Ethiopia, India, Israel, New Zealand, Tunisia, Morocco and West Africa. Philip directed personally the study of the Strategic Future of the Wool Textile Industry under the auspices of the National Economic Development Office (NEDO).

In 1968 he left the planning department to lead the Group's growing commercial operations. He had already been appointed chairman of Atkins Computing Services Limited and Woodcote Publications Limited. In 1971 he was promoted managing director of W.S. Atkins and Partners and in 1973 head of all the Group's consulting activities, including Atkins Planning and the architects – A.G. Shepard Fidler and Associates

– but excluding Research Department.[39] The Group then had about 2,000 staff.[39]

In November 1976 Philip became one of a steering group of eight people whose object was to establish the British Moroccan Society. The chairman was Ronald William Bailey, CMG, the former British ambassador to Morocco. The inaugural meeting was held at the Moroccan Embassy in London in October 1977, when Philip became a committee member. On 6 July 1976 he was elected a fellow of the British Institute of Management having been elected a member on 19 April 1967; he was later elected a companion. In 1977 On-Line Systems Inc. of 15 Evergreen Heights' Drive, Pittsburgh, Pennsylvania, USA, acquired Atkins Computing Services Limited for about £3,000,000.[*] Philip became a director of On-Line Systems for the next 15 months, travelling to Pittsburgh for board meetings at three-monthly intervals.

Towards the end of 1977 Gillian announced that she wished to end the marriage. Sir William Atkins then decided that, if Philip were to leave his family, he should also leave the firm. As there were no grounds for dismissal, negotiations started which lasted a year, in which Sir William, through solicitors, acted for his daughter as well as for his firm. One of the complications was Sir William's insistence that Philip should not act as a future consultant to any former client of the Atkins Group. He left the group in August 1978 and formed his own consulting company called 'P.M. Worthington and Associates Limited'. The decree nisi was granted on 14 September 1979 by the High Court of Justice and the decree absolute on 9 January 1980.

Soon afterwards Edwin Robert George Eyers (usually known as Sam Eyers) moved into Chobham Place. Gillian and he married on 28 June 1986 at the Surrey North-Western Region Register Office. He was then described as 'area manager (medical credit company)'. On 10 October 1992 they moved to Wilsham Farm, Wilsham, Countisbury, Devon.

On leaving Chobham, Philip resided for a year with his brother Andrew Ralph Worthington and Tessa Helen his wife (Article 8.5) at Abbotsmead, 49 London Road, Guildford. They allocated the second floor of their house for his use. On 18 December 1980 Philip acquired the ground-floor flat of Shirburn House, Ashbourne Road, Leek, which he renovated.

Within P.M. Worthington and Associates Limited, Philip's work was serving other organisations as an individual, usually having office facilities at each client. His first client was Babcock Turnkey Operations Limited, a newly formed subsidiary of Babcock International PLC. Another was the Major Projects Association, an organisation based at the Oxford Centre for Management Studies (which later became part of Oxford University as Templeton College). The association consisted

---

[*] Equivalent to 300,000 man-days of agricultural labour.

of British project owners, professional advisers, contractors, bankers, insurers, and government departments interested in major construction projects throughout the world. Philip was a member of the steering group to establish the association and then, in 1982, became its first executive director with an office at the college. He was also appointed an associate fellow of the college. This work took two or three days a week; he continued in the role for the first annual cycle, but continued as an associate fellow for a further year, until August 1983.

Following flotation of the A.J. Worthington group in 1954, the family held 12.5 per cent of the ordinary shares, all being in the hands of Lancelot Worthington (Article 8.1). Subsequently there was a concerted effort by Lancelot's five children to acquire shares, and by 31 March 1982 the family held 55.4 per cent of the issued ordinary shares, of which 23.7 per cent of the whole were held by Philip and his children. A further 12.4 per cent were held by his half-brother Stuart Gibson Worthington (Article 8.6) and his wife and children. Philip had become the non-executive chairman on 1 April 1972, while Stuart was the group's chief executive from 1978.

During the financial year ended 31 March 1980 a recession started to bite hard in the textile and clothing industries. Many companies were giving up the ghost, and two of them – one in Leek and one in Macclesfield – were acquired by the group for nominal sums. The Group then slid towards serious loss, so cost savings became urgent. The number of Group employees was reduced from 323 in July 1981 to 300 by July 1982 and to 221 by July 1983. However, in his annual statement to shareholders for 1982-3, Philip reported that the reductions were too late as the board had been 'reluctant to create redundancies at a time of high unemployment'. The pre-tax loss on ordinary activities in that year was £251,000.* The board took tough action in June 1983, but indeed it was too late. The bank started to investigate in July and a predator called Michael Hartland arrived on the scene in August. He succeeded in splitting the board, Stuart with the finance director and one other joined the Hartland camp, while Philip, his brother Andrew and the production director constituted the other camp. On 22 September 1983 it became known that Stuart had agreed to sell all his shares in the Group to Hartland. The chairmanship passed to Hartland on 16 January 1984, and Stuart resigned from the Group on 29 March 1984. Hartland's tenure as chairman was disastrous and the Group's position became perilous. However, Stuart's shares found their way to discretionary clients of C.L. Bank Nederland NV of London. Following Philip's pressure on C.L. Bank, one of their clients, Sidney Friedland, who had been a director of the bank, gave his support and provided a loan. Hartland left the group on 1 October 1984, the

---

* Equivalent to 14,300 man-days of agricultural labour.

73   *Philip Michael Worthington, about 1965.*

74   *Judith Sonia May, born Hamlin, in 2000.*

finance director having left a few weeks earlier. From 1 October there were only three directors. Sidney Friedland as non-executive chairman, Philip as part-time secretary and Anthony Ivory, a chartered accountant of Wilmslow, Cheshire, as non-executive. A long recuperation had begun.

On 4 October 1984 Philip was asked to help the City of London Police, who were investigating possible fraud concerning the handling of moneys which 'Michael Hartland Investment Brokers' had received from pensioners. The court later found Hartland guilty and sentenced him to four years' imprisonment.

Philip's part-time involvement in the group continued for a further 14 years, as a non-executive director and secretary. He was also part-time group human resources' director from 1993. He resigned as from 30 June 1998 as secretary and human resources' director, and as from 31 December 1998 as non-executive director, because he had for some years disagreed with policy decisions taken by the rest of the board. He was then 72 years of age.

On 4 June 1983 it was announced that Philip was engaged to be married to Judith Sonia May, the only daughter of Henry Peter Robson Hamlin and Mary Sonia his wife.[40] Judith was 16 years younger than Philip, having been born on 6 December 1942 at 90 Corporation Street, Stafford. In February 1950 the Hamlin family moved to Ashby-de-la-Zouch, living first at Lynstock, Moira Road, and from 1958 at Sandhurst, Tamworth Road. Judith attended the Church of England Junior School followed by the Girls' Grammar School, Ashby. She left the school in

July 1960, receiving a school prize for her performance in the A-level examinations – mathematics, physics and chemistry. The head mistress reported:

> Judith has a great potentiality. Her intelligence is well above average, she is a good student, and will, we think, develop into a natural leader. She takes an active part in all branches of the school's activities.

She had been captain of the school's first tennis team, and had produced the fifth-form play – Shakespeare's *The Winter's Tale* – which won the English cup. From September 1960 to July 1963 she was an undergraduate at Queen Mary College, University of London, and on 1 August 1963 attained the BSc (Special) degree in chemistry with second-class honours (lower division). During her last year there she was a joint author of a paper on 'The Ultraviolet Absorption of the Unconjugated Azomethine Group', published in the Journal of Chemistry and Industry.[41]

On 27 July 1963, when 20 years of age, Judith married Ian Anthony Donald Gale, BSc, (later PhD), at Holy Trinity Church, Ashby. Their first home was at Buckhurst Hill, Essex, and from September 1963 Judith taught chemistry at Woodford County High School for Girls, Woodford Green, Essex. In the summer of 1966 Judith and Ian moved to 36 The Green, Hurworth-on-Tees, County Durham and Judith was lecturer in chemistry at the Darlington College of Technology – from September 1966 to July 1971. Concurrently Judith worked with the Darlington Liberal Party and served on the local committee of the National Society for the Prevention of Cruelty to Children and the Campaign for the Advancement of State Education. She also became a governor of Hurworth Comprehensive School. She and Ian produced two children: Toby Jonathan, born on 18 September 1970, and Sophie Joanna, born on 24 July 1972. From September 1972 Judith taught at the Convent of the Assumption, Richmond, North Yorkshire. In July 1975 Ian was posted by his employer, ICI plc, to Belgium and the family moved with him. Judith then taught part-time at the British School of Brussels from September 1976 to July 1977. On returning to England in the summer of 1977 they lived at Elton West, 190 Coniscliffe Road, Darlington – a house they had bought and moved to in July 1973.

While teaching part-time from 1978 at Polam Hall School, Darlington, Judith started a business making and retailing children's clothing under her own label 'Ragamuffin', but in 1981 she left teaching to devote more time to the business. Working from retail premises in Grange Road, Darlington, she designed the clothing and had it made by outworkers in the area. The products for which she was best known were hand-smocked dresses for girls.

The marriage ended in divorce, on the grounds of Ian's adultery in Finland. The decree nisi was granted by Leicester County Court on 19 October 1982 and the decree absolute on 30 November 1982. Elton

West was sold, and Judith and her two children moved to 51 The Green, Hurworth. Her business was successful to the extent that she won a Midas Business Award organised jointly by Leicester County Council, Pedigree Petfoods Limited and Melton Borough Council. The prize was £4,001* but Pedigree Petfoods also provided a bank guarantee of £32,500,* and Judith's bank provided a loan of £100,000* under the government's small firms' guaranteed loan scheme. Under the terms of the award she gave up the Darlington business and concentrated on manufacturing at an industrial unit at 82 Snow Hill, Melton Mowbray, Leicestershire. From 23 May 1983 the business was transferred into a new company called 'Ragamuffin Children's Clothing Limited' which was owned 100 per cent by Judith.

Judith's father, Peter, was the only surviving son of Henry James Hamlin and his wife May (born Robson) of Burford, Mont à L'Abbé, Jersey. Peter served his whole career with H.M. Customs and Excise, achieving the rank of surveyor when he headed their unit at East Midlands Airport from 1950.[42] This career was interrupted by war service from 18 July 1940 to 20 May 1946. After training at the Royal Military Academy, Sandhurst, he was posted to India, embarking on 23 March 1942, a few weeks after marrying Sonia. He did not see his daughter, Judith, until 6 January 1945 when he arrived home on leave; she was then nearly three years of age. Peter then took part in the Burma Campaign, first as adjutant to the 2nd Battalion, the Welsh Regiment, and later as acting major commanding the HQ Company. He retired with the rank of captain having been mentioned in despatches.[8]

Judith's mother, Sonia, was the younger daughter of Victor Pickstock and Emily May his wife of Valley Farm, Dunstan, three miles south of Stafford. The Pickstocks had held land in Dunstan since time immemorial. In 1135, for example, 'Doneston' was held of Richard de Stretton by Thomas and William Picstoke and William de Draycote.

Judith and Philip's marriage took place at the Register Office, Coalville, Leicestershire, followed by a service at St Helen's Church, Ashby-de-la-Zouch. Their home was, and still is, The Knoll House, Knossington, Leicestershire. They produced one daughter:

Forenames	Date of birth	Date of baptism
Miranda Elizabeth	16 February 1985	14 July 1985

Miranda was born at the Leicester General Hospital, and baptised at St Peter's Church, Knossington.

On 18 May 1986 Philip was elected a fellow of the Institute of Management Consultants. He had been elected a member on 3 June 1980. He was elected a member of Lloyd's of London in 1987. This was just before the five-year period when Lloyd's was in serious

---

* Equivalent to 220, 1,820 and 56,000 man-days of agricultural labour.

financial difficulties and its members suffered enormous losses without the protection of limited liability. Philip's losses during this period – for which he had to borrow from his bank – were partly offset by three strong underwriting years from 1994 to 1996. Subsequently he transferred to limited liability through Talisman Underwriting plc, but he suffered large losses there mainly as a result of the terrorist attack on the twin towers of the International Trade Centre, New York, on 11 September 2001.

In 1994 P.M. Worthington & Associates Limited had been commissioned by Philip's first cousin, David Barry Sadler, to act for him in buying the business of Polycast Limited from M.S. Gibb & Co. Limited. Polycast, situated at Clock Tower Buildings, Warsash, Hampshire, was a foundry with about 50 employees, manufacturing for industrial customers castings in stainless steel and other metals by the lost-wax process. Philip was invited to take a holding of about 27 per cent of the shares of the company which he held for 18 years, selling them on 27 March 2002. He resigned as part-time director and secretary at the same time. He had been a non-executive director since 25 January 1985 and secretary since 23 April 1991.

Philip's main hobby since the age of 20 years has been genealogy. His first book on the subject – *The Worthington Families of Medieval England* – covering the 12th to 17th centuries was published in 1985. This second book, *The Worthingtons of Failsworth and their Descendants* – covers the 17th to 20th centuries.

Judith's new children's clothing factory at Melton Mowbray succeeded at first, serving prestigious retailers such as Scotch House, Burberry's and many high street boutiques.[43] After a time, the fall in the market for high quality dresses, coupled with strong competition from low-labour-cost countries, caused losses. The company ceased trading on 14 March 1985 and went into voluntary liquidation. Judith then purchased the business, stocks, and trade from the liquidators and continued to manufacture at the Snow Hill premises – especially to maintain trade with Scotch House and Burberry's. On 31 March 1987 she ceased trading.

In September 1988 she returned to teaching – this time at Oakham School and the Rutland Sixth Form College. Later she started and managed the training programme at the Vale of Catmose College, Oakham.[44] From 1992 to 1999 she was an examiner and moderator for various examining boards concerned with the General Certificates of Education.

In 1997 she joined the Human Resources department of the British Red Cross Society, London, to develop training for the society's staff, overseas delegates and volunteers.

In January 1991, Judith had been appointed a justice of the peace in the Leicestershire commission. She has since served as chairman on the Rutland bench at Oakham Castle and the combined Melton, Belvoir and Rutland bench at Melton Mowbray.[44] She is a member of the

Leicestershire family proceedings panel, sitting as chairman in Leicester, Loughborough and Melton Mowbray, having previously obtained the short-course diploma in child protection run jointly by King's College, London, and the London School of Economics. She is a lay member of the Lord Chancellor's judicial appointments panel, interviewing and selecting circuit and district judges and chairmen of tribunals.[45]

From 1996 she was a non-executive director of Leicester General Hospital NHS Trust. Since 1 April 2000, when this trust was merged with two others to form the University Hospitals of Leicester NHS Trust, she was retained as a non-executive director, and has been the vice-chairman since the autumn of 2002. As from 1 October 2002 she was a Privy Council nominee on the General Medical Council; that role lasted a year, until the council was restructured by Act of Parliament to consist of 35 members in place of the 104 members formerly. However, her work for the council continued through the chairing of committees on issues relating to the conduct and performance of doctors. In September 2003 she was appointed a member of the Investigating Committee of the General Osteopathic Council, and in June 2004 she also became a Privy Council nominee on the General Chiropractic Council. She is chairman of the Leicester-Warwick Medical School's Fitness to Practise Committee, and a lay member of investigations for the Healthcare Commission and the National Clinical Assessment Authority.

8.5 Andrew Ralph

Andrew Ralph Worthington, the second son of Lancelot Jukes Worthington and his first wife Phyllis Mary (Article 8.2), was born on 31 May 1928 at the War Memorial Hospital, Congleton, Cheshire. He was baptised on 5 July 1928. From 1932 to July 1935 he attended Moorfields School and Kindergarten, Leek, Staffordshire.

Andrew's mother left the family home, Rochemount, Leek, when he was six years of age. As a result he was placed as a boarder at Moorhill Preparatory School, Leek, at the age of seven. He was there for one year only, and in September 1936 transferred with his elder brother Philip (Article 8.4) to the Boys' Grammar School, Ashby-de-la-Zouch. He was the youngest boy to have entered that school as a boarder, then being eight years and four months. Thomas Woodcock the headmaster had written to Lancelot Worthington on 27 April 1936 to confirm acceptance of his two sons from September commenting: 'Andrew struck me as a very spirited young man. He is obviously the sort to mix with other boys ...'. A month into the first term, on 13 October 1936, the headmaster wrote:

> Andrew, of course, is the favourite of everyone – he is 'the baby' of the school but only in years. He has any amount of pluck. The matron was full of admiration for the way in which he stuck the painful operation of having some dirt taken out of his knee (the result of a fall in the playground) ...

By this time Rochemount had been temporarily closed, and Andrew and his brother had been living, since the summer of 1935, with their maternal grandparents – Dr Ernest Sadler and his wife Elizabeth (Article 8.1) at The Mansion, Ashbourne, Derbyshire – where school holidays were spent for four years. In the summer term of 1938 Andrew had a health problem which led to exchanges of many letters between Elizabeth and matron. He remained at The Mansion for the whole of the Christmas term for a complete rest under the medical guidance of his grandfather. During much of this time he had a bad foot, used a walking stick, and had to be carried downstairs. He attended a local school in St John's Road, Ashbourne, for mornings only. Although he returned to Ashby for the Easter term 1939, the illness lingered on for another year.

Andrew remained at the school for 10 years, during which time he became captain of the school's first-eleven cricket team, captain of house, and for the 1945-6 year 'captain of school and senior prefect'. He was also the colour sergeant of the school's company of the Army Cadet Force – part of the 1st cadet battalion, the Leicestershire Regiment. The company sometimes did exercises jointly with the Home Guard, and shared their Drill Hall. Andrew left the school in July 1946.

From October 1946 to the spring of 1952 Andrew attended Leeds University's School of Medicine and attained the degrees of MB and ChB in March 1952. For the whole six years he resided at Lyddon Hall, where he was a wine member for several years and hall president for a year. He was a member of the Leeds University Lawn Tennis Club throughout the period, being secretary for a time and later captain. He was awarded the university's colours. He was registered with the General Medical Council on 7 April 1952 and soon afterwards took up his first appointment as a house surgeon at the Haywood Memorial Hospital, Burslem, Staffordshire, where he worked for Mr J. Ramage, general surgeon, and Mr J. Grocott, a general and plastic surgeon. In mid-October the same year he transferred to the North Staffordshire Royal Infirmary, continuing as house surgeon to Mr Grocott who had there a burns' unit as part of his plastic surgery interest. After a further six months – about April 1953 – he moved to the Hull Royal Infirmary, Kingston upon Hull, East Yorkshire, as senior house officer – casualty.

In October 1953 he returned to Leeds University Medical School to be demonstrator in anatomy for one academic year. This was part of his plan to train as a surgeon, but at the end of the year he was unsuccessful when he sat Part I of the fellowship examination for the Royal College of Surgeons. During the year he lived again at Lyddon Hall where he was appointed sub-warden. His deferment of national service then ended, so on 3 August 1955 he joined the Royal Army Medical Corps, with a national-service commission as lieutenant.[46] His appointment was 'clinical officer in surgery'. After a few months he entered into a three-year short-service commission, and after a year he was promoted captain. His training started with two weeks at the RAMC Depot and Training Establishment at Church Crookham, near Aldershot, Hampshire, followed by four weeks at the Field Training School and Army School of Health at Keogh Barracks, Ash Vale, near Aldershot. This training continued at the Royal Army Medical College, Millbank, London, associated with Queen Alexandra Military Hospital, which then stood next to the Tate Gallery on Millbank but was later demolished to make way for the Tate Gallery extension.

75 *Andrew Ralph Worthington.*

His first assignment following his training had little to do with medicine or surgery; he was to take 120 soldiers to Hanover, West Germany, supported by an experienced warrant officer. On entering the parade ground where the soldiers had been drawn up he was asked by the warrant officer for 'Permission to carry on, sir?'. Andrew then gave what he claimed was his first army order: 'Carry on sergeant-major'! After sailing from Harwich to the Hook of Holland, Andrew found himself also in command of a troop train to Hanover.

About this time, a decision was made to form the Royal Army Medical Corps Apprentice Company at the Depot and Training Establishment, Church Crookham. Andrew became its first chief instructor. He wrote on 17 May 2000:

> ... Casting around for a chief instructor, someone noticed I had teaching experience and I was therefore invited to fill the post for the rest of my short service commission. I accepted but was then told that, if I took up the post, I might find it very difficult to get back into surgery. I decided there and then that if I did become a regular officer, which I was seriously considering, I would not want to do surgery but to join what was known as the command and staff cadre. This delightful post, at the Depot and TE, lasted three years during which I converted to a regular commission.

In 1953 Queen Elizabeth, the Queen Mother, visited the RAMC, of which she was the colonel-in-chief. The visit was to the Depot and Training Establishment, Queen Elizabeth Barracks, Church Crookham, and tea was to be taken at Redfields Officers' Mess. Andrew had been give a year's notice to organise, in his spare time, the renovation of the 16-acre garden of the mess, which had been neglected since the beginning of the Second World War. The work, which was done mainly by three national service soldiers and officer volunteers from the Mess, was completed in time. There was a parade, then tea in the garden. Alas, rain was unremitting but the marquees had been erected and the Queen Mother, with the aid of an umbrella, was able to talk to the staff and their families.

In August 1957 Andrew sailed in the troopship *Oxfordshire* from Liverpool to Singapore as the ship's senior medical officer with the acting rank of major: he was his own first patient, being seasick in the River Mersey. They sailed around the Cape of Good Hope because of the Suez War. On landing, he reverted to captain and made his way to Suvla Lines, Ipoh, in Malaya, to be the regimental medical officer of the 2nd Battalion, 6th Gurkha Rifles. (The regiment was styled 'Queen Elizabeth's Own' from January 1959.) The varied nature of his work is indicated in his 'circular letter no 5' of 10 October 1957 to his family:

> ... I had just over a third of a company in hospital at the same time. Indeed one night I had every ambulance in Ipoh on the road between here and the hospital at the same time. While this was going on, yet another two-month-old baby developed this fatal Gurkha respiratory disease, so that meant another quick dash to Taiping. Then a young wife had to go and hang herself in the quarters, so another few days went in endless conferences with the civilian and army police. An epidemic of 'flu in the British officers' quarters seems quite trivial ...

On 28 April 1958, after nine months at Ipoh, Andrew joined the headquarters staff of the British Gurkhas in India at Barrackpore, West Bengal, as senior medical officer (SMO). He sailed from Singapore to Calcutta on the 6,000-ton cargo ship SS *Easter Saga*. On arrival at the Officers' Mess in the Recruitment Depot at Darjeeling, 7,000 feet above sea level, he found that the previous SMO had extended his time there, so the appointment was delayed until 8 August 1958. In the meantime he was appointed regimental medical officer on 2 July 1958. When SMO, with the rank of acting major again, he was responsible for all the army medical services in the region which were mainly at four locations: Barrackpore and Darjeeling in West Bengal, Lehra in Uttar Pradesh, and Dharan in East Nepal. He visited each of his medical officers monthly which required a 2,000-mile round-trip taking two weeks. While on leave at Shilong, the capital of Assam, he studied for the promotion examination, the passing of which qualified him for selection to the Staff College at Camberley. He was promoted substantive major on 7 April 1960.

Andrew returned home in the P & O liner SS *Carthage* from Bombay, arriving on 12 June 1960 where he was met at Tilbury Docks, Essex, by Tessa Helen Thorowgood. Andrew's half-brother, Stuart (Article 8.5) was also on the dockside without knowing anything about Tessa. He tried to engage this girl dressed in yellow in conversation, but she would have none of it – only later to find they were meeting the same person. Andrew and Tessa had met at Tessa's coming-out ball held on 16 July 1954 at the Club of the Three Monkeys (more briefly called 'the Monkey Club') of Pont Street, London.[47] They had corresponded throughout Andrew's time in Malaya, India and Nepal. Their engagement was announced on 24 October 1960.[27] Tessa was six years younger than Andrew, having been born on 5 February 1935, at her parent's home, Downend, Fort Road, Guildford, Surrey. She was baptised on 27 December 1935 at Great Horton (Bethel) Methodist Church, Bradford. She was educated

76   *Tessa Helen, born Thorowgood.*

at Green Acre kindergarten school, followed by Tormeed in Guildford before boarding from 1947 at Effingham House School, Bexhill-on-Sea, Sussex. From 1951, at the age of 16 years, she moved to the Monkey Club where she remained for three years. The Monkey Club had been founded in 1923 with a dual function of providing further education and preparing girls for their coming-out year and for marriage. There were visits to museums, theatres and overseas countries, and there were annual events to attend such as Wimbledon tennis tournament and Queen Charlotte's Ball. The club, which closed in 1969, was thus part of the London social scene. Tessa was noted by the press as well as her friends for her fashionable dress. For example, the *Daily Sketch* of 22 June 1953 published a photograph of her with the caption:

> Want the zebra look? Then take some tips from Miss Tessa Thorowgood of Guildford. She went to Wimbledon yesterday in a white sweater which had striped sleeves and a striped neckband. Topping it off was a pixy hat – striped, of course!

At the time of the engagement, Tessa was a secretary at the Foreign Office, London. She was the elder daughter and co-heiress of Wilfrid Ernest Thorowgood and Dorothy Lois his wife. Wilfrid was chief civil and structural engineer with London County Council. He had previously served in the Bridge Department of Dorman Long and Co., working on the design and construction of the Sydney Harbour Bridge. He had attained an MA degree in the University of Cambridge and was an associate member (now termed member) of the Institution of Civil Engineers and a member (now termed fellow) of the Institution of Structural Engineers.[24] He was also an underwriting member of Lloyd's of London. Wilfrid had been born on 15 October 1904 at 25 Lewisham Park, Lewisham, London, his parents being Alfred Ernest Thorowgood, stock jobber, and his wife Florence (born Starling). Tessa's mother, Dorothy, was the elder daughter and co-heiress of Alderman Arthur Llewellyn Whittaker, JP and his wife Lois (born Thomas) of Kingston Grange, Kingston, Halifax, Yorkshire, and from 1935 of Saville Heath, Halifax. Arthur was a justice of the peace from 1918, mayor of Halifax in 1927-8 and a director of the Halifax Building Society.[48] He gave an organ to the Queen's Road Methodist Church, Halifax 2nd Circuit, which was inaugurated at a ceremony held on 28 November 1928. The gift was in memory of his parents, 'Mr and Mrs John Whittaker ... devoted members of the Primitive Methodist church'. By 1932 Arthur was one of the two stewards of the 2nd circuit.[49] He was chairman and managing director of John Whittaker and Sons (Kingston 1921) Limited (formerly John Whittaker and Sons Limited), bakers, confectioners and biscuit manufacturers of Kingston Works, Hopwood Lane, Halifax, a business which his father, John, had founded.[50] Arthur had also been deputy chairman of the Halifax Equitable Bank prior to its amalgamation with the Bank of Liverpool and Martins.[50]

Andrew and Tessa's wedding was on 15 April 1961 at St Margaret's Church, Westminster, followed by a reception for about 300 guests at the *Savoy Hotel*, London.[51] After a honeymoon in Italy they took up residence in Army quarters in Joseph Haydn Strasse, Bielefeld, West Germany. Andrew had already served three months with the British Army of the Rhine as second-in-command of 4 Field Ambulance at Munster, West Germany, after which he was officer commanding 11 Field Dressing Station, Bielefeld. After about a year in that post he became deputy assistant director of medical services at headquarters, First British Corps, British Army of the Rhine.

Andrew and Tessa produced one son and one daughter:

Forenames	Date of birth	Date of baptism
Rupert Lancelot	11 September 1962	18 October 1964
Charlotte Helen	26 April 1965	18 July 1965

Rupert was born at the British Military Hospital, Rinteln, West Germany, and Charlotte was born at their next home – Park Farm Cottage, Park Lane, Merrow, Guildford, Surrey, after their return to England. Both were baptised at St John the Evangelist's Church, Merrow. About 1967, the family moved to Abbotsmead, 49 London Road, Guildford.

In 1963 Andrew took a six-month senior officers' course at the Royal Army Medical College at Millbank, London, combined with a course at the London School of Tropical Medicine. As a result he was awarded the diploma in tropical medicine and hygiene (DTM&H) in the University of London. He then returned to the RAMC Depot and Training Establishment (now renamed RAMC Training Centre) at Mytchett, Aldershot, Hampshire. His two-year appointment there was as instructor in Field Training for RAMC officers. For 15 months, starting in the autumn of 1964, he attended the Army Staff College, the first three months being at the Royal Military College of Science at Shrivenham, Wiltshire, and the rest at the staff college at Camberley. He passed, thus being awarded the military qualification 'psc'. He was promoted to lieutenant-colonel on 7 April 1965 while at the college; this caused some consternation as it made him senior to all the other officers attending the college – mainly majors! The promotion was exactly 13 years after his registration with the General Medical Council, a privilege awarded to medical officers only. This was the highest rank based on length of service subject to recommendations; all future promotions would be by selection alone.

He then joined the Army Medical Directorate, Ministry of Defence, Lansdowne House, Berkeley Square, London, as deputy assistant director-general, dealing mainly with personnel work concerning all officers of the RAMC. From 1968 to 1970 he returned again to the RAMC Training Centre, this time as the chief instructor and deputy commandant.

On 14 May 1969 Andrew was admitted an Officer (Brother) of the Order of the Hospital of St John of Jerusalem (OStJ), his investiture taking place at the Grand Priory Church, St John's Square, London, on 14 October 1969.[52] On 16 July 1982 he was appointed president of the Ash Vale Ambulance and Nursing Division of St John's Ambulance. He was later vice-president for the county of Surrey and about to become president-elect when he resigned his St John's Ambulance appointment because the family was moving to Norfolk. The resignation took place from 31 December 1984.

From 1970 to 1973 Andrew was the officer commanding the Military Hospital at Colchester, Essex – the family taking up residence in Hospital House.[53] This gave Andrew and Tessa the opportunity to renew one of their abiding interests – boating on the Norfolk Broads. Andrew had taken several holidays on the Broads while at university, cruising first under sail and later motor. They acquired a motor cruiser which they named 'Tessina III'. By an agreement dated 24 February 1971, Tessa took a stake in the boat yard where the boat was kept, namely The Boatyard, Griffin Lane, Thorpe St Andrew, about three miles east of Norwich on the River Yare. The other shareholder was Roy Martin Smith, the yard manager. They formed a company called 'Harmony Boats Limited' which was incorporated on 1 April 1971. Tessa was chairman and Andrew, Roy and his wife were directors. The company ran a fleet of motor boats for hire, built new boats, and manufactured wooden steering wheels for sale to other boat yards. The company was not financially successful.

As a result, Tessa took control of the company by raising her equity holding to 75 per cent while Roy remained managing director. After the summer season she decided that the company should be sold, and an advertisement produced over 200 enquiries. The business was acquired by Hoveringham Leisure Limited of Hoveringham, Nottinghamshire, by a contract signed on 21 September 1973 and completed in December.

While at the Military Hospital, Andrew was appointed a founder member of the Faculty of Community Medicine (now called the Faculty of Public Health Medicine) of the Royal College of Physicians of the United Kingdom. In the same year he was elected a member of the British Institute of Management. On leaving Colchester he returned to the Army Medical Directorate, Ministry of Defence, as head of the personnel department, RAMC – being promoted to colonel on 7 April 1974. From 1976 to 1978 he was assistant director of medical services – West Midlands District and Wales District – and for that purpose the family moved residence for three years to Army quarters at 5 Sundowne Close, Shrewsbury.[23] Covering two districts led to much travelling, for most of which he had an Army driver. It also entailed being responsible to two major-generals which led to difficulties!

Meanwhile Andrew had continued his interest in tennis. In West Germany he had been selected for the British Army of the Rhine team on several occasions and was awarded the BAOR colours. Subsequently, in England, he played for the Army on many occasions, including once in the Inter-services Tennis Tournament at Wimbledon – as his first cousin once removed, Roger Worthington, had earlier. (Article 7.12)

On 20 February 1978 he went to the RAMC Training Centre for the fourth time, but now as the commandant; he was promoted brigadier the same day. He was also president of the Staff Band of the Royal Army Medical Corps, with a strength of 30 musicians. After three years, he moved to the headquarters of United Kingdom Land Forces, Salisbury, Wiltshire, as deputy director of Medical Services and as inspector training – Territorial Army Medical Services.[25] (The post was later re-designated 'Commander Army Medical Services –Territorial Army'.)

About September 1981 Andrew and Tessa sold Abbotsmead, after which another house was built in the garden. They moved to The Shooting Lodge, Whitmoor Common, near Guildford. The property included two fields which enabled them to keep Jacob sheep; they were members of the Jacob Sheep Society.

Andrew retired from the Army on 1 November 1982 with the rank of brigadier. He was then 54 years of age. He was appointed a non-executive director of A.J. Worthington (Holdings) PLC on 1 April 1983 and resigned on 16 January 1984 – the day Michael Hartland became chairman of the Group (Article 8.4). On 16 June 1983 Andrew was appointed executive director of BUPA Medical Centre Limited, the subsidiary company of the British United Provident Association responsible for providing complete health checks for members of the public on a fee-paying basis.[54] He was appointed to the board of governors of the whole association as from 1 July 1984. He served BUPA for nearly two years, leaving early in 1985.

In the spring of 1985 Andrew and Tessa bought Hunsett Mill, Stalham, Norfolk, on the River Ant about 15 miles north-east of Norwich. They lived there for 11 years, during which time they renovated the mill and its sails and the cottage. A previous owner had added a main reception room to the rear of the building with an en-suite bedroom above. The garden, which had a 145-yard front to the river, was brought to a high state of perfection – Andrew now having the time to devote to gardening. Gardening had been a life-long interest and he had for many years been a fellow of the Royal Horticultural Society. Their motor cruiser *Hunsett* was moored alongside the garden in front of the cottage. So picturesque and colourful was the whole that the property earned the reputation of being the most photographed on the Norfolk Broads.[55] Views of it were used for many cards, calendars and advertisements; Waddington Games Limited made a 1,000-piece jigsaw puzzle of it. Alas, Andrew developed a vertebral problem which prevented him from continuing gardening effort at the required level, so they sold the property and moved on 26 April 1996 to Abbotswood, Sandy Lane, West Runton, Norfolk, some 30 miles north of the mill, on the coast between Cromer and Sheringham.

8.6 Stuart Gibson

Stuart Gibson Worthington, the third and youngest son of Lancelot Jukes Worthington (Article 8.2) and the elder child by Lancelot's second wife, Marjorie Brown, was born on 30 October 1940 at Rochemount, Leek, and baptised on 8 December 1940 at St Edward the Confessor's Church, Cheddleton, Staffordshire. His education started on 14 September 1945 at Moorfields School and Kindergarten, Leek, which he attended for four years, being head boy in his last year. In 1949 he went to Aysgarth School, near Bedale, North Yorkshire, thus following in his father's footsteps. He was a member of the school's first-eleven soccer team in 1952 and its captain in 1953, during which year the team won all nine matches against other preparatory schools in the area. He was also in the first-eleven cricket team in 1953 and first-fifteen rugby football team in 1953 and 1954 and first-eight rifle shooting team. He won the senior high jump at the 1953 sports' day and was runner-up in the school's Rugby and Eton fives competitions of the same year. For two years he was set captain of the Olympians – one of the four sets into which the school was organised. When he left in March 1954, Robert William Thompson the headmaster wrote:

> He leaves behind him a good reputation, for throughout his years at Aysgarth he has always been a most loyal member of the school. He

will be much missed by the younger boys, which in itself is a great tribute; they looked up to him and trusted him.

From 1954 to December 1958 he attended Winchester College, Hampshire, where he boarded at Morshead's, becoming a house prefect. He won the junior high jump in 1955 and played in the school's second soccer eleven in 1956 and 1958, being out in 1957 because of a thigh injury. From 1954 to 1958 he was in the Combined Cadet Force, becoming a lance-corporal and a marksman.

From January to May 1959 Stuart attended, as the only male student, Madame de Sallier du Pin's residential girls' finishing school in Blois, 100 miles south-west of Paris, France. Whilst there he also attended the senior history class at the city's lycée for boys.

Stuart's career began in September 1959 when he started four months' unpaid work for Wm. Frost & Co. Limited, textile manufacturers of Macclesfield, Cheshire. The chairman and managing director of that company was William Read Wadsworth who was also a part-owner and non-executive chairman of A.J. Worthington (Holdings) Limited (Article 8.2). There, Stuart received on-floor training in silk and man-made-fibre yarn processing. In January 1960 he transferred to Worthington's where he worked sequentially in all departments to learn the business. From 1960 to 1962 he attended part-time at the Leek College of Further Education, where he gained the full technological certificate in 'silk and man-made fibres – throwing' of the City and Guilds of London Institute. In 1966 he was appointed deputy head of the Trimmings Department which manufactured crochet products for the clothing, furniture and lighting industries. He was promoted head of the department in the spring of 1970. He was also appointed a director of A.J. Worthington & Co. (Leek) Limited and the holding company on 1 August 1970.

During the 1960s Stuart contributed much to research on the history of the Worthington families. In January 1965 his paper on *The Life of an Elizabethan Recusant – Thomas Worthington, SJ, DD, BA*, was published in *Family History*.[56]

On 9 March 1967 he was elected to the Leek Rural District Council, on which he served for seven years. He represented the ward of Butterton, which included Swainsley where he was then living with his parents. At the age of 26 years he was the youngest member of the council. Whilst serving, he had an eye for national politics; for example, he wrote a long letter to the press which carried the headline 'A Tory looks at National Politics as They Affect Local Affairs – and Finds Socialists Don't Practise What They Preach'. As the council's representative he was a governor of both the Leek College of Further Education and the Leek School of Arts and Crafts from 1970 to 1974.

Towards the end of 1969 news broke that the Trent River Authority were considering the possibility of building a surface regulating reservoir in the upper reaches of the Manifold Valley in the Peak National Park.

It would submerge 15 farms and affect 18 others. Opposition was expressed at a meeting of 200 local residents who met at Warslow, Staffordshire, early in December 1969 where speeches were made by Harold Davies, MP for Leek (later Baron Davies of Leek), by John Lawrence Venables Vernon, 10th Baron Vernon, Captain, JP, of Sudbury Hall, Derbyshire, and by Lieutenant-Colonel Gerald Haythornthwaite of the Voluntary Joint Committee for the Peak National Park. After a unanimous vote opposing the scheme, Stuart proposed the vote of thanks to the speakers.[57] The Manifold Valley Action Committee (from 1970 renamed the Manifold Valley Preservation Committee) originally had 15 members including Stuart, who was immediately appointed public relations' officer. From early 1970 he was also the secretary. On 4 March 1970 the committee

77   *Stuart Gibson Worthington in 1990.*

visited the House of Commons to address members of parliament and show them a film specially produced by the National Farmers' Union. A blizzard causing a three-hour delay on the railway partially frustrated the event, but a pre-recorded interview was shown that evening on BBC News, in which Stuart made a three minute case against the reservoir. Although the committee met 25 MPs, another visit was arranged for 8 April 1970. An all-party delegation of MPs made a return visit about 10 days later when '... a motorcade of 11 vehicles wound its way round the twisting undulating roads of the Manifold Valley ...'. Later, a delegation of members of parliament and members of the Water Resources Board visited the Trent River Authority. The campaign was successfully completed in 1973 when it was announced that the reservoir would instead be built at Carsington, near Ashbourne, Derbyshire.

On 20 September 1972 came the announcement that Stuart was engaged to be married to Geraldine Judith Snowball, of Swallow Barn, Milford Green, Chobham, Surrey, the widow of Murray Roger Malcolm Snowball.[58] Geraldine was two years younger than Stuart, having been born on 10 January 1943 at Ivy Cottage, Hutton Henry, County Durham, and baptised on 31 January 1943 at the Roman Catholic church of Saints

78   *Geraldine Judith, born Seth.*

Peter and Paul, Hutton House, Castle Eden, County Durham. (Both Hutton Henry and Castle Eden are now in the county of Cleveland.) She was the only daughter of John James Seth and his wife Hylda, born North. At the time of Geraldine's birth, John was serving with the Royal Corps of Signals as a company quartermaster-sergeant. During the Second World War he was on active service with the 1st Army in North Africa, and later in Italy where he was present at the battle of Monte Cassino. Whilst in Italy he was mentioned in despatches and commissioned. After the war he transferred to the Royal Army Ordnance Corps, serving in Palestine, Malaya, Aden and West Germany. He was appointed a member of the Order of the British Empire on 11 June 1960 and promoted substantive lieutenant-colonel on 10 June 1963. He retired from the Army on 1 July 1969 to join, and later become a director of, United Builders Merchants PLC in Bristol. In 1976 he moved again to become a director of Debenhams plc, the retail store group, until his retirement in 1987. He was a member of the British Institute of Management.

As the daughter of a soldier, Geraldine had a mobile childhood. She lived for two years at Johore Bahru, Malaya, close to the causeway to Singapore. Later, for a similar period, the family were in Aden which Geraldine visited during some of her school holidays, when she was a boarder at Farnborough Hill Convent School for Girls at Farnborough, Hampshire. She attended that school from 1954 to 1960 during which time she was a member of the school's first teams for lacrosse, tennis and swimming. One year whilst at the school she was chosen to represent Hampshire in an under-18 inter-county swimming competition. Geraldine married Murray Snowball on 14 August 1965 at the Roman Catholic church of Kemerton, Worcestershire. He was the second son of Laurence Alfred Howard Snowball, MB, BS, FRCS, LRCP, and his wife Gwendolen Nellie, MB, BS, MRCS, LRCP. They practised surgery and medicine respectively at Eastbourne, Sussex. Murray had been born on 7 March 1938 and educated at Charterhouse School, Godalming, Surrey, followed by the University of London. There he read theology but left before graduating to become a chartered accountant. Later he joined the Drayton Group where he became managing director of one of the subsidiary companies. At the time of his death he was described as 'chief executive (builders' merchants)'. Geraldine and Murray produced two daughters – Melanie Sara April who was born on 19 April 1966 and Lucinda Charlotte Judith, born on 21 January 1969. At first living in London, the family moved to Merlebank, Knowle Green, Virginia Water, Surrey and finally to Swallow Barn, Milford Green, Chobham, Surrey. Geraldine was secretary of the Farnborough Hill Convent's Old Girls' Association from 1966 to 1968. She was a keen horsewoman and occasionally hunted with the Bisley and Sandhurst foxhounds in Surrey. Murray died on 13 May 1972 when his daughters were only six and three years of age.

Stuart had met Geraldine on one of his regular visits to the home of his elder half-brother and sister-in-law, Philip and Gillian Worthington at Chobham Place (Article 8.4). Indeed Gillian was godmother to Lucinda. Stuart and Geraldine were married on 2 December 1972 at St Mary's Church, Cadogan Street, Chelsea, London, according to Roman Catholic rites. After the service a reception was held for 170 guests at the *Carlton Tower Hotel*, Cadogan Place, Knightsbridge, London.[58] Their honeymoon was in Cyprus. Until his marriage Stuart had lived with his parents at Swainsley (Article 8.2), but after the wedding, he, Geraldine, and her two daughters took up residence at Swainsley Cottage, Stuart having purchased the property in 1972 from his father. The adjacent farm buildings and 10 acres of meadow were acquired later from Stuart's mother, when she was a widow and the owner of Swainsley. On 25 January 1973, seven weeks after the wedding, the names of Geraldine's daughters were changed by deed poll; they took the surname 'Worthington', 'Snowball' becoming an additional forename. Thus, they became: Melanie Sara April Snowball Worthington and Lucinda Charlotte Judith Snowball Worthington. The deed was enrolled on 9 February 1973 in the Supreme Court of Judicature. Stuart and Geraldine produced one child of their own, namely:

Forenames	Date of birth	Date of baptism
Victoria Louise Emma	7 October 1973	December 1973

Victoria was born at the Maternity Home, Green Road, Ashbourne, Derbyshire, and baptised at St Mary's Roman Catholic church, Leek.

In March 1976, after three years at Swainsley Cottage, they sold the property and purchased The Old Rectory at Blore, Staffordshire, four miles north-west of Ashbourne. This three-storey, six-bedroomed house stands adjacent to the church in 1.3 acres of land. A sale brochure on the property described it as:

> A particularly fine, stone built former rectory set in an idyllic location in the hamlet of Blore ... This period property dating from the early 19th century enjoys commanding views from all the principal rooms across the adjoining countryside of the Peak District National Park.

From there Geraldine was able to ride again, hunting occasionally with the Meynell and South Staffordshire foxhounds.

Meanwhile Stuart continued in his full-time role as a director of A.J. Worthington & Co. (Leek) Limited (later renamed A.J. Worthington (Leek) Limited). He was appointed joint managing director of this subsidiary in 1973 with special responsibility for marketing, sales and exports. On 1 April 1974 he was promoted chairman and joint managing director, and in 1978 chairman and managing director. He also became chairman of each of the other subsidiary companies – Heavers and Pace Limited, Wm. Gallimore & Co. Limited, and Watson & Co. (Leek) Limited. Later, as they were acquired, he also chaired Smith Bros. (Macclesfield) Limited and W.H. White and Son Limited. He attended the Cranfield School of Management's Senior Managers' programme in 1980.

Stuart took a leading part in the textile industry's trade associations. He was chairman of the junior committee of the Leek and District Manufacturers' and Dyers' Association in 1970-1, and a member of the senior committee from 1971, and he was vice-president of the association from 1977 to 1980. From 1971 to 1973 he was chairman of the British Federation of Trimmings and Braid Manufacturers. He was chairman of the Narrow Fabrics Federation from 1973 to 1976 and chairman of the Joint Industrial Council for the Leek and District Textile and Clothing Industries from 1980 to 1983. He also served on the councils of the British Man-made Fibres Federation from 1972 to 1977 and the British Textile Confederation from 1973 to 1976. He was a member of the comité directeur of the Association Européenne Rubans, Tresses et Tissus Elastiques (AERTEL). He became a fellow of the Institute of Directors in 1976 and a fellow of the British Institute of Management in 1980.

On 7 January 1976, Stuart was appointed a justice of the peace for the county of Stafford, taking the oath of allegiance and judicial oath at Shire Hall, Stafford, on 16 February 1976. Thereafter he sat on the Leek bench which covered the towns of Leek and Biddulph. He resigned his commission with effect from 16 January 1987 after serving 11 years. On 18 May 1978 he was admitted a freeman of the City of London.[59] He had been admitted a freeman of the Worshipful Company of Weavers on 4 April 1978, becoming a liveryman of the Company on 7 June 1978. He was renter warden in 1989-90 and upper warden (the third officer of the company) in 1990-1.

The 175th anniversary of the founding of the Worthington textile business on the Portland Mills site was celebrated on 11 August 1978 at the *Lake Hotel*, Rudyard, near Leek. All employees, many retired and former employees, and other people associated with the group were invited. There was a buffet luncheon followed by speeches and the presentation to each person of a pottery loving cup depicting the company's five oldest trade marks.[60] In the same year A.J. Worthington & Co. (Leek)

Limited received the Gold Medallion award of the International Export Association in recognition of substantial increases in exports to most continents of the world, the presentation being made by Squadron Leader Arthur Morgan Rees, CBE, QPM, KStJ, MA, DL, former chief-constable of Staffordshire. A second Gold Medallion award was presented to the company three years later, on 30 June 1981, by David Laidlaw Knox (later Sir David Knox, Kt), the member of parliament for Leek. Also present was Herbert Lisle, OBE, JP, general secretary of the Amalgamated Society of Textile Workers and Kindred Trades. On 24 November 1981 Field-Marshal Prince Edward George Nicholas Paul Patrick, 2nd duke of Kent, KG, GCMG, GCVO, accompanied by Sir Arthur Bryan, Kt, KStJ, DLitt, lord lieutenant for Staffordshire, visited Leek, arriving by Royal Air Force helicopter on the playing fields of Springfield Road School, Leek. His first engagement was with A.J. Worthington & Co. (Leek) Limited. He was greeted by Stuart and Geraldine, the other directors, and the group chairman Philip Worthington (Article 8.4), the general secretary of the trade union Herbert Lisle and Mrs Dorothy Carr, who was the longest serving employee. The duke toured Portland Mills.[60]

When the Group moved into loss in the early 1980s, serious differences of opinion emerged amongst the directors as to the way forward. The part played by Michael Hartland has already been described (Article 8.4) but the final outcome was that Stuart resigned from all positions in the Group as from 29 March 1984, having sold all his shares in the Group to Hartland in September 1983.

Within weeks Stuart set up a new business styled 'S.G. Worthington and Company Limited' with premises at Crowther Industrial Estate, Leek Road, Waterhouses, four miles west of Blore. The directors were Stuart and Geraldine and Robert J. Addison, the former sales director of A.J. Worthington & Co. (Leek) Limited. The business imported children's clothing and accessories for distribution in the United Kingdom in an operation running parallel to Kiddies (Pty) Limited of Australia, who had bought large quantities of babywear from the Worthington Group over the previous 10 years. Kiddies offered support, especially with sourcing expertise in Hong Kong, Taiwan and The Philippines; in return Stuart undertook to source British-made goods for Kiddies. Stuart and Geraldine provided all the share capital and some loan capital, while other loans were to be provided by the bank. Stuart later wrote:

> The local manager of the company's banker suggested that a loan be sought under the government sponsored Small Firms' Loan Guarantee Scheme, which at the time offered new developing enterprises, when supported by their bankers, advances of up to £75,000[*] on favourable terms. Such maximum figure was the borrowing need in the company's cash flow forecasts, which showed that the business was expected to move into profitability after 15 months ... The company's bank manager

---

[*] Equivalent to 4,200 man-days of agricultural labour.

> advised that he expected the relevant paperwork to be 'rubber stamped' by the authorities within a few weeks. Heartened by such news, the company's products were exhibited at the 1984 Autumn Fashion Fair at Alexandra Palace, London, where sales and interest shown by departmental stores exceeded expectations. It was therefore a devastating shock to learn from the bank manager a few days later that his Area Office had declined to endorse the fulsome support he had given ... With some goods from the Far East already landed in England and others on the high seas, cash flow difficulties immediately loomed ... In the interests of all, not least the suppliers themselves, I had no choice but to put the company into voluntary liquidation.

A meeting of creditors was held on 23 November 1984 at Basford House, Stoke-on-Trent, and the company was wound up early the following year.[61]

In 1985 Stuart started the business named Blore Associates, of which he was the sole proprietor. At first it traded in financial services, working closely with Ibis Financial Services of Windsor, Berkshire. By 1987 Blore Associates had been appointed the Staffordshire, Derbyshire and Nottinghamshire agents for the sale of cutlery from Sheffield-based Dine Design (later Dine Design Limited). Within three or four months, the agency was extended to the whole of the United Kingdom. Later still the agency included Europe, the Middle East and the Caribbean. When Dine Design was wound up following the owner's death, Stuart expanded his business by including other tableware products. He sourced directly from about 20 manufacturers. His customers included the Savoy Group, Norfolk Capital Hotels, Thistle Hotels, Toby Restaurants and hotel consortia such as Prestige, Consort and Best Western. The St. James Beach Group of hotels in Barbados was the largest overseas customer for cutlery, shipments there exceeding a ton a year.

Whilst Stuart developed this business, Geraldine ran The Old Rectory as a guest house, operating in the niche market of stylish entertainment with excellent food and wine. The first paying guests arrived in 1985, and henceforth the house was open except during Christmas and New Year. The business was listed in *Wolsey Lodges* from January 1987 and achieved entry in *The Good Food Guide*, *Good Hotel Guide*, and the *Michelin Guide*. The 1990 edition of *Wolsey Lodges* includes:

> ... Stuart and Geraldine Worthington, both well travelled, entertain with style and flair in their attractive stone-built home, with its gracious drawing room where guests are made to feel at home. Dinner is by candle light with fine silver and furnishings, in a house-party atmosphere.

House rules stipulated jackets and ties for the men at dinner, but guests coming as a group sometimes called for black tie. In an article on the venture published in 1998, Stuart was quoted as saying 'Geraldine is a marvellous hostess, so it's like one long party...'[62] Guests staying overnight rose from 250 in the first year to over 600 a year in the

1990s. Stuart was a director of Wolsey Lodges Limited from 1991 to 1994.

Stuart had been elected to the parochial church council of St Bartholomew's Church, Blore Ray, in 1976, and was appointed a churchwarden in 1983. Additional responsibility as treasurer was added in 1992. As the church was a member of a group of parishes with only one parson, Stuart often had the task of conducting the services. Stuart wrote:

> ... During all the time I was connected with the Church, only Book of Common Prayer services were allowed by the PCC (led by myself!): thus to the dismay of four incumbents, no ASB services were permitted ... Unquestionably Blore Church is the most traditional church in North Staffordshire ...

For these reasons, the Venerable Denis Ede, BA, MSocSc, archdeacon of Stoke upon Trent, sometimes referred to Blore church as 'Stuart Worthington's peculiar'!

From 1994 to 1997, Stuart took a leading role in the restoration programme for the church building. The cost was £123,000 and the corresponding appeal achieved a fund of £126,000* over the four years.[19] The earliest visible fabric of the church, which is Grade 1 listed, was built about 1100. The renovation work included repair of the sculptured alabaster tomb of William Bassett, who died in 1601, and his family – 'the last of the Bassetts of Blore'. Bassetts had fought with William the Conqueror at Hastings in 1066 and were lords of the manor of Blore from the 14th to the 17th centuries. One of the subscribers to the appeal fund was Charles Philip Arthur George, the Prince of Wales, KG, KT, GCB, AK, QSO, PC, – a 12th-generation descendant of William Bassett. In 1998 Stuart produced two published booklets: one on the history of the church, the other on the restoration project.[63]

In 1966, at the age of 25 years, Stuart had sought nomination as prospective parliamentary candidate for the Conservative Party in the Leek constituency, and was runner-up in the selection process. He maintained his interest in party politics, being president of the Staffordshire Moorlands Conservative Association from 1996 to 1998, and chairman from 1998 to 2000. He was a member of the National Conservative Convention and a member of the Staffordshire Area Council of the party.

Stuart and Geraldine left The Old Rectory in 2000, moving to 'Casa Orquidea', Guadalamina Alta 605, San Pedro de Alcantara, Malaga Province, Spain. The move took place on 30 October 2000 – Stuart's 60th birthday. Hylda Seth moved with them; she had been living at The Coach House of The Old Rectory since being widowed in January 1994. Previously she and John Seth had lived for 11 years at Las Mimosas, Guadalmina Alta 519, only half a mile from Casa Orquidea.

---

* Equivalent to 4,500 man-days of agricultural labour.

79 *Rosalie Frances, born Worthington, on Red Star.*

In preparation for this move, Blore Associates had ceased trading on 5 April 2000, when its goodwill was sold to Hiram Wild Limited of Sheffield, cutlery manufacturers.

From 2001, their new home was included in the *Wosley Lodges* brochure. In due course Stuart and Geraldine joined the Marbella and West branch of Conservatives Abroad. They also became regular worshippers at Guadalmina Chapel, Stuart being elected to the parochial church council of the Costa del Sol (West) chaplaincy in 2002.

8.7 Rosalie Frances

Rosalie Frances Worthington, the younger daughter of Lancelot Jukes Worthington (Article 8.2) and the younger child by Marjorie Brown his second wife, was born on 10 September 1944 at Rochemount, Leek, and baptised on 28 October 1944 at St Edward the Confessor's Church, Cheddleton, Staffordshire. After living at Rochemount for about seven years she moved with her family to Swainsley Cottage, and four years later to the hall at Swainsley.

Rosalie started her education at Hallscroft Kindergarten School, St Edward Street, Leek. The school building had at one time been the home of Rosalie's great-grandparents Andrew and Sarah Worthington (Article 3.3). From September 1953 to July 1957 she was a boarder at Portsdown Lodge School, Bexhill-on-Sea, Sussex; there she won the Leaver's Good Fellowship Cup for the best all-round pupil. She then transferred to Benenden School, near Cranbrook, Kent, where she boarded at Guldeford House for four years – until July 1961. One of her principal sports was riding, in which she concentrated on dressage. She was also a member of the school's lacrosse and tennis teams. From September 1961 until March 1962 she followed in the footsteps of her elder brother Stuart (Article 8.6) by attending the finishing school at Blois, France. There she studied French history and literature. Starting in September 1962, she took a year's secretarial course at the Oxford and County Secretarial College at Oxford, being awarded their secretarial diploma in July 1963.

Her career commenced on 7 October 1963 when she joined the British Broadcasting Corporation, starting as a junior secretary in the TV Enterprises' Department; there she worked for the general manager responsible for the buying and selling of television programmes. In October 1964 she became secretary to the producer (films) of the Production Unit, TV Enterprises, at Bush House, The Strand, London WC2. She worked there on the Lowell Thomas series of 39 travel programmes for American TV, her contributions including research, continuity and map-making. This lasted until February 1967 when she transferred to the TV Production Panel – Science and Features' Department – to work as a trainee production assistant on programmes such as the 'Science Fair' series and 'The Supersonic Adventure' (the Story of Concorde). After 18 months Rosalie qualified as a 'television production assistant' and worked in the TV Documentary Department as production assistant to Alan Whicker's three producers on his series 'Whicker's World'. She then worked on 'One Pair of Eyes', a series of programmes featuring well-known people on subjects about which they felt strongly. One programme featured Dr Benjamin Spock, the American paediatrician and author of many books including the best-seller of its time *Common Sense Book of Baby and Child Care*, published in 1946. Another example was Major John Christopher Dancy, MA, the master of Marlborough College (later professor of education at the University of Exeter and principal of St Luke's College of Education, Exeter). A third example was Laurens Jan van der Post, CBE, FRSL, Hon DLitt, author, farmer, soldier, explorer and conservationist (later Sir Laurens, Kt, Hon LLD). As production assistant, Rosalie worked with the producer from the inception of a programme until its transmission. She was responsible for research, costings, organising interviews and filming schedules, continuity and administration. After filming she worked with the film editor in the cutting rooms and found extra footage from film libraries. She also cued the presenters in the dubbing theatre and handled post-transmission work. To Laurens van der Post she was known as 'Mary Poppins' because she 'worked miracles'. Later she worked on 'The Tuesday Documentary' programmes including 'The Right to Silence', and 'The Po Valley', filming from the river's source to its mouth in Venice.

At the age of 28 years, Rosalie became engaged to Michael John Courage, the announcement being made on 20 March 1973.[64] She relates how she met him 'on a blind date'. When returning from a holiday in the Bahamas, Rosalie was asked to bring back a letter for Michael who had previously worked there. Michael came to her flat for the letter, stayed for dinner, and in Rosalie's words, 'that was that'. Michael was two years older than Rosalie, having been born on 16 April 1942 at Paddington East, London. From 1955 to December 1960 he had been educated at Eton College, Berkshire, thus following in the footsteps of his grandfather Miles Rafe Ferguson Courage. Michael boarded there in Mr Brocklebank's, of which he was house captain and games captain in his last year. He then spent a year with the Voluntary Service Overseas organisation, serving an Anglican mission in Papua New Guinea. In 1961 Michael joined his family's firm of Courage Barclay and Simonds – brewers. During the first five years he passed through most departments as a management trainee. From 1967 to 1969 he was seconded to Saccone & Speed, wine merchants in Nairobi, Kenya and later became branch manager in Mombasa. Then from 1969 to early 1973 he managed Courage's interests in the Bahamas, based at Nassau. On returning to England he became area manager for Courage's public houses in the City and West End of London. The dynasty of Courage brewers had been founded by Michael's great-great-great-grandfather, John Courage, who is believed to be of French-Huguenot extraction. John had been a shipping agent in Aberdeen, Scotland, and later the Wapping agent for the Carron Shipping Company at Glasgow Wharf, London. On 17 December 1787 John bought the 'private house and old brew house' at Horselydown on the River Thames opposite Wapping. Thus began the long and successful business at first called John Courage, later Courage and Donaldson, and from 1888 Courage & Co. Ltd.[65] Michael's father, Maurice Vandeleur Courage (generally known as Bay Courage), had been chairman of the company. Maurice's father, Miles Rafe Courage, who lived at Preston House, Preston Candover, was a director of the company and was master of the Hampshire Hunt. Miles also owned the Invergeldie estate near Perth, Scotland. The family's involvement on the board of directors ended in 1975, some years after the company was sold to the Imperial Tobacco Group.[66]

The marriage of Rosalie and Michael took place on 8 September 1973 at St Edward's Church, Leek.[67] The reception was held at Swainsley, a marquee being erected on the old tennis court. Their first home was 84 Orbel Street, London, SW11; then in May 1975 they purchased and moved to Chestnut Cottage, Axford, near Preston Candover. While at these two homes they produced their family of one daughter and one son:

Forenames	Date of birth	Date of baptism
Lucy Philippa	27 January 1974	1 September 1974
Simon Lancelot	10 July 1977	16 October 1977

Lucy was born at St Teresa's Hospital, Wimbledon, London, and baptised at St Bartholomew's Church, Butterton, near Leek, Staffordshire. Simon was born at Basingstoke District Hospital, Hampshire, and baptised at Preston Candover parish church.

Rosalie left the British Broadcasting Corporation in July 1974, having continued to work full-time there for six months after the birth of Lucy. In 1978 she started her own business called 'Elder Wines' in which she bought elderflower wine, bottled and labelled it, and distributed it to health food shops. Later she added mead as a second product, sold in small decorated crocks which she commissioned from a local potter. This business continued for three years.

On 6 August 1981, the family moved to Kit Lane House, in Bell Lane, Ellisfield, Hampshire, about three miles to the north-east of Chestnut Cottage. The property, which includes an acre of garden, is surrounded almost entirely by farmland. Michael and Rosalie enlarged the house in 1981 and again in 1982, and about 1998 they added an office above the garage.

In 1981, Rosalie started another business retailing designer knitwear. At first she took an agency for the sale of Dunlin Collection garments manufactured by W.H. White and Son Limited of Leek, a subsidiary company of A.J. Worthington (Holdings) PLC. The following year she became independent, buying wholesale and commissioning production to her own designs. She published an annual mail-order brochure, in which her products were described as 'designer knitwear, skirts, shirts and fashion accessories' trading under the name of 'Rosalie Courage' from Kit Lane House. The 1988-9 collection portrayed in a 16-page A5 brochure include skirts and shirts to enable buyers to '... make up a complete outfit'. In the 1989-90 brochure, her daughter Lucy appeared as one of the models, Lucy then being 16 years of age. On some occasions sales were held at Kit Lane House, a proportion of the takings going to charities such as the Multiple Sclerosis Society. For 12 years Rosalie provided stands at leading charity fairs all over England. The business continued until March 1995.

In the early 1990s Michael took responsibility for updating the Courage pedigree, covering the period from 1686. The pedigree was printed in the form of five charts which included 1,000 descendants and their spouses – through female as well as male lines. He published the work privately in 1993.[65] Michael Foster, who was then chairman of John Courage & Co. Ltd, marked the occasion by inviting 700 of John Courage's descendants and their spouses to a party held at the Berkshire Brewery on 11 September 1993. Many guests flew from overseas for the purpose. Michael updated the pedigree in 2004, when the company held a similar party.

Michael left the firm in June 1993 to develop his own chain of public houses. By September of that year he had his first two leased houses in place – *The Crown* at Kingsclere, Berkshire, and the *Great Western Hotel* near Basingstoke railway station. The business prospered and by the year 2000 he had six public houses, two of which he held freehold – *The Black Horse* at Byworth, West Sussex, and *The Artillery Arms* at Milton, near Portsmouth, Hampshire. By 2004 he also owned the *White Lion* at Aldershot, Hampshire.

In 2000 Rosalie attended healing development courses, followed by a two-year training period to become a member of the National Federation of Spiritual Healers. In 2001 she was appointed secretary of the Hampshire Dowsing Society.

CHAPTER 9

LINE OF GEORGE WORTHINGTON
OF WERNETH

9.1 George

George Worthington, the fourth son of Daniel Worthington (Article 1.21) by Rebecca his first wife, was born about 1691 and died in March 1772. His life has already been treated (Article 1.25). He and Anne (or Hannah) his first wife produced three daughters and a son.[1]

SECOND GENERATION – FAMILY OF GEORGE AND ANNE

9.2 Mary

Mary Worthington, daughter of George Worthington (Articles 1.25 and 9.1) by Anne (or Hannah) his first wife, was probably the eldest child, as she is the first mentioned in the Wills of both her brother George Worthington (Article 9.5) and his widow Rebecca (Articles 3.6 and 9.5). Her baptism has not been traced but all three of her siblings were baptised at St Mary's Church, Oldham, Lancashire, the eldest being baptised on 13 September 1719. Hence, Mary's birth is likely to have been before December 1718. The presumed marriage of her parents was 1 January 1717-8 at Birstall, Yorkshire, and it is possible that she was born and baptised there.

Mary married John Nicholls (or Nichols) on 9 January 1733-4 at St Mary's Church, Oldham, the entry in the register being 'John Nichols, butcher, and Mary Worthington, spinster, both of Oldham'. This marriage was only 16 years and eight days after the marriage of her parents, so either Mary was born within nine days of her parents' marriage, or her own marriage was prior to her 16th birthday. Marriage under the age of 16 was then unusual although it was legally possible after the age of 12 for a girl and 14 for a boy. John was the second son of Jonathan Nicholls, 'shoemaker and merchant of Manchester, and Lydia his wife'. Jonathan's Will dated 4 September 1714 shows that he held 'messuages, burgages and lands and tenements in Manchester', and that he was a close relative of a Mr Nicholls of 'the Great Fenton Estate'. Jonathan's two sons were bound apprentices at the time, and were appointed executors of the Will. Mary and John produced 10 children, all of whom were baptised at St Mary's Church:[2]

PEDIGREE 9 – LINE OF GEORGE WORTHINGTON OF WERNETH, LANCASHIRE

Anne (probably Hannah ⊤ **George Worthington**; b. circa 1691, m(2) without ⊥ **Susanna**, dau. of John Ogden;
Rayner, m. 1717-8)　issue, d. 1772. *(Pedigree 1 & Arts 1.25 & 9.1)*　bap. 1698, d. 1784

Mary; b. circa 1718,
m. 1733-4 John
Nicholls & had issue,
living 1791. *(Art. 9.2)*

Hannah; bap. 1719, m.
Samuel Bentley, living
1791, d. without issue.
(Art. 9.3)

Phoebe; bap. 1721, m.(1) circa 1741
Jonathan Jackson & had issue, m.(2)
1752 Jonathan Buckley & had issue,
d. 1793. *(Art. 9.4)*

George Worthington; ⸗ **Rebecca**, dau. of Jonathan
bap. 1723-4, m. 1749,　Worthington; bap. 1729, d.
d. 1788 without issue.　1791. *(Pedigree 3 & Arts*
(Art. 9.5)　*3.6 & 9.5)*

Forename	Date of baptism	Spelling of Nicholls
John	18 September 1734	Nichols
John	15 September 1736	Nicholls
Hannah	28 June 1738	Nicholas
Mary	8 July 1741	Nicholas
George	17 October 1744	Nichalls
Jonathan	4 June 1746	Nicholls
Jonathan	16 October 1747	Nicholls
George	13 February 1750-1	Nichols
Susey	18 April 1753	Nichols
Susey	27 October 1758	Nichols

In all entries in the register John is described as 'butcher'; in the first three entries John and Mary are described as 'of Hollinwood', in the next as 'of Little Town' and in the remainder as 'of Oldham'. It may be noted that the eldest child, John, was baptised on 18 September 1734, eight months and nine days after his parents' marriage; history may thus have been repeated with two premature births in successive generations.

'John Nicholls', butcher, was buried on 31 March 1763 at St Mary's Church, when Mary was only 44 years of age. Mary was still living in 1791. In her widowhood she received annuities from her younger brother George Worthington and from his widow Rebecca.

9.3 Hannah

Hannah Worthington, the second daughter of George Worthington (Articles 1.25 and 9.1) by Anne his first wife, was baptised on 13 September 1719 at St Mary's Church, Oldham. The entry in the register was 'Hanna daughter of Geo. Worthington from Wernith, carrier, by Ann his wife'.[2]

Hannah's husband 'Samuel Bentley, yeoman' was probably 'Samuel son of Joseph Bentley', Samuel having been baptised on 20 February 1706-7 at the Collegiate Church of Manchester; no other baptisms of a Samuel Bentley in due time and locality have been found. If so, Samuel was 12 years older than Hannah. Hannah and Samuel lived at Failsworth, Lancashire, but were probably childless, as no children are mentioned in either of their Wills.[3] In his Will dated 14 April 1785 and proved at Chester on 17 August 1786, Samuel bequeathed all his 'messuages, dwelling houses, lands, investments, hereditaments and premises' together with his personal estate, 'cattle, household goods and furniture' to Hannah and her heirs. The executors of the Will were Hannah herself and Joshua Taylor of Hollinwood, yeoman.

Hannah as a widow wrote her Will on 19 May 1788. The Will shows more clearly the properties which she and Samuel held:

(a) A messuage in Failsworth in the tenancy of John Rydings – to Joshua Taylor's son, George;

(b) Two other messuages in Failsworth in the tenancy of John Clough and Betty Harrison – to Joshua Taylor;

(c) Another messuage and garden in Failsworth in the tenancy of Robert

Hilton – to Richard Fletcher of Failsworth, weaver, son of James Fletcher;

(d) Another house and garden in Failsworth in the tenancy of Samuel Derry – to 'my niece Betty, wife of Joseph Newton'.

Betty Newton was to receive all the remainder of Hannah's estate. Joshua Taylor and Joseph Newton were appointed executors. Despite holding this property, Hannah lived as a widow in a 'messuage and tenement' belonging to her sister-in-law and first cousin Rebecca Worthington. By the Will of her brother George (Article 9.5), Hannah had received an annuity for life, and by the Will of his widow Rebecca she was given the option to repay the annuity with the right to occupy for life, rent free, the messuage and tenement in which she then lived as Rebecca's tenant.

9.4 Phoebe

Phoebe Worthington, the third and youngest daughter of George Worthington (Articles 1.25 and 9.1) by Anne his first wife, was baptised on 11 October 1721 at St Mary's Church, Oldham, the entry in the register being 'Phebe daughter of Geo. Worthington from Wernith'.[2] She married Jonathan Jackson and they produced four children as shown by the registers of St Mary's Church, Oldham:

Forename	Date of baptism	Date of burial
Jonathan	14 June 1742	25 June 1742
Phebe	14 June 1742	
Fanny (or Frances)	9 March 1743-4	
John	23 July 1746	

The entry for the twins was 'Jonathan and Phebe son and daughter of Jonathan Jackson, Oldham, saddler by Phebe his wife'. The marriage of Phoebe and Jonathan has not been traced, but Phoebe must have been a minor at the time, as she was only 20 years of age when the twins were born. Jonathan died when his son John was aged about 16 months; Jonathan was buried on 27 November 1747 at St Mary's Church. He had not made a Will, but Phoebe was appointed the sole administrator by letters of administration granted on 16 March 1747-8 at Chester. George Worthington, carrier, and John Wallwork, yeoman, both of the parish of Oldham, were her bondsmen.

After nearly five years as a widow, Phoebe married Jonathan Buckley on 21 November 1752 at the Collegiate Church of Manchester. The entry in the register is 'Jonathan Buckley and Phoebe Jackson, by license'. It has proved difficult to locate Jonathan in the Buckley family because there were at least two Jonathan Buckleys and two John Buckleys at the time. The burials of three of them at St Mary's Church, all styled yeomen, were 'John Buckely of Sholver Moor' on 9 October 1775, 'John Buckley of Sholver' on 18 July 1777 and 'Old Jonathan Buckley of Sholver Fold' on 6 February 1784. All wrote Wills, none of which contained enough information to ascertain the exact relationship to Phoebe. Her most likely father-in-law was Old Jonathan of Sholver Fold. In his Will, made on 27 November 1782, he referred to 'my late son Jonathan Buckley' and he made bequests to the lawful children of his 'said late son Jonathan Buckley'. Phoebe and Jonathan produced five children, all being baptised at St Mary's Church:

Forename	Date of baptism
Betty	9 January 1754
Hannah	25 August 1756
Isabel	14 January 1759
Mary	7 April 1762
Isabel	12 April 1767

The entry in the register for Betty was '... daughter of Jonathan Buckely late of Lime Yate, now of Bardsley Brow by Phoebe his wife'. For Hannah and the later children the entry showed that Jonathan was then an innkeeper at Primrose Bank. In the entry for Mary, Jonathan is described as 'yeoman' and Phoebe is spelt 'Febe'.

Rebecca Worthington (Article 3.6 and 9.5), who was Phoebe's first cousin and sister-in-law, made her Will on 12 April 1791. In it she wrote:

> ... I also bequeath unto John Jackson, Frances Smethurst widow, Sabitha Clegg Smethurst the wife of Henry Smethurst, Betty Newton widow, and Isabel Buckley spinster, the five children of the said Phebe Buckley, the sum of one hundred pounds* a piece ...

This shows that Phoebe had a child, Sabitha – in addition to the nine children already listed. As Sabitha's baptism has not been found, it is not known whether she was born Jackson or Buckley. However, study of the dates of baptism of the nine children, together with the sequence in which the surviving children are mentioned in Rebecca's Will indicates that Sabitha may have been the last of the Jackson children, born about the time of her father's death.

Phoebe died in 1793 and was buried on 23 May at St Mary's Church. The entry in the register was 'Phebe widow of the late John Buckley of Primrose Bank aged 72'. Jonathan had died before 1791. Following his death, Phoebe had moved to a house at Moor Lea, near Oldham, as a tenant of Rebecca. By her Will Rebecca confirmed that Phoebe could live there rent free for the rest of her life.

9.5 George
George Worthington, the only son of George Worthington (Articles 1.25 and 9.1) by Anne his first wife was baptised on 8 March 1723-4 at St Mary's Church, Oldham.[2] The entry in the register was 'George son of George Worthington of Wernith, carrier, by Anne his wife'. George married

---

* Equivalent to 1,300 man-days of agricultural labour.

80 *Werneth Hall, Lancashire.*

his first cousin, Rebecca Worthington (Article 3.6), the fourth daughter of Jonathan Worthington and Mary his wife (Article 1.24). A licence was obtained on 12 May 1749 when George's co-bondsman was John Haworth, innkeeper of Manchester. George and Rebecca were then aged about 25 and 20 respectively. The wedding was held on 14 May 1749 at the Collegiate Church of Manchester.[2] No children were born.

It is likely that George entered his father's carrying business at Oldham early in his career. He is described as 'carrier of Prestwich' on his marriage licence. Although the township of Prestwich is seven miles west of Oldham, the diocesan clerk may have been referring to the parish of Prestwich, which at that time included the townships of Oldham and Werneth. By 1778 George was certainly living at Werneth and managing the business, his father then being 87 years of age. At the time of his death, his residence was Werneth Hall, and it is probable that his father had lived there previously. The principal route for the business was between Manchester and York, via Leeds, a total distance of 60 miles as the crow flies. The horses had to draw the wagons up some 1,500 feet over the Pennine Range on rough roads. The rainfall on the Pennines is high, and snow sometimes caused a complete blockage. However, the business was strong in a growing market. One weekly run to York advertised in 1772 had grown to three per week by 1778.[4]

On 29 March 1788 George was robbed and murdered. He was on his way home from Manchester to Werneth and had called at a house between Miles Platting and Mile Stone on the Oldham Road. Some three minutes after leaving the house, when he was in Newton Heath, just over the Failsworth boundary, he was shot. An article in the *Manchester Mercury* read:[5]

Whereas on Saturday night the 29th day of March last, about the hour of Nine o'clock, George Worthington, late of Werneth, near Oldham, in the County of Lancaster, the Common Carrier between Manchester and York, was most inhumanely murdered, by being shot dead with a pistol, or some other fire arms, loaded with pewter slugs, on the Kings Highway, near a place called Miles Platting, about the distance of two miles from Manchester, on his Road from that Town Home, and a sum of money and a Silver Watch Makers Name John Oliver, Leeds No 301 or No 302, together with a pair of spectacles in a steel case, and Money Balance were taken from him. The Coroner's inquest have sat upon the body of the deceased and found that the said George Worthington was murdered by a certain person or persons at present unknown. In order that the perpetrators of so inhuman a deed may be brought to Justice, and made a public example of, the following rewards are offered: Mr Richard Tunnadine, of Manchester, doth herby promise a reward of One Hundred Guineas;* and the Town of Manchester doth promise a further reward of One Hundred Guineas, to any person or persons, whether an accomplice or otherwise, in the said murder and robbery (except the person who actually committed the said murder) who shall discover any of the parties concerned therein, to be respectively paid on the conviction of such offender or offenders; and an application will be made, in order to obtain his Majesty's pardon for the person making such discovery.

The statement was signed by Richard Tunnadine (Article 3.26) who was the first cousin-in-law of both George and Rebecca. It was also witnessed by Nathan Crompton and James Entwistle, constables of Manchester. According to another article 'the people of the town were horrified at this crime as Worthington was a popular man'.[2] George was buried on 31 March 1788 at St Mary's Church, Oldham. There is an unusually extended reference to him in the register of burials:

Mr George Worthington of Werneth yeoman who was shot dead and robbed in Newton Lane by some person or persons unknown as he was returning from Manchester on Saturday 29th about 9 o'clock in the evening.

Within six weeks Rebecca had disposed of the business to Welch & Hanley (sometimes spelt Welsh & Handley) who issued the following notice:[5]

Mrs Worthington, sole executrix of the late George Worthington, having disposed of the Carrying business betwixt Manchester, Leeds and York, to Welsh and Hanley, wishes to recommend them to her friends and the public, that they intend to carry on the said business and will be happy to receive their goods and favours. Goods delivered at their warehouse at Shudehill and Fountain Street, for York, Leeds etc with be forwarded every Tuesday and Saturday as usual. They likewise carry on the Newcastle upon Tyne business as usual.

---

* Equivalent to 1,350 man-days of agricultural labour.

George had prepared a Will on 3 July 1785 when he was described as 'gentleman of Werneth in the parish of Prestwich'. At the time he held two messuages and tenement lands in Oldham apart from his own residence. One was at Highfield, being in the occupation of Aaron Jackson. The other was occupied by Henry Booth. George provided annuities for his three sisters, Mary, Hannah and Phoebe (Articles 9.2 to 9.4). All the residue of his estate passed to Rebecca.

Rebecca continued to live for a further three years, during which time she moved to Hollinwood (Article 3.6). She was buried on 8 December 1791 at St Mary's Church, Oldham.[2]

With the murder of George, male representation in this cadet line had become extinct after the second generation. A silver medal inscribed 'George Worthington of Werneth' passed to Rebecca, and from her to her nephew Jonathan Worthington of Stourport (Article 3.11) and thence for a further two generations to Jonathan Yorke Worthington of Newbury, Berkshire (Article 3.31). Yorke bequeathed it in his Will to his niece Ruth Helen Worthington Keele (Article 3.35). The medal has not recently been located. It must have been awarded either to the George Worthington treated in this article or to his father George (Article 1.25). No medals were awarded to soldiers by the state during the period, but Mrs L. Smurthwaite, head of the Department of Uniforms, Badges and Medals at the National Army Museum, has suggested that it could be a medal struck by a regiment or society. In their younger years, these Georges would have been natural choices for cavalry, or military supplies or transport.

CHAPTER 10

LINE OF ROBERT WORTHINGTON
OF SHUDEHILL

10.1 Robert

Robert Worthington, the fifth son of Daniel Worthington and Rebecca his wife (Article 1.21), was born about 1693. Robert's life has already been treated (Article 1.26). He and his wife Elizabeth produced four children.[1]

SECOND GENERATION – FAMILY OF
ROBERT AND ELIZABETH

10.2 George

George Worthington, son of Robert Worthington and Elizabeth his wife (Articles 1.26 and 10.1), was baptised on 29 April 1722 at All Saints' Church, Newton, Lancashire.[2] The Will of his mother, made 48 years later on 12 May 1770, indicates that George was then the only surviving son, his two brothers having already died.[3] Curiously, George was not appointed executor and trustee of the Will – roles which were passed to her nephew-in-law George Worthington (Article 9.5) and her son-in-law Joseph Lyon (Article 10.5). George inherited from his mother £40[*] plus a quarter of the residue. No mention is made of his having a wife or children.

10.3 Jonathan

Jonathan Worthington, son of Robert Worthington and Elizabeth his wife (Articles 1.26 and 10.1), married Lydia, daughter of Richard Coe (sometimes written Koe) and Mary his wife of Audenshaw, Lancashire, on 2 September 1740 at St Michael's Church, Ashton-under-Lyne. Banns had been read. Lydia was then aged 25 years, having been baptised on 5 January 1714-5 at the same church. It appears that Jonathan and Lydia lived at Woodhouses for a time, but by 1744-5 they had moved to the town of Ashton-under-Lyne. They produced at least three children:

Forename	Date of baptism	Date of burial	Article
Jonathan	30 January 1742-3	22 March 1744-5	10.6
Rebecca			10.7
Jonathan	25 January 1753		10.8

The two baptisms and the burial quoted were registered at St Michael's Church.[2] The entry for the first son was 'Jonathan son of Jonathan

---

[*] Equivalent to 640 man-days of agricultural labour.

PEDIGREE 10 – LINE OF ROBERT WORTHINGTON OF SHUDEHILL, MANCHESTER

Robert Worthington; b. circa 1693, m. 1717, d. 1767 or 1768. *(Pedigree 1 & Arts 1.26 & 10.1)* ═══ **Elizabeth** Charlsworth; d. circa 1776

George Worthington; bap. 1722, living 1770. *(Art. 10.2)*

Jonathan Worthington; m. 1740, d. 1752 or 1753. *(Art. 10.3)* ═══ **Lydia**, dau. of Richard Coe; bap. 1714-5, re-m. 1759

Robert Worthington; m. 1743, d. by 1770 probably without issue. *(Art. 10.4)* ═══ **Elizabeth**, dau. of William Barlow; living 1770

Elizabeth; m. Joseph Lyon & had issue, living 1794. *(Art. 10.5)*

Jonathan Worthington; bap. 1742-3, d. 1744-5. *(Art. 10.6)*

Rebecca; living 1770. *(Art. 10.7)*

Jonathan Worthington; bap. 1753, living 1770. *(Art. 10.8)*

Worthington of Woodhouses by Lydia his wife', and for his burial was 'Jonathan son of Jonathan Worthington of the Town'. The entry for the second son was 'Jonathan son of Jonathan Worthington deceased by Lydia his wife'. Thus, Jonathan senior died in 1752 or early in 1753 and Jonathan junior was probably born posthumously.

About five years after becoming a widow, Lydia remarried by banns on 18 May 1759 at St Michael's Church, the entry in the register being 'Wm Walker and Lidia Worthington both of Ashton'. She may have married for a third time on 10 December 1778 to John Line or Lime of the parish of Glossop, Derbyshire, the wedding again taking place at St Michael's Church, Ashton-under-Lyne. Glossop lies about 40 miles south-east of Ashton.

10.4 Robert

Robert Worthington, son of Robert Worthington and Elizabeth his wife (Articles 1.26 and 10.1), married by banns Elizabeth Barlow on 24 May 1743 at St Michael's Church, Ashton-under-Lyne, both being described as 'of this parish'. Elizabeth is likely to have been the Elizabeth, daughter of William and Mary Barlow, who was baptised on 28 May 1727 at St Michael's Church. If so, she would have been married within a few days of the age of 16 years.

Robert was dead by 1770 when his mother made her Will with the words: 'To my daughter-in-law Betty otherwise Elizabeth widow of my late son Robert Worthington deceased ...'. Probably the alternative 'Betty' was used to avoid potential confusion of the two generations both bearing the names Robert and Elizabeth. It is thought that Robert and Betty did not have any children, or at least surviving children. Robert's mother mentioned no such grandchildren in her Will while mentioning three other grandchildren.

10.5 Elizabeth

Elizabeth Worthington, daughter of Robert Worthington and Elizabeth his wife, seniors (Article 1.26 and 10.1), married Joseph Lyon (or Lion) of Blackley, Lancaster. The township of Blackley lies two miles north-west of Failsworth and about five miles north-west of the town of Ashton-under-Lyne. Elizabeth and Joseph produced four children, but, alas, three of them died in infancy:

Forename	Date of baptism	Date of burial
Joseph	26 January 1752-3	Before 1754
Joseph	4 March 1753	
Sarah	1 June 1757	3 June 1757
Hannah	17 April 1761	19 April 1761

All the baptisms and burials quoted were at the parish church of Blackley and on all occasions Joseph senior was described as 'whitster'.[2] Another

Joseph Lyon, presumably the father of Joseph senior, was buried on 19 October 1745 when he was described as 'fustian whitster'.

In 1770 Elizabeth's mother, Elizabeth, made her Will with the words 'To my grandson Joseph son of the said Joseph Lyon ...' Joseph senior was one of the executors of this Will, but he himself died four years later; he died on 8 January and was buried on 12 January 1774 at Blackley church. Joseph had died without making a Will. The right to administer his estate was granted on 13 January 1794 by the Consistory Court of Chester to Elizabeth and to Ortho Hulme, warehouseman of Manchester, and Robert Saxton, chapman of Manchester.

THIRD GENERATION – FAMILY OF JONATHAN AND LYDIA

10.6 Jonathan
Jonathan Worthington, son of Jonathan Worthington (Article 10.3) and Lydia his wife, died young and was buried on 22 March 1744-5 at St Michael's Church, Ashton-under-Lyne.[2] The entry in the register of burials reads 'Jonathan son of Jonathan Worthington of the Town'.

10.7 Rebecca
Rebecca Worthington, the only known daughter of Jonathan Worthington and Lydia his wife (Article 10.3), was still living in 1770 when she was mentioned in the Will of her grandmother Elizabeth Worthington, born Charlsworth (Articles 1.26 and 10.1). The Will states:

> To my grandson and granddaughter Jonathan and Rebecca Worthington son and daughter of my late son Jonathan Worthington deceased the sum of ten pounds a piece ...[*]

10.8 Jonathan
Jonathan Worthington, presumed to be the only surviving son of Jonathan Worthington (Article 10.3) and Lydia his wife, was still living in 1770 when he was mentioned in the Will of his grandmother Elizabeth Worthington, born Charlsworth (Articles 1.26 and 10.1). Nothing more is known about him, nor whether, through him, the cadet line of Robert Worthington continued.

---

[*] Equivalent to 165 man-days of agricultural labour.

CHAPTER 11

LINE OF JOSEPH WORTHINGTON
OF WOODHOUSES

11.1 Joseph

Joseph Worthington who heads the line of the Worthingtons of Woodhouses, Lancashire, married Elizabeth Barlow on 13 January 1669-70 at the Collegiate Church, Manchester.[1] Joseph's life has already been treated (Article 1.15) and it has been shown that he is likely to have been the same man as Joseph, one of the younger sons of Ralph Worthington junior of Middlewood and Jane his wife (Article 1.6). Joseph and Elizabeth produced two sons and three daughters.

SECOND GENERATION – FAMILY OF JOSEPH AND ELIZABETH

11.2 Joseph (junior)

Joseph Worthington, the elder son of Joseph Worthington, senior, and Elizabeth his wife (Articles 1.15 and 11.1), was probably baptised on 30 May 1676 at All Saints' Chapel, Newton Heath. A slight doubt remains because the child's forename is missing from the damaged register. The remaining entry reads: '... Worthington son of Joseph Worthington'.

Joseph's wife was Margaret; the date and place of marriage have not yet been found, but the earliest known reference to a baptism of one of their children was on 2 June 1700 at Dob Lane Chapel, Failsworth.[1] However, there were two earlier burials at St Michael's Church, Ashton-under-Lyne, which may have been of children either of Joseph senior or Joseph junior. The burial records are: 'John son of Joseph Worthington of Woodhouses' on 12 December 1695 and 'Mary daughter of Joseph Worthington of Woodhouses' on 24 February 1695-6. Excluding these uncertainties, Joseph Worthington junior and Margaret his wife produced seven children:

Forename	Date of baptism	Date of burial	Article
Mary	2 June 1700		11.6
Esther		5 December 1701	11.7
John		8 May 1704	11.8
Richard	7 May 1705	7 September 1707	11.9
Ralph	14 July 1706		11.10
Esther	6 February 1708		11.11
Margaret	27 September 1713		11.12

Joseph Worthington; b. circa 1623, m. 1669-70, d. 1721. *(Art. 11.1 & probably Pedigree 1 & Art. 1.15)* = **Elizabeth Barlow**; d. 1721-2

- **Joseph Worthington**; bap. probably 1676, d. 1729. *(Art. 11.2)* = **Margaret**; d. 1753
- **Ralph Worthington**; bap. 1680, m. 1711. *(Art. 11.3)* = **Anne Knott**; d. 1730
- **Anne**; bap 1684, d. 1684-5. *(Art. 11.4)*
- **Elizabeth**; bap. 1686, d. 1686. *(Art. 11.5)*

Children of Joseph Worthington and Margaret:
- **John Worthington**; d. 1695
- **Mary**; d. 1695-6

Children of Ralph Worthington and Anne Knott:
- **Mary**; bap. 1700, m. probably 1723 John Peak. *(Art. 11.6)*
- **Esther**; d. 1701. *(Art. 11.7)*
- **John Worthington**; d. 1704. *(Art. 11.8)*
- **Richard Worthington**; bap. 1705, d. 1707. *(Art. 11.9)*
- **Ralph Worthington**; bap. 1706, m. 1730, d. 1791. *(Art. 11.10)* = **Elizabeth**, dau. of Thomas Hudson; bap. 1707, d. 1780
- **Esther**; bap. 1708-9, m. 1731 William Dawson. *(Art. 11.11)*
- **Margaret**; bap. 1713. *(Art. 11.12)*

Next generation:
- **Betty**; bap. 1731, d. 1742. *(Art. 11.13)*
- **Joseph Worthington**; d. 1792. *(Art. 11.14)*
- **Mary**; bap. 1736. *(Art. 11.15)*
- **Thomas Worthington**; bap. 1741-2, living 1784. *(Art. 11.16)*
- **Alice**; m. 1750-1 Jonathan Whitworth & had issue; d. before 1785. *(Art. 11.17)*
- **Molly**; living 1784. *(Art. 11.18)*
- **Betty**; d. 1747-8. *(Art. 11.19)*
- **Elizabeth**; living 1784. *(Art. 11.20)*
- **Rebecca**; bap. 1753, m. 1769 William Barlow & had issue, living 1784. *(Art. 11.21)*

All of the baptisms quoted took place at Dob Lane Chapel, and in all their father was described as 'Joseph Worthington of Woodhouses'.[1] In the case of the second 'Esther', Joseph was also described as 'junior'. The baptism of Ralph was also recorded in the register of St Michael's Church, Ashton-under-Lyne. The three young burials took place at St Michael's Church.

Joseph, who had variously been described as 'general badger and weaver', was buried at St Michael's Church. He was aged 59 years or less and had not made a Will. Letters of administration were granted on 20 October 1729 by the Consistory Court of Chester in favour of 'Margaret Worthington of Woodhouses' and 'Ralph Worthington of Woodhouses, weaver' – then their only surviving son.[2] Margaret lived for a further 24 years. She was buried on 3 December 1753 at St Michael's Church, and was entered in the register as 'Margaret Worthington from Woodhouses, widow'.

11.3 Ralph

Ralph Worthington, the younger son of Joseph Worthington senior and Elizabeth his wife (Articles 1.15 and 11.1), was baptised in November 1680 at All Saints' Church, Newton, the entry in the register being 'Ralph son of Joseph Worthington'.[1] At the age of 31 years, on 19 July 1711, he married Anne Knott. The wedding took place at St Michael's Church, Ashton-under-Lyne, the entry in the register being 'Ralph Worthington of Woodhouses and Anne Knott'. Nothing more is known about them.

When the Worthingtons of Woodhouses were being researched, five references came to light which could not be linked to the pedigree (Pedigree 11). It is just possible that some of the later ones are descendants of Ralph and Anne or are linked in some other way, so are listed here for future reference:

27 July 1698	Baptism of a daughter of 'John Worthington of Woodhouses', at All Saint's, Newton;
19 December 1740	Baptism of 'George son of Robert Worthington of Woodhouses, butcher', at St Michael's, Ashton;
11 April 1743	Burial of Rebecca 'daughter of Robert Worthington of Woodhouses', at St Michael's;
27 December 1777	Burial of 'Richard son of Ralph Worthington of Woodhouses', at St Michael's;
8 November 1779	Marriage of 'Eli Andrews of this parish, Mottram in Longdendale and Esther Worthington of Woodhouses of this parish', at St Michael's.

11.4 Anne

Anne Worthington, daughter of Joseph Worthington, senior, and Elizabeth his wife (Articles 1.15 and 11.1), died young and was buried on

11 March 1684-5 at St Michael's Church, Ashton-under-Lyne. The entry in the register was 'Anne child of Joseph Worthington de Woodhouses'. It is likely that Anne had been baptised in October 1684 at All Saints' Church, Newton Heath; the surviving part of the register reads '... daughter of Joseph Worthington'.[1]

11.5 Elizabeth

Elizabeth Worthington, the youngest daughter of Joseph Worthington, senior, and Elizabeth his wife (Articles 1.15 and 11.1), was baptised at All Saints' Church, Newton.[1] The day and month have decayed from the register which reads '...1686 Elizth dau of Joseph Worthington of ffailsworth'. It is curious that while the four known baptisms of Elizabeth and her elder siblings were at All Saints' Church, Newton, she and her sister (Article 11.4) who died young were buried at St Michael's Church, Ashton-under-Lyne. Newton church is about a mile and a half west of Woodhouses, while Ashton church is two miles south-east of Woodhouses. Perhaps Ashton had more appropriate burial arrangements, but whatever the reason for the first burial it would have been natural to wish for the three children to be buried together. Indeed, their parents and elder brother were later also buried at Ashton (Articles 1.15 and 11.2).

THIRD GENERATION – FAMILY OF JOSEPH AND MARGARET

11.6 Mary

Mary Worthington, the eldest surviving daughter of Joseph Worthington, junior, and Margaret his wife (Article 11.2), was baptised on 2 June 1700 at Dob Lane Chapel, Failsworth, the entry in the register being 'Mary Worthington the doutter of Joseph Worthington of wood houses'. It may be she who married John Peak, weaver, on 16 April 1723 at St Michael's Church, Ashton-under-Lyne when she was described as '... Mary Worthington spinster of this parish'.[1]

11.7 Esther

Esther Worthington, a daughter of Joseph Worthington, junior, and Margaret his wife (Article 11.2), was buried on 5 December 1701 at St Michael's Church, Ashton-under-Lyne.[1]

11.8 John

John Worthington, a son of Joseph Worthington junior and Margaret his wife (Article 11.2), was buried on 8 May 1704 at St Michael's Church, Ashton-under-Lyne.[1]

11.9 Richard

Richard Worthington, the second or third son of Joseph Worthington, junior, and Margaret his wife (Article 11.2), was baptised on 7 May 1705 at Dob Lane Chapel, Failsworth, the entry in the register being 'Richard ye son of Joseph Worthington of wood-houses'.[1] Richard was then the only surviving son, but he died aged two years and was buried on 7 September 1707 at St Michael's Church, Ashton-under-Lyne. It is noteworthy that still, in the third generation, St Michael's was the burial ground while baptisms were elsewhere.

11.10 Ralph

Ralph Worthington, the third or fourth son of Joseph Worthington, junior, and Margaret his wife (Article 11.2), was baptised on 14 July 1706 at Dob Lane Chapel, Failsworth, the entry in the register being 'Ralph ye son of Joseph Worthington of Woodhouses'. At the age of 14 months, on the death of his elder brother Richard Worthington (Article 11.10), Ralph became the only surviving son. In the letters of administration granted to his mother on 2 October 1729, following the death of his father, Ralph was described as 'Radulphum Worthington de Woodhouses weaver', but from then on, as Joseph's heir, he was perforce farmer as well as weaver.

On 18 August 1730, Ralph married Elizabeth Hudson at St Michael's Church, Ashton-under-Lyne, both parties being described as 'of this parish'.[1] Elizabeth daughter of Thomas Hudson of Ashton had been baptised at the same church on 20 August 1707. Thus Elizabeth, usually known as 'Betty', was one year younger than Ralph. They produced two sons and seven daughters namely:

Forename	Date of baptism	Date of burial	Article
Betty	27 November 1731	6 April 1742	11.13
Joseph		15 January 1792	11.14
Mary	12 December 1736		11.15
Thomas	10 March 1741-2		11.16
Alice			11.17
Molly			11.18
Betty	1742 or later	4 February 1747-8	11.19
Elizabeth	1747-8 or later		11.20
Rebecca	14 September 1753		11.21

All the baptisms and burials quoted took place at St Michael's Church, Ashton-under-Lyne.[1] The record for the first Betty was 'Betty daughter of Ralph Worthington of Woodhouses, weaver, and Elizabeth his wife'.

Ralph's wife, Elizabeth, was buried on 11 March 1780 at St Michael's Church, Ashton-under-Lyne, the entry in the register being 'Elizabeth wife of Ralph Worthington of Woodhouses'. Ralph was then 73 years of age. Sometime during the next three years Ralph moved to Greenside in Droylsdon, probably to retire. Presumably his eldest son, Joseph, had not shown an interest to continue with the farm, which Ralph then let to Philip Barwick. These changes are clearly described in Ralph's Will, which he made on 6 February 1784:[2]

I, Ralph Worthington of Greenside within Droylsdon in the parish of Manchester in the County of Lancaster, yeoman, being sick in bodye but of sound and disposing mind, memory and understanding praised be God for the same do make and publish this my last Will and testament in manner and form the following. That is to say ffirst I will and direct that all my just Debts my Funeral Expenses and the Charges of probate and Execution of this my Will shall be paid and discharged out of my Estate and Effects, and I give and devise All that my Messuage and Tenements with the land and Appurtenances thereunto belonging situate lying and being in Woodhouses in the Parish of Ashton-under-Lyne in the said county, now or late in the Tenure or Occupation of Philip Barwick his Assigns or Undertenants, unto my friends William Bardsly of Littlemoss in the said Parish of Ashton-under-Lyne Weaver and Thomas Moss of Audenshaw in the said Parish of Ashton-under-Lyne Schoolmaster their Executors Administrators and Assigns Upon Trust nevertheless that they, my said Trustees or the Survivors of them, do and shall within twelve months next after my Decease absolutely sell and dispose of my said Estate and premises for the best price and most money that can be had or got for the same. And money arising from the Sale thereof, as well as the money arising from the Sale of all and every part of my Household Goods and Furniture Cattle Corn Hay Straw, Husbandry Geer, and Implements of Husbandry, which I also will and direct to be sold within twelve months after my Decease, I give and dispose thereof as follows namely I give and bequeath unto my son Joseph Worthington the Sum of Five pounds* And I give and bequeath unto my son Thomas Worthington the Sum of five pounds And I give and bequeath unto my Son-in-law Jonathan Whitworth the Husband of my late Daughter Alice deceased the Sum of one Shilling if demanded, And I give and bequeath unto the living children of my said late daughter Alice the sum of one Shilling each if demanded And all the Rest residue and remainder of my worldly estate and effects of what kind or nature soever, after my just Debts, funeral Expenses and the Charges of the probate and execution of this my Will be fully discharged satisfied and paid I hereby will order and direct to be divided between and amongst my sons Joseph and Thomas and my Daughters Molly, Elizabeth and Rebecca share and part alike ...

Ralph lived as a widower for 10 years. He was buried on 9 January 1791 at St Michael's Church, Ashton-under-Lyne, the entry in the register being 'Ralph Worthington of Droylsden'.

Another 'Ralph Worthington of Droylesdon' was buried with coroner's licence on 28 January 1801 at St Michael's Church, but it is not yet clear who he was.

11.11 Esther

Esther Worthington, the second daughter of Joseph Worthington junior and Margaret his wife (Articles 1.15 and 11.1) was baptised on 6 February 1708 at Dob Lane Chapel, Failsworth.[1] The entry in the register was 'Ester

---

* Equivalent to 70 man-days of agricultural labour.

ye daughter of Joseph Worthington junior of Woodhouses'. She married by banns William Dawson of Manchester on 17 April 1731 at the Collegiate Church of Manchester, the entry in the bishop's transcript being 'Wm Dawson ... Esther Worthington of Ashton'. The words following 'Dawson', probably giving his location, are now too faded to read. No children by this couple have been found.

11.12 Margaret

Margaret Worthington, the third daughter of Joseph Worthington junior and Margaret his wife (Articles 1.15 and 11.1), was baptised on 27 September 1713 at Dob Lane Chapel, Failsworth.[1] The entry in the register was 'Margaret ye daughter of Joseph Worthington of wood houses'.

FOURTH GENERATION – FAMILY OF RALPH AND ELIZABETH

11.13 Betty

Betty Worthington, the eldest daughter of Ralph Worthington and Elizabeth his wife (Article 11.10), was baptised on 27 November 1731 at St Michael's Church, Ashton-under-Lyne. She died aged 10 years and was buried on 6 April 1742 at the same church.[1]

11.14 Joseph

Joseph Worthington, the elder son of Ralph Worthington and Elizabeth his wife (Article 11.10), was mentioned in his father's Will made on 6 February 1784. He was to receive £5 plus a fifth part of the residue. Joseph's baptism has not been found but it seems likely that he was born in the five-year gap between the baptisms of the first and second daughters – 1731 and 1736.

Joseph died in his late 50s and was buried on 15 January 1792 at St Michael's Church, Ashton-under-Lyne.[1] His father had been buried only 12 months previously. The entry in the register was 'Joseph Worthington of Droylesdon'; the family still maintained the custom of burial at Ashton-under-Lyne although Droylesdon lay within the parish of Manchester.

11.15 Mary

Mary Worthington, the second daughter of Ralph Worthington and Elizabeth his wife (Article 11.10), was baptised on 12 December 1736 at St Michael's Church, Ashton-under-Lyne.[1] She is not mentioned in her father's Will, so may have died young.

11.16 Thomas

Thomas Worthington, the younger son of Ralph Worthington and Elizabeth his wife (Article 11.10), was baptised on 10 March 1741-2 at St Michael's Church, Ashton-under-Lyne.[1] He was mentioned in his father's Will made on 6 February 1784, when he was to receive five pounds and one fifth of the remainder.

11.17 Alice

Alice Worthington, the eldest surviving daughter of Ralph Worthington and Elizabeth his wife (Article 11.10), married Jonathan Whitworth on 7 February 1750-1. The wedding took place at the Collegiate Church of Manchester, the entry in the register being 'Jonathan Whitworth and Alice Worthington both of this parish'.[1] The wedding was also noted in the register of St Michael's Church, Ashton-under-Lyne. Jonathan and Alice produced at least two children:

Forename	Date of baptism	Place of baptism
Jonathan	14 March 1724-5	Collegiate Church, Manchester
Jonathan	14 December 1729	St Michael's, Ashton-under-Lyne

In the second of these, the bishop's transcript is 'Jonathan son of John Whitworth of the Town, Collier, and Alice his wife'.

The Will of Alice's father made on 6 February 1784 (given in Article 11.11) shows that Alice had died by that date. The Will included:

> ... unto my Son-in-law Jonathan Whitworth the Husband of my late Daughter Alice deceased the sum of one shilling if demanded, And I give and bequeath unto the living children of my said late daughter Alice the sum of one shilling each if demanded ...

The reason for cutting off the Whitworths with a shilling* each is not known.

11.18 Molly

Molly Worthington, a daughter of Ralph Worthington and Elizabeth his wife (Article 11.10), was mentioned in her father's Will made on 6 February 1784. She was to receive a fifth part of the remainder of his estate. She was simply described as 'Molly' his daughter, so it is not known whether she was then a spinster, married or a widow.

11.19 Betty

Betty Worthington, the fifth daughter of Ralph Worthington and Elizabeth his wife (Article 11.10), died young and was buried on 4 February 1747-8 at St Michael's Church, Ashton-under-Lyne. The entry in the register was 'Betty daughter of Ralph Worthington of Woodhouses, by Betty his wife'.[1]

11.20 Elizabeth

Elizabeth Worthington, daughter of Ralph Worthington and Elizabeth his wife (Article 11.10), must have been born in 1747-8 or later, after both Bettys had died. She was still living on 6 February 1784 when her

---

* Equivalent to three-quarters of a day of agricultural labour.

father made his Will. She was to receive one fifth of his estate after the payment of certain bequests.

11.21 Rebecca

Rebecca Worthington, probably the youngest child of Ralph Worthington and Elizabeth his wife (Article 11.10), was baptised on 14 September 1753 at St Michael's Church, Ashton-under-Lyne. The entry in the register was 'Rebecca daughter of Ralph Worthington of Woodhouses, yeoman, by Betty.'[1] Rebecca was still living on 6 February 1784 when her father wrote his Will. She was to receive one fifth of his estate after the payment of certain bequests. The Will only refers to Rebecca by her forename, so no indication is provided as to whether she was already married. However, Rebecca had already married William Barlow, clockmaker, of Ashton-under-Lyne on 9 May 1769 at St Michael's Church, Ashton-under-Lyne. The register reads 'William Barlow m. Rebecca Worthington'. Rebecca would then have been about 15 years and eight months of age, assuming that she was baptised as customary within a few days of birth. Marriage was then permitted above the age of 12 years for a girl and 14 for a boy, subject to parental consent. This was legally the case until the Marriage Act of 1929 which forbade marriage below the age of 16 years. William and Rebecca produced six children:

Forename	Date of baptism
Ann	20 February 1770
Robert	19 January 1772
Henry	16 January 1774
Sarah	8 June 1777
Elizabeth	2 January 1785
Mary	25 March 1787

All the baptisms were at St Michael's Church, Ashton-under-Lyne, and in all the parents were described as 'William Barlow Opp. clock-maker by Rebecca'.[1] 'Opp.' or 'oppidan' signifies 'of the town'.

CHAPTER 12

LINE OF DANIEL WORTHINGTON
OF AUDENSHAW

12.1 Daniel

Daniel Worthington, one of the younger sons of Ralph Worthington junior and Jane his wife (Article 1.6), was born sometime between 1617 and the late 1620s. Daniel's life has already been treated (Article 1.16). He and Alice his wife produced one son, Ralph.

SECOND GENERATION - SON OF DANIEL AND ALICE

12.2 Ralph

Ralph Worthington, the only child of Daniel Worthington and Alice his wife (Article 1.16 and 12.1), was baptised on 22 May 1670 at St Michael's Church, Ashton-under-Lyne, Lancashire. The entry in the register was 'Ralph son of Daniel Worthington de Waterhouses'.[1] On 10 July 1691, at the age of 21 years, Ralph married Esther Oldham at St Michael's Church, the entry in the register being 'Ralph Worthington and Esther Oldham, Stopford pish'. There is no parish of Stopford or Stopforth, but J.D. Skepper has expressed the view that Stockport in Cheshire was intended. Stockport lies about four miles south of Audenshaw, Lancashire. Ralph and Esther produced 10 children:

Forename	Date of birth	Date of baptism	Date of burial	Article
Daniel			11 December 1714	12.3
Alice				12.4
Esther		9 February 1695-6	5 August 1696	12.5
Ralph	25 June 1697	4 July 1697		12.6
Thomas	29 June 1700	7 July 1700	27 February 1700-1	12.7
John	28 December 1701	6 January 1701-2		12.8
Esther	26 September 1704	8 October 1704		12.9
Thomas	21 December 1708	10 January 1708-9		12.10
Samuel	7 June 1711	26 June 1711	28 May 1719	12.11
Mary	6 May 1713	6 May 1713		12.12

All the baptisms were recorded at the Old Presbyterian Chapel at Dukinfield, Cheshire.[2] Some were also recorded at St Michael's Church, Ashton-under-Lyne. The chapel recorded the dates of birth of the seven youngest children, and in the case of Mary even recorded 'between 12 at night and one'. The burials of those who died young were at St Michael's Church. Esther the mother died when her youngest child was only 22 months of age; she was buried on 8 March 1714-5

PEDIGREE 12 – LINE OF DANIEL WORTHINGTON OF AUDENSHAW, LANCASHIRE

Daniel Worthington; m. 1669, d. 1708-9. *(Pedigree 1 & Arts 1.16 & 12.1)* ╤ **Alice**, dau. of Richard Jones; bap. 1644-5, d. 1709

Esther Oldham; ╪ **Ralph Worthington**; b. 1670, m.(1) 1691, m(2) ╪ **Elizabeth**, dau. of Peter Walker; bap. 1674,
d. 1714-5   1719-20, d. 1745. *(Art. 12.2)*   m(1) 1699 John Harrop & had issue, d. 1742

Daniel Worthington; d. 1714. *(Art. 12.3)*

Alice; m. 1717 John Heyward & had issue. *(Art. 12.4)*

Esther; bap. 1695-6, d. 1696. *(Art. 12.5)*

Ralph Worthington; b. 1697, m. 1720, d. 1767. *(Art. 12.6)* ╤ **Alice**, dau. & heiress of William Brewerton; d. 1785

Thomas Worthington; b. 1700, d. 1700-1 *(Art. 12.7)*

John Worthington; b. 1701, living 1744. *(Art. 12.8)*

Esther; b. 1704. *(Art. 12.9)*

Thomas Worthington; b. 1708, living 1744. *(Art. 12.10)*

Samuel Worthington; b. 1711, d. 1719. *(Art. 12.11)*

Mary; b. 1713, m. 1734 Joseph Walker, living 1774 *(Art. 12.12)*

Esther; bap. 1722-3, d. before 1743 un-m. *(Art. 12.13)*

Daniel Worthington; bap. 1724, living 1766. *(Art. 12.14)*

William Worthington; living 1766. *(Art. 12.15)*

Ralph Worthington; living 1766. *(Art. 12.16)*

Hannah; bap. 1735, m. John Byrom, living 1766. *(Art. 12.17)*

Alice; m. 1756 John Barlow, living 1766. *(Art. 12.18)*

John Worthington; living 1766. *(Art. 12.19)*

Esther; bap. 1742-3, d. 1745. *(Art. 12.20)*

George Worthington; b. 1746, m. 1778, d. 1828. *(Art. 12.21)* ╤ **Bridget**, dau. & co-heiress of James Warren; living 1824

Anne; m. 1804 Joshua Taylor, living 1824. *(Art. 12.22)*   **Alice**; m. 1807 William Bowland, living 1824. *(Art. 12.23)*

319

at St Michael's Church. The entry in the register was 'Esther wife of Ralph Worthington of Audenshaw'.

After being a widower for nearly five years Ralph married Elizabeth, daughter of Peter Walker of Milne. She was then aged 45 years, having been baptised on 12 April 1674 at St Michael's Church, Ashton-under-Lyne. She had previously married John Harrop on 9 November 1699 at St Michael's Church.[1] John died in 1719 having made his Will on 24 May of that year. In his Will he was described as yeoman of Ashton-under-Lyne. He held his property by a three-lives' lease from George, Earl of Warrington. From this Will and the inventory of his goods and chattels taken on 12 June 1719 it appears that he was a woollen weaver. The tools of his trade included a lead dye vat, 'loomes, combes, wheels, creels and wayes and weights'. John also had a shop in the same property, in which the main merchandise was woollen cloth valued at £18 0s. 6d., but there was also, 'blankiting, fladen', a caddow, serges, silk, and 'linnen cloath whitt and blew'. He also had three cows. £810 17s. 5d.[*] – a high proportion of his assets – was in the form of debts owing to him. Ralph and Elizabeth's wedding took place on 25 February 1719-20 at Gorton parish church, the entry in the register being 'Ralph Worthington and Elizabeth Harrop both of Eshton parish'[1] They did not produce any children, but Elizabeth already had, by her earlier marriage, five children, namely John Harrop junior, Mary, Elizabeth, Margaret and Catherine.

Ralph had succeeded to his father's farm in Audenshaw in 1708-9, having been living there with his parents sometime previously (Article 1.16). 'Elizabeth wife of Ralph Worthington of Audenshaw' was buried on 26 November 1742 at St Michael's Church, Ashton-under-Lyne, and Ralph was buried there two years later on 23 April 1745. In his Will made on 16 September 1744 he was described as yeoman. His son and heir Ralph Worthington was to repay £40 to the executors.[3] The residue of his personal estate was to be divided among his four children, Ralph, Thomas, John and Mary and his two grandchildren John and Daniel Heyward (Articles 12.6, 12.10, 12.8, 12.12 and 12.4 respectively). His stepson John Harrop was one of the executors: he was described as 'shopkeeper' and had probably discontinued his father's weaving business.

THIRD GENERATION – FAMILY OF RALPH AND ESTHER

12.3 Daniel

Daniel Worthington, the eldest son of Ralph Worthington (Article 12.2) by Esther his first wife, was probably born about 1692. His baptism has not been traced, but his parents married in 1691 and his younger brother, Ralph (Article 12.6) was baptised in 1697. He was mentioned in the Will of his grandfather, Daniel Worthington, which was made

---

[*] Equivalent to 16,200 man-days of agricultural labour.

in 1702-3 (Articles 1.16 and 12.1). Assuming he was born about 1692, he died aged about 22 years, and was buried on 11 December 1714 at St Michael's Church, Ashton-under-Lyne.[1] The entry in the register was 'Daniel son of Ralph Worthington of Audenshaw'.

12.4 Alice

Alice Worthington, the eldest daughter of Ralph Worthington (Article 12.2) by Esther his first wife, was probably born about 1694. She was mentioned in the Will of her grandfather, Daniel Worthington (Articles 1.16 and 12.1), made in 1702-3. She married 'John Heawood' on 24 April 1717 at the Collegiate Church of Manchester and they produced two sons:[1]

Forename	Date known to be living
John	16 September 1744
Daniel	16 September 1744

Both are mentioned in the Will of their grandfather, Ralph Worthington senior, made on 16 September 1744, the surname then being spelt 'Heyward'. Their mother Alice was not mentioned, so the implication is that she had died by that date. It has not yet proved possible to locate this family, partly because 'John Heyward' or 'John Haywood' was a common name in south Lancashire at the time. For example, there were three baptisms at St Michael's Church, Ashton-under-Lyne which could fit the year 1719 – John son of John Heyward of Edenshaw, John son of John Heward taylor of Oppenshaw, and Dan son of Jn Hewart of Hartshead. There was also a John son of John Heywood and Alice of Prestwich or Cobishaw baptised on 10 September 1730.

12.5 Esther

Esther Worthington, a daughter of Ralph Worthington (Article 12.2) by Esther his first wife, was baptised on 9 February 1695-6 at the Old Presbyterian Chapel at Dukinfield, Cheshire. She was buried on 5 August 1696 at St Michael's Church, Ashton-under-Lyne, the entry in the register being 'Esther daughter of Ralph Worthington'.[1]

12.6 Ralph

Ralph Worthington, the second son of Ralph Worthington senior (Article 12.2) by Esther his first wife, was born on 25 June 1697 and baptised on 4 July 1697 at St Michael's Church, Ashton-under-Lyne, the entry in the register being 'Ralph son of Ralph Worthington of Audenshaw'.[1]

As a younger son, Ralph grew up believing that he would have to leave the farm and develop a career of his own. He chose to train as a blacksmith and in due course set up in business as such. He is described as 'Blacksmith' at the baptism of his eldest son, Daniel, in 1724 when Ralph was aged 27 years. However, 10 years earlier his elder brother Daniel (Article 12.3) had died, leaving Ralph as the surviving heir.

Ralph married Alice, daughter of William Brewerton (or Brearton) on 11 October 1720. Although the marriage was by licence at St Chad's Church, Rochdale, both parties were described as 'of Ashton Parish'.[1] It is clear from the Will of William made on 4 May 1751 and proved on 16 May 1751 that Alice was his sole heiress.[3] In the Will, William is described as 'William Brearton of Audenshaw ..., yeoman'. He held lands of fee in Levenshulme, which lies about three miles south-west of Audenshaw. The lands were let out to the occupier – Aaron Blackshaw. William placed these lands in trust, to be passed absolutely to his grandson George Worthington on attaining the age of 21 years. William also bequeathed £100[*] to each of his granddaughters, Hannah Worthington and Alice Worthington, and the residue of the estate to his grandson, John Worthington. If George died without issue before reaching the age of 21 years, the Levenshulme estate was to pass in equal parts to Ralph's children – Daniel, William, Ralph, Hannah, Alice and John. It is noteworthy that William should have singled out Ralph's youngest son, George, to inherit the Levenshulme lands. It is also noteworthy that John, the next youngest son, was probably treated more favourably than his elder brothers by receiving the remainder. William appointed his son-in-law Ralph Worthington and his grandson, William Worthington, as executors and trustees. The family of Ralph and Alice can now be given. They produced five sons and four daughters over a 23-year period:

Forename	Date of baptism	Date of burial	Article
Esther	24 March 1722-3	Before 1743	12.13
Daniel	10 December 1724		12.14
William			12.15
Ralph			12.16
Hannah	27 April 1735		12.17
Alice			12.18
John			12.19
Esther	27 January 1742-3	25 August 1745	12.20
George	26 October 1746		12.21

The five baptisms and two burials recorded were at St Michael's Church, Ashton-under-Lyne.

Ralph the father died in 1767. He had made a Will on 20 May 1766 which was proved at Chester on 2 February 1767-8.[3] The Will is unusual in that it gives a picture of his buildings, although much of the real estate was to pass to his eldest son. He referred to:

(a) 'my Messuage or Tenement ... in Audenshaw' which were to be sold;

(b) 'the House in which we now live in, the shippen and the Bay adjoining the east end of the Barn, and the likewise Bay adjoining the west end of the said Barn within half a yard of the barn door, the Turf

---

[*] Equivalent to 2,000 man-days of agricultural labour.

house' which were for the use of his wife for life or until she should remarry, thereafter passing to Daniel and his heirs;

(c) 'the further Dow-croft, the How meadow, the Barn croft, the Little Intack and the Old Garden together with the Ancient-roads to all the said Inclosures' were also left to his wife for life or until re-marriage, thereafter passing to Daniel and his heirs;

(d) 'All the rest ... of my Messuage and Tenement in Audenshaw' was left to his son Daniel Worthington (Article 12.14) and his heirs;

(e) 'that Land and Housing which is mine at the Cold-house in Manchester' was left to his son John Worthington and his heirs;

(f) 'the Messuage and Tenement ... in Gorton', which he had lately purchased from John Robinson of Manchester, to be sold ...

Ralph was also in the process of buying a property in Ashton-under-Lyne; he had paid 'Money down upon a Tenement' there. It appears that the value of the property in (d) above was three times the combined value of (b) and (c) which were for Alice's use, since Alice was to pay a fourth part of the annual rent due to the lord of the manor. All Ralph's household goods, cattle and fodder were to pass to Alice for life and then to be equally divided among all his children. Daniel was to inherit the 'Carts, Wheels and Harrows'. The cash residue of Ralph's estate was then to be divided by unequal allocations between his wife and children. However, there was an interesting and unusual provision concerning the bequests to his two married daughters, Hannah and Alice, to prevent the money being retained by their respective husbands under the law then prevailing. The money would only pass to the husbands if they first entered into bonds to settle it on their wives and children. Furthermore, if a wife produced no child, then her money was to return to Ralph's executors on the wife's decease. Ralph's executors were to be his second son William Worthington of Openshaw and George Fletcher of Audenshaw.

Alice lived as a widow for 17 years. She was buried on 25 August 1785 at St Michael's Church, Ashton-under-Lyne.

12.7 Thomas

Thomas Worthington, the third son of Ralph Worthington senior (Article 12.2) by Esther his first wife, was born on 29 June 1700 and baptised on 7 July 1700 at the old Presbyterian Chapel at Dukinfield, Cheshire.[2] He died young and was buried on 27 February 1700-1 at St Michael's Church, Ashton-under-Lyne.[1] The entry in the church register was 'Thomas child of Ralph Worthington Audenshaw, husbandman'.

12.8 John

John Worthington, the fourth son of Ralph Worthington senior (Article 12.2) by Esther his first wife, was born on 28 December 1701 and baptised on 6 January 1701-2 at St Michael's Church, Ashton-under-Lyne.[1] He was described as 'John son of Ralph Worthington husbandman'. He was mentioned in the Will of his grandfather, Daniel Worthington, made in 1702-3 when John was only a year old (Article 1.16). By the Will of John's father, Ralph Worthington senior (Article 12.6), John was to receive 'that Land and Housing … at the Cold house in Manchester'. Nothing more is known of John's life.

12.9 Esther
Esther Worthington, the third – or second surviving – daughter of Ralph Worthington senior (article 12.2) by Esther his wife, was born on 26 September 1704 and baptised on 8 October 1704 at St Michael's Church, Ashton-under-Lyne.[1] The entry in the church register was 'Esther daughter of Ralph Worthington Agricol'. She was not mentioned in her father's Will made on 16 September 1744 and is presumed dead by that time.

12.10 Thomas
Thomas Worthington, the fifth – or fourth surviving – son of Ralph Worthington senior (Article 12.2) by Esther his wife, was baptised on 10 January 1708-9 at St Michael's Church, Ashton-under-Lyne. The entry in the register was 'Thomas son of Ralph Worthington of Audenshaw'. When Thomas was aged 35 years he was mentioned in his father's Will made on 16 September 1744. Thomas was to receive a fifth part of the residue of the personal estate of his father.

12.11 Samuel
Samuel Worthington, the sixth – or fifth surviving – son of Ralph Worthington, senior (Article 12.2) by Esther his first wife, was born on 21 December 1708 and baptised on 26 June 1711 at St Michael's Church, Ashton-under-Lyne.[1] The entry in the register was 'Samuel son of Ralph Worthington of Audenshaw'. Samuel lived for seven years and was buried on 28 May 1719 at the same church. The entry in the register was 'Samuel son of Ralph Worthington of Odenshaw'. The place 'Odenshaw' could be read as Audenshaw or Openshaw, but there is no doubt that Audenshaw was intended. Openshaw lay in the parish of Manchester and was too-distant from St Michael's Church.

12.12 Mary
Mary Worthington, the fourth – but third surviving – daughter of Ralph Worthington senior (Article 12.2) by Esther his first wife, was born and baptised on 6 May 1713 at St Michael's Church, Ashton-under-Lyne.[1] The entry in the register was 'Mary daughter of Ralph Worthington of Audenshaw (born 6 May)'. Perhaps Mary's parents had her baptised so quickly because they feared for her life. Perhaps that was also the reason for the entry made at the Presbyterian Chapel at Dukinfield quoting the hour of Mary's birth. At the age of 21 years, on 16 September 1734, she

married 'Joseph Walker, Manchester' at St Michael's Church, Ashton-under-Lyne.

FOURTH GENERATION – FAMILY OF RALPH AND ALICE

12.13 Esther
Esther Worthington, the eldest daughter of Ralph Worthington and Alice his wife (Article 12.6), was baptised on 24 March 1722-3 at St Michael's Church, Ashton-under-Lyne.[1] The entry in the register was 'Esther daughter of Ralph Worthington and Alice'. Esther died before 1743; that is known because Ralph and Alice gave the same name to another child baptised on 27 February 1742-3 (Article 12.20).

12.14 Daniel
Daniel Worthington, the eldest son of Ralph Worthington and Alice his wife (Article 12.6), was baptised on 10 December 1724 at St Michael's Church, Ashton-under-Lyne.[1] The entry in the register was 'Daniel son of Ralph Worthington junior of Audenshaw, blacksmith, by his wife Alice'. Daniel had great opportunity; he was the son and heir of Ralph, who now had a blacksmith's business as well as a farm. Also, his mother was heiress of William Brewerton who held substantial properties. But it is not clear how Daniel fared. William, in his Will dated 4 May 1751, treated Alice's youngest son, George, as his favourite. The lease of Ralph's farm was due to expire after Ralph's death, as he was the last holder of a three-lives' lease. In his Will dated 20 May 1766 Ralph Worthington appears worried as to whether Daniel would or could renew the lease. Ralph wrote:

> … And after the death of my said Wife or her Marriage, which shall first happen, I give and devise the before mentioned Premises to my Eldest Son Daniel Worthington and his Heirs … All the rest, residue and remainder of my Messuage and Tenement in Audenshaw Aforesaid … I Also give and devise unto my said son Daniel Worthington and his Heirs, he first paying before he enters the said Premises into the Hands of my Executors hereafter named One Hundred and ten Pounds.* And also shall pay or give proper security for the payment of the Sum of Ninety Pounds, together with what Interest may be then due for the same, unto Mr James Grimshaw of Audenshaw aforesaid or his Heirs Executors or Administrators or which soever of them may be then in power, for the payment of which said sum of ninety pounds, with the Interest as Aforesaid, I have made an assignment of part of my tenement in Audenshaw aforesaid, unto the said Mr James Grimshaw. But if my said son Daniel refuses or neglects to pay the said sum of One hundred and ten Pounds, and Likewise to pay or secure to pay the Sum of Ninety pounds as Aforesaid and both or either of the said Sums be unpaid at the Time fixed for his Entering upon the said Premises which shall be on the twelfth day of May next after my decease. Then my Will

---

* Equivalent to 1,900 man-days of agricultural labour.

and mind is and I hereby Order and Authorise my Executors hereafter mentioned to keep possession of that part of my said Messuage and Tenement which I have hereby given and devised unto my said Son Daniel ... And I order and Authorise my Executors herinafter named to renew the Lease with the then Lord or Lady of the Manor and out of the New Lease to give proper security for paying the said Sum of Ninety Pounds with the Interest as Aforesaid together with the money required for renewing the Lease, and the Rents, Issues and profits thereof from time to time to take and receive until they have raised the Aforesaid Sum ... I give and devise the Reversion of the Aforesaid Messuage and Tenement unto my said son Daniel Worthington ...

While the instructions to Ralph's executors are clear, the reasons for the complexities are not. Why had plans for the renewal of the lease not already been made and why was there some difficulty in finding the money for renewal? Ralph was really keen that Daniel should succeed, but was worried that he would not. No details of what happened have come to light, but equally there is no evidence that the farm remained in the family. Ralph's executors were his second son, William Worthington of Openshaw and George Fletcher of Audenshaw.

12.15 William
William Worthington, the second son of Ralph Worthington and Alice his wife (Article 12.6), was entrusted at the age of about 25 years with the responsibility of being a joint executor and trustee of the Will of his grandfather William Brewerton (Article 12.6). He was also a trustee of his father's Will made on 20 May 1766. William was described as 'of Openshaw', a township lying adjacent to the west side of Audenshaw.

    A marriage of William has not yet been found, but 'Jane daughter of William Worthington of Openshaw' who was baptised on 19 July 1760 at St Michael's Church, Ashton-under-Lyne, may be connected.[1]

12.16 Ralph
Ralph Worthington was the third son of Ralph Worthington and Alice his wife (Article 12.6). The international genealogical index of baptisms shows a 'Ralph son of Ralph Worthington' baptised on 1 February 1734-5 at Winwick which lies 20 miles west of Audenshaw. However, the original registers of Winwick do not show the baptism. It is possible that the date of baptism is correct but that the wrong parish has been stated.

    By the Will of his father, dated 20 May 1766, Ralph was to receive a bequest of £80* plus a fifth part of the remainder.[3]

12.17 Hannah
Hannah Worthington, the second daughter of Ralph Worthington and Alice his wife (Article 12.6), was baptised on 27 April 1735 at St Michael's

---

* Equivalent to 680 man-days of agricultural labour.

Church, Ashton-under-Lyne.[1] She inherited £100 from her grandfather, William Brewerton (Article 12.6), and £40 from her father. Her father's Will dated 25 May 1766 shows that Hannah's husband was John Byrom.

12.18 Alice

Alice Worthington, the third daughter of Ralph Worthington and Alice his wife (Article 12.6), married John Barlow on 11 October 1756 at St Michael's Church, Ashton-under-Lyne. She would then have been a minor, aged perhaps 19 or 20 years. She inherited £100 from her grandfather, William Brewerton (Article 12.6), and £30 from her father. Her father's Will dated 25 May 1766 mentions John her husband.

12.19 John

John Worthington, the fourth son of Ralph Worthington and Alice his wife (Article 12.6), was mentioned in the Will of his father made on 20 May 1766. He was to inherit 'all that Land and Housing which is mine at the Cold-house in Manchester', subject to John first paying £25 to Ralph's executors. He was also bequeathed £40 and a fifth part of the residue.

12.20 Esther

Esther Worthington, the fourth daughter of Ralph Worthington and Alice his wife (Article 12.6), was baptised on 27 February 1742-3 at St Michael's Church, Ashton-under-Lyne.[1] She is not mentioned in the Will of her father made in 1776 nor that of her grandfather, William Brewerton, made in 1751, so she is likely to have died young. There is a record of a burial on 25 August 1745 which reads 'Esther daughter of Ralph Worthington of Audenshaw'. That description could have fitted Esther's aunt Esther, who was baptised in 1702 (Article 12.9). However, Aunt Esther's father had died four months previously and it would have been more accurate to describe her father as deceased, especially as her brother Ralph was then head of the family. It therefore seems likely that the Esther treated in this article died at the age of two years.

12.21 George

George Worthington, the fifth son and youngest child of Ralph Worthington and Alice his wife (Article 12.6), was baptised on 26 October 1746 at St Michael's Church, Ashton-under-Lyne.[1] The bishop of Lichfield's transcription of the register records 'George son of Ralph Worthington of Audenshaw, baptised by a dissenting minister'. Dissenting, or nonconformist ministers, were found in many parishes in the north-west of England during the 18th century. Some of them had been permitted and re-licensed to preach by the Declaration of Indulgence of 1672.

When George's maternal grandfather, William Brewerton (or Brearton), wrote his Will on 24 May 1751, he provided that George should inherit, on reaching the age of 21 years, the 'Lands hereditaments and premises' which William held of fee in Levenshulme.[3] He was to pay £60 to William's executors on succeeding to the property. This bequest to the youngest of William's daughter, Alice, is interesting. George was obviously being favoured, although only four years of age at the time. Perhaps the difficulty in the way of the eldest son Daniel (Article 12.4) succeeding to his father's real estate was already apparent, but then why was not the bequest to the second son? The law of primogeniture only applies to the eldest son surviving at the moment of inheritance. Thus, if the eldest abdicates or is disinherited, there is no law or custom which requires the inheritance to pass to the second son. Accordingly, the father (or mother) is then free to choose which other son should succeed.

On 20 January 1778, at the age of 32 years, George married Bridget, daughter and co-heiress of James Warren, of The Toll-Gate, Audenshaw. James's Will, made on 18 September 1790, shows that Bridget was one of four daughters of James and Mary. James, described in his Will as 'yeoman', was a property owner and victualler. He owned eight houses in Audenshaw, all with tenants. George and Bridget's wedding took place by licence at St Michael's Church, Ashton-under-Lyne. They produced two daughters, whose baptisms have not been traced:

Forename	Date of marriage	Article
Anne	29 April 1804	12.22
Alice	27 February 1807	12.23

James's Will shows that George and Bridget then lived at a house with outbuildings and garden called 'Blise Pig', on which George paid rent of £12 a year to James.[3] James held that property of the earl of Stamford and, as the lease would break with James's death, James instructed his executors to apply to the earl for renewal. Perhaps George and Bridget were already involved in the victualling business run from Blise Pig; under the terms of the Will, if George and Bridget '… decline the Business of a Victualler or otherwise quit and remove from out the same messuage or dwelling house and premises …', the house was to be let for the highest rent.

George followed in the footsteps of his father-in-law by investing in and owning property. When he made his Will on 11 October 1823, he held:

a) an estate called Hilton's in Audenshaw then occupied by James Moss;

b) 15 cottages near Hugh's Smithy in Audenshaw;

c) chief rents arising from land and buildings in Audenshaw and seven properties under tenancy;

d) three cottages and a field in Back Lane, Audenshaw;

e) Carrington Farm in Audenshaw, the house being the home of George and Bridget, but the land being let to James Moss;

f) the estate in Levenshulme which he had inherited from William Brewerton;

g) various mortgage loans made to others to enable them to acquire property.

Only four months later, when he made a codicil to his Will, he had built two dwelling houses at Park Parade in Ashton-under-Lyne. They were on land he leased for three lives from George Henry Gray, 6th earl of Stamford, 2nd earl of Warrington and lord-lieutenant of Cheshire. His earldom of Warrington was by the second creation of 1796, his father's mother having been sole heiress of the second and last earl by the original creation (Article 1.21). George Worthington appointed as his executors and trustees Bridget, Nathaniel Howard of Ashton-under-Lyne, cotton spinner, and Daniel Howarth of Audenshaw, shopkeeper.

George died in 1828 at the age of 82 years. He was styled 'gentleman' in his Will made on 11 October 1823 with a codicil made on 14 February 1824.[3] All his assets, real and personal, were to be placed in trust, mostly to provide income for his two daughters and for the maintenance and education of their children. Bridget, still living in 1824, was to receive all the income from the mortgage loans – but only so long as she did not remarry. On the deaths of Bridget and the two daughters, the assets were to pass to the grandchildren.

FIFTH GENERATION – DAUGHTERS OF GEORGE AND BRIDGET

12.22 Anne
Anne Worthington was the elder daughter and co-heiress of George Worthington and Bridget his wife (Article 12.21). On 29 April 1804 she married Joshua Taylor at St Michael's Church, Ashton-under-Lyne.[1] In 1824 they were living in one of the two new houses in Park Parade, Ashton-under-Lyne, as tenants of her father, George. It is not yet clear whether Anne and Joshua had children, but there is a burial of 'Alice daughter of Joshua Taylor oppid' on 27 February 1812 at St Michael's Church, Ashton-under-Lyne.

When her father, George, died in 1828, Anne became the life tenant of part of his estate, namely, the Hilton's, the 15 cottages near Hugh's Smithy, various chief rents and three cottages and a field in Back Lane, all in Audenshaw (Items (a) to (d) in Article 12.21). She was to enjoy the profits for life, but when she died the properties were to pass to her children equally. Failing such children, the properties were to pass to the children of her sister, Alice.

12.23 Alice
Alice Worthington was the younger daughter and co-heiress of George Worthington and Bridget his wife (Article 12.21). On 27 February 1807 she married William Bowland (or Bowler) at the Collegiate Church of Manchester.[1] The entry in the register was 'William Bowland of

Southworth, yeoman, and Alice Worthington, spinster of Audenshaw'. The spelling 'Bowland' in the register compares with 'Bowler' in George Worthington's Will. George's codicil dated 14 February 1824 shows that Alice and William were then living at Stockport, Cheshire, having moved recently from Ashton-under-Lyne. A search for baptisms of any children of theirs has not proved successful. The entry 'John son of William Bowler and Alice of Adswood, Hatter' in the register of baptisms at St Michael's Church, Ashton-under-Lyne, on 19 September 1824, may not be relevant. The event occurred 17 years after their wedding and 10 months after they were known to be living in Stockport.

When her father George died in 1828, Alice became the life tenant of part of his estate, namely Carrington Farm and the estate in Levenshulme (Items (e) and (f) in Article 12.21). She was to enjoy the profits for life, but when she died the properties were to pass to her children equally. Failing such children, the properties were to pass to the children of her sister Anne. George's Will specifically provided that the profits of his various properties should be for the benefits and uses of his daughters and for the maintenance and education of their children. The profits were not to be treated as part of the incomes of their respective husbands. Presumably the properties remained in trust to safeguard these provisions and to ensure that, if one of the daughters died childless, her share would transfer to the other daughter and her children rather than to a surviving husband. George made a special provision that his daughters should not be allowed to mortgage the properties, or encumber them in any way.

CHAPTER 13

PROBABLE CONNECTIONS

13.1 The Worthingtons of Oldham

Oldham is three miles north-east of Failsworth. Thus, a Worthington family living in Oldham in the late 18th and early 19th centuries may be related to the Worthingtons of Failsworth. Further research is required, but the information currently available is summarised here.

Nathan Worthington of Oldham, shown in the second generation of the following pedigree, may have been baptised on 23 June 1754 at the Collegiate College, Manchester, as 'Nathaniel son of Nathaniel Worthington'. If so, he had an elder brother and an elder sister as shown by baptismal records. 'John son of Nathaniel Worthington and Sarah' was baptised on 14 February 1747-8 at Holy Trinity Church, Salford, and 'Ann daughter of Nathaniel Worthington and Sarah' was baptised on 9 February 1752 at the Collegiate Church.

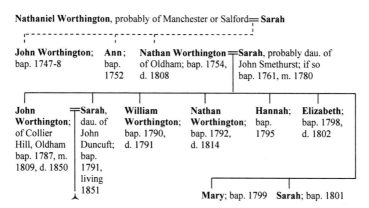

The wife of Nathan (the younger) was also called Sarah and it is likely that she was 'Sally daughter of John Smethurst in Oldham, throwster, by Nancy his wife' baptised on 15 February 1761 at St Mary's Church, Oldham. John's occupation as a throwster could be relevant because Nathan and Sarah's eldest son became a cotton manufacturer. This Sally married on 27 January 1780 at St Michael's Church, Ashton-under-Lyme, the entry in the register being 'Nathan Worthington of this parish & Sally Smethurst of this same parish'.[1]

Nathan Worthington of Oldham and Sarah his wife produced seven children, all of whom were baptised at St Peter's Church, Oldham:

Forename	Date of baptism	Date of burial
John	19 October 1787	
William	23 June 1790	29 May 1791
Nathan	11 December 1792	
Hannah	2 October 1795	
Elizabeth	1 February 1798	14 April 1802
Mary	18 July 1799	
Sarah	3 September 1801	

At the first baptism Nathan was described as 'weaver', at four others as 'mercer' and at the remaining two as 'shopkeeper'. His Will, made on 27 February 1808 and proved on 24 October 1808 at Chester, shows that he occupied a 'dwellinghouse, shop and premises' in Oldham where he conducted business as a draper.[2] At the time of his death his children ranged in age between six and 20 years, so he placed the business in the hands of his trustees, Joseph Rowland of Oldham, cotton manufacturer, and Edward Halkyard, surgeon. Referring to his wife, he directed that:

> ... my said Trustees do and shall permit and suffer her to ... carry on the Business of Draper for so long time as they in their Discretion shall think proper for and towards the maintenance, Education and support of herself and my said Children...

The family did retain the business.

John Worthington the eldest son married on 14 December 1809 Sarah, daughter of John Duncuft of Hathershaw, near Oldham, and Ann his wife (born Hilton). The Will of John Duncuft made on 26 May 1826 and proved on 13 February 1829 described him as yeoman. He was a farmer of 'Collier Hill or Whitehouse in the township of Oldham'. However, he also had interests in coalmines at Broadway Lane, Oldham. As a partner in 'The Werneth Coal Company' he also worked several other mines in the township of Oldham. Sarah was not an heiress, since John Duncuft had a son James who had two daughters, but James pre-deceased John, leaving John without an heir male. The wedding of John Worthington and Sarah took place at St Mary's Church, Oldham. John was then 22 years of age while Sarah was 18, having been baptised on 3 April 1791 at St Mary's Church. They lived at Collier Hill, Oldham, on the south side of the town and produced three sons, the eldest of whom became a justice of the peace and a deputy lieutenant for the county.[3] John died aged 62 years on 20 March 1850 and was buried five days later at St Peter's Church, Oldham. In his Will, proved on 20 April 1850 at Chester, he is described as 'gentleman of Collier Hill'. He still held his parents' old 'dwelling house, shop and stables' at Cheapside, Oldham, but they were then let out. He also held 'freehold and leasehold messuages or dwelling houses, buildings, land and tenements' in Oldham, dwelling houses in Werneth and mineral rights in Chadderton.

13.2 The Worthingtons of Newton

A 17th-century family of Worthingtons was living in the township of Newton, which lies adjacent to the south-west border of Failsworth. The earliest known reference to the family is the marriage of 'George Worthington – Martha Hyde' on 6 September 1640 at the Collegiate Church of Manchester.[1] P.W.L. Adams held the view that this George was a

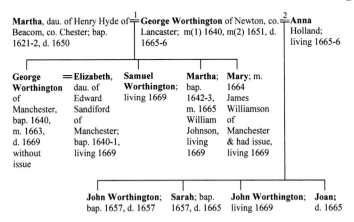

younger son of Ralph Worthington of Failsworth.[4] The evidence in favour of this connection has already been discussed (Article 1.2). Whilst being likely, the connection cannot be regarded as proved.

Martha had been baptised on 6 January 1621-2 at St Mary's Church, Stockport, Cheshire, thus being 18 years of age at the time of her marriage.[1] She was the second daughter of Henry Hyde, yeoman, and Elizabeth his wife of Beacom, Cheshire. Henry had died two years before Martha's marriage. His Will, made on 20 February 1638-9, and the inventory of his goods taken later the same year, show that he was a farmer with a messuage, tenements and lands in 'Becom and Wernith', Cheshire, and another messuage at Beacom Houses.[2] Werneth is on the outskirts of Stockport, to the south-east; Beacom and Beacom Houses are adjacent to Werneth further south-east. George and Martha produced four children:

Forename	Date of baptism	Date of marriage
George	25 December 1640	11 June 1663
Samuel		
Martha	15 January 1642-3	About 12 September 1665
Mary		27 December 1664

The baptisms of George and Martha junior took place at the Collegiate Church of Manchester.

Both George and Martha senior were included in the protestation roll of 1641 taken at the chapel of Newton Heath. This roll included 12 Worthingtons, the other ten being Anne, James junior, Margaret, Margaret, Nicholas, Thomas, Thomas, Thomas junior, William and William.[5] Some of these names are recognisably those of the Worthingtons of Failsworth (Chapter 1).

Martha senior died in 1650 and was buried on 25 October at the Collegiate Church, the entry in the register being 'Martha wife to George Worthington of Newton'. About 14 months later, on 11 December 1651, George married Ann (or Anna) Holland, at the Collegiate Church. They produced four children the first two of whom were twins:

Forename	Date of baptism	Date of burial
John	September 1657	September 1657
Sarah	September 1657	23 October 1665
John		
Joan		26 July 1665

The twins were baptised at the Newton chapel, the entry in the register being 'John & Sarah children of George Worthington'.

When George senior made his Will on 12 February 1665-6, he was described as 'yarn whiter' of Newton. At that time he had three surviving sons, namely George, Samuel and John, and two surviving daughters, namely Martha and Mary.[2] George died within 30 days of signing his Will, as shown by the inventory of his assets taken on 15 March 1665-6 and the granting of powers of administration on 19 March 1665-6. Some ten months before his death George, then described as yeoman, had entered into articles of agreement with Richard Grantome, Esquire of Manchester, in the form of an indenture. Unfortunately the agreement has not survived, but a supporting bond in £100* dated 27 April 1665 has survived.[6] In it, George bound himself, his heirs, executors and administrators to keep all the terms of the agreement. The inventory taken following George's death shows that he was still in business at the time. Much of the inventory is concerned with his debtors and creditors which were dealt with by George's 'accomptant', John Sandiforth. This John Sandiforth and George Worthington junior were joint administrators of the Will. Of the creditors, five were employees for wages, and some others were for work done. Further creditors show that George had farming interests; for example he owed money to 'Richard Martley for drying malt, Thomas Hault for leading hay and Edward Wroe for tithe corn'. One creditor was 'Doctor Smith for physicke' at £6†; another was 'Doctor Hartby for physicke at £1 4s 0d'. George also owed money to Thomas Worthington by bill, to John Heape for smithy work and to Mr Hoaton for chapel wages.

---

* Equivalent to 2,000 man-days of agricultural labour.
† Equivalent to 120 man-days of agricultural labour.

George's eldest son, George, married Elizabeth Sandiford (or Sandiforth) on 11 June 1663 by licence at the Collegiate College, Manchester.[7] She was nearly the same age as George, having been baptised on 21 February 1640-1 at the Collegiate Church, the entry in the register being 'Elizabeth daughter of Edward Soondieforth of Manchester'.[1] George died without issue aged 29 years, and was buried on 20 January 1669-70 at the Collegiate Church. His Will, dated 29 July 1669 and proved on 14 May 1670 at the Chester Consistory Court, describes him as a 'linen weaver of Manchester'.[2] He made bequests to his sisters – Martha and Mary – and his brothers – Samuel and John. The remainder was bequeathed to Elizabeth his widow. The inventory of his goods, taken on 21 February 1669-70, showed that he had three Dutch looms.

Samuel Worthington, the second son of George senior and Martha, thus succeeded as representative of the line. Samuel's marriage has not yet come to light, but twins were baptised on 3 December 1654 at the Collegiate Church, Manchester, described as 'Martha and Mary daughters of Samuel Worthington'. If this were the same Samuel, the twins would have been named after their young aunts – still spinsters. P.W.L. Adams showed him as marrying Sarah Kenyon on 5 January 1657-8, but this could not have been the case.[4] Sarah Kenyon in fact married another Samuel Worthington as shown by the register of marriages at the Collegiate Church: 'Samuel Worthington, Gorton, carpenter, son of James Worthington late of Salford ... deceased & Sarah Kenion, Droylesden, daughter of George Kenion, late of Salford, deceased.'[1]

Martha, the elder daughter of George Worthington senior by Martha his first wife, married 'William Johnson, grocier, of Manchester' – the licence bond being issued on 12 September 1665 with permission to marry at either Newton or Gorton.

Mary, the younger daughter of George Worthington senior and Martha his wife married James Williamson, painter of Manchester, on 27 December 1664 at St Mary's Church, Oldham. This James may have been the 'James son of James Williamson of W. Hall' who was baptised on 7 December 1634 at the Collegiate Church. Mary and James produced one daughter, namely:

Forename	Date known to be living
Mary	8 October 1660

Mary senior was mentioned in her father's Will dated 8 October 1660 and proved in 1670.

13.3 The Worthingtons of Manchester
Records of three generations of a Worthington family of Manchester have been preserved at the College of Arms, London.[8] One record there is a

funeral certificate of Dr John Worthington taken on 30 November 1697 by Sir Henry St George, Kt, Clarenceux King of Arms, and attested by Edward, bishop of Gloucester, Sir Paul Whichcote, Bt, Kt, and Benjamin and Jeremy Whichcote. This certificate runs to four pages of vellum. A second record is a pedigree of two generations of the family taken during the early years of the 18th century.

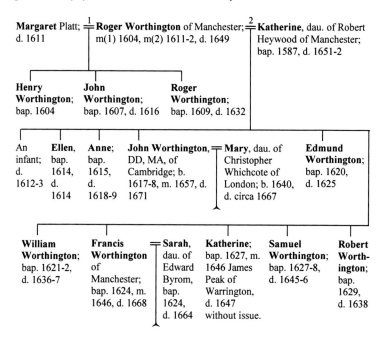

The earliest known member of this line is Roger Worthington, a woollen draper of Manchester, who in 1604 was also a reader at the Collegiate Church of Manchester. He married firstly Margaret Platt on 20 May 1604 at the Collegiate Church.[1] There are two appropriate baptisms of a Margaret Platt, both taking place at the Collegiate Church: the first was on 7 January 1579-80 – 'Margaret daughter of Robert Platt' – and the second on 12 February 1581-2 – 'Margaret daughter of George Platt'. Roger and Margaret produced three sons:

Forename	Date of baptism	Date of burial
Henry	10 July 1604	
John	6 September 1607	4 August 1616
Roger	19 November 1609	26 October 1632

All of these baptisms and burials took place at the Collegiate Church.[1] Margaret died in 1611 and was buried on 2 April 1611 at the same church. Roger married secondly Katherine daughter of Robert Heywood on 25 February 1611-2 at the Collegiate Church. Katherine was 25 years of age at the time, having been baptised on 28 October 1587 at the same church. She bore Roger ten more children:

Forename	Date of baptism	Date of burial
An infant	14 February 1612-3	
Ellen	6 May 1614	12 June 1614
Anne	29 September 1615	30 January 1618-9
John	8 February 1617-8	
Edmund	27 April 1620	16 November 1625
William	24 March 1621-2	26 February 1636-7
Francis	15 October 1624	
Katherine	21 December 1627	
Samuel	10 January 1627-8	
Robert	17 April 1629	22 April 1638

Again, all the baptisms and burials quoted were at the Collegiate Church. The certificate of the heraldic funeral of their son Dr John Worthington, kept at the College of Arms, describes Roger and Katherine as:

> ... vertuous and Religeous parents, persons of Chief Note and Esteem in the Town ... Roger Worthington extracted originally out of Worthington within the Parish of Standish in the County Palatine aforesaid; and Katherine ... from the Heywoods of Heywood in the same county ...

Roger died in 1649 and was buried on 23 August of that year at the Collegiate Church. Katherine was buried there on 19 February 1651-2.

John Worthington, the eldest son of Roger's second marriage, left home on 27 March 1632 at the age of 16 years. He '... went towards Cambridge ... and came thither on 30 March and was admitted sizar in Emmanuel College the next day'.[9] He attained his BA degree in 1636 and MA in 1639. In 1641 he was appointed a lecturer in the college for a year, and was elected a fellow as from 1642. In 1646 he attained a BD degree and was appointed university preacher. He attained the degree of doctor of divinity in 1665. He had been elected master of Jesus College, Cambridge, on 14 November 1650, a position he held for 10 years. On 13 October 1657, at the age of 39 years, he married Mary, daughter of 'Christopher Whichcote, Esquire, sometime a Spanish Merchant in London, Brother to Sr Jeremy Whichcote Bart ...'. The wedding service was conducted by Mary's uncle, the Reverend Benjamin Whichcote, DD, MA, vice-chancellor of Cambridge University, who had been one of John's tutors. John and Mary produced one son and four daughters. In November 1657 John was elected vice-chancellor of the university and held the office for one year. He then retired from the university to hold a succession of livings as parson. He held such a post in London at the time of the Great Fire in September 1666, when his church and house were burnt down.[9] Mary died within a year of the fire in August 1667. John died aged 54 years and was buried on 30 November 1671 in the chancel of St John's church, Hackney, near London. His funeral certificate includes a painting of his coat of arms: *Argent three dung forks Sable in chief a chaplet of roses proper*, impaled with the arms of Whichcote.

Francis Worthington, who from the age of 12 years was Roger's second surviving son by his second marriage, continued his father's business of woollen draper in Manchester. On 15 September 1646, aged 22 years, he married Sarah, daughter of Edward Byrom. She was then 21 years of age, having been baptised on 20 March 1624-5 at the Collegiate Church. A pedigree of the Byrom family taken by Sir William Dugdale, Norroy King of Arms, during his visitation of Lancashire in 1664 and 1665 shows that Edward Byrom was of Salford and that his wife – Sarah's mother – was Helen, daughter of Thomas Worsley of Carr, Bowden, Cheshire.[10] When Edward Byrom wrote his Will on 27 February 1654-5, he was described as 'Lynnen Draper' of Manchester.[11] He bequeathed £20* to his daughter Sarah Worthington, and appointed his son-in-law Francis Worthington an overseer. Francis and Sarah produced six children, all baptised at the Collegiate Church. Sarah was buried on 3 October 1664 and Francis on 10 September 1668, both at the Collegiate Church. In the register of burials Francis is described as 'woolendraper'. One of his sons – another Francis – continued the business.

Katherine Worthington, the youngest daughter of Roger Worthington and Katherine his second wife, married James Peak, a woollen draper of Warrington, Lancashire. The wedding took place on 31 August 1646 at St Elphin's Church, Warrington. Alas, she died the following year. He died in 1676 and was buried on 30 December 1676 at St Elphin's Church when he was described as 'Mr James Peake, woolen draper'. It appears that he had re-married and had issue.

Samuel Worthington, the third surviving son of Roger Worthington and Katherine his second wife, was educated at Manchester School. He was admitted to Emmanuel College, Cambridge, on 11 July 1644 but died in 1645-6 before achieving a degree.

13.4 Early Worthingtons near Failsworth

The earliest known reference to a Worthington in the Failsworth area – within, say, seven miles of Failsworth – is in the lay subsidy roll of 1524.[12] Under the parish of Manchester appears 'Nicholas Worthington xls xijd†'. Unfortunately, the township is not stated, and the parish at that time had 25 townships, including Failsworth and Manchester. The 1524 subsidy was levied at the rate of one-sixth of the value of moveable goods to enable King Henry VIII to settle debts left by his military campaigns in France over several years.

Rauffe Worthington of Droylsden, which is adjacent to the southern border of Failsworth, was assessed to pay 10 shillings for £20 in goods in the subsidy of 1541.[13] This was a much more lenient subsidy levied

---

* Equivalent to 400 man-days of agricultural labour.

† Equivalent to 135 man-days of agricultural labour.

at the rate of one fortieth; that of 1524 had led to deep resentment and resistance. Rauffe also contributed to the subsidy of 1543.[12] It appears that a Worthington family was settled in the township; a 'James Worthington of Droylsden in the parish of Manchester, singleman' made his Will on 19 December 1611.

A James Worthington of Gorton, three miles south of Failsworth, also contributed to the 1543 subsidy.[12] A James Worthington, labourer, of Gorton made his Will in 1576 and presumably the same James Worthington of Gorton was buried on 3 January 1576-7 at the Collegiate Church of Manchester. A Thomas Worthington of Gorton had made a Will on 25 March 1572 which was proved at Chester on 22 January 1576-7.[2] A Samuel Worthington, yeoman of Gorton, appears as an executor in the Will of Robert Kenion, whitster of Gorton, made on 16 August 1690.

Edward Worthington is mentioned as a 'Chorister of the College of Manchester', in 1547-8.[14]

It appears that there was also a family of Worthingtons in the township of Middleton, six miles north-west of Failsworth. William Worthington and Anne Neuton married at the parish church there on 28 April 1559. Also an Adam Worthington contributed to the subsidy of 1563 under 'Mediltoun'. He was assessed to pay five shillings* for goods valued at £3*.[12]

No other Worthington references prior to 1570, within seven miles of Failsworth, have yet come to light. From 1570 onwards references become much more frequent.

13.5 The Worthingtons of Crawshaw

The Worthingtons of Crawshaw held the Crawshaw estate in the southern parts of the township of Adlington, Lancashire, from 1433 to 1770. The line is probably more ancient than 1433, as a 'William de Worthington of Crawshaw' was living in 1401, and the family may previously have sprung as a cadet line of the Worthingtons of Worthington. Crawshaw Hall, where they lived, lies less than a mile north-east of Worthington Hall. The history of this armigerous family is treated in *The Worthington Families of Medieval England*.[15]

When Alexander Leyver (or Lever) of Chamber in the township of Oldham made his Will on 20 April 1539, he referred to covenants he had made with Christopher Worthington of Crawshaw concerning the marriage of Christopher's son and heir Laurence Worthington with Joan the daughter of Alexander.[15] This was probably a childhood betrothal because the son and heir of Laurence and Joan was not baptised until the 15 November 1562, 23 years after the betrothal. Chamber Hall lay 22 miles east-south-east of Crawshaw Hall, but less than a mile from the border of the township of Failsworth. The geography of this marriage would have presented a strange coincidence if there were

---

* Equivalent to 11 and 129 man-days of agricultural labour respectively.

not some family link between the Worthingtons of Crawshaw and the Worthingtons who had already settled in the Failsworth area (Article 13.3). A conjectural scenario of the situation could be that the father or grandfather of Thomas Worthington of Failsworth (Article 1.1) was a younger brother of Christopher Worthington of Crawshaw. Such a relationship could have led to occasional visits both ways between Crawshaw and Failsworth – a four-hour ride – and thus provided an opportunity for the betrothal.

MONEY VALUES

The following table gives the movements in purchasing power of the £ sterling from 1250 to 2000. The figures for agricultural labour, wheat, and cattle in the earlier centuries have been deduced from data given in *A History of Agricultural Prices in England*, by J.E.T. Rogers (1866). See also *Economic History Of England*, by H.O. Merideth, 4th Edition (1939), Page 415. Gold prices were stationary from 1700 to 1900 as the gold standard was in force. The figures for agricultural labour at decade intervals during the 20th century are from *A Hundred Years of British Food and Farming*, by H.F. Marks (1989).

Purchasing power of £1

Year	Agricultural Labour (days work)	Wheat (kilograms)	Live cattle (kilograms)	Gold (fine ounces)
1250	300	910	1,300	1.11
1300	240	760	1,100	0.91
1350	140	660	970	0.67
1400	90	560	900	0.62
1450	70	560	900	0.56
1500	60	560	860	0.50
1550	48	300	420	0.33
1600	27	200	160	0.33
1650	20	110	91	0.26
1700	19	110	91	0.24
1750	20	110	110	0.24
1800	11	45	51	0.24
1850	11	27	36	0.24
1900	7.8	18	29	0.24
1910	7.1			
1920	2.8			
1930	3.5			
1940	3.0			
1950	1.0	38	9.6	0.01
1960	0.53			
1970	0.28			
1980	0.059			
1990	0.049			
2000	0.03	12	0.9	0.005

In terms of agricultural labour, the rate of inflation averaged less than one per cent a year from 1250 to 1900. From 1900 to 1950 yearly inflation averaged four per cent and from 1950 to 2000 it averaged seven per cent. The rates were by no means uniform during the two halves of the 20th century; the Second World War and the period 1972 to 1982 suffered particularly high rates.

An agricultural labourer's daily wage would purchase three kilograms of wheat in 1250 and 400 kilograms in 2000 – that is 130 times as much. For beef on the hoof a day's work would buy only seven times as much in 2000 as in 1250. Mechanisation was the main cause of the extraordinary fall in the relative price of wheat.

APPENDIX B

REFERENCES

Titles of published works are quoted in italics and those of manuscripts in roman type. Where the source of the material is not delineated by a number in text it is kept in the Worthington family archives now stored at The Knoll House, Knossington, Oakham, Rutland, England. These archives include letters and other manuscripts, memoranda on discussions with people, photographic copies of documents, annual reports of companies and newspaper cuttings (some of which have been separated from their dates and names of newspaper). The archives are filed by person, each file bearing the same number as the corresponding number in this book.

Chapter 1
1. *A History of the Newton Chapelry in the Ancient Parish of Manchester*, by H.T. Crofton, Chetham Society New Series, vols 52 to 55 (1904 to 1905). Newton Court rolls, 1530 to 1596, are given in Chapter 2 of vol.53.
2. *The Genealogists' Atlas of Lancashire*, by J.P. Smith (1930), p.71.
3. The pedigree of Thomas Worthington is published in *A History of the Adams Family of North Staffordshire*, by P.W.L. Adams (1914), Table K; also *Burke's Genealogical and Heraldic History of the Landed Gentry*, edited by L.G. Prince (1952), pp.2795 and 2796.
4. Lancashire Record Office, WCW (Wills and Admons).
5. *The Story of Failsworth*, by D. Ball, 2nd edition (1987), p.16.
6. Church registers of baptisms, marriages and burials in Lancashire kept at Lancashire Record Office are available on microfilm. See also bishops' transcripts and the International Genealogical Index, sometimes known as the Mormon Index. Many of the records are published in the volumes of the Lancashire Parish Register Society.
7. The Clowes Deeds, John Rylands University Library, Manchester, 922, Numbers 4-1 to 12-3. Most of the texts are in Latin.
8. *Chadderton Chapters*, by M. Lawson (1972), pp.17 and 51.
9. Owen Manuscripts, Lancashire Record Office, MFI302, vol.41. John Owen, born in Bolton-le-Moors in 1815, devoted much of his life transcribing registers, mainly in the Manchester area.
10. *5,000 Acres of Old Ashton*, by W. Bowman (c.1950), p.241.
11. Registers of the Old Presbyterian Chapel, Dukinfield, Cheshire, are at Manchester Central Library, MFPR 294.
12. Cheshire Record Office, WS1682 (Wills and Admons).
13. Registers of Rostherne Parish Church, Cheshire Record Office, Chester, P47 and MF81.
14. Marriage licence bonds, Cheshire Record Office, EDC 8. Indexed abstracts to 1719 are in *Record Society of Lancashire and Cheshire*, vols. 53, 56, 57, 61, 65, 69, 73, 77, 82, 85, 97 and 101.

15. Stretford Court Baron Book, Lancashire Record Office; also *Chetham Society*, New Series vol. 45 (1901), pp.46 to 118.
16. Pocket books of John Collier senr and jnr 1736 to 1764, Manchester Central Reference Library, BR 928.28 and C35.
17. *The Manchester Directory for the year 1772*, by Elizabeth Raffald (1889), Manchester Central Library, microfilm.
18. *Historical Account of Dob Lane Chapel, Failsworth, and its Schools*, by A. Gordon (1904).

Chapter 2
1. Volumes of the *Lancashire Parish Register Society*.
2. Marriage licence bonds, Cheshire Record Office, EDC 8. Indexed abstracts to 1719 are in *Record Society of Lancashire and Cheshire*, vols. 53, 56, 57, 61, 65, 69, 73, 77, 82, 85, 97 and 101.
3. Lancashire Record Office, WCW (Wills and admons).
4. *History of the Parish of Rochdale*, by H. Fishwick (1889), p.6.
5. Manchester Central Library, Banns Register MFPR37.

Chapter 3
1. Church registers of baptisms, marriages and burials in Lancashire are kept at the Lancashire Record Office and are available on microfilm. See also bishops' transcripts and the International Genealogical Index. Many of the records are published in the volumes of the *Lancashire Parish Register Society*. In exceptional cases resort may be had to the Owen Manuscripts, Lancashire Record Office, Mf1/302.
2. Lancashire Record Office, WCW (Wills and Admons).
3. Marriage licence bonds, Cheshire Record Office, EDC8.
4. Lancashire Record Office, DRM5.
5. Worcestershire Record Office, 705: 413 and 414 BA 6033; proceedings of the manorial court of Bewdley.
6. Worcestershire Record Office, X850 Wribbenhall BA 8479.
7. Worcestershire Record Office, bishops' transcript of the marriage register of Ombersley.
8. Worcestershire Record Office, 008.7 BA 3585, Box 544.
9. *The Manchester Directory for the Year 1772*, by Elizabeth Raffald (1889), Manchester Central Reference Library; also *Lewis's 1788 Directory of Salford and Manchester.*
10. Manchester Central Reference Library, M/c 52 682 and 683.
11. Lancashire Record Office, DD Tr Box 22; also *Trafford Park – the First Hundred Years*, by R. Nicholls (1996).
12. *Chetham Society*, New Series, vol.45, p.151.
13. *Manchester Mercury*, 4 March 1780 and 4 February 1783; also *Chetham Society*, New Series vol.51, p.151.
14. *Visitation of England and Wales*, edited by F.A. Crisp, vol.19 (1917), p.79.
15. *The Canals of the West Midlands*, by C. Hadfield, 2nd edition (1969), pp.38 and 128; also *The Canals of North West England*, by C. Hadfield and G. Briddle.
16. *Agents of Revolution: John and Thomas Gilbert, Entrepreneurs*, by P. Lead (1989).
17. *Transactions of the Cheshire and Lancashire Antiquarian Society*, vol.71 (1961), pp.145 and 146.
18. British Waterways Archives, Gloucester, 512-94 and 342-94.
19. *Early Victorian Warehouses of Manchester Waterways*, by V.I. Tomlinson. A photograph of the warehouse is shown in *The Bridgewater Canal*, p.60.
20. Thomas Kent's General Account with His Grace the Duke of Bridgewater for the year 1791, Chetham Library, ms3, Manchester.
21. Worcestershire Record Office, X850 Stourport-on-Severn BA 8432/1-2.
22. *An Answer to the Comparative Statement Lately Circulated by the Schemers of the Intended Worcester Canal*, by A. York (1789), Worcestershire Record Office, 899 31 BA 3762/2.
23. *Stourport – Its Rise, Decline and Final Triumph*, by I.L. Wedley, Kidderminster Shuttle (1933); also *Old Stourport*, by I.L. Wedley (1912), p.60; also *The Passing of Mitton*, by

I.L. Wedley (1921).

24. 'A Plan of Stour Port and Part of the Hamlet of Lower Mitton Situate in the Parish of Kidderminster and County of Worcester', surveyed in May 1802 by James Sherriff, Waterways Museum, Gloucester; also 'Plan of Land and Buildings Belonging to the Staffordshire and Worcestershire Canal Company', surveyed 18 January 1810 by T. Smith, Worcestershire Record Office, BA 6507/4, 900.9.3.

25. Aaron York's Will was proved on 15 April 1797 at the Principal Probate Registry, Public Record Office, Prob 11/1290.

26. *The Birmingham Directory* (1777).

27. *A History of the Jukes Family of Cound, Shropshire*, by P.W.L. Adams (1927).

28. *The Life and Times of Sir Charles Hastings*, by W.H. McMenemey (1959), p.4; also *Worcester General and Commercial Directory* (1820), p.273; also Lower Mitton Poor Rate Books (1820 and 1833). Kendric Watson made a study of the geographical and medical topography of the district, published in *A Topographical Account of Stourport, Worcestershire, and its Immediate Neighbourhood*.

29. *Cambrian Travellers Guide*, by G. Nicholson, 2nd edition (1813); also *Stourport-on-Severn in Old Picture Postcards*, by T.J.S. Baylis (1983).

30. *Crosby's Complete Pocket Gazeteer of England and Wales* (1815), p.453.

31. A newspaper announcement of 5 August 1739. The name of the newspaper was not preserved.

32. Worcestershire Record Office, Palfrey Papers, b899.31 BA 3762, Parcel 11c, folio 348.

33. Boulton and Watt Collection, Birmingham Reference Library.

34. The list of 70 contributors to the town clock is kept by the Stourport-on-Severn Civic Society.

35. *British Canals: An Illustrated History* by C. Hadfield, 4th edition (1969), p.72; also 'History of Ceramics' by S.W. Fisher, *Country Life*, 22 December 1951.

36. Worcestershire Record Office, 705 413 BA 6033.

37. *Lewis's 1820 Directory*.

38. *Berrow's Worcester Journal*, 28 June 1821, 1 February 1827 and 26 June 1884; also Stourport on Severn Civic Society Newsletter, Number 13 (June 1994).

39. *A Short History of the Worthington and Jukes Families*, by P.W.L. Adams (1902), p.20.

40. *North Staffs Post and Times*, 5 September 1985.

41. *St Luke's Church Leek – A Brief History*, booklet to commemorate the 150th anniversary of the construction of the church (1998), pp.8, 18 and 20.

42. Manchester Central Reference Library, M/c 683.

43. *Bentley's History, Gazetteer, Directory and Statistics of Worcestershire*, vol.2 (1840); also *Wrighton's Annual Directory of Birmingham* (1829-30), p.122.

44. Public Record Office, Prob 11/1805 24703; also 1851 national census, Lower Mitton, p.37, Entry 156.

45. *Pigott and Co's London Provincial New Commercial Directory* (1822-3), pp. 577, 558, and 579: also 1835 edition, pp.663 and 664.

46. Worcestershire Record Office, Quarter Sessions Order Book, b118 BASP.6/13 and BA 769/1 and 2.

47. National Census of 1841, Public Record Office, 107/1197, Worcestershire, Book 4, p.25; also national census of 1851, Lower Mitton, p.37, entry 156.

48. *Littlebury's Directory and Gazeteer of Worcester and District*, third issue (1879).

49. A photograph of Moor Hill as extended is at Worcestershire Record Office, 899: 954, BA 10255/2.

50. *Archaeologia Cambrensis*, series 6, vol.1 (1901), p.14.

51. *The Cheltenham Annuairs* for 1848 onwards, by H. Davies; also national census for 1851, Cheltenham, p.772; also national census for 1861, Cheltenham, Enumeration Districts 1 and 25; also national census for 1871, Cheltenham, Enumeration District 36.

52. *The Cheltenham Examiner*, 6 April 1864, 27 May 1874, 5 April 1876, 17 May 1876, 18 July 1877, 6 June 1883 and about 1 April 1885.

53. *Plarr's Lives of Fellows*, p.434; also *A Roll of the British Army Medical Officers, 1660-1960*, by R. Drew, pp.249, 308, 330, 837; also *London and Provincial Medical Directory – 1848*.

54. Records of the school secretary, Marlborough College.
55. National census for 1851, Wiltshire and Swindon Record Office, H0107/1838, pp.298 and 299.
56. Will of John Gardner dated 24 August 1852 and proved on 2 December 1872 at Gloucester, Family division, High Court of Justice.
57. Worcestershire Record Office, 705380 BA 2309/24. There are about 40 land deeds, most relating to Baron Sandys (lord of the manor) and the Gardner and Watkins families.
58. Land Tax Returns, Savernake Park, 1789 to 1852, Wiltshire Record Office, A1/345/335 A and B.
59. *The Book of Devizes – the Life Story of an Ancient Borough*, by E. Bradby (1985), pp.53 and 95; also early trade directories of Wiltshire and *Universal British Directory* 1793 to 1805.
60. *Story of the Masefield Family 1678-1978*, by G.B. Masefield, pp.15 and 18. Biographies of Frederick Halcomb and his eldest son are given in *The Cyclopedia of South Australia*, by H.T. Burgess, vol.1 (1907) and vol.2 (1909); also *Australian Dictionary of Biography*, vol.9, p.159.
61. Wiltshire Record Office, Duke of Marlborough collection, 1033/6/13 and 873/41/332.
62. *A History of Marlborough*, by J.E. Chandler (1977), p.68.
63. Staffordshire Record Office, D 4316.
64. *The British Medical Journal*, 13 July 1872, p.55.
65. National census for 1871, Staffordshire Record Office, RG10/2881, folio 6, p.4; also *Slater's Directory of the Midlands* (1850) and *Post Office Directory of Staffordshire* (1868).
66. *Leek Times*, 29 June 1872.
67. *Victoria History of the County of Stafford*, vol.7 edited by M.W. Greenslade (1996), p.236; also *Old Leek*, edited by M.H. Miller (1891), vol.1, pp.147, 271 and 281.
68. *Natal Almanac and Register* (1904), p.550; *The Natal Who's Who* (1906); and KwaZulu-Natal Archives, Pietermaritzburg, MSCE 12154/1927.
69. *Notes on Some North Staffordshire Families* by P.W.L. Adams (1930), pp.97-6, 119.
70. *Pemberton Pedigrees* by Major-General R.C.B. Pemberton and the Reverend R. Pemberton (1923); also *Birmingham Weekly Post*, 14 January 1900.
71. Commission of the Peace, Birmingham Magistrates' Court, 14 February, second year of Victoria.
72. National census for 1851, Staffordshire Record Office, H0107/2008/4, Folio 213, p.10; 1861 census RG/1946 Folio 82, p.17; 1871 census RG 10/2880 Folio 12, p.18; 1881 census RG11/2738, Folio 7, p.5.
73. *A History of the Adams Family of North Staffordshire*, by P.W.L. Adams (1914) Supplement III, Additions and corrections.
74. *St Luke's Church, Leek – A Short History*, by Mrs P. Johnson.
75. *Leek Parish Church of St Edward the Confessor – History and Guide*, p.xxxii.
76. Unknown Leek or other local newspapers of 22 December 1854 and 22 May 1873.
77. Cadet papers of the East India Company, British Library, Orient and India Office, L/MIL/9/206, Folios 802 and 809.
78. British Library, Orient and India Office, L/MIL/10/43 to 67, Folio 543 and L/MIL/10/75, Folio 151.
79. 14 letters written by Mary Jane Worthington to Mary Jane Burne between 1843 and 1853 descended to Miss Burne's nephew S.A.H. Burne, barrister-at-law, who passed them to P.W.L. Adams of Woore Manor, Shropshire. Manuscript copies taken in 1951 are now in the Worthington family archives.
80. *History of the Organisation, Equipment and War Services of the Regiment of Bengal Artillery*, by Major-General F.W. Stubbs, vol.3 (1895), pp.181, 224, 252 and 461; also *The New Annual Army List*, by Lieutenant-General H.G. Hart (1879), p.574.
81. *The County Families of the United Kingdom*, by E. Walford, 2nd edition (1864).
82. *Burke's Genealogical and Heraldic History of the Peerage, Baronetage and Knightage*, edition 105, edited by P. Townsend (1970), pp.83-7.
83. *List of the Officers of the Army and the Corps of Royal Marines*, for 1849, 1851 and 1853-4.
84. Public Record Office, Kew, Military Records, Widow's Pension Applications, WO

42/49/261.

85. *Kelly's Post Office Directory* (1896).
86. *Hunt's Mineral Statistics*
87. *Western Mail,* 7 July 1881.
88. *A Historical Account of the Services of the 34th and 55th Regiment,* by G. Noakes (1875), p.117.
89. *Roll of Commissioned Officers in the Medical Service of the British Army,* 1727 to 1898, edited by Lieutenant-Colonel H.A.L. Howell (1917), Number 5270; also the Monthly Army Lists.
90. *The Life of John Rushworth, Earl Jellicoe,* by Admiral Sir R.H. Bacon (1936), in which pedigrees of the Keele, Rushworth and Patton families are given in Appendix I; *The Grand Fleet 1914-1916,* by Admiral Viscount Jellicoe of Scapa (1919); *Jellicoe – A Biography,* by A.T. Patterson (1969), p.15; *Burke's Genealogical and Historical History of the Peerage, Baronetage and Knightage,* Edition 105 (1970), p.445.
91. *New Zealand Gazette,* about February 1862, p.91.
92. *Bardigo Advertiser* (Australia), 15 October 1862.
93. *Otago Daily Times* (New Zealand), 8 and 26 November 1862, 7 January 1863 and 17 June 1863.
94. *Lourenco Marques Guardian,* 27 December 1927. Charles Worthington is included in a photograph taken 50 years previously of the two cricket teams with umpires.
95. KwaZulu-Natal Archives, Pietermaritzburg, MSC 1/59 31 and 1/140 190.
96. Deeds Office, Pietermaritzburg, 1462.
97. *Historical Record of the Eighty-Ninth Princess Victoria's Regiment* by R. Brinkman (1888); *The New Annual Army List,* by Lieutenant-General H.G. Hart.
98. Museum Archives of the Grande Chancellerie de la Légion d'Honneur, Paris, France.
99. *The Cheltenham Onlooker,* 9 June 1883, p.363 and 12 June 1897, p.560.

Chapter 4

1. *Visitation of England and Wales,* edited by F.A. Crisp, vol.19 (1917), pp.79-84.
2. *Golden Memories of Barberton,* by W.O Curror, revised and enlarged by H-Bornman; aslo *Reader's Digest: Illustrated Guide to South Africa,* 2nd edition (1980) pp.262-7.
3. National Archives Repository, Pretoria, TAB DRD 420/05, 851/07, 32/08, 29/09, 466/09, 2,061/09, 113/10, 561/10 and 1,029/10.
4. Transvaal Provincial Division of the Supreme Court of South Africa, Wills 45,030 and 67,064.
5. National Archives Repository, Pretoria, TAB MHE 0/12654 and 67,064; MHG 0/12,654 and 1,710/1946; MKB 1179m (A3/34); RAD 26 0549 1902; TPO 5/20 164/1911; WLD 5/43 498/1904; ZKB 10/76m (A1/49); ZTPD 5/394 3,131/1896; 8/478 8367/1896, 5/569 354/1904, 5/628 239/1906, 5/669 173/1909, 5/11 366/1909, 5/673 49/1910 and 5/20 104/1911.
6. *The Washing of the Spears,* by Lieut-Commander D.R. Morris (1958), pp.33 and 303.
7. Kwa Zulu-Natal Archives, Pietermaritzburg, NAB NMP, vols. 2 and 9; Natal Civil Service Lists, 1895 and 1897.
8. *The Natal Witness,* 12 May 1888, 17 July 1913, 7 July 1915, 6, 7 and 8 September 1917, 4, 5, 12 and 13 June 1936, 13 October 1938, 22 March 1943, 13 December 1951, 4 May 1955, 16 April 1962, 21 November 1991 and 31 January 2001.
9. Estcourt Births Register, 14 February 1868 to 24 January 1894; Ladysmith Birth Register, 9 January 1868 to 2 December 1897 and Durban Deaths Register 3 June 1920 to 6 February 1821, Estcourt Death Register, June 1893 to January 1901; Dundee Deaths Register, 28 April 1938 to 3 September 1945; KwaZulu-Natal Archives, Pietermaritzburg.
10. *Natal Almanac and Directory* (1890 to 1917).
11. KwaZulu-Natal Archives, Pietermaritzburg, NAB MSCE 368/47, 17/175, 898/62, 44/106, 33/189, 37/215, 8,353/92, 555/1914, 3,174/1918, 1,769/1919, 4,833/1920, 5,284/1920, 9,436/1924, 28,012/1938, 29,729/1939, 46/1943, 555/1944, 863/1948, 1,816/1950, 1,269/1951, 51/1952, 2,853/1953, 1,201/1955, 1,977/1955, 2,306/1958, 2,316/1661, 1,291/1962, 1,501/1966, 110/1971, 4,062/1971, 232/1973, 2,774/1973, 975/1983, 5,099/1983, 5,486/1990, 8,721/1990, 8,485/1991, 8,353/1992, 1,201/1995 and 3,647/1999; also NRD5/3 V3339(A) 1908.

12. *The Natal Mercury*, 2 September 1903, 29 May 1920, 10 February 1947, 28 June 1948 and 28 August 1973.
13. KwaZulu-Natal Archives, Pietermaritzburg, NAB CSO 997 1884/4,377, 1178 1888/359 and 1180 1888/685.
14. *Encyclopedia of South Africa*, edited by E. Rosenthal, 4th edition (1967), pp.182 and 365; *The Natal Moors*, by M. Tarr (1999), p.130.
15. *South African Country Life*, October 1999.
16. *The Hiltonian Magazine* (1905), p.72.
17. *Old Pietermaritzburg* by R. Haswell.
18. KwaZulu-Natal Archives, Pietermaritzburg, RSCE 12,180/1927, 18,140/1933 and RSC 1/7/6 77/1941.
19. *The Natal Directory* (1918 to 1950), followed by *Blaby's Natal Directory* (1952 to 1974).
20. Diocesan Archives, Cathedral of the Holy Nativity, Pietermaritzburg.
21. *Sports and Sportsmen – South Africa and Rhodesia*, compiled by the *Cape Times* (1929).
22. *South African Military Who's Who 1452 – 1992* by I. Uys, p.209.
23. *Bram Fischer: Africaner Revolutionary*, by S. Clingman (1988); also *Encyclopedia of Southern Africa*, by E. Rosenthal (1967), p.181.
24. *Long Walk to Freedom*, by N. Mandela, pp. 461, 462, 561 and 562.
25. *Cape Times*, 19 December 1916; also National Archives Repository, Pretoria, TAB MHG 30,514 296/1917 and 1710/46.
26. *Natal Farmer*, May 1927 – article by J.W. McCullough.
27. Department of Home Affairs, South Africa – death certificate.
28. Deeds Office, Pierter Maritz Street, Pietermartizburg.
29. *The Volunteer Regiments of Natal and East Griqualand*, by G.T. West (1945), pp.20-39.
30. KwaZulu-Natal Archives, Pietermaritzburg, Natal Illiquid Record Book, RSC 1/7/6, 1932-1946, Numbers 2, 5 and 33; also Criminal Record Book RSC 1/4/42, 1909-1954.
31. Records of military service, South Africa, 265/895 and 268/595.
32. *Australian Dictionary of Biography*, vol.3, p.474 and vol.8, p.127; also *A Biographical Register of the Queensland Parliament – 1860-1929* by D.B. Watson (1972).
33. *Victory in Italy*, by N. Orpen (1975), being vol.5 of *South African Forces in World War 2*, pp.31, 220 and 222; *War in the Desert*, by N. Orpen, p. 276; *Carbineer*, by A.F. Hattersley, pp. 121, 137, 138, 153 and 176.
34. *Newcastle Advertiser*, Natal, 31 July 1981.
35. *The Natal Daily News*, Durban, 7 May 1941, 1 October 1946, 17 and 18 July 1990; *The Natal Mercury*, 17 July 1990.
36. Department of the Interior, South Africa, 76/27,725.
37. African Defence Force Records, Documentation Centre, Pretoria, Private bag X289.
38. *Who Was Who* (1951-1960), p.915.
39. Crosskill Records at Beverley Library, Humberside County Council.
40. *First Beginning* by W.E. Crosskill (1987), pp.1-4.
41. Divorce files, Durban, TBD RSC 5A/779 I1,059/1965.
42. *The Natal Daily News*, Durban, 20 May 1936 and 2, 4, 5, 7 and 8 September 1992. A photograph of the Natal golf team, including Timothy Yorke Worthington, appears in the issue of 3 November 1961.
43. *Westville News*, April 1976 and July 1977.
44. *The Homefinder Supplement* to *The Natal Mercury*, Durban, 12 January 1985 and 25 July 1987.

Chapter 5
1. *Visitation of England and Wales*, edited by F.A. Crisp, vol.19 (1917), p.81.
2. Cape Archives Repository, death notice, MOOC 6/9/1596 4,365.
3. National Archives Repository, Pretoria, TAB W4455/59.
4. National Archives Repository, Pretoria, Mental Estate 1,784/1956.
5. Durban Archives Repository, 8/1945 and Case I 169/1971.

6. Voters Roll, Natal 1989.
7. KwaZulu-Natal Archives, Pietermaritzburg, NAB MSCE 409/73, 1,742/1959, 2,442/1961, 4,904/1982 and 1,377/1990.
8. *Natal Daily News,* 7 March 1979.
9. L.W.J. Hartman's published books include under his own name: *Bande van Bloed* (1965), *Die Woestynrowers* (1965), *Die Geel Koevert* (1966), *Waar de Tremspore Doodloop* (1967), *Kopiereg Deur Mev. H.M. Hartman* (1981), *Die Mense van Zuiderkruis, Hoe Terug Die Daeraad, Die Huis to Gaan Was Darr* and *Die Boerebedrieer.* Under the name Ferona Bosman: *Rukwinde* (1953), *Totdate Die Skaduwees Oorwaai* (1967), *Aan Woelige Waters* and *Die Transportryers.* Under the name Louwrens de Kock: *Blombare van Bloed* (1966) and *In Diens van Die Veldpond.*
10. *Blaby's Natal Directory,* 1946 and 1947.

Chapter 6
1. *Visitation of England and Wales,* edited by F.A. Crisp, vol.19 (1917),p.81.
2. Diocesan Archives, Cathedral of the Holy Nativity, Pietermaritzburg.
3. *The Natal Moors,* by M. Tarr (1999), p.206.
4. KwaZulu-Natal Archives, Pietermaritzburg, NAB 813/77 and MSCE 31,134/1940, 1,412/1948 and 4,172/1968.
5. Pietermaritzburg marriages register, 70/1928, KwaZulu-Natal Archives, Pietermaritzburg.
6. *The Natal Witness,* 22 December 1928.

Chapter 7
1. *Visitation of England and Wales,* edited by F.A. Crisp, vol.19 (1917), pp.82-4; *Burke's Genealogical and Heraldic History of the Landed Gentry,* edited by L.G. Price (1952), pp. 6 and 7.
2. *A History of the Adams Family of North Staffordshire,* by P.W.L. Adams (1914); Second Supplement to the book, p.Z and Third Supplement, pp.10-11.
3. *Notes on Some North Staffordshire Families,* by P.W.L. Adams (1930) pp. 67 to 79.
4. *Ten Generations of a Potting Family,* compiled by R. Nicholls; also *William Adams – An Old English Potter,* by W. Turner (1923); also *Visitation of England and Wales,* edited by F.A. Crisp, vol.13, p.26.
5. *North Staffordshire Advertiser,* soon after 27 April 1914.
6. *Wolstanton Parish Magazine,* about May 1914.
7. Staffordshire Record Office, D 4316.
8. *Trade Marks Journal,* Number 40, 6 December 1876, p.6C.
9. *The Times,* 2 October 1880, 20 March 1937, 6 October 1964 and 13 May 1998.
10. National census of 1881, Staffordshire Record Office, RG11/2,738, Folio 7, p.5; also census of 1891, RG12/2,186, Folio 47, p.18.
11. *The History of the Leek Embroidery Society,* published by the Department of Adult Education, University of Keele (1969); *Embroider,* Spring 1988, p.10 being an article on *Leek Embroidery* by Mrs A.G. Jacques, MBE, MA, JP; *Leek Embroidery* by Mrs A.G. Jacques, Staffordshire Libraries, Arts and Archives (1990).
12. *Walford's County Families of the United Kingdom* (1916), p.1,337.
13. *The Leek Post,* 26 July 1919 and 7 and 14 May 1927.
14. Leek Urban District Council, Register 1965, Plot 8,088.
15. *Burke's Genealogical and Heraldic History of the Landed Gentry,* edited by L.G. Price (1952), p.1005.
16. Manchester School Register, *Chetham Society,* New Series, vol.93.
17. *High Peak News,* 12 June 1875 and 23 August 1913.
18. A pedigree of the Pearson family is given in *Visitation of England and Wales,* edited by F.A. Crisp, vol.15 (1908), pp.164-6.
19. *Dictionary of South African Biography,* vol.3 (1977), p.849.
20. Published works by A.T. Wirgman include: *The Prayer Book, with Historical Notes and Scripture Proofs* (1873), *Thoughts on Harmony between the Lord's Prayer and the Beatitudes* (1877), *Catechism on Confirmation* (1881), *The English Reformation and*

Book of Common Prayer (1882), *The Seven Gifts of the Spirit* (1889), *A Short History of the Church and Parish of St Mary* (1892), *The Church and the Civil Power* (1893), *The Spirit of Liberty and Other Sermons* (1893), *The English Church and People in South Africa* (1895), *Doctrine of Confirmation in Relation to Holy Baptism* (1897), *The Constitutional Authority of the Bishops* (1899), *The Blessed Virgin and all the Company of Heaven* (1905), *The Life of Dean Green* (1909), *The History of Protestantism* (1911) and *A Catechism of Christian Science* (1917).

21. *Storm and Sunshine in South Africa*, by A.T. Wirgman (his autobiography).
22. *Eastern Province Herald*, Friday ... December 1926; *Port Elizabeth Advertiser*, about the same date.
23. *Looking Back – Journal of the Historical Society of Port Elizabeth*, November 2000.
24. *Lectures, Verses, Speeches, Reminiscences &c.*, by W. Challinor (1891), p.327; *The Staffordshire Advertiser*, 31 August 1872; *Leek News*, Christmas Shopping Number, December 1932.
25. *Leek Times*, 25 July 1874, 10 June 1876 and September 1889. A photograph of the band of the Leek Volunteers is shown in *A History of Leek – Images of a Bygone Age*, by R. Poole (2002), p.116.
26. *Thomas Wardle and the Kashmir Silk Industry*, by Mrs A.G. Jacques, Staffordshire Studies, vol.6 (1994), University of Keele; also *The Wardle Story*, by Mrs A.G. Jacques (1996); also *The Journal of Indian Art Industry*, vol.13, number 108, October 1909, which includes *The Silk Industries of India and the Personal History of Sir Thomas Wardle, JP, FCS, FGS &c.*, by Colonel T.H. Hendley, *Memoirs of the Late Sir Thomas Wardle and the Formation of the Silk Association of Great Britain and Ireland*, by G.C. Wardle, and *Sericulture and Silk Weaving in India and Kashmir*, by Sir Thomas Wardle. Sir Thomas's other publications include: *On the Geology of the Neighbourhood of Leek, Staffordshire* (1863); *On the History and Growing Utilization of Tassar Silk* (1891); Report on the English Silk Industry, Royal Commission on Technical Instruction (1885); *The Breaking of Copmere*, Proceedings of the North Staffordshire Field Club (1901); *Kashmir, its New Silk Industry, Natural History, Geology, Sports etc* (1904); *An Examination into the Divisibility of the Brin or Ultimate Fibre of the Silk of Bombyx Mori, or Silk Commerce* (1908); 'Free Trade, Protection and Unemployment', *Leek Post*, 28 November 1908.
27. Lady Wardle's published books were: *Guide to the Bayeux Tapestry* (1886), and *366 Easy and Inexpensive Dinners for Young Housekeepers* (1901). Her obituary is given in *Leek Post*, 13 September 1902 and *Staffordshire Evening Sentinel*, 13 September 1902.
28. *The Leek and Manifold Valley Light Railway*, by K. Turner (1980).
29. *Australia Dictionary of Biography*, vol.9 (1591-1993), p.159.
30. *A History of the Ancient Parish of Leek in Staffordshire*, by J. Sleigh (1883), p.7; *Who Was Who*, vol.5 (1951-1960), p.411; G.R.A. Gaunt's autobiography is *The Yield of the Years* (1940).
31. *Staffordshire Evening Sentinel*, 9 and 10 February 1949 and 19 December 1978.
32. *Leek Post and Times*, 8 December 1944, 2 March 1945, 18 February 1949, 26 October 1967, 20 May 1971, 20 May 1976, 21 and 28 December 1978 and 1 May 1980.
33. *The Natal Who's Who* (1906); *Natal Almanac and Register* (1904), p.550.
34. KwaZulu-Natal Archives, NAB MSCE 12,154/1927.
35. *Shrewsbury School Register*, vol.1, edited by J.E. Auden (1928), pp.419, 434; *The Salopian*, March 1900.
36. Imperial War Museum, London, Box 79/5/1; also *The 5th North Staffords and the North Midland Territorials*, by Lieutenant W. Meakin (1920), pp.9-61.
37. *The Metfield Magazine*, number 1, vol.1, Autumn term 1921; *The S.Anne's Guild Magazine*, May 1922, May 1924 and June 1927.
38. *Building Society Who's Who – 1963-4*, p.338.
39. *Leek and Moorlands Building Society – 1856-1956*, a booklet issued by the society.
40. *International Union of Building Societies and Savings Associations – Proceedings of the Tenth Congress* (1965), p.360; *The Building Societies' Gazette*, October 1933, December 1937, October 1938 and the Special Congress Issue, 1965.
41. *Staffordshire Weekly Sentinel*, 8 June 1971 and 16 September 1955.
42. *Burke's Handbook to the Most Excellent Order of the British Empire*, edited by A.W.

Thorpe (1921).

43. *Congleton Chronicle*, 5 December 1952.
44. *The London Gazette*, 28 September 1917.
45. *Who Was Who*, vol.3, 1929-40 (1967), p.538 and vol.6, 1961-70, p.1,231.
46. Public Record Office, ADM 196/44, vol.6, p.204 and ADM 196/53; *The Times*, 20 March 1937.
47. *W.G. Grace: A Biography with a Treatise on Cricket contributed by W.G. Grace*, by W.M. Brownlee (1887); *The Memorial Biography of Dr W.G. Grace*, by Lord Hawke, Lord Harris and Sir H. Gordon (1919); *W.G. Grace*, by B. Darwin (1934); *The Great Cricketer*, by A.A. Thompson (1957); *W.G. Grace – His Life and Times*, by E. Midwinter (1981); *W.G.: A Life of W.G. Grace*, by R. Law (1988). A work by W.G. Grace is *Cricket* (1891).
48. *The Bystander*, 5 May 1926.
49. *The Evening News*, 6 March 1920, 14 February 1952 and 10 October 1964.
50. *Navy List*, April 1944; *Leek Post and Times*, 21 January 1944.
51. *Kelly's Handbook of the Titled, Landed and Official Classes* (1945); *Burke's Peerage, Baronetage, Knightage and Companionage* (1952).
52. *Hampshire Telegraph and Post*, 6 September 1962.
53. *A History of Leek*, by R. Poole (2002), p.162.
54. *North Staffordshire Post and Times*, 17 February 1950.
55. *Abstract of the Accounts of the Leek Urban District Council* for the financial years ending 31 March 1940, 1941 and 1942.
56. *Daily Telegraph*, 6 October 1964 and 18 January 1965; also *Evening News*, 10 October 1964.
57. *The Beverley Family of Virginia – Descendants of Major Robert Beverley (1641 to 1687)*, compiled by J. McGill (USA 1956).
58. *The Washington Post – The District Weekly*, 10 April 1980.
59. *Curio*, Summer 1984, pp.31-3, School of Fine Arts and Communication, James Madison University, Harrisonburg, Virginia.
60. *London Times-Mirror*, 12 June 1996.

Chapter 8
1. The Pedigree of Philip Jukes Worthington is registered at the College of Arms, Surrey 27, p.79.
2. *Visitation of England and Wales*, edited by F.A. Crisp, vol.19 (1917), p.84.
3. *Wykehamist War Service Roll*, 6th edition (1919), p.229; *Kelly's Handbook of the Titled, Landed and Official Classes* (1945).
4. Biographies of T.E. Lawrence are: *With Lawrence in Arabia*, by L. Thomas (1921); *Lawrence and the Arabs*, by R. Graves (1927) and *The Secret Lives of Lawrence of Arabia*, by P. Knightley and C. Simpson (1969).
5. An Account of the Gallipoli campaign is given in *Gallipoli*, by A. Moorhead (1956).
6. *The Royal Corps of Signals*, by Major-General R.F.H. Nalder, CB, OBE (1958), pp.155-65 and pp.612-13.
7. *The Palestine Campaigns*, by A.P. Wavell, 2nd edition (1929), p.35.
8. *London Gazette*, December 1914, 9 March 1917, 20 April 1917, 15 December 1917, 9 November 1918, 13 November 1931, 19 September 1946, 14 April 1950 and 13 and 16 March 1951.
9. *Egyptian Gazette*, 19 December 1916.
10. *The Leek Post*, 26 July 1919, 24 November 1923 and 20 and 27 April 1929.
11. *Stags and Serpents*, by J. Pearson (1983), pp.196-204.
12. *Monthly Army List*, December 1938.
13. L.J. Worthington's Territorial Army papers are at the Derbyshire Record Office, D5593/1 to 17.
14. Published works of E.A. Sadler include: *Velayed Toxic Effects of Sulphonal, Birmingham Medical Review* (1901); 'The French Prisoners of War in England and in Ashbourne, 1808-1815', *Derbyshire Archaeological Journal* (1934); *The Parish Church of St Oswald, Ashbourne* (1934).
15. *Some Records of the Holland Family*, collected by W.R. Holland (1929).

16. *The Ashbourne News,* 10 March 1955.
17. *Derby and Chesterfield Reporter,* 9 February 1923; *Derby Daily Express,* 26 January and 1 and 6 February 1923; *The Ashbourne News,* 9 and 16 February 1923; *Ashbourne Telegraph,* 9 February 1923, *Leek Post,* 27 January and 3 and 10 February 1923; *Leek Times,* 10 February 1923; *Staffordshire Sentinel,* 6 February 1923; *Staffordshire Weekly Sentinel,* 10 February 1923; *Staffordshire Advertiser,* 10 February 1923; *Barton Advertiser,* 10 February 1923; *The Herald,* 10 February 1923; *Army, Navy and Airforce Gazette,* 17 February 1923; *The Times,* 7 and 8 February 1923 and *Gentlewoman,* 17 February 1923.
18. A biography of M.E. Sadler by his son M.T.H. Sadler is *Michael Thomas Sadler* (1949); *The Times,* 30 December 1927 and 16 and 20 December 1957.
19. *Leek Post and Times,* 11 May 1935, 5 August 1949, November 1963, 12 June 1975, 2 July 1981, 23 December 1981, October 1984 and 14 September 1994.
20. 'The Postage Stamps of South-West Africa', by L.J. Worthington, *Stamp Collecting,* 11 and 18 April 1925, pp.47, 63, 66, 69 and 89.
21. *Crockford's Clerical Directory* (1929), p.1229.
22. *Daily Dispatch,* 30 June 1936; *Daily Sketch,* 30 June 1936; *Daily Herald,* 30 June 1936; *The Times,* 30 June 1936; *Daily Express,* 30 June 1936; *Birmingham Post,* 30 June 1936; *Daily Mirror,* 30 June 1936; *Leek Post and Times,* 4 July 1936; *Staffordshire Weekly Sentinel,* 4 July 1936; *Empire News,* 5 July 1936; *News of the World,* 5 July 1936.
23. *The Leek Times,* 19 and 26 April 1929, 9 October 1931 and 27 October 1933; *Leek Post and Times,* 22 May 1934, 22 and 29 December 1934 and 26 June 1936; *Staffordshire Evening Sentinel,* 19 December 1934; *Staffordshire Weekly Sentinel,* 2 February 1935 and 30 March 1935.
24. *Daily Dispatch,* 5 January 1955; *Staffordshire Evening Sentinel,* 5 October 1955 and about September 1977.
25. *Daily Telegraph,* 23 June 1961, 16 February 1981, 12 December 1981, 27 December 1988, 8, 9 and 14 December 1999.
26. *Noel Coward – A Biography,* by P. Hoare, pp.217, 345, 516 and 526; *The Noel Coward Song Book,* pp.73 and 107-12; *Who Was Who,* 1971-1980, p.177.
27. *London Evening News,* 30 April 1977.
28. *Daily Mail Weekend Supplement,* 25 March 2000.
29. A photograph of about 1931 of the 14 pupils at Moorfields School, including Valentine and Philip Worthington, appears in *The Spirit of Leek: 2* by C. Walton and L. Porter (2001), p.115.
30. *The 59th Division – Its War Story,* by P. Knight (1954); *Army Lists,* January 1942, p.554, and January 1945, p.558c.
31. *Business Post,* 18 August 1973.
32. *Leek Post and Times,* 28 March 1947; *Staffordshire Evening Sentinel,* 24 March 1947; *Staffordshire Weekly Sentinel,* 29 March 1947.
33. *Hull Daily Mail,* 8 May 1965; *Yorkshire Post,* 13 July 1965; *Driffield Times,* 15 July 1965.
34. *Financial Times,* 1 July 1978; *The Times,* 1 July 1978; *Guardian,* 1 July 1978.
35. *Examination Results and Prize List,* Boys Grammar School, Ashby-de-la-Zouch (1938-9) p.8.
36. *Partners – Fifty Years of WSA and P* (1988).
37. P.M. Worthington's published papers include: *An Experiment on the Theory of Voids in Granular Materials,* Magazine of Concrete Research (1953); *The Elastic Stability of I-Beams Subjected to Complex Load Systems,* Journal of the Institution of Civil Engineers, January and September 1954; *The Effects of Wheel Tread Profiles and Other Factors on the Long-Travel Motion of Gantry Cranes,* Journal of the Institution of Structural Engineers, December 1957; *The Economics of Handling Materials in the Iron and Steel Industry,* Journal of the Iron and Steel Institute, October 1962; *The Economics of Process Selection in the Iron and Steel Industry,* Journal of the Iron and Steel Institute, September 1964 (in joint authorship with M.D.J. Brisby and R.J. Anderson); *Feasibility Studies – a Consultants Role,* Proceedings of the Conference on Civil Engineering Problems Oversees, June 1966 (in joint authorship with D.R.R. Dick); *Strategic Planning in the Wool Textile Industry,*

Journal of Systems Engineering, September 1970; *The Career Triangle*, Engineering, April 1971; *On the Home Ground – the Form and Structure of the British Consulting Profession*, Consulting in the European Community, March 1974 (in joint authorship with A.L. Brake).

38. *The Times*, 1 January 1966; *Financial Times*, 12 June 1976; *New Civil Engineer*, 18 March 1976 and 17 June 1976; *Daily Telegraph*, 17 August 1989 and 31 October 1989; *Who Was Who*, 1981-1990, p.27.
39. *People of Today* (1998), pp.78 and 2129.
40. *The Times*, 14 June 1983; *Daily Telegraph*, 14 June 1983; *Guardian*, 14 June 1983.
41. 'The Ultraviolet Absorption of the Unconjugated Azomethine Group' by R. Bonnett, N.J. David, J.S.M. Hamlin and P. Smith, *Journal of Chemistry and Industry*, 16 November 1963, pp.1836 and 1837.
42. *Daily Telegraph*, 4 September 1962; *Leicester Graphic*, October 1963.
43. *Melton Times*, 24 June 1983; *Pins and Needles*, August 1983, p.14.
44. *Rutland and Stamford Mercury*, 6 August 1991 and 22 December 1995; *Rutland Times*, 22 November 1991 and 22 December 1995.
45. Book reviews by Mrs J.S.M. Worthington are given in *The Magistrate*, July-August 1996, p.141 and June 1997.
46. *The Army Lists*, under Royal Army Medical Corps, 1954 to 1985.
47. *Evening Standard*, 17 July 1954: there is a photograph of Tessa Thorowgood and her sister Christine in one edition.
48. *Halifax Courier and Guardian Almanac* (1928), p.5; *A Hundred Years of the Halifax – the History of the Halifax Building Society 1853-1953*, by O.R. Hobson, p.85.
49. *Primitive Methodist Church; Quarterly Guide of the Halifax I, II, Sowerby Bridge, Brighouse and Greetland Circuits*, July to September 1932. A photograph of John and Elizabeth Whittaker is kept at the Calderdale Reference Library, Halifax.
50. *Halifax County Borough Directory* (1936); also *Halifax Daily Courier and Guardian*, 2 November 1935, 6th edition, 5 and 9 November 1935.
51. *Leek Post and Times*, 3 March 1961 and 20 April 1961; *Staffordshire Evening Sentinel*, 17 April 1961; *Staffordshire Weekly Sentinel*, 21 April 1961.
52. A history of the order is given in *The Knights of St John in the British Empire*, by Colonel E.J. King, CMG, ADC, MA (1934).
53. *Colchester Evening Gazette*, 6 June 1971.
54. *Financial Times*, 2 July 1984; *Leicester Mercury*, 29 August 1983; *Board Room*, November 1984.
55. An article on Hunsett Mill, 'The Unbeatable Beauty of Hunsett' is given in *Eastern Property News*, June 1995.
56. 'The Life of an Elizabethan Recusant – Thomas Worthington, SJ, DD, BA', by S.G. Worthington, *Family History*, the bi-monthly journal of the Institute of Heraldic and Genealogical Studies, vol.3, Number 13, January 1965, pp.9-14.
57. *Leek Post and Times*, 4 December 1969, 12 March 1970, 16 and 23 April 1970, 4 June 1970 and 5 August 1970; *Staffordshire Evening Sentinel*, 16 December 1969, 5 March 1970, 9 April 1970, 15 December 1970 and 5 August 1970; *Cheadle and Tean Times*, 19 December 1969, 2 and 23 January 1970, 13 February 1970 and 17 April 1970; *The Field*, 5 February 1970; *Staffordshire Weekly Sentinel*, 18 April 1970; *Buxton Advertiser*, 5 June 1970; *Farmer's Guardian*, 18 September 1970; *Birmingham Post*, January 1971; *Daily Telegraph*, 4 August 1971; *Country Life*, 19 August 1971. A 20-page booklet, *The Manifold – A Fight for Life*, was published in 1971.
58. *The Times*, 20 September 1972; *Daily Telegraph*, 20 September 1972; *Leek Post and Times*, 17 December 1972.
59. *Debrett's People of Today* (1955), p.2180; *Leek Post and Times*, 15 June 1978.
60. *Leek Post and Times*, 17 August 1978 and 26 November 1981; *Staffordshire Weekly Sentinel*, 18 August 1978.
61. *Staffordshire Evening or Weekly Sentinel*, 13 November 1984.
62. *Daily Express Colour Supplement*, 8 August 1998; *Daily Telegraph*, late September or October 1999.
63. *The Parish Church of St Bartholomew, Blore Ray – A History and Guide*, by D. and

M. Swincoe, revised and updated by S.G. Worthington (1998); *The Restoration of St Bartholomew's Church, Blore Ray 1994-1997*, by S.G. Worthington.

64. *The Times*, 20 March 1973; *Daily Telegraph*, 20 March 1973.
65. *The Courage Family – Descendants of Alexander Courage, born at Foveran near Aberdeen 1686*, a published folder of pedigrees, by M.R. Courage (1993).
66. Obituary of Richard Courage, *Daily Telegraph*, 15 September 1994.
67. *Leek Post and Times*, September 1973; *Daily Telegraph*, September 1973. A photograph of the bridal party leaving the church appears in *The Staffordshire Sentinel*, September 1973.

Chapter 9
1. *A History of the Adams Family of North Staffordshire*, by P.W.L. Adams (1914), Pedigree K.
2. Registers of St Mary's Church, Oldham, Lancashire Record Office, Preston; *Lancashire Parish Register Society* volumes.
3. Lancashire Record Office, WCW (Wills and admons).
4. *Manchester Directories*.
5. *Manchester Mercury*, 8 April 1788 and 6 May 1788; *Oldham Annals*, compiled by G. Shaw; *The Old Leeds and York Wagons*, p.21; 'A History of the Newton Chapelry in the Ancient Parish of Manchester', by H.T. Crofton, Chetham Society New Series, vol.53; *Waugh's Roads Out of Manchester*, p.366.

Chapter 10
1. *A History of the Adams Family of North Staffordshire*, by P.W.L. Adams (1914), Pedigree K.
2. Church registers of baptisms, marriages and burials, Lancashire Record Office; *Lancashire Parish Register Society* volumes.
3. Lancashire Record Office, WCW (Wills and admons).

Chapter 11
1. Church registers of baptisms, marriages and burials, Lancashire Record Office; *Lancashire Parish Register Society* volumes; Owen Manuscripts, Lancashire Record Office.
2. Lancashire Record Office, WCW (Wills and admons).

Chapter 12
1. Church registers of baptisms, marriages and burials, Lancashire Record Office; also *The Registers of the Parish Church of Gorton 1599-1741*, transcribed by H. Brierly, Lancashire Parish Register Society, vol.47 (1913). The original registers of St Michael's Church, Ashton-under-Lyne, are at Manchester Central Reference Library.
2. Registers of the Old Presbyterian Chapel, Dukinfield, at the Manchester Archives and Local Studies Library, MFPR 294, Manchester Central Library.
3. Lancashire Record Office, WCW (Wills and admons).

Chapter 13
1. Church registers of baptisms, marriages and burials, Lancashire Record Office; *The Registers of the Collegiate Church of Manchester, 1573-1653*, Lancashire Parish Register Society, vol.31; Owen Manuscripts, Lancashire Record Office.
2. Lancashire Record Office, WCW (Wills and admons).
3. *The County Families of the United Kingdom*, by E. Walford, 2nd edition (1864); also other editions of the same work.
4. *A History of the Adams Family of North Staffordshire*, by P.W.L. Adams (1914), Pedigree K.
5. *Chetham Society*, New Series, vol.52 (1904), pp.131-8.
6. Manchester Central Reference Library, M35/7/6/11.
7. Marriage licences at the Diocese of Chester.
8. College of Arms, London, Funeral Certificates and Pedigrees, Norfolk, 12/195-6.
9. *Alumni Cantabrigienses*, by J. Venn, ScD, FRS, and J. Venn, MA, part I, vol.4, pp.382 and

465; *The Dictionary of National Biography*, edited by Sir L. Stephen and Sir S. Lee, vol.21 (1917), pp.955-75; *A History of Jesus College Cambridge*, by A. Gray MA, and F. Brittain, LittD (1979), pp.84-9 and 118; *The Diary and Correspondence of Dr John Worthington, Master of Jesus College, Cambridge, Vice Chancellor of the University of Cambridge*, vol.I; Chetham Society, vol.13 (1847), edited by J. Crossley, and vol.II, Chetham Society vol.114 (1886), edited by J. Crossley and R.C. Christie.

10. *Visitation of Sir William Dugdale, 1664-5*, Chetham Society, vol.8, p.67.
11. Will of Edward Byrom, Public Record Office.
12. *Taxation in the Salford Hundred 1524-1802*, Chetham Society, New Series, vol.83, pp.4, 27 and 62.
13. *Miscellanies*, Lancashire Record Society, vol.12, p.139.
14. *Chetham Society*, vol.59, pp.7 and 20.
15. *The Worthington Families of Medieval England*, by P.M. Worthington (1985), pp.23, 24, 206 and 214.

CORRIGENDA TO AN EARLIER WORK

The following two corrections are required to the author's previous book, *The Worthington Families of Medieval England*, published in 1985.

Page 44
In Pedigree 1, generations 7 and 8, 'Henry de Worthington; living 1373 & 1407' should be shown as the son of Alan de Worthington (not of Hugh de Worthington).

Page 206
In Pedigree 6, generations 3 and 4, 'Joan dau. of Alexander Lever of Chamber' should not be shown as child of Christopher Worthington and Alice his wife. Joan was their daughter-in-law.

The texts dealing with these two matters are correct.

Pages 206, 207 and 214
There has been confusion about the name 'Joan', the daughter of Alexander Lever. At the visitations of Lancashire in 1613 and 1664 and 1665, the heralds recorded her as 'Jane'. At the baptism of her eldest son, Thomas, she was entered in the register as 'Joanae', and in the abstract of her father's Will she was named 'Jone'. The abstract was published in *Chetham Society*, New Series, vol.3 (1884), but recent attempts to find the original Will have failed. The matter remains unresolved.

INDEX